Faulkner and Money
FAULKNER AND YOKNAPATAWPHA

2017

Faulkner and Money

FAULKNER AND YOKNAPATAWPHA, 2017

EDITED BY
JAY WATSON
AND
JAMES G. THOMAS, JR.

UNIVERSITY PRESS OF MISSISSIPPI
JACKSON

The University Press of Mississippi is the scholarly publishing agency of the Mississippi Institutions of Higher Learning: Alcorn State University, Delta State University, Jackson State University, Mississippi State University, Mississippi University for Women, Mississippi Valley State University, University of Mississippi, and University of Southern Mississippi.

www.upress.state.ms.us

The University Press of Mississippi is a member of the Association of University Presses.

Copyright © 2019 by University Press of Mississippi
All rights reserved

First printing 2019
∞

Library of Congress Cataloging-in-Publication Data

Names: Faulkner and Yoknapatawpha Conference (44th: 2017: University of Mississippi) | Watson, Jay, editor. | Thomas, James G., Jr., editor.
Title: Faulkner and money / Faulkner and Yoknapatawpha, 2017; edited by Jay Watson and James G. Thomas, Jr.
Description: Jackson: University Press of Mississippi, [2019] | Includes bibliographical references and index. |
Identifiers: LCCN 2019003193 (print) | LCCN 2019006268 (ebook) | ISBN 9781496822536 (epub single) | ISBN 9781496822543 (epub institutional) | ISBN 9781496822550 (pdf single) | ISBN 9781496822567 (pdf institutional) | ISBN 9781496822529 (cloth)
Subjects: LCSH: Faulkner, William, 1897–1962—Criticism and interpretation—Congresses. | Finance in literature—Congresses. | Money in literature—Congresses.
Classification: LCC PS3511.A86 (ebook) | LCC PS3511.A86 Z783211393 2019 (print) | DDC 813/.52—dc23
LC record available at https://lccn.loc.gov/2019003193

British Library Cataloging-in-Publication Data available

Contents

Introduction vii
   Jay Watson

Note on the Conference xxix

"Bookless Mississippi" 3
   Sarah E. Gardner

War, Labor, and Gasoline in "Carcassonne" 15
   Michael Zeitlin

The Anatomy of Thrift: Markets, Media, and William Faulkner's Great Depression 31
   Robert Jackson

Pictorialism, Prolixity, and Spatial Form in Faulkner's Post-Hollywood Racial Imaginary 45
   Peter Lurie

Financialization and Neoliberalism: A Snopes Genealogy 59
   John T. Matthews

Legacy: The Currency of Eternity 78
   Gloria J. Burgess

The Friction of Money: Poverty and Failure in Early Faulkner 90
   Gavin Jones

Too Small to Fail: Jason Compson's Precarious Self-Worth 110
   Ted Atkinson

What Price a "Cheap Idea"? Money, *Sanctuary*, and Its Intertexts 122
   Richard Godden

Mink Snopes's *Shavasana*: Body, Relation, and Exchange in
Faulkner's Economies of Being   138
   RYAN HERYFORD

Faulkner's Stores: Microfinance and Economic Power
in the Postbellum South   156
   DAVID A. DAVIS

The Gifted Presence of *Intruder in the Dust*   169
   MICHAEL WAINWRIGHT

Racial Debts, Individual Slights, and Sleights of Hand in
Faulkner's *Intruder in the Dust*   186
   MARY A. KNIGHTON

Answering the Call: Telephonic Fascism and Faulkner's
Angel of History   208
   MYKA TUCKER-ABRAMSON

Contributors   231

Index   235

Introduction

Jay Watson

"When the curtain truly goes up" on Western civilization in fifth-century Greece, writes anthropologist and historian of debt David Graeber, "we find everybody arguing about money."[1] Something similar happened when the curtain went up on Yoknapatawpha County. One Sunday in October of 1927, William Faulkner wrote a letter to his publisher, Horace Liveright. Biographer Joseph Blotner describes the mood of the letter as "euphoric."[2] And justifiably so, as Faulkner announced a new work that represented a turning point, indeed a takeoff point, in his creative life, a breakthrough that would reorganize and re-energize his imaginative economy. "At last, and certainly, as El Orens' sheik said, I have written THE book, of which those other things were but foals. I believe it is the damdest best book you'll look at this year, or any other publisher."[3] "Those other things" were *Soldiers' Pay* and *Mosquitoes*, which Liveright had brought out to appreciative reviews over the past twenty months. The new book was *Flags in the Dust*, the first completed full-length work to harvest the imaginative bounty of Faulkner's fictional north Mississippi town of Jefferson, in the county he christened Yocona but later renamed Yoknapatawpha. Hindsight has revealed this to be one of the most auspicious literary events of the twentieth century. Faulkner knew he was on a roll. He crowed about his title for the manuscript: "I dont think that even the bird who named 'Soldiers' Pay' can improve on it." The material was so fertile that it had already germinated another book idea, "a collection of short stories of my townspeople" (*SL* 34), many of which would appear four years later in *These 13*. (And though he didn't mention it to Liveright, the unfinished *Father Abraham* was also there, waiting to be "foaled" into the Snopes trilogy.) The creative juices were even flowing in other media, recalling Faulkner to earlier vocations of painting and illustrating. "I also have an idea for a jacket," he told Liveright. "I will paint it and send it up for your approval soon" (38). Only one small note clashed with the letter's ebullient tone: "As usual, I am broke, and as usual, I want some money" (qtd in *FAB* 557).

VII

To put it mildly, Liveright's response was unexpected. Late in November, Faulkner received the following reply: "It is with sorrow in my heart that I write to tell you that three of us have read Flags in the Dust and don't believe that Boni and Liveright should publish it. Furthermore, as a firm deeply interested in your work, we don't believe you should offer it for publication" (qtd in *FAB* 559). Where Faulkner had seen a great leap ahead into artistic maturity, with the promise of a wealth of future material, Boni and Liveright saw only decline followed by a precipitous plunge:

> Soldier's Pay [sic] was a very fine book and should have done better. Then Mosquitoes wasn't quite as good, showed little development in your spiritual growth and I think none in your art of writing. Now comes Flags in the Dust and we're frankly very much disappointed by it. It is diffuse and non-integral with neither very much plot development nor character development. We think it lacks plot, dimension and projection. The story really doesn't get anywhere and has a thousand loose ends. If the book had plot and structure, we might suggest shortening and revisions but it is so diffuse that I don't think this would be any use. My chief objection is that you don't seem to have any story to tell and I contend that a novel should tell a story and tell it well. (qtd *FAB* 560)

Faulkner's measured reply on the last day of the month fails to disguise his disappointment: "It's too bad you dont like Flags in the Dust. . . . I still believe it is the book which will make my name for me as a writer" (*SL* 39). He was also still worried about money, specifically the $200.00 advance against which he had apparently failed to deliver a work that measured up. Faulkner would get the last laugh, of course, first a wry chuckle when his novel, renamed *Sartoris* and much excised, was published by Harcourt in 1929; then a posthumous chortle when Random House brought out the unabridged manuscript under his intended title in 1973. But all that was years away. The blow to his self-confidence, and his material prospects, must have been devastating. The somber tone of his note to Liveright reminds us of the affinities between emotional and financial distress that lie at the heart of terms like *depression*.[4]

What had gone wrong? Faulkner believed that he had produced a stallion among foals, or more to the point, a mare, a dam: a matrix of story material that would stand tall now and give and give into the future, a mother lode of imaginative wealth that would yield and yield. Yet Liveright was telling him that this fount of literary value was valueless, that the thickly populated territory he had conceived was short on "character." With his eye on reputation—his firm's and his author's—and the bottom line, the publisher had seen in the manuscript not an abundance of story line but "deficit of plot." Not a work teeming with possibility but a "non-integral" dead end. How could two men so devoted to the art of the book have such wildly discrepant notions of value?[5] I linger over this crisis to underscore the incongruous way in which Faulkner, at the advent of Yoknapatawpha, had stumbled onto what social geographer David Harvey calls the "madness of economic reason."[6]

For centuries, classical economists have been selling us a bill of goods with a primal scene of economic activity featuring characters and conditions that have never existed anywhere: human free agents coming together to exchange items in a spirit of pure rational self-interest, in a social field—consecrated as the market—cleansed by definitional fiat of any other human motive or consideration. Even more implausibly, through a second founding fiction, the omnipotent agency of Adam Smith's "invisible hand," the millions upon millions of individual exchanges that constitute the market economy are mysteriously coordinated and directed toward the common good: a rising standard of living that fosters personal happiness and, despite the overt competitiveness of market activity, social harmony. Rational individuals performing rational acts give rise to a rational society, which in turn safeguards the sanctity of market conditions. It's a beautiful Enlightenment-era fable: the pursuit of self-interest isn't just compatible with collective well-being but the very means of it.[7] Or perhaps it's more of a parable, a primer in and apology for a capitalist system in which market competition is the engine of prosperity, progress, and public concord.

There's just one problem. In real life, away from the artificially straitened parameters of economic theory, market transactions rarely behave this way and rarely ever did.[8] There are a number of reasons for this. For one thing, as Marxist economists have been most vociferous and effective in pointing out, economic activity, even of the most rational variety, generates contradictions and all sorts of other unintended consequences that run counter to the interests of the participants. Consider for example the predicament of a capitalist entrepreneur. As a producer of goods or services, her interest lies in keeping labor costs low, driving down the wages of her employees in order to drive up potential profits. On the other hand, she can only realize these profits by taking her goods to market. She's not only a producer of commodities, in other words; she's also necessarily a proprietor. And as a vendor, her interest (also) lies in reaching as broad a market as possible, since driving up demand creates opportunities to increase production, raise prices, or both. Driving down the disposable income of her employees risks squeezing them out of the potential consumer base for her firm's products. And this is because those employees aren't just laborers but consumers as well. The self-interest that a business owner brings to the labor market conflicts with the self-interest she brings to the consumer market. Perfectly rational interests and transactions, then, turn out to be complexly overdetermined, even self-defeating at times. What's a poor capitalist to do?[9]

Complementary predicaments abound in the lives of workers. The same unfair, deeply unfree terms of the "free" market for labor that suppress wages and drive an existential wedge between workers and their own powers of creation ("the products of their own hands") also drive them together—at worksites, in company towns, in associations and unions—while driving their employers farther and farther from the skills and technical know-how that keep machines running, production lines moving, crops growing. As Hegel would have predicted, the lords of the workplace grow dependent on their bondsmen. In the modern economy, then, alienation cuts more than one way, and the same labor arrangements that set out to disempower the working class also foster new sources of empowerment with the potential to shift the balance of power between classes. The capitalists may "own" the land, the equipment, the worksite—a legal fiction—but as a result of inexorable and quite rational processes and principles, the hirelings may come to control them—a political fact. Economic reason yields a topsy-turvy world.[10]

There's a second important reason why the classical model of market economics rings false. Market transactions are at bottom forms of human behavior. This is why the discipline of economics falls among the social (or as the French like to call them, the *human*) sciences, alongside psychology, sociology, anthropology, and so on. The human beings who come to market aren't the purely economic monads of Smith's fable, governed solely by reason. Markets and the social forms they engender are hardly so one-dimensional as that, hermetically sealed away from the ignoble, the illogical, the unruly. Economic subjects carry with them at every moment all manner of secondary motives, psychic baggage, unfinished business, complicating if not obliterating entirely the rationality of their decisions and choices. "There is no question," writes Niall Ferguson, "that the heuristic biases of individuals play a critical role in generating volatility in financial markets. . . . [Such] heuristic biases . . . distinguish real human beings from the *homo oeconomicus* of neoclassical economic theory, who is supposed to make his decisions rationally, on the basis of all the available information and his expected utility."[11] Moreover, human economic activity is typically shortsighted, poorly attuned to the long waves and macroeconomic cycles that govern economic phenomena at their most lawful.[12] We see the fruits of this fundamental economic attention deficit on April 6, 1928. Jason

Compson's decision to sell short on the cotton market, to bet against a rise in the price of cotton, is not, from a macroeconomic viewpoint, an unsound one.[13] Cotton prices were falling over the decade-long run-up to the Depression that lies just over Jason's (and Faulkner's) horizon in 1928. But Jason isn't playing the long game. As an economic actor, he's just not wired that way, and in his haste to make a quick score and get out, he leaves himself in the vulnerable position of having his margin called, and a momentary aberration in cotton's long slide, a mere blip on the macroeconomic radar—perhaps a lingering ripple effect from the quite literal waves of the great Mississippi River flood that had wiped out the previous summer's crop—takes him down. Like Jason's fortunes, the science of economics might be a lot less "dismal"[14] were it to factor the vagaries of human behavior—the competing motivations, the characteristic affects[15] and tempos—more conscientiously into its calculations, predictions, and schemes.[16]

Jason's loss is Faulkner's gain. The dirty little secret he never tires of repeating in his fiction is that *homo oeconomicus* is not a rational man. In Faulkner, economics is always behavioral, and thus all too human. The plantation ledgers of *Go Down, Moses*, for example, reveal not only the brutal arithmetic of planter power but also the sibling rivalry and petty bickering—and, in one influential reading, the homoerotic desire[17]—of a fractious pair of twin brothers, all of which gets worked out, or at least worked *on*, through a series of economic transactions and notations. (A similar set of cold equivalences figures, and competitive juices flow, in the poker games of "Was.") In the pony auction of *The Hamlet*, marginal dirt farmers are willing to empty their pockets in pursuit of the most evanescent sort of personal status—or, in Henry Armstid's case, to bid up a horse simply to deny a neighbor the gratification of doing so. A figure of such probity as Lucas Beauchamp employs a series of subtle financial maneuvers to conduct complex genealogical, psychological, and ethical business with his white ancestors and kinsmen, and in *Intruder in the Dust*, he manipulates economic transactions, from the beginning of the narrative to the end, to conduct urgent racial business with Chick Mallison and Gavin Stevens, with lives including his own hanging in the balance. In so doing, Lucas is perhaps lifting a page—though to more benevolent and dignified ends—from the book of his slaveholding McCaslin grandfather, who recognized in the economics of bequest and bribery a way to appease his own conscience—such as it were—about the sexual commodification of his own enslaved daughter, without ever directly acknowledging the abuse. Even scrupulous, frugal V. K. Ratliff allows financial moves to be contaminated by pride, one-upmanship, and impulsiveness in his dealings with Flem Snopes, letting self-aggrandizement and—let's face it—greed usurp economic self-interest when he falls for the salted-mine trick at the Old Frenchman Place. Conversely, in Flem, the author gives us a character whose economic behavior is so impeccably rational and methodical in its pursuit of self-interest that other characters, and many readers, have difficulty recognizing it *as* human. Nor was Faulkner himself exempt from the fundamental irrationality that plagues economic behavior. To cite only one example, he made himself house- and farm-poor for two decades, sometimes desperately so, in part to show his "townspeople" that he was somebody, that "Count No 'Count" counted after all. (In this respect, his example points forward to his character Thomas Sutpen, who in *Absalom, Absalom!* embarks for the West Indies, "to which poor men went in ships and became rich,"[18] then returns to the US South to build the largest plantation in Yoknapatawpha, out of quite similar motives.) Such was the madness of economic reason in Lafayette as well as Yoknapatawpha County.

Alongside his sharp eye for such local and intensely personal exercises in economic unreason, however, lies an expansiveness and prescience of economic vision that singles Faulkner out among twentieth-century Anglophone writers and gives his works continuing relevance for our time. Macroeconomists could do worse than to study Faulkner's fiction for memorable dramatizations of the economic currents, institutions, and systems that have shaped the modern world. Sutpen's itinerary, for example, veers away from the Virginia-to-Mississippi axis along which so many antebellum white men traveled toward cheap cotton land—and so many African Americans traveled as part of the internal slave trade—to route Haiti and Martinique into his path to power, plugging economic and political histories of New World colonialism and postcolonial revolution into the American rags-to-riches story. Along the way, Faulkner's tales of the Native South, for all their awkwardness of tone and scenario, point to the damage inflicted on and by southeastern Indians as a result of their incorporation into the modern world system, with its cultivation of new consumer desires and its monetization of human life in chattel slavery.

Then, as Native plantations eventually give ground to white-owned ones, the speed and scale of Sutpen's rise in the antebellum Mississippi Valley stands as vivid testament to the role of that region in powering up the global industrial economy. In its relationship to the mills of Manchester, the finance sectors of London and Manhattan, and the shipping centers of Liverpool and New York, Sutpen's cotton South was more core than periphery, driver than driven: a locus of technological and financial innovation so dynamic and dominant in its day that one contemporary historian has christened it the Silicon Valley of the nineteenth century.[19]

Proceeding to postbellum developments, critic Richard Godden has demonstrated how Faulkner's mature work traces the structural transformation of the southern agricultural economy from the labor-intensive arrangements of slave capitalism and postbellum sharecropping and debt peonage to the capital-intensive arrangements made by turns possible and necessary by New Deal programs and policies and by the technological development of mechanized farm equipment, with effects that sift down into the lives of southerners at a granular level, from habits of speech to nuances of racial ontology.[20] Within that larger transition, Flem Snopes's rise from sharecropper's son to bank president; old Bayard Sartoris's diversification of the family portfolio by channeling surplus plantation and railroad capital into the opening of that very bank; Will Varner's rural empire building around a country store; the thwarted ambition of Jason Compson IV, grandson of an antebellum planter, to work in a bank; and even his actual career first as co-owner of a store and then as a clerk there—all offer revealing glimpses of how the balance of economic power in the South shifted in the postbellum decades, from planters to merchants and bankers. Meanwhile, the career of sewing-machine salesman Ratliff, the fierce attachment of Mrs. Abner Snopes to her cream separator—to the point of trading away the cow that would have provided milk for it—and the yearning of Vardaman Bundren for an electric train set (when in all likelihood the family home does not yet have electricity) are just a few of the many examples in Faulkner's writing that witness the penetration of the modern consumer market deep into the rural countryside of north Mississippi.

As the twentieth century unfolds, of course, Faulkner conducts a decade-long fictional interrogation of the Great Depression, the most convulsive event in the nation's economic history, in works ranging in scale and incisiveness from *Light in August, Pylon,* "Wild Palms," and *The Hamlet* to "Lo!" (the 1934 short story whose Indigenous march on Washington conjures up the historical specter of the Bonus Army from only two years before), "Pennsylvania Station," and "Two Dollar Wife."[21] As World War II and the "permanent arms economy" it inaugurated ushered the developed world into the "long boom" of the 1940s, 1950s, and 1960s, the prologues of *Requiem for a Nun* staged a saga of economic, legal, and technological transformation that allowed Faulkner to engage imaginatively with the Marshall Plan for the reconstruction of postwar Europe.[22] And as the Cold War heated up, Faulkner used *A Fable*, as John T. Matthews has argued, to sound an early warning about the rise of the military-industrial complex, the multinational cartel of industrialists (chief among them arms manufacturers), financiers, statesmen, and generals whose roots the novel traces to the Great War.[23] And as Matthews and Myka Tucker-Abramson argue in these pages, other postwar fictions like *Intruder, Requiem,* and *The Town* point to the midcentury origins of American neoliberalism, with its recrudescent rhetoric of market individualism, its distaste for state-supported social programs, and its other characteristic forms of soft and not-so-soft power. It all adds up to an extraordinary imaginative record of the economic life of a local world, a region, a nation, and global modernity itself—a record in turn shaped by the economic exigencies of a national market for stories, books, and movies whose own evolving contours Faulkner skillfully negotiated over five decades of prolific writing. Following the proverbial money through Faulkner's personal and professional life is in many ways as intriguing, as revealing, and as necessary as following it through his art.

And follow it we will in the chapters ahead, charting the flows of commodities, currency, and credit that tie people to people, places to places, and people to places across the broad arc of Faulkner's life and work, and along the way tracing the strange career of Faulknerian objects as they wind their way across fictional, historical, and biographical landscapes, forging relations, defining value, shifting shape. We open the volume with a six-part "economic biography" of Faulkner's life, work, and times. Sarah E. Gardner's "Bookless Mississippi" introduces us to the economies of publishing and readership at the time Faulkner launched his career, pointing out a significant though not entirely surprising hurdle he faced on his path to authorship: a dearth of readers and book buyers from his native region. Depression-era commentators from the book industry and the academic world noted that the economic poverty of the region was accompanied by a cultural poverty that made the development of a book-purchasing public there next to impossible. Literacy rates lagged behind the rest of the nation. Distribution networks underserved the rural areas where most southerners still resided, and low newspaper and magazine circulation in the region meant that southern readers lacked access to the reviews, notices, advertisements, and other forms of "book news" that marketed the product. Faulkner's own Mississippi ranked last in the nation in bookstores per capita, and nearly 70 percent of its citizens lived in counties that lacked access to public libraries. Reading had to compete for precious time with new leisure outlets like radios, automobiles, and football. Small wonder, then, that one professional librarian suggested that book sales in the South had been higher in 1850 than in 1920 or that another study from the 1930s credited the eleven states of the former Confederacy with only 7 percent of the nation's book sales. Faulkner's own tales often pause to survey the contents of his characters' personal libraries, but the cold equations of the publishing industry suggest that his own works were far more likely to end up on bookshelves outside the region.

Economic exigencies take on a more personal cast for Faulkner in Michael Zeitlin's "War, Labor, and Gasoline in 'Carcassonne.'" Focusing on Faulkner's first decade as a writer, 1918–1927, Zeitlin identifies a central motif running like a thread through works of the period: a fantasy of upward soaring—on horses, in aeroplanes, or simply in and through imaginative creation. Yet this dream of flight is invariably held in check by immanent forces whose gravitational pull keeps its promise of transcendence unfulfilled. Faulkner, for instance, cites the medieval *Song of Roland* and its account of the Battle of Roncesvalles to acknowledge war's capacity literally to cleave in two the fiery steed that symbolizes the yearning for apotheosis; in much the same way, Johnny Sartoris's Camel plummets back to earth after soaring over the Western Front in *Flags in the Dust*, and his twin brother, Bayard, follows suit a year and a half later in an experimental aircraft in Ohio. Other all-too-material realities intrude in early Faulkner to thwart the dream of escape velocity: the facticity of labor, the drag of financial obligations, the nauseating odor of gasoline, with its reminder that modern flight and speed are intrinsically dependent on fossil-fuel regimes wedded firmly to earth. Even Faulkner at his most youthful and romantic, then, can't divorce his lyric intensities from the clamor, press, and stink of economic forces. To convey the insistence of these image-patterns, Zeitlin experiments with essayistic form, edging his discussion toward intellectual montage effects once espoused by Walter Benjamin, which rely heavily on the juxtaposition of quotations—from "The Hill," from *Soldiers' Pay*, from *Mosquitoes*, from *Flags*, from Max Weber, and above all from "Carcassonne"—to spark unsuspected insights and new questions.

Moving ahead into the thirties, Robert Jackson traces the "signature move[s]" of a writer whose "most intense creative development" coincided with global economic upheaval. "The Anatomy of Thrift: Markets, Media, and William Faulkner's Great Depression" points out the market-conscious writer's penchant for projecting greed onto various outsider figures—Jews, Scotsmen, Yankees—during this period and for placing "money and romance" in mutually antagonistic relation. Though Jackson finds Faulkner's stance toward the dominant economic order to be "passive-aggressive," he also notes that "the economic" figures prominently in the fictions and screen work of the thirties as "a subtle, highly complex means of expression" there, nowhere more than in the case of money itself, which Faulkner recognized as a form of media in its own right, "as definitively modern . . . as motion pictures." Jackson nominates *Absalom, Absalom!* as "the most ambitious and comprehensive literary statement of Faulkner's economic thought" during the Depression years, but he reserves his closest scrutiny for a minor work, the 1930 story "Thrift," which even Faulkner pronounced "not too good." Jackson finds in "Thrift" a "sharp analysis of the market conditions of modernity" as they shape not only the period's print culture but its "wars, religions," and modes of cultural identity. The story may make light of its protagonist's all-consuming (which is to say, anticonsumerist) pence pinching as a stereotypically Scottish trait, but it also, significantly, allows the hero, unlike so many characters from Faulkner's Great War fiction, to emerge from the conflict untraumatized, both "culturally and psychologically intact." Where for Zeitlin the aircraft of Faulkner's early work hold out a seductive but false promise of sanctuary from labor, for Jackson's Depression-era Faulkner the airplane becomes the very scene of labor. But in the "curbing influence" money here exerts "against flights of solipsism and despair," we also find evidence of a writer's probing engagement with the market conditions of his moment.

Peter Lurie offers a related take on the "economics" of Faulkner's greatest novel in "Pictorialism, Prolixity, and Spatial Form in Faulkner's Post-Hollywood Racial Imaginary." Pointing out that Faulkner composed *Absalom, Absalom!* "in the midst of [his] highest remuneration to date" as an MGM and Fox screenwriter, Lurie links this "experience of financial ease" to the assurance and ambition of the novel, its aesthetic, thematic, and historical "expansiveness." Moreover, "the outsized spectacle of the Hollywood film image" of the period may have contributed more directly and formally to "the enlarged scope of vision" that his novels begin to exhibit after the author's introduction to Hollywood in 1932. Lurie finds a powerful emblem of this process in the map Faulkner created for the endpapers of *Absalom*. Reflecting at once the "pictorial turn" of twentieth-century print culture, the universalizing ambitions of the photographic and cinematic eye, and the commercial savvy of Faulkner's new publisher, Random House, the map indicates the "new imaginative space" that Yoknapatawpha County "was becoming in the midthirties and beyond." Its visual survey of the entire Yoknapatawpha domain, populated by characters from half a dozen novels, and its notations of the sort of "violent and sensational action" favored by the film studios—"dangerous, modern, and . . . narratively interesting"—all point to new "scalar dimensions" for Faulkner's "writerly vision," along with a "richer perspective" on his Mississippi material, especially its racial complexities. It also reveals a growing interest, perhaps fueled by his Hollywood experiences as well, in the theme identified by W. J. T. Mitchell as "the artist as world-maker." *Absalom*'s grandness of conception indicates that Faulkner may have owed the studios a debt—aesthetic, attitudinal, and, yes, economic—he could never repay.

Turning to Faulkner's late career, John T. Matthews reveals how the movement from *The Hamlet* (1940) to *The Town* (1957), and the parallel shift in narrative focus from the 1890s to the 1920s, allows the novelist to explore one of the most significant developments in twentieth-century economic history: the rise of financialization. Whereas the first installment in the Snopes trilogy details Flem Snopes's successful apprenticeship in the "speculative mercantilism" of the Varner dynasty in Frenchman's Bend, "Financialization and Neoliberalism: A Snopes Genealogy" plots Flem's ascendancy in Jefferson against a more sophisticated regime of accumulation, in which the systematic monetization of every sort of material and immaterial asset in the local environment allows savvy students of behavioral economics like Montgomery Ward Snopes and Mrs. Hait (of the celebrated "Mule in the Yard" incident) to "mak[e] money off nothing," with Flem, of course, at the top of that particular pyramid. In valorizing the "goods-based trade" of an earlier era over the "traffic in abstract economies" that is quite literally the stock in trade of modern banks, insurance companies, and other concerns that monetize "social information," *The Town*'s trio of narrators, Chick Mallison, Gavin Stevens, and V. K. Ratliff, manage to look twentieth-century finance capitalism squarely in the eye yet miss the point—miss it completely, Ratliff might say. But Faulkner doesn't miss it. Alongside the undeniable comedy of the various rackets and schemes that propel Flem from the role of human fire insurance policy at the Varner store to the presidency of old Bayard Sartoris's bank is a profound running commentary on the financialized American capitalism of the interwar twenties *and* Cold War fifties, in which the sources of profit in brutal labor regimes are literally papered over by a "traffic in stocks, bonds, and debt" that in turn "limns a genealogy" for the neoliberalism of our own moment.

Gloria J. Burgess introduces us to a different facet of Faulkner's economic life during this era: his role as a benefactor. "Legacy: The Currency of Eternity" tells the story of Burgess's father, Earnest McEwen Jr., who, as a young husband, parent, and maintenance worker at the University of Mississippi in the early 1950s, was introduced to William Faulkner. On learning of McEwen's lifelong dream of attending college, Faulkner offered to pay for his tuition, books, and room and board at Alcorn A&M, an historically black college in Lorman, Mississippi, and to help McEwen and his wife find work there to meet family expenses. A proud man, McEwen initially hesitated to incur a financial debt he feared he would be unable to repay, whereupon the author assured him that the only repayment he expected was that McEwen find ways in his life to pass the kindness and assistance on to others. The results were transformative for the McEwen family. Earnest graduated from college in 1957 with a degree in architecture, the first in his family line to do so, and went on to careers in hematology, at a Detroit-area hospital, and in engineering, with the Ford Motor Company. He passed down his love of learning, along with the family creed of living a useful life, not only to his five daughters, all of whom went on to complete college and, in some cases, graduate degrees, but to many members of his community as well. "Legacy: The Currency of Eternity" complicates received wisdom about Faulkner's fraught stance toward the segregation and institutionalized racism rampant in the midcentury South, revealing a more complex figure than many scholars will have expected. It also attests to the surprising moments of "vision, compassion, generosity, and kindness" that surfaced in the 1950s and other difficult periods in our history, moments that sometimes fostered lasting legacies.

Exiting economic biography, we re-enter the Faulkner canon at the genesis of some of the earliest and most worked-over material the author generated out of the Yoknapatawpha turn in his imagination, material in which the Armstid family plays a surprisingly central role. In "The Friction of Money: Poverty and Failure in Early Faulkner," Gavin Jones takes up what he calls "the Spotted Horses material," a "constellation" of published and unpublished narratives ranging from the 1926 "Father Abraham" fragment at the very birth of Yoknapatawpha, through published stories like "Spotted Horses" and "Lizards in Jamshyd's Courtyard," and on to *As I Lay Dying*, *The Hamlet*, and even Malcolm Cowley's *Portable Faulkner* volume of 1946, where the tale of the Texas pony auction was excerpted from *The Hamlet*. In addition to illustrating how Faulkner's own authorial identity "grew in [an] impoverished economic of barter and reuse," these tales of Frenchman's Bend introduce us not only to the genealogical and economic "multiplying power" of the Snopes clan and the exuberant generativity of the ponies themselves as they "attract spectatorship," "narrative attention," and, of course, eager buyers, but also to the abject and long-suffering Armstids, who appear across all versions of this material. The family brings a world of misery, hunger, and shame into the Frenchman's Bend story that Faulkner clearly found compelling but also "difficult to tell, and to sell." Some of the manuscripts break off upon scenes featuring the Armstids, "revealing a reticence, perhaps, in approaching the[ir] pain" that led to "unsatisfying termination[s]" and asymptotic narrative paths. The "tonal uncertainty," experiments with shifting or multiple perspectives, and thematics of violence, "dependency," and "disempowerment" surrounding the Armstids attest to Faulkner's repeated "if faltering attempts to theorize the impact of poverty" and dramatize the "unseen, multiplying, abstract" power of money "to determine our relationships and structure their inequality." The Armstids shadow the Snopeses throughout the Yoknapatawpha story like a haunting photographic negative, a testament to the *friction*, and not just the liquidity, of money.

Ted Atkinson turns to the psychology of economic downturn in "Too Small to Fail: Jason Compson's Precarious Self-Worth." As Atkinson demonstrates, the characterization of the most odious of the Compson brothers resonates tellingly with period concerns about the middle-class American's ability to navigate the perilous waters of the modern economy. When Jason pulls out his strongbox at night, he doesn't just count "his" money, the funds he has embezzled from his sister and niece. He counts *on* it as well, "for compensation in a ritual of financial and psychological insecurity" intended to shore up a fragile ego threatening to come apart under the uncertainties and outright assaults of the commodities market and other complex instruments of twentieth-century capitalism. Atkinson tells us that if Jason's mother associates being a Bascomb with the ability "to thrive in modern business," then Jason remains a Compson through and through, no less marked than his suicidal brother, Quentin, by "deep-seated feelings of inadequacy" that in his case "the conditions of the modern marketplace only exacerbate." The fantasy he clings to, that "turning a profit will be a quick fix for his feelings of declining stature at home and in the community," confirms the diagnosis of contemporaneous popular economist Stuart Chase that, at the end of a decade characterized by a bull market on Wall Street whose enormous paper profits only fitfully drifted down into the middle and working classes, money—more specifically currency—was becoming "the prime ontological determinant of experience" for the era. So much the worse for Jason, whose thoroughly monetized psyche, under the buffetings first of April 6 and then of April 8, 1928, dissolves toward a most unwelcome ontological liquidity.

Richard Godden takes up the fate of the commodified, monetized modern body in Faulkner's most notorious novel. "What Price a 'Cheap-Idea'? Money, *Sanctuary*, and Its Intertexts" inverts Faulkner's offhand remark that his arch-villain Popeye should be played in the film adaptation by Mickey Mouse to hold up *The Karnival Kid*, the 1929 animated short that introduced Mickey to the world of the talkies, as a gloss on the weird forms of animatedness and anamorphosis on display in Faulkner's 1931 novel. The whirling, springing, elongating, contorting bodies of *Sanctuary*, especially those of Popeye and Temple Drake, may owe something to the advent of the movie camera and its optical unconscious, which steal "physical cohesion" from the human form. But, according to Godden, they owe even more to the impact of modern capital as "value in motion," morphing, with more and more violence and speed, through the money and commodity forms and back again, and along the way "producing thingified persons and personified things" through exploitive labor arrangements and runaway consumption habits. This necromancy (which anticipates Mickey's later role in *The Sorcerer's Apprentice*) and the "physical incoherence" it introduces are telling symptoms of the "prevalent monetization of the real" in the Depression era, fittingly at their most conspicuous in the Faulkner novel conceived above all others "to make money." "In writing *for* money," Godden argues, Faulkner also "wrote *through* money," and with great candor and acumen. As Godden's characteristically granular analysis reveals, *Sanctuary* takes us for a wild ride in the fast lane of modern value in motion.

Ryan Heryford approaches Faulknerian bodies in quite a different context, though with related economic and political implications. If it might seem difficult at first glance to link the practices of Hatha yoga to the economics of the Faulkner oeuvre in a meaningful way, "Mink Snopes's *Shavasana*: Body, Relation, and Exchange in Faulkner's Economies of Being" proves up to the task. As Heryford memorably explains, the *shavasana*, or "corpse pose," offers the body release from itself at the end of a yoga session, "feeling its own weight supported by the earth entirely, each point of contact dissolving, free from any assembled notion of a thinking self, enmeshed into anonymity." As such, the practice of *shavasana* "bel[ies] the individuation underwriting our dominant economy of accumulation and exchange" and thereby offers a conceptual model for an important subset of "economic relations within and beyond" Yoknapatawpha County. According to Heryford, the shavasanic bodies of Thomas Sutpen, Darl Bundren, Mink and Ike Snopes, and Eula Varner, along with shavasanic acts of enfleshment, fusion, and release, recur across Faulkner's work in "cris[e]s of ontological ambiguity" that pose a direct challenge to expansionist regimes of accumulation predicated on "contained and fixed units of difference, hierarchy, and . . . value." Sutpen's ordeal outside the walls of the sugar planter's compound dramatizes "the crisis posed to colonial ontology by postrevolutionary Haiti." Darl follows the vitalistic lead of the swollen Yoknapatawpha River and its creative-destructive force into the "powerful and destructive anarchy" of barn burning, releasing the energy and radiance trapped within the Gillespies' accumulated agricultural capital. Both Snopeses, in their sensuous intimacy with the earth that others of their world seek to monetize, live out a version of selfhood "born in relation to its outsides" and in continuous, transcorporeal traffic with them. The "relationality of being" these characters experience points to "subaltern routes" beneath or away from "our reiterated economies of exchange."

David A. Davis makes a case for Faulkner's *bona fides* as an economic historian of his region's post-Emancipation cotton economy. "Faulkner's Stores: Microfinance and Economic Power in the Postbellum South" turns to three of Faulkner's most distinguished works, *Absalom, Absalom!*, *The Hamlet*, and *The Sound and the Fury*, to illustrate the strange career of the southern country store as it became a locus of wealth and power with the reorganization of agricultural labor arrangements after the Civil War. Whereas the antebellum cotton economy hinged on the use of land and slaves as collateral, cotton factors as financial liaisons, and the legalized mastery conferred by slave ownership as the chief form of labor control, this system shifted with the evaporation of slave capital brought about by Emancipation. With the rise of the sharecropping system, "the rural merchant became a financial intermediary" in the system, whether as independent entrepreneur or as the landowner himself operating a commissary. By extending credit to croppers, tenants, and small farmers, enticing them with a new world of consumer goods on store shelves, and placing liens on their cotton crops, southern merchants rose to status and influence while insuring that the labor supply remained available and compliant. In this way, "the store became the nexus for labor control," and the key to that control was no longer "mastery" but "debt." *Absalom* offers before-and-after portraits of this process: the antebellum merchant Goodhue Coldfield is a social nonentity in Jefferson, whereas postbellum Thomas Sutpen holds his plantation together by refocusing his attention and energy on his store. Similarly, Flem Snopes learns the social power and economic utility of debt while clerking in Will Varner's store in *The Hamlet*; then he parlays his own private credit operation into a ticket to Jefferson by novel's end. By contrast, Jason Compson IV remains a lowly store clerk in *The Sound and the Fury* in part because he never learns to leverage the debt of his customers, only to accumulate debt of his own through speculative blunders. We may think of Yoknapatawpha primarily as a world of plantations and small farms, but as Davis shows, merchants and their stores play an outsized economic role there.

Two chapters explore the subtle economics of *Intruder in the Dust*, the postwar racial thriller that tellingly begins and ends with the counting of coins in charged interracial exchanges. In "The Gifted Presence of *Intruder in the Dust*," Michael Wainwright draws on Jacques Derrida's theoretical work to argue that the education young Chick Mallison receives under the mentorship of his African American elder Lucas Beauchamp redirects the boy from an economy of money to an economy of the gift, which "demands neither exchange nor return of payment." This novel-long course of instruction, a gift in its own right, begins with Chick's misguided attempt to repay Lucas for the gift of hospitality that opens the narrative, but as Wainwright explains, "the reciprocation of exchange" simply "translates gifts into presents" that cut short the recognition of responsibility to the other and the extension of this relation into the uncertain future. The essence of the gift is its excess, a surplus that signals to giver and recipient alike, contra American myths of self-reliance and self-sufficiency, that subjectivity is constituted in a crucial *more* that comes from outside the self—that selfhood *depends* on otherness. For the white southerner, the sources, both financial and ontological, of that supplemented selfhood reach back into the slaveholding South, whose antebellum code of southern honor ironically rested in part on gift-giving abilities reserved for elite gentlemen and denied the enslaved, and still farther to an "accredited history of *American* foundation . . . spawned by the financial transactions encompassing the Middle Passage" and the plantation colonies of the Chesapeake Bay region. Lucas suggests as much, perhaps knowingly, when he reaches into an old tobacco pouch at novel's end for the coins that will discharge his obligations to Chick and his uncle and theirs to him—for now, at least, and only if they truly understand the nature and implications of the "receipt" he requests of them.

Where Wainwright stresses the importance of gifting in *Intruder*, Mary A. Knighton focuses on debt. "Racial Debts, Individual Slights, and Sleights of Hand in Faulkner's *Intruder in the Dust*" explores how the novel figures "debt resolution as racial kinship," in an "aphasic story of racial reparations" that Faulkner had to occlude behind—or bury beneath—the popular formulas of the murder mystery and the lynching narrative. As Chick struggles to balance his personal moral account with Lucas, and as it slowly dawns on him that the debt he owes Lucas is "not just for food and shelter" but for his white privilege and indeed his very life, Chick comes to stand in for his benefactor in the novel's plot, "walking where he would walk, seeing what he would see," even digging into the earth of Yoknapatawpha as if to mimic the nocturnal activities of Lucas in "The Fire and the Hearth." Such interracial, intertextual mimicry "mediat[es] our access to Lucas" as readers, "magnif[ies] what Lucas means" to Chick and to the county, and forges "racial kinship ties" with which Chick and the reader must increasingly reckon. As we do, a personal debt begins to "swell to encompass Yoknapatawpha's historical reparations" via Lucas's long McCaslin-Beauchamp lineage, and we come to understand that Chick can attain manhood only at the cost of acknowledging, and assuming, his part of "his race's, and his nation's, collective debt," one reaching back to the origins of American capitalism in the monetization of the bodies and persons of Lucas's ancestors and their enslaved cohorts. In unearthing the "debts spawned by past violations of human and family value," *Intruder* anticipates recent arguments for reparations by Ta-Nehisi Coates and other African American intellectuals.

Myka Tucker-Abramson argues that it also anticipates the neoliberal economics and white nationalist politics that animate the contemporary American scene. "Answering the Call: Telephonic Fascism and Faulkner's Angel of History" follows Hosam Aboul-Ela's important work in linking the post-Reconstruction South of Faulkner's fiction with the neocolonial logic of the post–World War II United States: both regimes relied on industrial development, ramped-up financial investment, and centralized planning to consolidate imperial power. As an emerging technology and media form in the earlier era and a leading commodity in the latter one, the telephone functioned as "a foundational object through which phantasms and fantasies of modern life emerge," as Tucker-Abramson illustrates by turning to Faulkner fictions from the 1930s, 1940s, and 1950s. In *Light in August*, telephone calls are directly connected "to births . . . and to racialized deaths" in ways that prefigure Nazi fascism's insidious fusions of "supertechnical" power and "ethnic nationalism" in the militarized state; key scenes of the novel turn on examples of telephonic, indeed quasitelepathic, transmission in which crowds become "anaesthetized into violence" and Percy Grimm is moved about on a murderous chessboard by an authoritarian Player figure that operates like a voice in his ear. After the fall of Nazism, *Intruder in the Dust* turns to automobiles and telephones to introduce us to emergent forms of urbanism "organized around dispersion, mass consumption, single-family homes, and the reassertion of separate domestic and racial spheres," as a chain of party-line calls assembles an urban gathering that "fades in and out of [a] lynch mob." In its image of African American domestics making phone calls of their own, however, the novel also holds out a more hopeful glimpse of a "working-class history" of "transformative collective organizing" that will bloom in the decades ahead. Finally, the story of Essie Meadowfill, telephone operator and landed entrepreneur, in "Hog Pawn" (1954) and *The Mansion* (1959), points at once to a midcentury "suburban sensorium" that "militarizes all aspects of daily life" and to "a new cycle of wealth extraction . . . launched on the battlefields of real estate and oil," a nascent neoliberal order hospitable to fascist energies. "This is the call," Tucker-Abramson concludes, "that Donald Trump answered."

Well into his magisterial *Capitalism in the Twenty-First Century*, French economist Thomas Piketty turns literary critic for a moment.

"Until World War I," he writes, "money had meaning, and novelists did not fail to exploit it, explore it, and turn it into a literary subject."[24] Piketty argues that this state of affairs changed when the belligerent nations of the Great War took their currencies off the gold standard and piled up huge public debts to finance their militaries, destabilizing not just the value but the very *meaning* of money, "not only in the realms of economics and politics but also in regard to social, cultural, and literary matters. It is surely no accident that money—at least in the form of specific amounts—virtually disappeared from literature after the shocks of 1914–45. . . . This is true not only of European and American novels but also of the literature of other continents."[25]

Piketty is a superb economist whose book deserves the accolades it has received, but the example of Faulkner's career suggests he may be a bit out of his depth as a literary scholar. Even in currency-strapped Frenchman's Bend, where the specter of eight "actual Yoknapatawpha county cash dollars" set "rattling around loose" in the village economy by a horse-dealing stranger looms for years afterward as an affront to local honor, and where Mrs. Armstid has pored so intently over the meager sum she has earned from weaving that she "would know them five dollars anywhere"—or perhaps *especially* in such hard-pressed Faulknerian locales—money, indeed specific sums of it, is ever on the minds of Faulkner's people and on the pages of his work.[26] So are the more complex but never abstract economic forces that money traces through their lives and traced through his. Faulkner finds in those forces a hothouse mixture of violence, derangement, fantasy, and strangeness that courses behind the cool, sober façade of economic rationality. Which brings us back to the impasse with his publisher that gave the young Faulkner that early crash course in economic unreason: imaginative and aesthetic riches pronounced devoid of market value. "That human wealth," writes Harvey, "which should have all manner of social meanings, is increasingly imprisoned in the unique metric of money power . . . is the insane and troubling world in which we live."[27] Faulkner went on to show us that world in unparalleled detail and depth. He even managed to make a living at it.

NOTES

1. David Graeber, *Debt: The First 5,000 Years* (2011; repr., Brooklyn, NY: Melville House, 2012), 187.

2. Joseph Blotner, *Faulkner: A Biography*, 2 vol. (New York: Random House, 1974), 557. Hereafter cited parenthetically as *FAB*.

3. Joseph Blotner, ed., *Selected Letters of William Faulkner* (New York: Random House, 1977), 38. Hereafter cited parenthetically as *SL*.

4. As economic historian Niall Ferguson explains, "Money amplifies our tendency to overreact, to swing from exuberance when things are going well, deep depression when they go wrong. Booms and busts are products, at root, of our emotional volatility" (*The Ascent of Money: A Financial History of the World* [2008; repr., New York: Penguin, 2009], 15–16).

5. Value, writes David Harvey, is "like gravity, an immaterial but objective force. . . . Both are immaterial relations that have objective material consequences" (*Marx, Capital, and the Madness of Economic Reason* [New York: Oxford University Press, 2018], 5). He's not saying anything that Faulkner, thanks to Liveright, wasn't painfully aware of.

6. See especially Harvey, *Marx, Capital, and the Madness of Economic Reason*, 172–205.

7. As Stephen M. Best, argues, the mystifying work of this fable, and the master trope Smith installed at the center of it, was to rationalize "consumer desire" in all its contingency and affective volatility "as a sort of natural and ontological force in the economy" (*The Fugitive's Properties: Law and the Poetics of Possession* [Chicago: University of Chicago Press, 2004], 109; see also 119–22, 160–63).

8. As Graeber observes, "Markets aren't real. They are mathematical models, created by imagining a self-contained world where everyone has exactly the same motivation and the same knowledge and is engaged in the same self-interested calculating exchange. Economists are aware that reality is always more complicated. . . . The problem comes when it enables some (often these same economists) to declare that anyone who ignores the dictates of the market shall surely be punished—or that since we live in a market system, everything (except government interference) is based on principles of justice" (*Debt*, 114–15).

9. The contemporary explosion of easy credit and massive consumer debt may be allowing today's capitalist class to dodge this bullet, at least for now, in what Harvey might call a debt "fix." On consumer debt as an increasingly important economic stimulus for flagging regimes of accumulation, and not incidentally as a powerful way of disciplining a work force, see Harvey, *Marx, Capital, and the Madness of Economic Reason*, 78–87 and 204–5; Ferguson, *The Ascent of Money*, 63; Graeber, *Debt*, 368; Chris Harman, *Zombie Capitalism: Global Crisis and the Relevance of Marx* (2009; repr., Chicago: Haymarket, 2010), 289; Thomas Piketty, *Capitalism in the Twenty-First Century* (Cambridge, MA: Harvard University Press, 2014), 297; and Peter Sloterdijk, *In the World Interior of Capital* (2005), trans. Wieland Hoban (Malden, MA: Polity, 2014), 50.

10. Chris Harman points out another important source of fundamental economic contradiction: in "a system based on commodity production," he writes, "everything that happens in it is subject to two different sets of scientific laws." First, "there are the laws of the physical world—of physics, chemistry, biology, geology and so on. . . . On the other side, there is the way things relate to each other as exchange values" that (supposedly) follow the principles of economics. These laws "operate according to different, often contradictory, logics and a failure to see this leads to a failure to understand the most basic thing about a commodity producing economy. It does not operate smoothly, just through the flow of exchange values, but is always subject to bumps, to stopping and starting, due to the embodiment of exchange values in use values with physical properties that limit their fluidity" (*Zombie Capitalism*, 23–24; see also 320–28).

11. Ferguson, *The Ascent of Money*, 346–47. As a result, economic agents "succumb too readily to . . . cognitive traps" that upset the rational basis of decision-making (347).

12. See Piketty, *Capital in the Twenty-First Century*, 359, on the personal and social forms of "time preference" that shape investment strategy and consumer activity.

13. On the financial intricacies of Jason's Black Good Friday, see Wayne W. Westbrook, "Skunked on the New York Cotton Exchange: What Really Happens to Jason Compson in *The Sound and the Fury*," *Southern Literary Journal* 41, no. 2 (Spring 2009): 53–68.

14. See Stephen A. Marglin, *The Dismal Science: How Thinking Like an Economist Undermines Community* (Cambridge, MA: Harvard University Press, 2008). The phrase "dismal science," of course, is Thomas Carlyle's pithy put-down of the economic and demographic calculations of Thomas Malthus.

15. Indeed, once we turn from the productive and commercial economies favored by classical economic theory to consider financialized systems built on credit, debt, and speculation, we find ourselves floating on a veritable sea of affect: trust, hope, confidence, passion, and so on. "The circulation of affect," writes Stephen M. Best, "is no more and no less than the very trope of credit economy (an early and foundational trope, we could argue, for the inflation endemic to speculative financial cycles)" (*The Fugitive's Properties*, 159). In addition to Best's eye-opening study, another particularly rich and illuminating account of the affect-driven credit economy's impact on literary form and racial representation is Ian Baucom's *Specters of the Atlantic: Finance Capital, Slavery, and the Philosophy of History* (Durham, NC: Duke University Press, 2005).

16. Ferguson agrees: "If any field has the potential to revolutionize our understanding of the way financial markets work, it must surely be the burgeoning discipline of behavioral finance" (*The Ascent of Money*, 347; see also 15).

17. Noel Polk and Richard Godden, "Reading the Ledgers," *Mississippi Quarterly* 55, no. 3 (2002): 301–59.

18. William Faulkner, *Absalom, Absalom!* rev. ed. (1986; repr., New York: Vintage International, 1990), 195.

19. Walter Johnson, "The 'Negro Fever,' the South, and the Ignominious Effort to Re-Open the Atlantic Slave Trade," Gilder-Jordan Lecture in Southern Cultural History, University of Mississippi, 2013. For more on this economic history, see Johnson's *River of Dark Dreams: Slavery and Empire in the Cotton Kingdom* (Cambridge, MA: Harvard University Press, 2013); and Edward E. Baptist, *The Half Has Never Been Told: Slavery and the Making of American Capitalism* (New York: Basic Books, 2014).

20. See Richard Godden, *Fictions of Labor: William Faulkner and the South's Long Revolution* (New York: Cambridge University Press, 1997), and *William Faulkner: An Economy of Complex Words* (Princeton, NJ: Princeton University Press, 2007).

21. See Ted Atkinson, *Faulkner and the Great Depression: Aesthetics, Ideology, and Cultural Politics* (Athens: University of Georgia Press, 2006).

22. Harman, *Zombie Capitalism*, 229, 178. According to Harman, massive state-orchestrated defense spending was the crucial factor that enabled postwar nations to avoid "slumps" like the Depression and keep the "long boom" going by "reduc[ing] the pressures leading to over-accumulation (by diverting a portion of capital into nonproductive military channels); tak[ing] direct action to try to maintain a high rate of exploitation (through wage controls); interven[ing] to slow down the boom before it led key firms to become unprofitable; and maintain[ing] a minimum guaranteed level of demand through military orders" (178). With help from Harman and Harvey, we can identify a series of strategic "fixes" that modern capitalists have employed in order to stave off declining profit rates and crises of over-accumulation: a turn-of-the-century "spatial fix" geared toward imperial or colonial expansion into new markets and resource bases (Harvey, *Marx, Capital, and the Madness of Economic Reason*, 133–34, 189–90); a *speed* fix focused

on accelerating turnover time by means of speeding up and stretching out production, directing consumption toward fashion and planned obsolescence, or both (31–32); the *defense* fix of mid-and late-century arms economies described by Harman above; and the contemporary *debt* fix discussed in note 9.

On *Requiem* and the Marshall Plan, see Spencer Morrison, "*Requiem's* Ruins: Unmaking and Making in Cold War Faulkner," *American Literature* 85, no. 2 (2013): 303–31.

23. John T. Matthews, *William Faulkner: Seeing through the South* (Malden, MA: Blackwell-Wiley, 2009), 267–79, 285–87.

24. Piketty, *Capitalism in the Twenty-First Century*, 106.

25. Ibid., 108–9.

26. William Faulkner, *The Hamlet*, rev. ed. (1940; repr., New York: Vintage International, 1991), 38, 360.

27. Harvey, *Marx, Capital, and the Madness of Economic Reason*, 206.

Note on the Conference

The forty-fourth Faulkner and Yoknapatawpha Conference, sponsored by the University of Mississippi in Oxford, took place Sunday, July 23, through Thursday, July 27, 2017. Fourteen presentations on the theme "Faulkner and Money" are collected as chapters in this volume. Brief mention is made here of other conference activities.

The program began on Sunday with a reception at the University Museum for the exhibition *Love = Love*, by Kent Rogowski. The exhibition was a collage of more than sixty store-bought puzzles that created entirely new compositions. Following the reception, a panel convened in Nutt Auditorium on the subject of "A Speculative, Four-Part Economic Biography of William Faulkner," which included papers by Michael Zeitlin, Robert Jackson, Peter Lurie, and John T. Matthews. A talk, "What Price a 'Cheap Idea'? Money, *Sanctuary*, and Its Intertexts," by Richard Godden, followed the panel.

Following a buffet supper at Rowan Oak that evening, Robyn Tannehill, mayor of Oxford, and University of Mississippi provost Noel Wilkin welcomed participants, and Ted Atkinson, president of the William Faulkner Society, introduced winners of the 2017 John W. Hunt Scholarships. These fellowships, awarded to graduate students pursuing research on William Faulkner, are funded by the Faulkner Society and the *Faulkner Journal* in memory of John W. Hunt, Faulkner scholar and emeritus professor of literature at Lehigh University. The Center for the Study of Southern Culture's Rebecca Lauck Cleary presented the 2017 Eudora Welty Awards in Creative Writing. The panel "Two More Episodes from William Faulkner's Economic Biography," which included Ike S. Trotter, Cham Trotter, and Gloria Burgess, rounded out the evening.

Monday's program began with Charles A. Peek and Terrell L. Tebbetts leading the first "Teaching Faulkner" session, "Not for Love or Money! . . . Well, Maybe for Money!" followed by a panel on "Urban, Rural, and Ontological Economies," with Matthew Bolton, David A. Davis, and Ryan Heryford. The day's program also included a Brown Bag Lunch presentation by Seth Berner on "Collecting Faulkner"; a keynote lecture, "Answering the Call: Telephonic Fascism and Faulkner's Angel of History," by Myka Tucker-Abramson; and papers on the topic of "Economies of Entertainment and Play," presented by Daniel Anderson, James Deutsch, and D. Matthew Ramsey.

Tuesday's program included the second "Teaching Faulkner" session, "Beginning with Money," led by James B. Carothers and Theresa M. Towner, followed by a progress report by John Michael Corrigan, Lorie Watkins, and Stephen Railton on the Digital Yoknapatawpha project at the University of Virginia. That afternoon John N. Duvall, Ted Atkinson, and Christopher Rieger presented papers on the topic of "Currency Conversions: Calculating Performances in Faulkner's Yoknapatawpha," followed by a panel with Sarah E. Gardner and Han Qiqun on the subject of "Books and Things." A cocktail party at the Oxford Depot completed the day.

Wednesday's program began with the third "Teaching Faulkner" session, "Faulkner in the AP/IB Classroom," led by Brian McDonald. Michael Wainwright, Mary A. Knighton, and Zoran Kuzmanovich then presented papers on the topic of "Gifting and Debt." Kathleen Woodruff Wickham spoke on "Searching for Faulkner during the Ole Miss Integration Crisis: A Tale of Two Brothers" at the J. D. Williams Library, followed, in Nutt Auditorium, by Gavin Jones's lecture "Faulkner's Failed Economies" and a panel on "Money and Alienation," which included presentations by Caroline Miles and Terrell L. Tebbetts. A late-afternoon walk through Bailey Woods ended at Rowan Oak, where the annual picnic on the grounds concluded the day's events.

Guided tours of north Mississippi, including Oxford and Lafayette County, the Mississippi Delta, and New Albany and Ripley, took place on Thursday, and the conference ended with a closing party and book signing at Square Books. The University Press of Mississippi exhibited Faulkner books published by members of the American Association of University Presses.

The Faulkner and Yoknapatawpha Conference at the University of Mississippi is sponsored by the Department of English and the Center for the Study of Southern Culture and coordinated by the Division of Outreach and Continuing Studies. The conference planners are grateful to all the individuals and organizations that support the Faulkner and Yoknapatawpha Conference annually. In addition to those mentioned above, we wish to thank the College of Liberal Arts, the Office of the Provost, Square Books, the City of Oxford, and the Oxford Convention and Visitors Bureau.

Faulkner and Money
FAULKNER AND YOKNAPATAWPHA

2017

"Bookless Mississippi"

Sarah E. Gardner

Midway through "Ambuscade," the opening story of William Faulkner's collection *The Unvanquished* (1938), Bayard Sartoris, the story's twelve-year-old narrator, lists the books held in his father's library. At least Granny called the room a "library"; it had "one bookcase in it."[1] Bayard's brief survey of the shelves' contents reveals an odd assortment of texts, including "a Coke upon Littleton, a Josephus, a Koran, a volume of Mississippi Reports dated 1848, a Jeremy Taylor, a Napoleon's Maxims, a thousand and ninety-eight page treatise on astrology, a History of Werewolf Men in England, Ireland and Scotland and Including Wales by the Reverend Ptolemy Thorndyke, M.A. (Edinburgh), F.R.S.S., a complete Walter Scott, a complete Fenimore Cooper, a paper-bound Dumas complete, too, save for the volume which Father lost from his pocket at Manassas (retreating, he said)."[2] Colonel Sartoris, it seems, owned the expected, the improbable, and the impossible. Still, what most likely surprised Faulkner's Depression-era readers was not the idiosyncratic composition of Sartoris's library—"Werewolf Men in England"?—but that Sartoris owned a library at all. Nothing that informed "book-conscious readers" of the day, those who kept up with the news of the publishing world, suggested that Mississippians even read, let alone owned a library.

Perhaps encouraging that incredulity, Faulkner intimated that Colonel Sartoris's library was a relic of the past. Readers learn in *Flags in the Dust* that Bayard had inherited his father's library. Now approaching seventy, "Old Bayard" retires to his library, a room, this time described by an omniscient narrator rather than by Bayard himself, "lined with book-cases containing rows of heavy legal tomes bound in dun calf and emanating an atmosphere of dusty and undisturbed meditation, and a miscellany of fiction of the historical-romantic school."[3] By now, readers learn, the missing volume of Dumas had been replaced. But it does not appear as if Bayard read it or any other of his father's old books. "The steady progression of the volumes now constituted Bayard Sartoris' entire reading," the narrator clarifies, "and one volume lay always on the night-table beside his bed."[4] Bayard's library grew through the acquisition of professional reading material. At the dawn of a new era, when the modern commercial press experienced the kind of tremendous growth that made Faulkner's literary career possible, Old Bayard did not seem to acquire the kind of books that would interest a general reader.

Old Bayard's office stands in marked contrast with that of Dr. Peabody, his contemporary and confidante. Here, too, Faulkner does not give readers an enumeration of titles—it was not that kind of library— but merely says a word or two about genre. Peabody's reading material, we learn, consisted of "a stack of lurid paper-covered nickel novels. This was Dr Peabody's library," the narrator continued, "and on this sofa he passed his office hours, reading them over and over. Other books there were none."[5] These three libraries and three passages, each less detailed than its predecessor, tell us something about how Faulkner imagined books' varied purposes. Some were owned and displayed. Others were consulted. Others still, of an utterly different sort, were indistinguishable and read for pleasure. The categories, Faulkner implies, were mutually exclusive. Perhaps more to the point, "middlebrow" fiction, which was coming into its own in the second quarter of the twentieth century, was wholly missing.

For Faulkner, this absence mattered. And it mattered because it was personal. As Jay Watson and Jaime Harker note in the introduction to their edited collection *Faulkner and Print Culture*, Faulkner was "ever on the lookout for new ways of making books and getting them into the hands of consumers."[6] His hopes were unrealized more often than not. Jay Satterfield has noted that Random House, for example, developed a strategy to promote Faulkner to readers throughout the 1930s, "though with each successive book, a little less attention was given to Faulkner, whose sales were disappointing."[7] Random House hyped Faulkner's artistry and his "literary importance" throughout the 1930s and 1940s, but the firm acknowledged that Faulkner's books "would probably represent a loss." Not until Faulkner published *Intruder in the Dust* in 1948 did he become "a break-even author" for Random House.[8]

Faulkner's concern with his own financial success was particular; the problem of developing a reading public was much larger than he probably imagined. This chapter contextualizes Faulkner's concern for books by examining the ways in which academics along with industry insiders—publishers, critics, and booksellers—understood depressed rates of book buying and borrowing in the US South. These were no idle concerns. During the 1930s, the South accounted for a little more than 7 percent of the nation's book purchases. High rates of poverty and illiteracy accounted for much of the problem, but not all. Those with a vested interest in fostering "book consciousness" in the South devised creative schemes to promote reading in the region. Yet their efforts proved largely unsuccessful, in large measure because those concerned solely with the bottom line were content to write the South off. The implications, as we shall see, were considerable.

One example will suffice. In early 1935, Elsie W. Stokes of Stokes and Stockell Bookstore in Nashville, Tennessee, wrote to the editors of *Publishers' Weekly*, complaining of the book industry's neglect of the southern market. "It has long been one of our notions that the reason the South does not buy books is because the publishers do no advertising in the South. Automobiles, breakfast goods, cigarettes, etc., are sold as well in the South in proportion as elsewhere, but since no book advertising to speak of goes on here," she concluded, "we blamed that fact for the small amount that is spent for books in this section." How else to explain, she intimated, Simon and Schuster's claim that it had sold "exactly $8.08 worth of books in Mississippi" since its founding eleven years earlier?[9]

Determined to prove the book industry wrong, Stokes set out on a mass-marketing campaign targeted at Mississippi alumni of Vanderbilt University. She wrote "hundreds and hundreds of letters, entirely by hand, and in the most persuasive manner," encouraging recipients to buy Mississippian Stark Young's blockbuster novel *So Red the Rose*.[10] She sold not one book. Perhaps the book industry's neglect of the region, she conceded, was justified after all.

Indeed, the desire to foster a middle-class book-buying public intensified during the interwar years. An expansion of the publishing industry made books increasingly available to urban Americans at the same time as other, competing forms of leisure activities became popular. From all corners, wails could be heard about America's booklessness. "People don't read as much as they used to before they began to run around in automobiles and listen to radios," an industry insider mocked. "Look at how little we spend on books as compared to ice-cream sodas and lipsticks." "Books mean nothing to the life of the country—America is not book-conscious." These cries were meaningless, however, without data. Those in the trade began to call for investigations of "where books are bought and who buys them." Commissioned by the National Association of Book Publishers, O. H. Cheney's exhaustive *Economic Survey of the Book Industry* became the most important study to emerge in this period.[11]

From the outset of Cheney's investigation, it was clear that the "book-buying public," whatever its size, was actually a "collection of publics." Among other insights, this recognition acknowledged that different regions of the country were "differently unconscious."[12] Cheney's assessment of potential and actual book markets in each state offers one of the clearest demonstrations of these "differing publics." For those concerned with the South's reading public, the Cheney report was sobering. Cheney first compiled two indices, one of "relative cultural level," based on education, use of library facilities, and reading habits, and the other of "relative economic level," based on available income, retail purchases, and automobile ownership. A number greater than 1.0 suggested relative strength in either cultural or economic attainment. Perhaps unsurprisingly, southern states ranked at or near the bottom. South Carolina had a cultural index of 0.51 and an economic index of 0.39, for example; Mississippi's numbers were 0.43 and 0.34 respectively. Those two numbers averaged equaled the potential sales index. Thus, South Carolina's potential sales index was 0.45 and Mississippi's 0.38. Among southern states, only Florida had a potential sales index that approached 1.0, coming in at 0.8. True, the potential for book sales in each southern state was higher than the number of actual sales (which was based on the distribution of books from publishers' and wholesalers' accounts), but the totals were still grim. As Cheney reminded his readers, although the potential sales index demonstrated the difficulties the book industry faced in some states, those difficulties were relative. For Cheney, the question remained whether these states were "inherently poor markets." In other words, do the numbers indicate that the South is "hopeless?"[13] For Cheney, the jury was still out.

For others, the evidence was clear. The cover of the April 2, 1938, issue of the *Saturday Review of Literature* featured a map drawn from Cheney's data, titled "A Bookman's Idea of the United States of America." Each state had been distorted to represent "in exact proportion" its percentage to the nation's book purchases. New York is nearly twenty times its actual size; Mississippi is one-tenth its size. New York accounted for more than 30 percent of the nation's book purchases; Mississippi accounted for two-tenths of 1 percent. Combined, the eleven states of the former Confederacy accounted for 7.12 percent of the country's book sales.[14] The magazine carried no article to accompany the map. Rather, it merely offered a static, visual guide that suggested to viewers that book readers were concentrated in only a handful of states. A barely perceptible Louisiana or Mississippi held up against a puffed-up New York or Massachusetts hardly encouraged those in the book industry to regard the South as a thriving book market. If Cheney held out the possibility that the South could overcome its limitations, the map suggested no such thing. For all practical purposes, the map indicated that the book market in the South was nonexistent.[15]

Saturday Review of Literature, April 2, 1938.

Southern book men and women hardly needed a map on the cover of the *Saturday Review of Literature* to remind them of the anemic state of readership in their region. Well before Cheney published his survey, concerned southerners began to study the problem. In the fall of 1922, Louis Round Wilson, librarian at the University of North Carolina, published the findings of his investigation of his fellow Tar Heels' reading habits. His conclusions were hardly encouraging. Designed to provoke, his article revealed that the state had one automobile for every book on the shelves of public libraries, that declining book sales suggested readers had purchased more books in 1850 than they did in 1920, that New York publishers considered North Carolina one of the poorest book markets in the nation, that less than 5 percent of the population had borrowed a book from a lending library in the previous year, and that North Carolina lacked a literary center to inform the state's reading tastes. Editorialists from around the state picked up Wilson's article, reprinting it in part or whole in a gesture of either sympathetic hand-wringing or defense of their fair state against such unwarranted attacks.[16] Whatever the response of local newspaper editors, Wilson believed that his preliminary work had identified a serious problem that demanded greater attention.

Wilson continued his investigation and began drafting "Reading as a Southern Problem" in 1926. In it, he argued that the fostering of southern readership depended on strengthening university presses, literary journals, and journals of opinion. He also advocated the establishment of bookstores that "provide for their readers books of distinction and character" and the creation of "book review pages in the dailies of the South capable of creating an interest in the news of the world of magazines and books."[17] The method of carrying out these programs eluded Wilson, however. At this stage of his work, he could merely recommend "men of means" to endow presses and journals, to patronize discriminating bookstores, and to praise managing editors "brave enough to maintain against all the arguments of the accounting room that news concerning magazines and books is news, and news in which readers are interested."[18] Wilson anticipated resentment in the South to his findings but also professed great faith in the power of "facts" to convince a reluctant population to act. Unfortunately, he did not have the opportunity to test his theory immediately. Although "solving the problem" of reading became the "principal objective" of his professional career, he was forced to abandon the project for nearly a decade in order to address other administrative concerns.[19]

Before Wilson had a chance to return to his work, others weighed in on the conversation. In large measure, their conclusions matched those of Wilson. Howard Mumford Jones, for example, reiterated the point that publishers considered southern readers irrelevant. There simply were not enough of them to affect the market. Like Wilson, Jones noted the absence of "literary agencies in Dixie," such as the *Saturday Review of Literature* and the *Bookman*, which meant that the southern author had to wait for the approval of northern literary critics before "being accepted by his home folks."[20] Southern writers, he concluded, mattered little to their compatriots, for "the average southerner does not care passionately for reading."[21]

Wilson became increasingly less interested in these sorts of anecdotal reports and impressionistic conclusions. By the time he returned to his work in the mid-1930s he was able to draw heavily on the studies conducted by the Chapel Hill regionalists, a new brand of sociologists led by Howard Odum and his graduate students at the University of North Carolina. Wilson broadened his project's scope and appealed to Odum for data that would support his suppositions. Odum enthusiastically complied, sending Wilson much of the draft material that would appear later in his magnum opus, *Southern Regions*. Wilson was immediately impressed by Odum's findings, and his subsequent publication, *The Geography of Reading*, bore the heavy imprint of the regionalists.[22]

Among other things, Wilson investigated the inequality of access to "book outlets," namely public libraries, bookstores, and book subscription services, among the states and regions of the country. He was interested, for example, in whether the bookstore was largely an urban phenomenon, whether libraries stimulated the purchase of books, and whether bookstores flourished in areas with few libraries. He also wondered whether class influenced the ways in which patrons used bookstores and libraries. Finally, he asked whether bookstores and libraries cooperated in "elevating taste in reading and stimulating reading interest."[23] Although many of these questions went unanswered, the conclusions he did reach were discouraging.

Part of the problem rested with rates of basic literacy. Wilson estimated that only half of the adult population had "attained a sufficiently high level of reading skill" to allow them to read books with comprehension and ease. As Wilson acknowledged, rates of illiteracy were higher in the South. In North Carolina, Alabama, Mississippi, Louisiana, and South Carolina, the rates were 10 percent or more. Even grimmer, only 25 percent of the reading population actually read books.[24] The prospect of developing southern readership, then, seemed daunting.

The problem went beyond depressed literacy rates, however. As Wilson noted, book manufacturers had the capacity to produce "millions and millions of books," but maldistribution prevented those books from reaching large segments of the population. "In the midst of potential plenty there is actual want," he explained.[25] As one might expect, rural areas were most underserved. The implications were thus particularly dire for the South. Six southern states ranked at the bottom of number of bookstores per capita, with Mississippi coming in last. Rhode Island, which topped the list, had one bookstore for every 7.5 residents; Mississippi had one for every 84,035.[26] Put another way, 77.4 percent of Mississippians lived in counties without bookstores. As Wilson discovered, public libraries did not pick up the slack. Sixty-nine percent of Mississippians, for example, lacked access to public libraries. Book subscription services such as the Book-of-the-Month Club and the Literary Guild fared no better in rural areas. In general, these services attracted readers in places that had the best library facilities. In other words, bookstores, libraries, and subscription services reinforced one another. Populations that had access to one of these book outlets generally had access to all three.[27] As Wilson explained privately, "on all counts the Southeast is the most backward of any of the six major regions of the United States."[28]

For his part, Wilson encouraged publishers and booksellers to develop an aggressive campaign to target rural (including southern) readers. To his way of thinking, the book industry had been too timid in fostering this potential market. He recommended that publishers "discover what constitutes a readable book" to those with limited reading abilities, that booksellers risk selling certain books below cost, and that all concerned "experiment" with new ways of marketing books to those in underserved areas.[29] Because Wilson considered the development of reading a constitutive element in improving general social and economic conditions for rural Americans, he implored "all forces dealing with rural life" to cooperate in attacking this problem.[30] He sent copies of *The Geography of Reading* to, among others, Harry Hopkins, head of the Federal Works Progress Administration, and Henry A. Wallace, the US secretary of agriculture. He also sent a copy to Jonathan Daniels, editor of the *Raleigh News and Observer*, whose travelogue of the South was scheduled to appear later that summer. As part of that trip, Daniels also undertook his own study of reading in the South, more qualitative and much less quantitative.

In addition to editing North Carolina's second largest newspaper, Daniels had been reviewing books about the South for the *Saturday Review of Literature* for a decade. As a member of the literary establishment, he shared its preoccupation with encouraging middle-class Americans to spend disposable income on books. In response to William Couch's program to develop "a reading public in North Carolina and in the South," for example, Daniels registered skepticism.[31] "It is really no part of the function of a Press such as yours to create the readers that we need in North Carolina, but it is a tragedy that book consumption is so limited in this state. North Carolinians," he continued, "still regard books as luxuries and book stores are still unable to exist on the patronage of the few who are willing to go in for this type of luxury."[32]

The key to fostering better reading habits, Daniels believed, rested in "developing individual buying and private libraries."[33] Alas, the North Carolina "parvenu" preferred a "home with all the gadgets of good living . . . and a fine car in the garage." One would find "hardly a book on the shelf."[34] Couch was even less sanguine. In a letter sent to northern philanthropists, he outlined his desperate need to attract northern capital to support the workings of his press. "We cannot expect aid from wealthy North Carolinians or wealthy southerners," he lamented. "Their chief interest is bigger and better football."[35]

Daniels soon had the opportunity to test his theories. Shortly after the release of *A Southerner Discovers the South*, *Publishers' Weekly* asked Daniels if, during his travels, he had learned "some interesting things" about southerners' book-buying and-reading habits.[36] As Daniels prepared an essay to respond to the query, he requested data from Norman Berg, a book agent for Macmillan. Berg's reply, portions of which Daniels worked into his essay, was devastating: "The book buying and reading tastes of the South at large are deplorable and pathetic!" Berg proclaimed.[37] Note that all the evidence seemed to point in one direction, which helps explain why these reports sound so similar.

Daniels published his findings in an essay titled "Zero Times Zero Equals Zero," which appeared in late 1938. Invoking Mencken, Daniels noted that the "traveling bookman's" report "ran like a desert to the Atlantic and the Mississippi, the Potomac and the Gulf. There were oases," Daniels confessed, but they were too few to provide sustenance to the book-deprived.[38] The situation might seem odd, given that "the South sometimes seems almost delivered to literature," Daniels acknowledged.[39] Publishers' catalogs were crowded with the works of southerners "depicting a colorful, confusing and occasionally confounding South. There is no scarcity of books about the South by Southerners," Daniels observed; but, as he "discovered long ago, books in the South, like cotton in the South, are produced for the export trade."[40] No wonder Daniels remained skeptical.

Nor were southerners likely to stay abreast of current literary trends. Granted, the degree to which southerners followed the "book news" in national newspapers and magazines was difficult to determine. Data on newspaper and magazine circulation in the South, however, did not warrant optimism. Eleven of the twelve states that came in last in circulation figures for forty-seven national magazines were in the South, for example.[41] By and large, therefore, critics wrote principally, although by no means exclusively, for a northern reading audience. This reality had profound repercussions for the ways in which reviewers wrote about southern writing.

Those who had hoped to develop an informed book-buying public in the South found little to cheer by the decade's end. To be sure, book production skyrocketed during the war years, and the major publishing firms reported net profits. New communities of readers had been created. And, as Jay Satterfield suggests, this was enough for Faulkner.[42] Yet book sales in the South remained anemic. In 1948, ten years after the "Bookman's Idea of the United States" appeared on the cover of the *Saturday Review of Literature*, Mississippi still accounted for two-tenths of a percent of the nation's book sales; South Carolina, three-tenths; Alabama, six-tenths. Combined, the eleven states of the former Confederacy represented 10.9 percent of the nation's book sales, up by more than fifty percent from 7.12 percent in 1931, but still well below any other region in the nation.[43] The South was beginning to break out of its economic and cultural poverty, yet the distance it had to go meant that it continued to lag behind the nation. Necessarily, then, southern authors still produced largely for outsiders, and how those outsiders "read" the South continued to worry southern book men and women as their region stood poised to enter the second half of the twentieth century.

Faulkner's 1932 introduction to the Modern Library's edition of *Sanctuary*, in which he imagines the novel's sales possibilities in Depression-era America, takes on a new meaning, given the economic and cultural realities of book buying in the decade leading up to World War II. As Faulkner contemplated the novel's potential appeal, so the story goes, he said to himself, "It might sell; maybe 10,000 of them will buy it."[44] He ends the introduction by pleading with his imagined reader: "I hope you will buy it and tell your friends and I hope they will buy it too."[45] Whatever Faulkner imagined, Cheney's and Wilson's findings reveal just how difficult Faulkner's "cheap idea" would be to pull off. The chances of finding ten thousand book buyers in one of the leanest years of the Depression were slim. The chances of finding them outside of literary Manhattan were slimmer still. Faulkner's realization of his "cheap idea" would have to wait.

NOTES

Portions of this chapter are from my book, *Reviewing the South: The Literary Marketplace and the Southern Renaissance, 1920–1941* (Cambridge, UK: Cambridge University Press, 2017). Reprinted with permission.

1. William Faulkner, *The Unvanquished*, rev. ed. (1938; repr., New York: Vintage International, 1991), 16.
2. Ibid.

3. William Faulkner, *Flags in the Dust* (1973; repr., New York: Vintage, 1974), 35.
4. Ibid.
5. Ibid., 106.
6. Jay Watson and Jamie Harker, introduction to *Faulkner and Print Culture: Faulkner and Yoknapatawpha, 2015*, ed. Jay Watson, Jaime Harker, and James G. Thomas, Jr. (Jackson: University Press of Mississippi, 2017), xv.
7. Jay Satterfield, "Building the Brand: Faulkner at Random," in *Faulkner and Print Culture: Faulkner and Yoknapatawpha, 2015*, ed. Jay Watson, Jaime Harker, and James G. Thomas, Jr. (Jackson: University Press of Mississippi, 2017), 103.
8. Ibid., 105.
9. Elsie W. Stokes, letter to the editor, *Publishers' Weekly* 127 (January 26, 1935): 409.
10. Ibid.
11. All quotations in this paragraph are cited in O. H. Cheney, *Economic Survey of the Book Industry, 1930–1931* (New York: R. R. Bowker, 1931), 17.
12. Ibid., 18.
13. Ibid., 60–64.
14. See cover illustration, "A Bookman's Idea of the United States of America," *Saturday Review of Literature* 17, no. 23 (April 2, 1938). A key to the map appears on 42.
15. For another account of the South's irrelevance to the book industry, see Melrich V. Rosenberg, "One Book Traveler Looks at the South," *Publishers' Weekly* 119, January 3, 1931, 39–41.
16. Editorials appeared in many of the state's newspapers. See clippings in the Louis Round Wilson Papers, Southern Historical Collection, Louis Round Wilson Library, University of North Carolina (hereafter SHC).
17. Louis Round Wilson, TS, "Reading as a Southern Problem," 1926, 46, in the Louis Round Wilson Papers, SHC.
18. Ibid., 47.
19. Louis Round Wilson, prefatory note to "Reading as a Southern Problem," 1967, 2, in the Louis Round Wilson Papers, SHC. See also Wilson to William S. Gray, March 17, 1928, and Wilson to H. L. Mencken, October 6, 1931, both in the Louis Round Wilson Papers, SHC.
20. Howard Mumford Jones, "Is There a Southern Renaissance?" *Virginia Quarterly Review* 6 (April 1930): 185.
21. Ibid.
22. See Howard W. Odum to Louis Round Wilson, January 15, 1934, and Wilson to Howard W. Odum, January 19, 1934, both in the Howard W. Odum Papers, SHC; and Odum to Wilson, June 14, 1938, in the Louis Round Wilson Papers, SHC.
23. Louis Round Wilson, *The Geography of Reading* (Chicago: University of Chicago Press, 1938), 200.
24. Ibid., 226, 272.
25. Ibid., 412.
26. Ibid., 203.
27. Ibid., 203, 219.
28. Wilson to Dumas Malone, May 25, 1938, in the Louis Round Wilson Papers, SHC.
29. Wilson, *The Geography of Reading*, 439.
30. Wilson to Glenn Frank, June 8, 1939, in the Louis Round Wilson Papers, SHC.
31. William T. Couch to Jonathan Daniels, January 28, 1936, in the Jonathan Daniels Papers, SHC.
32. Daniels to Couch, February 1, 1936, in the Jonathan Daniels Papers, SHC.
33. Ibid.

34. Ibid.

35. Couch to Jacob Billikopf, October 28, 1936, in the Oswald Garrison Villard Papers, Houghton Library, Harvard University.

36. Eugene Armfield to Daniels, August 10, 1938, in the Jonathan Daniels Papers, SHC.

37. Norman Berg to Daniels, August 24, 1938, in the Jonathan Daniels Papers, SHC.

38. Jonathan Daniels, "Zero Times Zero Equals Zero," *Publishers' Weekly* 134 (October 15, 1938): 1430.

39. Ibid.

40. Ibid.

41. See Wilson, *The Geography of Reading*, 227, 231, 237.

42. Satterfield, "Building the Brand," 105.

43. O. H. Cheney, *Economic Survey of the Book Industry, 1930–1931 with 1947–1948 Statistical Report* (New York: R. R. Bowker, 1949), 362. The updated statistical report did not include figures for library patronage.

44. William Faulkner, "Introduction to the Modern Library Edition of *Sanctuary*, 1932," in *William Faulkner: Essays, Speeches, and Public Letters*, ed. James B. Meriwether, rev. ed. (1965; repr., New York: Modern Library, 2004), 178.

45. Ibid.

War, Labor, and Gasoline in "Carcassonne"

MICHAEL ZEITLIN

And on another cot not far from him was a boy of his own age, an aviator with a broken back and both feet burned off. . . . The aviator had been carried away. Whether he died or not Elmer did not know nor care.
—Elmer, *William Faulkner*

[J]ust another rocket to glare for a moment . . .
—Flags in the Dust, *William Faulkner*

In 1931, Faulkner's French translator Maurice Edgar Coindreau asked Faulkner why he had titled one of his stories "Carcassonne." "He was unable to give me a clear-cut answer," Coindreau wrote. "'It's a vision,' he said, 'a poetic vision . . . a young man who sees a horse'": "And me on a buckskin pony *with eyes like blue electricity and a mane like tangled fire, galloping up the hill and right off into the high heaven of the world.*"[1] Coindreau was merely the first on record to ask Faulkner to explain this "poetic vision" in which a young man not only sees a horse but also seems to become one.[2] After the Algonquin Hotel episode of November 1937, when Faulkner collapsed against a steam pipe in the bathroom and suffered "a third-degree burn the size of the palm of a hand," he was escorted back to Oxford by Eric Devine.

To try to combat the nervousness, Devine read to his friend. One of the stories he chose was "Carcassonne." Faulkner listened silently.

"What does it mean?" Devine asked when he finished.

"It means anything you want it to mean," Faulkner answered curtly. He had read a lot in the Bible and Shakespeare that he didn't understand, he added defensively.[3]

Strike two. Faulkner (burned aviator) suffers in silence and refuses to explain. ("Don't complain, don't explain," his mother, Maud, had taught him.)[4] Still, we feel the pressure of some "private meaning" "in his most perplexing and enigmatic story," the one that "was obviously of special private significance for Faulkner."⁵ The sources of the story's "complex of images," it has often been felt, must lie "hidden in the labyrinth of Faulkner's biography."⁶

If a sense of private opacity has always attended interpretations of "Carcassonne," Cleanth Brooks posits (though he does not pursue) a reading of "Faulkner's young tramp-poet" in relation to "his material condition and prospects as compared to his high-flying thoughts."⁷ When pressed at the University of Virginia in 1957, Faulkner seemed to suggest that such an angle might be productive: "That was—I was still writing about a young man in conflict with his environment. I—It seemed to me that fantasy was the best way to tell that story. . . . I imagine there are so many things that went into it that probably nobody could say. This is where the resurgence of writing in the South came from. I myself am inclined to think it was because of the bareness of the Southerner's life, that he had to resort to his own imagination, to create his own Carcassonne."⁸

Like the protagonist of "Black Music" who "dressed as a tramp" and "had no job,"⁹ the dreamer of "Carcassonne" is a vagrant who is allowed to sleep above a "cantina" in a building owned by "the Standard Oil Company, who owned the garret and the roofing paper," and who "owned the darkness too" (897). This much may be "clear-cut," then, in Coindreau's terms: the transcendent vision of a flying horse seems something of an "ideological reflex and echo"[10] of "the barrenness of the Southerner's life" and the emergent hegemony of gasoline.[11]

The interplay of interior and exterior realities, rising and falling movements, air and water elements, small enclosures, and celestial expanses disorients the spatial perspectives of the story. Prone "beneath an unrolled strip of tarred roofing made of paper" (895), the man looks up toward the "ceiling of the garret slanted in a ruined pitch to the low eaves" (896).[12] From this position, he sees beyond the ceiling by contriving a kind of stereoscope out of his rough coverings:

> [H]e thought of his tarred paper bed as a pair of spectacles through which he nightly perused the fabric of dreams:
>
>> Across the twin transparencies of the spectacles the horse still gallops with its tangled welter of tossing flames. (896)

At another point he floats above the scene looking down: "Across the twin transparencies of the glassy floor the horse still galloped" (897). From here he sinks to the bottom of the ocean: "His body slanted and slanted downward through opaline corridors groined with ribs of dying sunlight upward dissolving dimly, and came to rest at last in the windless gardens of the sea. About him the swaying caverns and the grottoes, and his body lay on the rippled floor, tumbling peacefully to the wavering echoes of the tides."¹³ The next moment, as if in cinematic jump cut, he is mounted on *"a buckskin pony with eyes like blue electricity and a mane like tangled fire, galloping up the hill and right off into the high heaven of the world"* (899). Thus are the walls, floor, and ceiling of the garret resolved out of their integrity by the illuminated psychodrama.¹⁴

With Paul Virilio on war and cinema, one may think here of "Edison's famous tar-paper hut, the 'Black Maria,'—another camera obscura—which served as both studio and projection room,"¹⁵ in relation to this early instance in Faulkner's work in which "the afterlives of romance" are projected into an interior space by "the new mechanical and electronic media themselves,"¹⁶ simulated here by improvised filmic material, cheap and mass produced:

> Each morning the entire bed rolled back into a spool and stood erect in the corner. It was like those glasses, reading glasses which old ladies used to wear, attached to a cord that rolls onto a spindle in a neat case of unmarked gold; a spindle, a case, attached to the deep bosom of the mother of sleep.
>
> He lay still, savoring this. (895)

The image is developed in *Flags in the Dust*, where Miss Jenny's "glasses hung on a slender silk cord that rolled onto a spring in a small gold case pinned to her bosom. She snapped the cord out and set the glasses on her high-bridged nose, and behind them her gray eyes were cold and piercing as a surgeon's . . . letting her glasses whip back into the case" (Faulkner, *Flags in the Dust*, 593–94). As Murphet has observed, Miss Jenny is the primary visionary in *Flags in the Dust* of the romantic past within the present time of "an earth shaped and furnished for punier things" (543): "Virginia Du Pre, née Sartoris, the widow Miss Jenny, aids and abets the chivalric demiurge of old Simon's talks about those titanic Sartoris brothers."¹⁷ "The slender silk cord" of her glasses is the umbilicus that attaches her visionary life to "the past, like a spool being rewound" (857) and to a future to be "moulded," as Freud might put it, "into a perfect likeness of the past."¹⁸ "And now she is trying to make me one of them," Narcissa thinks, "to make of my child just another rocket to glare for a moment in the sky, then die away" (857)—the child born on the day of his father's fiery death as a test pilot in an experimental aeroplane.¹⁹ The overall metaphor is resolutely cinematic. Bayard sees the inexorability of his fate in "its entirety like the swift unrolling of a film, culminating in that which he had been warned against and that any fool might have foreseen" (816).

In "Carcassonne," the reclining figure sees "across the twin transparencies" from the perspective of a felled foot soldier as imagined in *The Song of Roland*, "the final integer in a long and varied sequence of lost works on the Roncesvalles theme";[20] "For there is death in the sound of it, and a glamorous fatality, like silver pennons downrushing at sunset, or a dying fall of horns along the road to Roncevaux" (Faulkner, *Flags in the Dust*, 875).[21] Gazing at horse and rider looming above him, the poet of "Carcassonne" "can see the saddlegirth and the soles of the rider's feet in the stirrups. The girth cuts the horse in two just back of the withers" (896). The horse is then imagined as cut in two by "the wrist which swung the blade, severed the galloping beast at a single blow, the several halves thundering on in the sacred dust . . . not knowing that it was dead." This is a repeated image in *The Song of Roland*:

> he slices downward through the coif and hair
> and cuts between the eyes, down through his face,
> the shiny hauberk made of fine-linked mail,
> entirely through the torso to the groin,
> and through the saddle trimmed with beaten gold.
> The body of the horse slows down the sword,
> which, seeking out no joint, divides the spine
> [. . .]
> he slashes through the center of his head
> and cleaves the trunk, the saffron-yellow byrnie,
> and well-made saddle set with gems and gold,
> and slices through the backbone of the horse;
> both fall down dead before him on the field.[22]

The poem, reimagined in the course of Faulkner's reckoning of the immense carnage of the late war in *Soldiers' Pay* and the war stories of *These 13*, is a principal source of the cavalier dromology in Faulkner's work.[23]

Throughout the poem Charlemagne,

> the mighty emperor, is sleeping.
> He dreamed. . . .
> And Charles sleeps on; he still does not wake
> Up.
> He dreams another vision after this.[24]

As he sleeps and dreams, scenes around him are "acted out" (as they are around Pierrot in *The Marionettes*, Julian Lowe and Donald Mahon in *Soldiers' Pay*, or Gowan Stevens in *Sanctuary*). Charles sleeps, and the war continues,

> piling corpses one upon the other.
> . . . the carnage is immense.

The fighting is incredible and heavy:
none harsher has occurred before or since.²⁵

In "Carcassonne," the man imagines himself as a corpse: "in his mind's eye his motionless body grown phosphorescent with that steady decay which had set up within his body on the day of his birth" (896–97). A "skeleton l[ying] motionless" (896), he is an anonymous dead soldier become Agamemnon murdered by Clytemnestra, "the woman with the dog's eyes"²⁶ who in *The Odyssey* leaves her dead husband's mouth agape and his staring eyes unclosed: *"where fell where I was King of Kings but the woman with the woman with the dog's eyes to knock my bones together and together"* (898). The allusion, I think, is a signature of the "Estelle complex" that runs across Faulkner's work of this early period.²⁷

The story ends as it begins with the man, spurring himself "to perform something bold and tragical and austere" (899), mounted and rising: "Me on a buckskin pony with eyes like blue electricity and a mane like tangled fire, galloping up the hill and right off into the high heaven of the world. Still galloping, the horse soars outward; still galloping, it thunders up the long blue hill of heaven, its tossing mane in golden swirls like fire. Steed and rider thunder on" (899–900).²⁸

The fantasy is dialectical in its interimplication of "base and superstructure," its transfiguration of the wounded foot soldier into the murdered king, the cuckolded tramp poet into the flaming cavalier: "[T]he phantoms of the human brain . . . are necessary sublimates of men's material life-process, which can be empirically established and which is bound to material preconditions."²⁹

In the sister story "Black Music," dialectical fantasy, or perhaps a kind of delusional madness, lifts the protagonist, "a small, snuffy, nondescript man whom neither man nor woman had ever turned to look at twice, in the monotonous shopwindows of monotonous hard streets," above his degraded reality (Faulkner, "Black Music," 799), whereupon "his apotheosis soar[s] glaring, and to him at least not brief, across the unfathomed sky above his lost earth like that of Elijah of old"—Elijah who in his "chariot of fire, and horses of fire . . . went up by a whirlwind into heaven" (2 Kings 2:11). In *Flags in the Dust*, Bayard's horse of fire also rises into the air from a depressing street scene in which some of the pavement is only just in the process of becoming hardened: "That mad flaming beast he rode almost over [Narcissa's] car" (Faulkner, *Flags in the Dust*, 662),³⁰ as the stallion "soared like a bronze explosion . . . in a myriad flicking like fire. . . . The beast burst like bronze unfolding wings . . . soared over a small negro child . . . and . . . struck clashing fire from wet concrete" (647–49).

Inevitably, the high flyers come crashing to the ground. Of the tramp in "Carcassonne," Noel Polk suggests that "perhaps he is an ex-pilot," linking him with the flyers of "Ad Astra" (Latin for "to the stars," a destination that Polk claims is also "the goal of the buckskin pony of 'Carcassonne'").[31] Citing the subadar's comment in "Ad Astra" that "[a]ll this generation which fought in the war are dead tonight. But we do not yet know it," Polk goes on to observe that "the characters of 'Ad Astra' are thus very much like the Norman steed in 'Carcassonne,' which even after he is cut in two thunders on, 'wrapped still in the fury and the pride of the charge, not knowing that it was dead.'"[32] Veteran war pilot and poet Bayard Sartoris is one of these already-dead ex-pilots whose postwar life is dominated by depression, death wishes, and alcohol.[33]

Having killed his grandfather, and unwilling to show his face at home, Bayard rides out to the MacCallums on his horse, Perry, the "Carcassonne" fantasy of *"galloping up the hill and right off into the high heaven of the world"* on an "unflagging" mount (895) now exposed as all played out: "Up the last hill the tireless pony bore him, and in the low December sun their shadow fell longly across the ridge and into the valley beyond" (Faulkner, *Flags in the Dust*, 811–12). As he lies in bed and listens to Buddy MacCallum talking about the war, it seems to Bayard "that he could feel the planks of the ceiling as they sloped down to the low wall on Buddy's side" (822). No transcendent visions dissolve the "strange roof" under which, like war veteran Darl Bundren, he lies.[34] There is only claustrophobia: "You got an impression of people, creatures without initiation or background or future, caught timelessly in a maze of solitary conflicting preoccupations, like bumping tops, against an imminent but incomprehensible nightmare" (823). In this process of working-through, the primal scene of Johnny's crash suddenly emerges with vivid and striking effect: "He watched the flame burst like the gay flapping of an orange pennon from the nose of John's Camel" (824).

Insofar as "the quest for social honor and avoidance of social shame are prime motives of . . . warriors" from Homeric times forward, Bayard already knows upon coming home that his trauma will endure irreparably.[35] In Simon Strother's second-hand report, Bayard returns from the war without fanfare and (unlike Faulkner himself) out of uniform: "'Jumped off de wrong side [of the train] and lit out th'ough de woods. . . . Jumpin' offen de bline side like a hobo. He never even had on no sojer-clothes. Jes a suit, lak a drummer er somethin'" (546). "Carcassonne" also draws on the memory of Faulkner's immediate postwar period in which (despite his costume and his tales) he failed to return from the war resolutely transfigured as a knightly aviation hero. With no significant martial achievements (*"bold and tragical and austere"*) to bank on or substantial social, erotic, or economic prospects to look forward to, he tasted nothing but ashes on his return.

Private Joe Gilligan puts it sardonically in *Soldiers' Pay* (the novel Faulkner was writing during his New Orleans period in 1925), on the demobilization train south: "Listen, think of having to go to work again when you get home. Ain't war hell? I would of been a corporal at least, if she had just hung on another year" (Faulkner, *Soldiers' Pay*, 5). As an integer of the war's surplus, Bayard, like Caspey Strother, returns "to his native land a total loss, sociologically speaking, with a definite disinclination toward labor, honest or otherwise" (Faulkner, *Flags in the Dust*, 588). In "Carcassonne" Mrs. Widdrington formulates the matter thus: "With her, if you were white and did not work, you were either a tramp or a poet" (897).[36]

As Robert Jackson observes in this volume, "It might be . . . accurate to characterize Depression-era Faulkner's attitude towards the prevailing economic philosophy and system of the United States as passive-aggressive," an attitude reinforced by Faulkner's itinerancy and chronic underemployment throughout the 1920s. "Obstructed by spiritual obstacles," in Max Weber's terms, "the development of rational economic conduct . . . met serious inner resistance" in the soul of the Faulknerian poet-tramp.[37] As Weber further explains, for such a social type, "The opportunity of earning more was less attractive than that of working less. He did not ask: how much can I earn in a day if I do as much work as possible? but: how much must I work in order to earn the wage . . . which takes care of my traditional needs? A man does not 'by nature' wish to earn more and more money, but simply to live as he is accustomed to live and to earn as much as is necessary for that purpose" (*The Protestant Ethic*, 60). In this passive-aggressive attitude coupled with his passion to soar "*off into the high heaven of the world*," Faulkner shared something essential with the spotted Texas ponies that "huddled like gaudy ghosts in the remote gloom, passive and watchful," signaling their violent refusal to do any work for the master (*Father Abraham*, 34). The Texas handler knows the cause is already lost, "the spiritual obstacles" noted by Weber insurmountable, as he begs the folks of Yoknapatawpha County to take the ponies off his hands: "'All you want to do is handle 'em a little and work 'em like hell for a couple of days, and they'll be gentle as a dog. . . . Pretty lively, aint they?' he said, breathing heavily. 'But it'll work out of 'em in a couple days. Then you'll have as good a saddle and work pony as you'll want'" (25, 28).

The early prose sketch "The Hill," written during this period, offers another impression of what Godden has called "the primal scene of bound southern labor" in the 1920s,[38] "a world of endless toil and troubled slumber" in which "the tieless casual" is ceaselessly reminded of "the devastating unimportance of his destiny" during long days dominated by "harsh labor with his hands, a strife against the forces of nature to gain bread and clothing and a place to sleep, a victory gotten at the price of bodily tissues and the numbered days of his existence."[39] In *Flags in the Dust*, "the skeletons of labor" lie all around the scene in which Bayard drinks moonshine whiskey with Hub and Suratt:

> Beyond the bordering weeds a fence straggled in limp dilapidation, and from the weeds beside it the handles of a plow stood at a gaunt angle while its shard rusted peacefully in the undergrowth, and other implements rusted half concealed there—skeletons of labor healed over by the earth they were to have violated . . . and Suratt drove on into the barnyard where stood . . . the rusting skeleton of a ford car. Low down upon its domed and bald radiator the two lamps gave it an expression of beetling patient astonishment, like a skull. . . . (651)

Bayard listens silently as Surrat describes the typical laboring life of Mississippi's proximate white others:

> But I swo' then, come what mought, that I wouldn't never plant nothin' in the ground, soon's I could he'p myself. It's all right fer folks that owns the land, but folks like my folks was dont never own no land, and ever' time we made a furrow, we was scratchin' dirt fer somebody else. . . . I was raised a pore boy, fellers, while Mr Bayard's folks has lived on that 'ere big place with plenty of money in the bank and niggers to wait on 'em. But he's all right. . . . He aint goin' to say nothin' about who give him this here whisky. (654–55)[40]

As an heir to "that 'ere big place," Bayard may not be facing a postwar life of rural labor. But the novel opens a view of the abyss into which demobilized soldiers like himself, along with all those moving off the land and into the towns, were likely to fall in massive numbers, as members of the reserve army of labor in the empire of gasoline: "There was a family of country people moved recently to town—a young man and his pregnant wife and two infant children. They abode in a rejuvenated rented cabin on the edge of town, where the woman did her own housework, while the man was employed by the local distributor for an oil company, laboring all day with a sort of eager fury of willingness and a desire to get on" (600).

For this man and all those like him, with nothing to sell but their own labor power,

> The capitalist economy of the present day is an immense cosmos into which the individual is born, and which presents itself to him, at least as an individual, as an unalterable order of things in which he must live. It forces the individual,

in so far as he is involved in the system of market relationships, to conform to capitalistic rules of action. The manufacturer who in the long run acts counter to these norms, will just as inevitably be eliminated from the economic scene as the worker who cannot or will not adapt himself to them will be thrown into the streets without a job. (Weber, *The Protestant Ethic*, 54–55)

This hard lesson arrives as a shock to Faulkner's Elmer Hodge, "five long years after [he] had returned interesting and limping from his rather vain participation in the war" (Faulkner, *Elmer*, 360). Like the tramp in "Carcassonne" who can be "allegorically splendid"[41] only in fantasy, Elmer "sets the internal world, tending towards satisfaction by means of illusion, against an outside world which gradually imposes the reality principle upon the subject."[42] "But who really wants experience, when he can get any sort of substitute—even a dream? To hell with experience Elmer thought knowing that all truth is unbearable" (Faulkner, *Elmer*, 359). He keeps thinking of himself "dead and pale and blond beneath a flag while soldiers marching past dropped flowers on his coffin" (435). He wants to be a painter but finds himself "sink[ing] gradually into the proletariat," as Marx and Engels would put it, upon his release from the air service and Camp Taliaferro near Fort Worth, Texas.[43] He ends up pumping gas in Houston as "mechanics in greasy overalls with red lettering across the back moved here and there or crawled like yellow worms on the filthy floor" (441). Breathing the fumes, he recalls an exchange with his former wife, now married to another man:

> She stopped talking and gave him a swift calculating glance, impersonal as if he had been a motor car and she in the middle of the street. She rushed on: "But tell me about yourself. When we were children together you told me all sort of things you planned to do. Now tell me what you've done. You went to the war, or something, didn't you?"....
> "I'm going to be a painter," he said with a sort of belligerence.
> "A——" her voice faded away in a hushed astonishment.
> "Paint pictures," he explained uncomfortably.
> "Oh. I thought——" she went again into immoderate nervous laughter. (445–46)

Amid these humiliating, art-crushing days a bitter inner dialogue unfolds:

> Why dont you paint? You've got plenty of time: you only work from eight to four, and grinding gasoline into automobiles isn't hard suggested that remote

gleeful thing within him that couldn't even be reached with a Mills bomb....
[He] remain[ed] static beside his gasoline pump, filling car after identical car
champing and vaporous and eager to be off and burn its ten gallons ere night-
fall.... Amid a continuous fretful stream of cars passing endlessly, filling his
mind with a broken and dreadful flashing of Texas sunlight on new and shiny
metal, filling his body with that nauseating smell of recently burned gasoline,
something would touch his heart. (437, 439–40)

Naturally, who should pull into the station one day but Elmer's ex-wife and her new husband, their figures seen at first through "an idiotic vibration of glass that obscured the occupants" (437). The scene unfolds as a blur of furtive glimpses, of lips, blank eyes, cloaked and shapeless bodies: a bad dream of masochism and humiliation. And then they are gone: "The car drew away vaporously, smelling of newness and spilt gasoline.... After a while he rediscovered his hand, finding that Grover had given him a dollar and fifty two cents instead of a dollar and seventy seven. He took a quarter from his overalls and added it to the coins in his palm with a bitter pleasure" (439). The narrative breaks off, and the novel is abandoned soon after, as if an impasse has been reached. An impasse, perhaps, not unlike the one described by Weber in 1905: "The tremendous cosmos of the modern economic order ... determines the lives of all the individuals who are born into this mechanism ... with irresistible force. Perhaps it will so determine them until the last ton of fossilized coal is burnt" (*The Protestant Ethic*, 181).

The Pegasus pony, the knight-aviator, the dream of soaring free from earth toward apotheosis—these motifs from Faulkner circa 1918–1927 all promise a transcendence that never fully arrives, ultimately yielding to the exigencies of the mundane, the immanent, the economic: earthbound labor, earthbound energy, earthbound modernity. In this vision of the end, in at least two senses, of the gasoline economy, rising and crashing in flames, the poet of "Carcassonne," Elmer Hodge, Johnny and Bayard Sartoris of *Flags in the Dust*, and William Faulkner the artist participate equally in the desire "*to perform something bold and tragical and austere*," and to be seen performing it by a Narcissa figure standing "there feeling her breath going out faster than she could draw it in again" (Faulkner, *Flags in the Dust*, 597). The erotic power of the horse and the gasoline engine is consumed in the spectacle of the fiery ascension and the fiery crash. "Carcassonne" crystallizes these images, themes, and trajectories into six pages of lyric beauty and fury, filled with war's remembrance, labor's gravity, the poet's transcendence, and "that nauseating smell of recently burned gasoline."

NOTES

I thank Jay Watson for his valuable comments on earlier versions of this work and for editing this published version.

The epigraphs in this chapter are from William Faulkner, *Elmer*, ed. Dianne Cox, *Mississippi Quarterly* 36 (1983): 382. Hereafter cited parenthetically. William Faulkner, *Flags in the Dust*, in *Novels 1926–1929*, ed. Joseph Blotner and Noel Polk (New York: Library of America, 2006), 857. Hereafter cited parenthetically.

1. Maurice Edgar Coindreau, "The Faulkner I Knew," trans. George McMillan Reeves, in Reeves, ed., *The Time of William Faulkner: A French View of Modern American Fiction* (Columbia: University of South Carolina Press, 1971), 21. William Faulkner, "Carcassonne," *Collected Stories of William Faulkner* (1950; New York: Vintage, 1977), 895. Hereafter cited parenthetically.

2. See Julian Murphet on "the fusion of human sense perception and equine motility" in *Flags in the Dust*: "The cavalier and his stallion are made one in the classical figure of the centaur" (*Faulkner's Media Romance* [New York: Oxford University Press, 2017], 102, 103). On "Faulkner's equation of the imaginative act with aerial equitation," see M. E. Bradford, "The Knight and the Artist: Tasso and Faulkner's 'Carcassonne,'" *South Central Bulletin* 41 (Winter 1981): 88–90; see also Richard A. Milum, "Faulkner's 'Carcassonne': The Dream and the Reality," *Studies in Short Fiction* 15 (Spring 1978): 133–38; Richard A. Milum, "Continuity and Change: The Horse, the Automobile, and the Airplane in Faulkner's Fiction," in *Faulkner: The Unappeased Imagination: A Collection of Critical Essays*, ed. Glenn O. Carey (Troy, NY: Whitson, 1980), 157–74. In his 1955 essay on the Kentucky Derby for *Sports Illustrated*, Faulkner himself wrote, "It is a sublimation, a transference: man, with his admiration for speed and strength, physical power far beyond what he himself is capable of, projects his own desire for physical supremacy, victory, onto the agent" ("Kentucky: May: Saturday," in *William Faulkner: Essays, Speeches and Public Letters*, ed. James B. Meriwether, rev. ed. [1965; repr., New York: Modern Library, 2004], 58). On "the United States Aircraft Production Board in its promise to produce 'regiments and brigades of winged cavalry mounted on gas-driven flying horses' in order to 'sweep the Germans from the sky' as the U.S. entered the war in April 1917," see Edward Jablonski, *Warriors with Wings: The Story of the Lafayette Escadrille* (Indianapolis, IN: Bobbs-Merrill, 1966), 158.

3. Joseph Blotner, *Faulkner: A Biography* (New York: Random House, 1974), 975–76.

4. Michel Gresset relates Faulkner's silence to his alcoholism and a "profound feeling of solitude that often became unbearable": "What heartrending, what incurable despair did drinking hide? Perhaps nothing can ever say it better than the books themselves" (Michel Gresset, *A Faulkner Chronology* [Jackson: University Press of Mississippi, 1985], 33).

5. Blotner, *Faulkner: A Biography*, 635; Noel Polk, "William Faulkner's 'Carcassonne,'" *Studies in American Fiction* 12 (Spring 1984): 29; Michael Millgate, "'A Cosmos of My Own': The Evolution of Yoknapatawpha," in *Fifty Years of Yoknapatawpha: Faulkner and Yoknapatawpha, 1979*, ed. Doreen Fowler and Ann J. Abadie (Jackson: University Press of Mississippi, 1980), 34.

6. Cleanth Brooks, *William Faulkner: The Yoknapatawpha Country* (New Haven, CT: Yale University Press, 1963), 65; see also Bradford, "The Knight and the Artist," 90. "The analytic experience allows us to feel the pressure of an intention. We read it in the symbolic meaning of symptoms" (Jacques Lacan, "Aggressivity in Psychoanalysis," *Écrits*:

A Selection, trans. Alan Sheridan [New York: Norton, 1977], 10). For Brooks, "the almost free association of thoughts and images, the recurrence of what appear to be obsessive metaphors—all these invite speculation—and indeed sheer guesses, since the author has left so many loose ends fluttering" (*William Faulkner*, 65). For more insightful commentary on the story, see Theresa M. Towner and James B. Carothers, "Carcassonne," *Reading Faulkner: Collected Stories: Glossary and Commentary* (Jackson: University Press of Mississippi, 2006), 460–74.

 7. Brooks, *William Faulkner*, 62–63.

 8. Frederick L. Gwynn and Joseph L. Blotner, eds., *Faulkner in the University: Class Conferences at the University of Virginia 1957–1958*, rev. ed. (1959; repr., New York: Vintage, 1965), 22, 136. In his 1933 introduction to *The Sound and the Fury*, Faulkner defined the artist's essential alternatives thus: "We seem to try in the simple furious breathing (or writing) span of the individual to draw a savage indictment of the contemporary scene or to escape from it into a make-believe region of swords and magnolias and mockingbirds which perhaps never existed. . . . I seem to have tried both of the courses. I have tried to escape and I have tried to indict" (William Faulkner, "An Introduction to *The Sound and the Fury*," ed. James B. Meriwether, *Mississippi Quarterly* 26 [1973]: 412).

 9. William Faulkner, "Black Music," in *Collected Stories of William Faulkner* (New York: Vintage, 1950), 800, 799. Faulkner, "Carcassonne," 897.

 10. Karl Marx, "Existence and Consciousness," trans. T. B. Bottomore, in *Karl Marx: Selected Writings in Sociology and Social Philosophy*, ed. Bottomore and Maximilien Rubel (New York: McGraw-Hill, 1956), 75.

 11. John T. Matthews, citing biographer Frederick Karl, notes that "in 1927, the year after he composed this portrait of the oil-dependent poet, his father sold two parcels of family land in Oxford—one became a gasoline station, the other the local office of the Standard Oil Company" ("Recalling the West Indies: From Yoknapatawpha to Haiti and Back," *American Literary History* 16 [Summer 2004]: 242). In "Black Music," a twin story to "Carcassonne," it is called "the Universal Oil Company" (Faulkner, "Black Music," 799). For Noel Polk, "[t]he setting of 'Carcassonne' comes directly from Section II of *The Waste Land*. The port of Rincon, which means, literally, in Spanish, 'corner,' 'nook,' or 'narrow valley,' is a waste land dominated by the darkness and by the monolithic Standard Oil Company, symbol of the mechanized and sterile modern world" ("William Faulkner's 'Carcassonne,'" 32). On "the romance figure of the cavalier" in relation to "the insidious normality of a spreading industrial culture" and "the new petrochemical economy" during and after "the world's first industrialized war," see Murphet, *Faulkner's Media Romance*, 44, 20, 66, 50. On figuration in these stories of "the South's obscured origins" along its "Caribbean horizon" and "the problematic of US neocolonial imperialism," see Matthews, "Recalling the West Indies," 256, 239, 243. "[I]n 1926 new corporate compulsions were driving former colonial places into the custody of agents of American neo-colonialism like the Standard Oil Company. The poet cannot create beauty without encountering the deadly history of new-world oppression that supports him. The fustian of 'Carcassonne' indicates Faulkner's critical reflection on his own fetish of style as a dangerous flight of fancy" (ibid., 243).

 12. Gordon's studio in *Mosquitoes* also features a "ruined pitch of walls which had housed slaves long ago, slaves long dead and dust with the age that had produced them" (William Faulkner, *Mosquitoes*, in *Novels 1926–1929* [New York: Library of America, 6], 262). For the ghost of slavery in such Faulknerian garrets, see Matthews, "Recalling the West Indies," and Kristin Fujie, "Hurt So Bad: The Crisis of Female Embodiment in William Faulkner's *Mosquitoes*," *Faulkner Journal* 29 (Fall 2015): 27–48. Blotner observes that the garret of "Carcassonne"—"slanted in a ruined pitch to the low eaves"—is "thus

not entirely dissimilar from the room Faulkner was sharing with [William] Spratling" in New Orleans in January 1925 (*Faulkner: A Biography*, 502; see also Gresset, *A Faulkner Chronology*, 18), a plausible date for the story's narrative consolidation. Towner and Carothers note "Carcassonne's" "murky composition history" (*Reading Faulkner: The Collected Stories*, 463). "Possibly the first of the *Collected Stories* to be written" (ibid., 460), "Carcassonne," they suggest, dates from "1926 or 1927" and was revised in 1931 for inclusion in *These 13*. David Minter and Cleanth Brooks push the date further back, linking the story with "The Hill," "Moonlight," "Nympholepsy" and other prose sketches "likely to belong to the period between 1920–1925" (David Minter, "'Carcassonne,' 'Wash,' and the Voices of Faulkner's Fiction," in *Faulkner and the Short Story: Faulkner and Yoknapatawpha, 1990*, ed. Evans Harrington and Ann J. Abadie [Jackson: University Press of Mississippi, 1992], 84); and see Brooks, *William Faulkner*, 60. This earlier date makes sense to me. I argue below that the story reflects Faulkner's immediate postwar experiences as a demobilized Royal Air Force (Canada) cadet.

13. "The poet-narrator of 'Carcassonne' is evidently dying himself, and I think it is reasonable to infer that Faulkner at some point had the idea of Quentin as a dying narrator before whose eyes his whole world would pass in almost instantaneous review" (Millgate, "'A Cosmos of My Own,'" 34). In *Soldiers' Pay* lovesick George Farr lies out on the grass beneath trees at night waiting for a glimpse of his lover, Cecily Saunders: "From this position the sky became a flat plane, flat as the brass-studded lid of a dark blue box. Then as he watched it assumed depth again, it was as if he lay on the bottom of the sea while sea-weed clotting blackly lifted surface-ward, unshaken by any current, motionless; it was as if he lay on his stomach staring downward into water through which his gorgon's hair clotting blackly sank straight and black and motionless. Eleven thirty" (William Faulkner, *Soldiers' Pay*, in *Novels 1926–1929* [New York: Library of America, 2006], 188). Hereafter cited parenthetically. In *Flags in the Dust*, Horace Benbow muses that "if . . . you could only crash upward, burst; anything but earth," while the mule's "flesh soars unawares against the blue in the craws of buzzards" (Faulkner, *Flags in the Dust*, 715, 780). In "Carcassonne," rising is falling, falling rising: "*[T]he flesh is dead living on itself subsisting consuming itself thriftily in its own renewal will never die for I am the Resurrection and the Life*" (897).

14. Horace Benbow is another of these dreamers who transforms his small room into a planetarium: "In the adjoining room Horace lay while that wild fantastic futility of his voyaged in lonely regions of its own beyond the moon, about meadows nailed with firmamented stars to the ultimate roof of things, where unicorns filled the neighing air with galloping, or grazed or lay supine in golden-hooved repose" (Faulkner, *Flags in the Dust*, 683).

15. Paul Virilio, *War and Cinema: The Logistics of Perception* (1986), trans. Patrick Camiller (New York: Verso, 1989), 18.

16. Murphet, *Faulkner's Media Romance*, 6.

17. Ibid., 52.

18. Sigmund Freud, *The Interpretation of Dreams*, in *The Standard Edition of the Complete Psychological Works of Sigmund Freud*, vol. 5, ed. and trans. James Strachey (London: Hogarth Press, 1953), 783.

19. Faulkner, *Flags in the Dust*, 857.

20. Robert Harrison, introduction, *The Song of Roland*, trans. Robert Harrison (New York: Signet, 2012), 6.

21. In Faulkner's work, Roland first appears tongue-in-cheek as Flem Snopes in *Father Abraham*: "He is a living example of the astonishing byblows of man's utopian dreams actually functioning; in this case the dream is Democracy. He will become legend-

ary in time, but he has always been symbolic. Legendary as Roland and as symbolic of a form of behavior" (William Faulkner, *Father Abraham*, ed. James B. Meriwether [New York: Random House, 1983], 13). Hereafter cited parenthetically. As Snopes comes to symbolize the impersonal mechanistic spread of capitalist modernity into the pastoral domain, Roland, in Faulkner's public pronouncements at the University of Virginia, is the anti-Snopes whose crusade takes the form of a commitment to art: "[T]here's always someone that will never stop trying to cope with Snopes, that will never stop trying to get rid of Snopes. . . . [T]he impulse to eradicate Snopes is in my opinion so strong that it selects its champions when the crisis comes. When the battle comes it always produces a Roland. . . . Whatever it is that keeps us still trying to paint the pictures, to make the music, to write the books—there's a great deal of pressure not to do that, because certainly the artist has no place in nature and almost no place at all in our American culture and economy, but yet people still try to write books, still try to paint pictures." (Gwynn and Blotner, *Faulkner in the University*, 34).

22. *The Song of Roland*, 95–97.

23. Fernando Esposito observes that the figure of the aeronautical cavalier in the First World War was "derived from a semantic counterposition to the ground war" and Europe's dead millions. "It was trench warfare that produced the aviator-hero. The dynamic hero with technical skills made up for the stalemate on the ground. . . . [T]he Kingdom of Italy, for example, ended the war with 2,000 airmen and a ground army of 3,500,000. . . . And whereas hardship, sacrifice and anonymous death typified warfare among the trenches and shell craters, the 'heroes of the air' had fame, medals and photos and magazines to show for themselves. . . . [I]f a machine-gunner mowed down hundreds of enemy troops in a single action not one word was lost about it, but every plane that an airman shot down won him honor and recognition in the press" (*Fascism, Aviation, and Mythical Modernity* [2011], trans. Patrick Camiller [New York: Palgrave Macmillan, 2015], 169, 178, 186, 187).

24. *The Song of Roland*, 75.

25. Ibid., 161–62.

26. "But she, that whore, she turned her back on me / well on my way to Death—she even lacked the heart / to seal my eyes with her hand or close my jaws" (Homer, *The Odyssey*, trans. Robert Fagles [New York: Penguin, 1996], 11:481–83).

27. The composition of "Carcassonne" and the remembered emotional past it draws upon coincide with a renewed sense of crisis surrounding Estelle Oldham Franklin: "Although Cornell and Estelle did not begin formal divorce proceedings until mid-November 1928, when Cornell filed for divorce in Shanghai, Estelle had left her husband four years earlier. Arriving in Oxford in early December 1924, she stayed almost a year. Then, pressured by both families and Cornell, she returned to Shanghai in late November 1925. Three months later (her marriage a shambles) Estelle and her children returned to Oxford for good" (Judith L. Sensibar, *Faulkner and Love: The Women Who Shaped His Art* [New Haven, CT: Yale University Press, 2009], 243).

28. The multicolored horse of "Carcassonne," like Jewel Bundren's in *As I Lay Dying*, is surely one of those "parti-colored" Texas ponies that, beginning in *Father Abraham* (35), watch you with "wild-eyed frenzy" (27) out of "a pale cerulean eye" (23) or "wild mismatched eyes" (26), "azure eyes" (33), "flying vari-colored eyes" (38), or "wild glaring eyes" (48). These "'circus hosses'" (34) form "a kaleidoscopic maelstrom" (27) of "mad tossing shapes like gaudy flames downrushing" (35), "feinting and dodging" (28) in "dizzy calico rushes" "with the consummate skill of a Red Grange" (28). This "Galloping Ghost"—as Red Grange was called!—"not knowing that it was dead" (Faulkner, "Carcassonne," 896), soars "into the moon like an unbelievable and wingless goblin in a

nightmare" (Faulkner, *Father Abraham*, 59). If you can latch on, the horse—if it doesn't kill you—can lift you "to sublime heights, like an apotheosis" (26). The "gaudy flames downrushing" are another link to *The Song of Roland*, to the "silver pennons downrushing" at the end of *Flags in the Dust,* and to the image in that novel of Johnny Sartoris's gasoline-filled aeroplane crashing in flames.

29. Marx, "Existence and Consciousness," 75.

30. Faulkner's fictions frequently pause to note, and comment on, paved streets and roads, as in this example from his story "Tomorrow": "and we were on the highway now, the gravel; we would be home in an hour and a half, because sometimes we could make thirty and thirty-five miles an hour, and Uncle Gavin said that someday all the main roads in Mississippi would be paved like the streets in Memphis and every family in America would own a car" (William Faulkner, *Knight's Gambit* [1949; repr., London: Chatto and Windus, 1960], 94–95. Also see Murphet on the "pace of petro-driven modernization" in *Flags in the Dust* and Faulkner's "withering satiric depiction of the town of Kinston" there (*Faulkner's Media Romance*, 91).

31. Polk, "William Faulkner's 'Carcassonne,'" 39.

32. Ibid., 34.

33. "Were they poets?" Horace Benbow asks of the Sartoris twins. "I mean, the one that got back. I know the other one, the dead one, was" (Faulkner, *Flags in the Dust*, 694). Faulkner's portrait of the "post-traumatic" soldier is one of the most profound of the modernist period. See T. H. Adamowski, "Bayard Sartoris: Mourning and Melancholia," *Literature and Psychology* 23 (1973): 149–53.

34. William Faulkner, *As I Lay Dying*, rev. ed. (1930; repr., New York: Vintage International, 1985), 81.

35. Jonathan Shay, *Achilles in Vietnam: Combat Trauma and the Undoing of Character* (New York: Atheneum, 1994), 14.

36. *If you were white.* Here is an early glimpse into what Godden has termed "a generative . . . labor trauma, centered on a primal scene of recognition during which white passes into black and black passes into white" (*Fictions of Labor: William Faulkner and the South's Long Revolution* [Cambridge, UK: Cambridge University Press, 1997], 1). On Faulkner as a "funny little black man" and on the motif of "whiteface minstrelsy" across his work, see John N. Duvall, "'A Strange Nigger': Faulkner and the Minstrel Performance of Whiteness," *Faulkner Journal* 22 (Fall 2006–Winter 2007): 106–19. The "poet as tramp" figured prominently among the "impersonations, imitations, fabrications, fictional personas, role-playing, and legends about himself that Faulkner employed in both life and art" and that he projected into those biographical sketches of himself that the public ceaselessly demanded after the publication of *Sanctuary* especially (Thomas L. McHaney, "Faulkner and Autobiography in Fiction," in Carmen Rueda-Ramos and Susana Jimémez Placer, eds., *Constructing the Self: Essays on Southern Life-Writing* [Universitat de València, 2018], 163). Louis Cochran's "personal sketch," published in the *Memphis Commercial Appeal's* Sunday feature section, November 6, 1932, is typical: "He had been, in turn, a student, loafer, dish washer, carpenter, house painter, book store clerk, post office employee, an aviator serving under the Union Jack, a poet, a writer of prose so difficult that two publishers thought him a bad bargain, and at last a novelist hailed on two continents as a genius. That is a long road for any man to travel who quit school in the fifth grade" (quoted in James B. Meriwether, "Early Notices of Faulkner by Phil Stone and Louis Cochran," *Mississippi Quarterly* 17 [Summer 1964]: 143). Faulkner recalled of himself in "Mississippi," a 1954 reminiscence, "At this time the young man's attitude of mind was that of most of the other young men in the world who had been around twenty-one years of age in April, 1917, even though at times he did admit to

himself that he was possibly using the fact that he had been nineteen on that day as an excuse to follow the avocation he was coming more and more to know would be forever his true one: to be a tramp, a harmless possessionless vagabond" (Faulkner, "Mississippi," in *William Faulkner: Essays, Speeches and Public Letters*, ed. Meriwether, 21). Robert Linscott reports of his conversations with Faulkner in 1953, "He went on to say that for years people in Oxford thought he was trash, doing no work to speak of, just writing books that nobody read" (Robert N. Linscott, "Faulkner without Fanfare," in *Conversations with William Faulkner*, ed. M. Thomas Inge [Jackson: University Press of Mississippi, 1999], 102). After winning the Nobel Prize, Faulkner wrote to Dot Wilcox Conkling about her copy of *The Marble Faun*: "Don't let anybody get it away from you. . . . The tramp has become famous" (quoted in Blotner, *Faulkner: A Biography*, 1373). "By temperament I'm a vagabond and a tramp," he told Jean Stein in 1956 (James B. Meriwether and Michael Millgate, eds., *Lion in the Garden: Interviews with William Faulkner, 1926–1962* [New York: Random House, 1968], 249).

37. Max Weber, *The Protestant Ethic and the Spirit of Capitalism* (1905), trans. Talcott Parsons (New York: Scribner's 1958), 26–27. Hereafter cited parenthetically.

38. Godden, *Fictions of Labor*, 4.

39. William Faulkner, "The Hill," in *William Faulkner: Early Prose and Poetry*, ed. Carvel Collins (Boston: Little, Brown, 1962), 92.

40. Simon Strother, in turn, driving his master in a horse-drawn carriage, "glanc[ed] now and then at the field niggers laboring among the cotton rows with tolerant and easy scorn" (Faulkner, *Flags in the Dust*, 740).

41. Edith Wharton, "In the North" (June 19, 1915), in *World War I and America: Told by the Americans Who Lived It*, ed. A. Scott Berg (New York: Library of America, 2017), 135. The fuller quotation reads, "They seemed allegorically splendid: as if, under the arch of sunset, we had been watching the whole French army ride straight into glory."

42. J. Laplanche and J. B. Pontalis, *The Language of Psycho-Analysis* (1967), trans. Donald Nicholson-Smith (New York: Norton, 1973), 315.

43. Karl Marx and Frederick Engels, *The Communist Manifesto* (1848), trans. Samuel Moore (1888) (Chicago: Henry Regnery, 1954), 29.

The Anatomy of Thrift: Markets, Media, and William Faulkner's Great Depression

Robert Jackson

> *Lastly, thrift shopping produces its own "organic intellectuals"; thrift is a field of knowledge production outside the academy and has tentacles into zine culture, Gen-X culture, Martha Stewart features, Internet discussion groups, and the like. More than a rest stop on the information highway, thrift "sites" reveal modes of pleasure in and coping with the morphing dimensions of late capital.*
> —Matthew Tinkcom, Joy Van Fuqua, and Amy Villarejo

If, indeed, William Faulkner had really set out in his youth, as he claimed in "Mississippi" (1954), "to be a tramp, a harmless possessionless vagabond," and to remain one all his days, the onset of the Great Depression put this vocation to the most severe sort of test.[1] Faulkner had been gradually coming to terms with the fact that he would never be a great poet—the writer's vocation he most fully equated with freedom from laws of economic gravity—during the late 1920s. And as biographer Frederick R. Karl points out, this realization was inseparable from what we might call Faulkner's market awareness: "When we speak of shifts in Faulkner's imagination which took him from poetry to fiction, we should not neglect the financial dimension. It had become clear to him, no matter how much he wished to be known as a poet, that he could not survive that way."[2] This was a period when Faulkner turned to prose most definitively and took up the subject of the Snopes clan in "Father Abraham," the material of which would surface in numerous short stories in subsequent years and finally in *The Hamlet* (1940), and which would make Faulkner's concerns with southern, white economic and social-class issues central to his entire career. The proximity of this turn to the early years of the Great Depression invites another perspective on Faulkner's deepening fictional world, one that takes into consideration the upheavals of the world economic order during the years of the writer's most intense creative development.

As a prose writer, too, Faulkner struggled to survive, and he recognized that adaptation to the market was absolutely essential. In a letter to his publisher, Harrison Smith, in the winter of 1932, during the bleakest stretch of the Depression, for example, Faulkner asked about the terms of a contract, writing: "Give me the best you can, tho. I am going cold-blooded Yankee now; I am not young enough anymore to hell around and earn money at other things as I could once. I have got to make it by writing or quit writing."[3] All Yankees are cold-blooded, of course, and it is precisely their lack of warm blood that predisposes them to greed and acquisitiveness, which makes them Yankees. Critics might assume that Faulkner would be above the derivative regional caricatures on display in this circular logic, since he had so recently dreamed up Flem Snopes and Jason Compson, those thoroughly cold-blooded *southerners*. But such critics would be mistaken; indeed, Faulkner's displacement of greed onto the Yankee, albeit with this humorous edge that implicitly acknowledges his own complicity in the same process, represents a signature move, one that shapes much of his treatment of money across his writings. For Faulkner, money and romance (which is to say, warm-bloodedness) are often mutually exclusive: money curtails rather than expands a man's ability to have sex with women, money prevents humans from loving and respecting nature (including human nature) properly, and money irreparably damages the course of history itself. Beneath all these conflicts, and critiques, lies a fundamental question: was Faulkner a capitalist? It would be difficult to answer in the affirmative without serious, perhaps even insurmountable, qualifications: for Faulkner produced, often with great admiration, numerous economic cooperatives and collectives in his fiction, and he made recurrent links in fiction and public letters between capitalism and racism, the Original Sin of New World Euro-American societies, especially the US South.

Privately, of course, Faulkner was hopelessly incapable of balancing his own books—overspending, buying on impulse, giving money away, accumulating debts, failing to read contracts carefully, finding himself in work situations he likened to prostitution and slave labor, getting fired or spontaneously quitting all sorts of paying jobs—all of which reveal a pattern and a relation to capital that look neither random nor accidental. The tramp in Faulkner, to be sure, never quite died out. But if his earliest stance on money was passive, even indifferent, it might be more accurate to characterize Depression-era Faulkner's attitude towards the prevailing economic philosophy and system of the United

States as passive-aggressive. In a long 1940 rant to Robert Haas at Random House, Faulkner writes of "these fits of sort of raging and impotent exasperation at this really quite alarming paradox which my life reveals: Beginning at the age of thirty I, an artist, a sincere one and of the first class, who should be free even of his own economic responsibilities and with no moral conscience at all, began to become the sole, principal and partial support—food, shelter, heat, clothes, medicine, Kotex, school fees, toilet paper and picture shows" of a large extended family including his mother, wife, daughter, two stepchildren, his brother's widow and child, and several white and black dependents.[4] Faulkner's resentment of mass culture, and his unsubtle comparison of it to the nether regions of human experience, scatological—"toilet paper and picture shows"—as well as misogynistically gendered—"Kotex"—serves here to redirect responsibility for his financial straits onto others—coded as inveterate consumers of sanitary products and movies alike—even as he insists on his right, as an artist, to a total exemption from economic concerns. Indeed, this was not Faulkner's first pejorative association of "Kotex" with the humiliatingly flighty, implicitly female, mass market: in 1936, brooding about magazine fiction he considered "trash," he wrote to his agent Morton Goldman of his desire "to cook up something for Cosmopolitan," but worried that such a lucrative venue might be out of reach because "I seem to be so out of touch with the Kotex Age here that I cant seem to think of anything myself."[5] (Faulkner might have been surprised to learn that kotex, a term derived from "cotton texture," was originally a product invented to bandage wounds in the Great War, and consequently that Kotex had significantly more combat experience in that conflict than Faulkner himself did.[6])

Faulkner also struggled with the fact that it was not his beloved novels but short stories and screenplays, subsidiary rights leading to film adaptations of his works, and the government of Sweden that represented the real source of whatever financial security he enjoyed. At the University of Virginia in 1957 he was asked who in the Deep South read his books, and why. Some readers in Oxford were friends, he said, others, detectives trying to recognize themselves or other townspeople in the books:

> Others read the books in a sort of outraged bafflement. Our country is poor country. Nobody is rich there and few people ever have as much as thirty thousand dollars. They know they'll never have as much as thirty thousand dollars, and if they ever did they would have got it out in the sun, doing hard work. And a foreign government suddenly gives me thirty thousand dollars just for sitting on my backside, writing books, and they simply cannot get over that and they will really never forgive me or Sweden for that. That

somehow that was an outrage to all the proprieties. And they read the book to see why in the world anybody should have give anybody thirty thousand dollars for writing the books like that.[7]

Like his neighbors, but from a slightly different angle, Faulkner himself was outraged at the commodification of his art, and this became one of the great themes his work explored. "What does it mean to Faulkner's writing," asks John T. Matthews, "for him to produce it under conditions he deeply resists yet to which he must subscribe?"[8] This central question undergirds the work of Matthews and other scholars whose research has considered the broad market pressures of Faulkner's career.[9]

As the writer's well-known, if exaggerated, renunciation of the market after the disappointing reception of *Sartoris* (1929) liberated him to produce *The Sound and the Fury* (1929) and *As I Lay Dying* (1930) (both full of people harboring serious economic grudges, of course, and the latter's composition begun the day after the Wall Street crash of 1929), so did his aggressive—indeed, *overcompensating*—return to what we might refer to as a market consciousness centrally inform *Sanctuary* (1931), the prolific production of short stories in the early 1930s, and the nascent Hollywood screenwritings of 1932 and thereafter. The situation of Faulkner in Hollywood deserves far more attention than is possible here, but, at the very least, it invites a highly suggestive comparison: for Faulkner in the Great Depression, money has become as definitively modern a medium as motion pictures. In the Faulknerian imagination, money mediates, it travels, it encodes and transmits communications, it structures ideology and affect and emotion, it constructs racial identities, and it does all of these things in the same ways that film and other modern media do—disruptively, and at once menacingly and alluringly. In this regard, the work of contemporary scholars on Faulkner and media, a topic enjoying a considerable boom in the early decades of the twenty-first century, might be revisited specifically in pursuit of new ways of formulating a media theory of money.[10] "While he may have been successful to some extent in maintaining the great divide of high art and industrial practice," writes Sarah Gleeson-White of Faulkner's "parallel writing careers" of novelist and screenwriter, "there is nonetheless some significant leaching between the two arenas."[11] Indeed, as the "industrial" contributed to Faulkner's aesthetics, so did the economic register powerfully as a subtle, highly complex means of expression in much of Faulkner's greatest work.

As a Mississippian, Faulkner saw the Great Depression's privation firsthand. Yet he also rode out the era in surprisingly comfortable financial circumstances. Money from magazines and Hollywood marked him off starkly both from the undermonetized, comparatively financially carefree years of his earliest work and from the financial desperation besetting many of his neighbors in Oxford during the 1930s. His embeddedness in the mass-media print culture and film institutions of both coasts, as well as in the agricultural and mercantile contexts of north Mississippi, gave him a number of important perspectives on economic history and change—local, regional, national, and global—which made their way into his writings. And these personal connections were complemented by the period's intensive focus on economic affairs. From Communism and Fascism in Europe to isolationism, New Deal liberal-interventionist economic policy, and such movements as Fordism, Taylorism, and agrarianism in the United States, debates about economics raged during these years.[12]

A sustained, historically informed, full-length study of Faulkner and money in the early 1930s would attend to Faulkner's own paradoxical economic fortunes as well as the state of the world economy, while focusing on the mutually constitutive relations among the short stories, screenwritings, and novels. It is tempting to imagine this work's culmination in *Absalom, Absalom!* (1936), which represents the most ambitious and comprehensive literary statement of Faulkner's economic thought during this period and which, not insignificantly, was produced in the multiple contexts of Hollywood and Mississippi in a period that included a substantial interruption during which Faulkner also produced *Pylon* (1935). Especially in its attention to the short stories and screenplays, the sites and conditions surrounding their production, and their critiques of the market, such a prospective study would complement Ted Atkinson's *Faulkner and the Great Depression: Aesthetics, Ideology, and Cultural Politics* (2006) in important ways. Atkinson's work convincingly demonstrates Faulkner's immersion in the social and political contexts of the Depression and focuses primarily on the tensions between aesthetics and ideology, examining a series of novels from *Mosquitoes* (1927) to *The Unvanquished* (1938).

Consider, more discretely, the year 1930. After completing the manuscript of *As I Lay Dying* in January, Faulkner's work on novels was interrupted for the better part of two years, during which he wrote dozens of short stories and submitted them to magazines simply because he needed the income. In 1930 he published the first four of these stories: "A Rose for Emily," "Honor," "Thrift," and "Red Leaves." He earned good money for "Thrift" and "Red Leaves," $750 each from the *Saturday Evening Post*—$750 in 1930 would be worth more than $10,000 in 2018—and smaller sums for the other two stories. These windfalls enabled the purchase and restoration of Faulkner's home, Rowan Oak. These four stories reveal Faulkner's wide range of subjects and styles, yet they cohere as a group not least on the basis of their economic concerns. "A Rose for Emily" turns on the humiliation of its title character, an aging spinster whose father's death reduces her to narrowly economic terms in the eyes of her neighbors. "At last they could pity Miss Emily," notes the narrator. "Being left alone, and a pauper, she had become humanized. Now she too would know the old thrill and the old despair of a penny more or less."[13] Miss Emily's resistance to her own commodification takes a particularly gothic expression, but the nature of that commodification is quite commonplace. "Red Leaves," a meditation on slavery, mortality, and nature, represents one of Faulkner's most penetrating studies of the corrupting effects of an increasingly abstract capitalist economy. Its climax consists of a slave's acceptance of his status as another man's property, which is also a capitulation to his own death. And "Honor," one of numerous stories from these years that might be called "aviation love triangle narratives," features one of Faulkner's favorite figures, the World War I veteran whose death drive is exacerbated in a postwar society where economic relations have become so formalized and rote as to be dehumanizing.[14] The veteran, Monaghan, uses a young secretary's perspective to express the futility of his own assimilation into the workforce: "So Miss West comes in; she is a good kid, only somebody told her I had had three or four other jobs in a year without sticking, and that I used to be a war pilot, and she'd keep on after me about why I quit flying and why I didn't go back to it, now that crates were more general, since I wasn't much good at selling automobiles or anything else, like women will. You know: urgent and sympathetic, and you can't shut them up like you could a man" (Faulkner, *Collected Stories*, 564). In each of these stories, despite their different historical periods, locales, and topics, the market effectively crushes a human being.

Perhaps most interesting in these contexts, however, is "Thrift," which Faulkner excluded from two collections in subsequent years (*These 13* [1931] and *Doctor Martino and Other Stories* [1934]). Faulkner apparently maintained a rather dismissive view of the story long after its publication, which he held despite its recognition and reprinting in *O. Henry Memorial Award Prize Stories of 1931*.[15] His only recorded comments on it came in a 1948 letter to Haas as they discussed what to include in *Collected Stories* (1950): "OMIT it if you like. Not too good."[16] As a result, "Thrift" wasn't republished until its inclusion in *Uncollected Stories* in 1979. Even James B. Carothers and Hans H. Skei, scholars specializing in Faulkner's short fiction, have had relatively little to say about it.[17] But "Thrift" is a deceptively complex story and is worth serious attention in the context of the other things Faulkner was working on at the same time—the other short stories, the novels from *The Sound and the Fury* to *Light in August* (1932), and the nonliterary activities that occupied him in the early years of the Great Depression.

"Thrift" tells the story of Willy MacWyrglinchbeath, a Scottish Highlander who participates in World War I and whose stereotypical Scottish fixation with money organizes every aspect of his life. As Skei writes, "Mac's obsession with money thus not only constitutes the plot of the story—it *is* the story."[18] "Thrift" is very largely lifted from James Warner Bellah's "The MacGillicuddie" (1927), suggesting that Faulkner may have read the latter not just because of his interests in aviation and the war but also for hints at how to produce short fiction suitable for the *Saturday Evening Post*, where Bellah's story first appeared.[19] As Richard T. Dillon has detailed, the two stories share many elements: both "are about Scottish pilots with jaw-breaking names"; both men "are fighting the English war only for personal reasons"; both "are pipesmoking loners who appear a bit queer to the younger pilots in the squadron"; both "fail to get official recognition for their outstanding achievements in aerial combat"; and finally, after the armistice, both Scotsmen "return to their small native villages where the locals know little of the foreign war, and both stories end with the heroes making a symbolic change of clothing, from the breeches of their English uniforms to Scottish kilts."[20] The fact that Faulkner borrowed so heavily from Bellah in these ways perhaps also suggests why "Thrift" constitutes such an outlier among Faulkner's aviation stories. There is no love triangle to complicate Mac's life nor much Oedipal tension to drive him to desperate ends.

MacWyrglinchbeath instead thinks exclusively about money. Early in the war, he purposely injures himself to obtain a transfer from the infantry to the higher-paying Royal Flying Corps, where he first works as a mechanic. He shows more concern for the expense and waste of crashed airplanes than for all their dead pilots, and indeed, in his almost autistic fixation on figures, both mechanical and economic, he often seems not to apprehend the presence of other people at all. He volunteers for the most dangerous missions and trains as a pilot because these positions pay better. He breaks both hips when he forces a German plane down with his own aircraft in order to try to save the life of an officer—but even this act of genuine heroism only occurs in the context of the officer's having taken out an insurance policy with Mac, whose last words before the crash—"Sax shillin'"—announce the precise amount of his loss.[21] Later, Mac turns down an officer's commission, a refusal widely misinterpreted by others as an admirable expression of pride and even a powerful anti-war critique, when in fact Mac had merely calculated that the rise in rank would cost him money. Mac has few intimates, and certainly no sexual identity; he spends his nights on his only passion—his figures.

After news of the armistice reaches the airfield, a group of drunken soldiers arrives to break down Mac's door and engulf him in their revelry. Typically, even at this moment of triumph, Mac is himself; Faulkner writes: "MacWyrglinchbeath was sitting on his cot, his ledger upon his knees and his pencil poised above it. He was taking stock" (397).

So, it is the differences between Bellah's and Faulkner's Scotsmen—most prominently, Faulkner's substitution of money for religion—that provide the greatest insight into Faulkner's thinking in 1930. When one of MacGillicuddie's cohort expresses enthusiasm for whiskey, for example, the outraged Scot retorts, "Dinna say that, mon! . . . Whiskey is for-r cowld and dampness—nae for-r ribaldry and nae for-r making the Lord's work th' easier-r!"[22] Bellah's hero, a devout Christian who prays over the enemy pilots he shoots down, suggests that religious faith is the key to maintaining a healthy psychological distance from trauma during and after the war. Faulkner's Mac, likewise, is known to have contempt for others who drink—"I have seen his face as he watched the men drinking beer in the canteen," a bemused officer recalls—but only on account of Mac's single-minded approach to saving money (386). Mac is never endowed with any sort of religious faith; instead, the central focus on religion in Bellah's story is replaced with a comparable devotion to financial matters. Christianity is supplanted by thrift, but the overall behavior of the two men is otherwise largely indistinguishable. Both men are genuine war heroes who place themselves in grave danger and contribute substantially to the Allied cause. Both are viewed askance by those around them. Both prove impossible fully to assimilate into military life, raising thorny problems for the war planners and bureaucrats.

Faulkner might be understood here, in the terms of a rather overstated cliché about the modernist era, as apprehending the replacement of religious values with secular ones. Yet in drawing so heavily on Bellah, Faulkner goes much farther, rejecting the uncomplicated pieties of "The MacGillicuddie" even as he undertakes in "Thrift" a sharp analysis of the market conditions of modernity, conditions shaping not just his own literary efforts, of course, but also those of wars, religions, and entire civilizations. MacGillicuddie's simple, if not quite sanctimonious, faith in the rightness of his cause, grounded in the local color of his Deep North, becomes MacWyrglinchbeath's postcolonial critique, which is endorsed by a neighbor who, learning that Mac has returned from Europe without "spoil," sounds a note of appropriately skeptical historical awareness at the end of "Thrift": "No Hieland Scots ha' ever won aught in English war-rs" (398). In this light, "Thrift" is more than a genial tall tale, belying its appearance in the pages of the middlebrow *Post*, and ought to be taken far more seriously. In relation to issues of religion, mortality, and trauma, and institutions from the military establishment to the global economic order, the story maintains a delicate balance between farce and pathos, its deadpan delivery masking the fact that humor and seriousness are inextricable from one another. Faulkner seems to be telling his *Post* readers: Your own interpretation depends on what you think about money.

It is vital to acknowledge that "thrift" is hardly a pejorative term here. Mac's defining trait seems to be "racial" in a loose (and, we ought to know by now, dangerous) sense, which critics have acknowledged mostly in passing: Hans H. Skei refers to his "stubborn, proverbial Scottish greed"; James B. Carothers and Jay Watson refer to Mac, respectively, as "the mercenary Scot" and "the epitome of the penurious Scotsman"; and Joseph Blotner, comparably invoking this economic connotation of Scottishness without elaboration, cites Mac's "quiet parsimony, his taciturnity in the face of good fortune and bad, his close computation in money matters" as connecting links between Scotland and Yoknapatawpha County's remote Beat Four.[23] Mac's thrift seems a very distant relation to the sort of miserliness more widely associated with Jews than Scots during this era of rampant racial, ethnic, regional, and religious stereotyping.[24] Indeed, several of Faulkner's other narratives during the early 1930s, including "Death Drag" (1932), "There Was a Queen" (1933), and *Pylon* (1935), utilize anti-Semitic gestures in the service of simplistic characterization, offering a crucial point of comparison to Faulkner's method in "Thrift." The key distinction, perhaps best imagined as one between industriousness and avariciousness, is unsatisfying when placed under even mild scrutiny and breaks down quickly: Mac's obsession with money keeps him from recognizing the mortal danger of his situation at the moment of an airplane crash, which he improbably survives, just as Ginsfarb, the Jewish wing-walker in "Death Drag," is so outraged at the small size of his paycheck that he feels no fear during a harrowing, but mostly harmless, fall from an airplane into a barn. Ginsfarb "wasn't thinking about being killed, or even hurt," a witness, Captain Warren, attempts to explain. "That's why he wasn't hurt. He was too mad, too in a hurry to receive justice. He couldn't wait to fly back down. Providence knew that he was too busy and that he deserved justice, so Providence put that barn there with the rotting roof" (Faulkner, *Collected Stories*, 202).

The strange recycling and conflation of Scottish and Jewish stereotypes in these stories complicate any simplistic formulation of Faulkner's anti-Semitism and raise important questions about some of the key economic actors across Faulkner's writings of the 1930s. For unlike Jason Compson (himself a vocal and unambiguous anti-Semite) and Flem Snopes, Mac is honest and industrious. Unlike Anse Bundren, Mac is unafraid of hard work. More than that, Mac's undeviating attention to money enables him to emerge from the war culturally and psychologically intact. Like Ginsfarb's furious faith in "justice," it has an almost spiritual quality, giving Mac an impervious sense of self and of his position in the universe. And unlike Alec Gray, another Scottish aviator and the protagonist of Faulkner's short story "Victory" (1931), Mac is not traumatized by the war. In aspiring to an officer's commission, Alec ignores his father's warning about *"the pride and vainglory of going for an officer. Never miscall your birth, Alec. You are not a gentleman. You are a Scottish shipwright"* (Faulkner, Collected Stories 447–48). Alec is spiritually dead when the war ends, doomed to drift homelessly through the ruins of old battles. Of Mac's tenacious and uncomplicated ethos, by contrast, we might simply say, as Faulkner did not of Ginsfarb and the Jews but of another oppressed and endlessly caricatured people, "He endured." At the conclusion of "Thrift," Mac returns to his native village—which, as Blotner rightly hints, quite resembles parts of the upland South—visits a neighbor who has been keeping his savings for him, and accepts a loss in a minor financial dispute with this neighbor whose honest financial acumen is equal to his own.[25] Mac has no trouble assimilating back into civilian life. Alec Gray, by contrast, represents a more recognizable figure in Faulkner, especially in the World War I stories (and, we might add provocatively, the Civil War stories), most of which emphasize postwar disillusionment and trauma; and significantly for Faulkner's future readers and interpreters, "Victory" was included in both *These 13* and *Collected Stories*, while "Thrift" was excluded from both collections.

If we take up the influential terms of economics rather than existentialism—or, perhaps better, if we discern the economic as existential—this marginalization makes the presence of "Thrift" in the middle of Faulkner's cold-blooded Yankee years of market-conscious fiction writing even more significant. Mac's undeviating focus on money has something of Quentin Compson's father's insight, too, when, attempting to talk his son down from his suicidal flights in *The Sound and the Fury*, he advises him to concentrate on saving his money for a trip to New England and suggests that "watching pennies has healed more scars than jesus."[26] This is not advice that Quentin followed, of course. But if Quentin never bodied forth from his warm-blooded reverie, and never abandoned his own romantic ideal of the tramp, Faulkner himself did, in his writings. "Thrift" is evidence of the writer's serious reflection on the influence of the market itself, both as a curbing influence against flights into solipsism and despair and as a pragmatic, even constructive source of new individual and social identities. This is perhaps the most monumental paradox of Faulkner's Great Depression: in keeping him grounded in ways Faulkner did not choose but ultimately, and grudgingly, did accept, the market enabled his greatest creations to take flight.

NOTES

My thanks to Mike Zeitlin, Peter Lurie, and Jack Matthews for much collaborative energy during our 2017 Faulkner and Yoknapatawpha conference session, as well as to others at the conference who provided valuable insights into my work: organizer Jay Watson, as well as Jim Carothers, David Davis, Leigh Anne Duck, John Duvall, Richard Godden, Michael Gorra, Caroline Miles, and Myka Tucker-Abramson. Thanks, too, to Sarah Gleeson-White for typically incisive suggestions and to Claire Olson for research assistance.

The epigraph is found in Matthew Tinkcom, Joy Van Fuqua, and Amy Villarejo, "On Thrifting," in *Hop on Pop: The Politics and Pleasures of Popular Culture*, ed. Henry Jenkins, Tara McPherson, and Jane Shattuc (Durham, NC: Duke University Press, 2002), 469.

1. William Faulkner, *Essays, Speeches, and Public Letters*, ed. James B. Meriwether, rev. ed. (1965; repr.,New York: Modern Library, 2004), 21.

2. Frederick R. Karl, *William Faulkner: American Writer* (New York: Weidenfeld & Nicolson, 1989), 287.

3. Joseph Blotner, ed., *Selected Letters of William Faulkner* (New York: Random House, 1977), 60.

4. Ibid., 122.

5. Ibid., 95–96. For more on this gendered aspect of Faulkner's view of mainstream literary and popular culture, see Anne Goodwyn Jones, "'The Kotex Age': Women, Popular Culture, and *The Wild Palms*," in *Faulkner and Popular Culture: Faulkner and Yoknapatawpha, 1988*, ed. Doreen Fowler and Ann J. Abadie (Jackson: University Press of Mississippi, 1990), 142–62.

6. For more on this history, see Autumn Stanley, *Mothers and Daughters of Invention: Notes for a Revised History of Technology* (New Brunswick, NJ: Rutgers University Press, 1995), 215.

7. Jefferson Society Meeting, University of Virginia, April 30, 1957. *Faulkner at Virginia* (2010), Rector and Visitors of the University of Virginia; author Stephen Railton, http://faulkner.lib.virginia.edu/display/wfaudi010#wfaudi010.32.

8. John T. Matthews, "Shortened Stories: Faulkner and the Market," in *Faulkner and the Short Story: Faulkner and Yoknapatawpha, 1990*, ed. Evans Harrington and Ann J. Abadie (Jackson: University Press of Mississippi, 1992), 7.

9. See also Lawrence H. Schwartz, *Creating Faulkner's Reputation: The Politics of Modern Literary Criticism* (Knoxville: University of Tennessee Press, 1988); Susan V. Donaldson, "Dismantling the *Saturday Evening Post* Reader: *The Unvanquished* and Changing 'Horizons of Expectations,'" in *Faulkner and Popular Culture: Faulkner and Yoknapatawpha, 1988*, ed. Doreen Fowler and Ann J. Abadie (Jackson: University Press of Mississippi, 1990), 179–95; and Phil Smith, "'The Megaphone's Bellowing and Bodiless Profanity': *If I Forget Thee, Jerusalem* and the Culture of Cacophony," *Faulkner Journal* 26, no. 1 (Spring 2012): 75–96.

10. See Peter Lurie, *Vision's Immanence: Faulkner, Film, and the Popular Imagination* (Baltimore: Johns Hopkins University Press, 2004); Peter Lurie and Ann

J. Abadie, eds., *Faulkner and Film: Faulkner and Yoknapatawpha, 2010* (Jackson: University Press of Mississippi, 2014); Julian Murphet and Stefan Solomon, eds., *William Faulkner in the Media Ecology* (Baton Rouge: Louisiana State University Press, 2015); Julian Murphet, *Faulkner's Media Romance* (New York: Oxford University Press, 2017); Stefan Solomon, *William Faulkner in Hollywood: Screenwriting for the Studios* (Athens: University of Georgia Press, 2017); Sarah Gleeson-White, ed., *William Faulkner at Twentieth Century-Fox: The Annotated Screenplays* (New York: Oxford University Press, 2017); Robert Jackson, *Fade In, Crossroads: A History of the Southern Cinema* (New York: Oxford University Press, 2017).

11. Sarah Gleeson-White, "Faulkner Goes to Hollywood," in *William Faulkner in Context*, ed. John T. Matthews (New York: Cambridge University Press, 2015), 195.

12. Faulkner's skepticism about capitalism did not come from the left in the straightforward manner of much New Deal–era critique. Indeed, Faulkner feared the New Deal itself and seems to have associated it, as a massive historical upheaval and threat to traditional order, with the Civil War. The war and its exigencies introduced the income tax, created legal tender money and the banking system, allocated vast sums of money to public works and infrastructure projects such as the transcontinental railroads, created a huge system of veterans' pensions that grew exponentially for the rest of the century, and created the Freedmen's Bureau, the first federal agency of its kind and a model for others that addressed a wide range of issues that the government had never addressed before. For more on these topics, see, for example, James M. McPherson, *Battle Cry of Freedom: The Civil War Era* (New York: Oxford University Press, 1988); Eric Foner, *Reconstruction: America's Unfinished Revolution, 1863–1877* (New York: Harper & Row, 1988); and Theda Skocpol, *Protecting Mothers and Soldiers: The Political Origins of Social Policy in the United States* (Cambridge, MA: Harvard University Press, 1992). To recognize the economic and racial implications of this revolution from the perspective of the 1930s is also to apprehend the racial threat to the South portended by the New Deal. Southern Congressional leaders' successful efforts to exclude southern black laborers from New Deal programs, as documented in Ira Katznelson, *When Affirmative Action Was White: An Untold History of Racial Inequality in Twentieth-Century America* (New York: Norton, 2005), revealed the degree to which many white southerners feared and resisted any external influence that might alter their racial order. As the Civil War had irrevocably cast the slave South into a dizzying future of new labor regimes and reactionary struggles of whites to regain economic control without the legal enslavement of blacks, so did Roosevelt's New Deal suggest that the cure could be worse than the disease. In this context, *Absalom, Absalom!* which Faulkner wrote as the major New Deal programs of Roosevelt's first term were implemented, might well be read as a record of white, southern ambivalence, resistance, denial, and disavowal in the face of inexorable, and necessary, economic transformation.

13. William Faulkner, *Collected Stories of William Faulkner* (New York: Random House, 1950), 123. Hereafter cited parenthetically.

14. See Murphet, *Faulkner's Media Romance*, chapter 1, for a sustained analysis of what Murphet suggests is "flight's functional return in peacetime to a critical *mediator* of modernity" between the world wars (56). Murphet's reading of Faulkner's aviation narratives as "compulsive transpositions between feudal and futuristic structures of feeling" (56–57) offers a comparable way of understanding both the unassimilable veteran, Monaghan, in "Honor" and, as my reading below suggests, the more adaptable MacWyrglinchbeath in "Thrift."

15. See Blanche Colton Williams, ed., *O. Henry Memorial Award Prize Stories of 1931* (New York: Doubleday, Doran & Co., 1931).

16. Blotner, *Selected Letters of William Faulkner*, 274.

17. A brief but important exception to this critical neglect is Hans H. Skei, "A Forgotten Faulkner Story: 'Thrift,'" *Mississippi Quarterly* 32 (Summer 1979), 453–60.

18. Ibid., 456.

19. See James Warner Bellah, "The MacGillicuddie," *Saturday Evening Post*, January 15, 1927, 6+; reprinted in James Warner Bellah, *Gods of Yesterday* (New York: D. Appleton, 1928), 105–34.

20. Richard T. Dillon, "Sources for Faulkner's Version of the First Air War," *American Literature* 44, no. 4 (January 1973): 630–31.

21. William Faulkner, "Thrift," *Uncollected Stories of William Faulkner*, ed. Joseph Blotner (New York: Random House, 1979), 392. Hereafter cited parenthetically.

22. Bellah, *Gods of Yesterday*, 113.

23. Skei, "A Forgotten Faulkner Story," 455; James B. Carothers, *William Faulkner's Short Stories* (Ann Arbor: UMI Research Press, 1985), 102; Jay Watson, "Escapes and Diversions, Whoring and Trash: Two Case Studies in the Aesthetics, Psychology, and Economics of the Twentieth-Century American Short Story," *Flannery O'Connor Review* 8 (2010): 13; Joseph Blotner, *Faulkner: A Biography* (1984; repr., Jackson: University Press of Mississippi, 2005), 256.

24. For more on anti-Semitism in modern Anglo-American literary history, see, for example, Bryan Cheyette, ed., *Between "Race" and "Culture": Representations of "the Jew" in English and American Literature* (Stanford, CA: Stanford University Press, 1996); Jonathan Freedman, *The Temple of Culture: Assimilation and Anti-Semitism in Literary Anglo-America* (New York: Oxford University Press, 2000); Donald Pizer, *American Naturalism and the Jews: Garland, Norris, Dreiser, Wharton, and Cather* (Urbana: University of Illinois Press, 2008).

25. The specifics of this dispute, and the creative and economic logic of interruption, are worth considering at greater length. When Mac's cow and his neighbor's bull produce a calf, whose rightful owner is thus not entirely clear, sexuality and reproduction are revealed to be problematic within the larger capitalist model in which property rights are legally defined. Mac learns of the calf's birth while away at the war and decides to let the situation play itself out for the time being; and he finally relinquishes ownership not because he doesn't think he has a claim to it, but because he calculates that the cost of asserting his claim would be higher than the calf's value.

This turn of events brings to mind the Civil War's interruption of Charles Bon's courtship of Judith Sutpen and the subsequent period during which, as Mr. Compson speculates, everyone agrees to let the war play itself out: "And who knows? there was the War now; who knows but what the fatality and the fatality's victims did not both think, hope, that the War would settle the matter, leave free one of the two irreconcilables, since it would not be the first time that youth has taken catastrophe as a direct act of Providence for the sole purpose of solving a personal problem which youth itself could not solve" (William Faulkner, *Absalom, Absalom!* rev. ed. [1936; repr., New York: Vintage International, 1990], 95).

In biographical terms, these scenarios resemble several of Faulkner's own interruptions. In the winter of 1930, when Faulkner had just completed *As I Lay Dying*, he was interrupted from writing novels—work he valued above all else—by the economic demands of family life, which compelled him to write and sell short stories. Several years later, Faulkner's slow progress on *Absalom, Absalom!* was interrupted with comparable results, leading to his writing of *Pylon* and the successful completion of *Absalom*. Later still, Faulkner produced both *Intruder in the Dust* (1948) and *Requiem for a Nun* (1951) during what I have described elsewhere as the "tortured, oft-interrupted gestation" of *A*

Fable (1954). So Faulkner's often-financially motivated interruptions—his turn to writing the short stories in 1930, his turn to *Pylon* in 1934, and his turn to the midcentury novels—express the same paradoxical logic (indeed, the same *productivity*) as these fictional interruptions, in which a personal problem of deep human import, often linked to sex and reproduction, is delayed by more immediate exigencies, and the things Faulkner has to spend his time on (the short stories, the "minor" novels) become infused with this sense of suspended work on presumably more meaningful things (the "major" novels). See Robert Jackson, "Balance, Bonus, Bastard: William Faulkner's B-sides," in *Faulkner and Print Culture: Faulkner and Yoknapatawpha, 2015*, ed. Jay Watson, Jaime Harker, and James G. Thomas, Jr. (Jackson: University Press of Mississippi, 2017), 18.

26. William Faulkner, *The Sound and the Fury*, rev. ed. (1929; repr., New York: Vintage International, 1990), 178.

Pictorialism, Prolixity, and Spatial Form in Faulkner's Post-Hollywood Racial Imaginary

Peter Lurie

When Faulkner completed the manuscript for *Absalom, Absalom!* in 1936, he famously delivered it to his friend Dave Hempstead with the boast, "It's the best novel yet written by an American."[1] At nearly the same time, he also furnished a tidy $100,000 price tag (a cool $1.8 million in today's value) for film rights to the novel because, he claimed, he "d[id] not need to sell it" immediately and, presumably, because he thought it could fetch such an amount on the Hollywood market.[2]

Faulkner's expansive sense of his novel's worth, both artistic and commercial, is worth noting not only because it signaled his recognition of his talent's full maturation. As I discuss below, this expansiveness—which, importantly, shapes the enlarged historical as well as formal and stylistic scale of the book—came in the midst of Faulkner's highest remuneration to date, his work as a studio writer for MGM and then for Fox Studios. His assessment of the potential value of *Absalom* as a property to lure Hollywood executives may have been somewhat inflated. But the conflation of his first experience of financial ease in the mid-1930s with the novel's own richness and ambition is hard to overlook.

As we know, Faulkner's early career revealed his striking interest in pictorialism, both in his line drawings for *Marionettes* and in the momentary icons in *As I Lay Dying* and *The Sound and the Fury*. So too do visual references and analogies throughout *Light in August* and *Absalom, Absalom!* to photography, the illustrator Aubrey Beardsley, or genres like the woodcut. These images, and Faulkner's interest in the image per se as a conveyor of meaning, have been much discussed, most recently and most extensively by Candace Waid in her wide-ranging treatment of Faulkner's visual proclivities, *The Signifying Eye*.[3] I will turn shortly to another well-considered example of Faulkner's visual rendering of Yoknapatawpha, his map of the county that appeared in the first edition of *Absalom, Absalom!* in 1936 and that he reprised in several other versions over the course of his career. What my remarks here consider more fully is the role of Faulkner's encounter with a very different example of visual culture, namely, the outsized spectacle of the Hollywood film image.

Without asserting a causal link between his work as a screenwriter and his approach to the narrative of Thomas Sutpen (which critics such as Joseph Urgo, Charles Hannon, and others have already done), I think we would do well to consider what Faulkner's hands-on experience with the motion picture industry may have added to the enlarged scope of vision for his novel-writing.[4] *Absalom*'s narrative covers a greater historical range than had any of his novels before it. Importantly, it also demonstrated Faulkner's most ambitious stylistic prose experiment to that point in his career (perhaps at any point of it). The novel's syntactical, lexical, and structural demands are clear from its opening pages and chapters; as any reader of the novel also knows, they play an important role not only in *Absalom*'s aesthetic effect but also in its meaning.[5] What I would like to suggest, and what I will use models from film and image theory to elaborate, is that Faulkner's experience with the film industry in this period played a role in his fiction's more encompassing workings.

Faulkner's formal ambitions in *Absalom* were not initiated with his work on this novel. *Light in August* too may be distinguished in his work to that point by its own structural prolixity, the sheer proliferation of narratives across its pages, many portions of which do not directly converge or do so only belatedly, and marked as it is by yet another putative "beginning" in the book's final chapter with the story of the furniture repairer about Byron and Lena. *Pylon* bears its own new formal aspects by virtue of its frequent neologisms and its self-referential tropes about authorship and writing. And *Absalom* hardly marks an outer limit to this expanded "scale" to Faulkner's novelistic practice, as *Go Down, Moses*, the Snopes trilogy, or even *A Fable* demonstrates. But matters and themes such as race relations, racial identity, the history of slavery, or the day-to-day functioning of the peculiar institution, not to mention ventures into depicting black subjectivity such as we find in *Go Down, Moses* and *Intruder in the Dust* and beyond the more limited confines of Compsons, Sartorises, or Sutpens—in short, Faulkner had essayed little of this prior to his own movement outward and west from Oxford in May of 1932.

The greater remuneration Faulkner enjoyed at MGM would likely have eased his mind from financial burdens, allowing a more far-reaching formal experiment than what he had to that point pursued. Yet a more immediate influence of Hollywood was aesthetic, the opening out to spatial reaches that the film frame always and *perforce* yields. As Stanley

Cavell puts it in *The World Viewed*, distinguishing photography and film from painting, "The camera, being finite, crops a portion from an infinitely larger field; continuous portions of that field could be included in the photograph in fact taken; in principle it could all be taken."[6] Stephen Heath offers a similar take in his essay "Narrative Space." Referring to early film theory's exalting of cinema as the "universal language," Heath writes, "As its source and authority . . . the universal language has no less than the universe itself, the world embraced by the eye of the camera and delivered over on screen."[7]

One of the more suggestive accounts of the sense of the image generally and its implied plenitude comes from W. J. T. Mitchell in his early book *Picture Theory*. Mitchell's concept of what he calls the "metapicture" is especially apt to Faulkner's broader (and broadening) efforts to depict Yoknapatawpha in the period following his first stint in Hollywood, an affinity that we can better grasp by way of the *Absalom* map. Mitchell defines a metapicture as an image—whether a drawing, a painting, a photograph, or a cinematic photogram—that draws attention to itself as a visual construction rather than as an invisible or transparent "window" onto reality or the scene depicted. These are pictures, he says, "that are used to show what a picture is."[8] He cites theorists of art such as Clement Greenberg and Michael Fried, who long ago posited that the proper subject of modern painting is the medium itself, and postmodern thinkers like Thierry de Duve in terms that will be particularly apt for considering Faulkner's post-Hollywood writing. Here Mitchell refers to the idea of art as "self-analytic," an analysis that "is directed, not only at the medium, but at the determining conditions of the work—its institutional setting, its historical positionality, its address to beholders" (*Picture Theory*, 35–36).

Mitchell's first example of a metapicture is a deceptively simple 1964 drawing by Saul Steinberg titled *The Spiral*. Mitchell is at pains to indicate that he chose Steinberg's drawing (and his several other examples of metapictures) not because of its artistic merit or aesthetic accomplishment. As he puts it, "the drawing is not 'art,' but a *New Yorker* cartoon; it is not sublime but ridiculous" (41). Nevertheless, it conveys a measure of self-awareness as a drawing and quite deliberately invokes the notion of the greater world that lies only putatively outside its border. Steinberg's drawing, Mitchell points out, "first appeared in the *New Yorker* with the title *New World*. This title established the drawing as an exemplar of a whole series of drawings on the theme of the artist as world-maker" (40). Mitchell offers ways to read the drawing in two "directions" temporally: one follows the image's circular motion clockwise, which to Mitchell offers "an allegory of a familiar history of

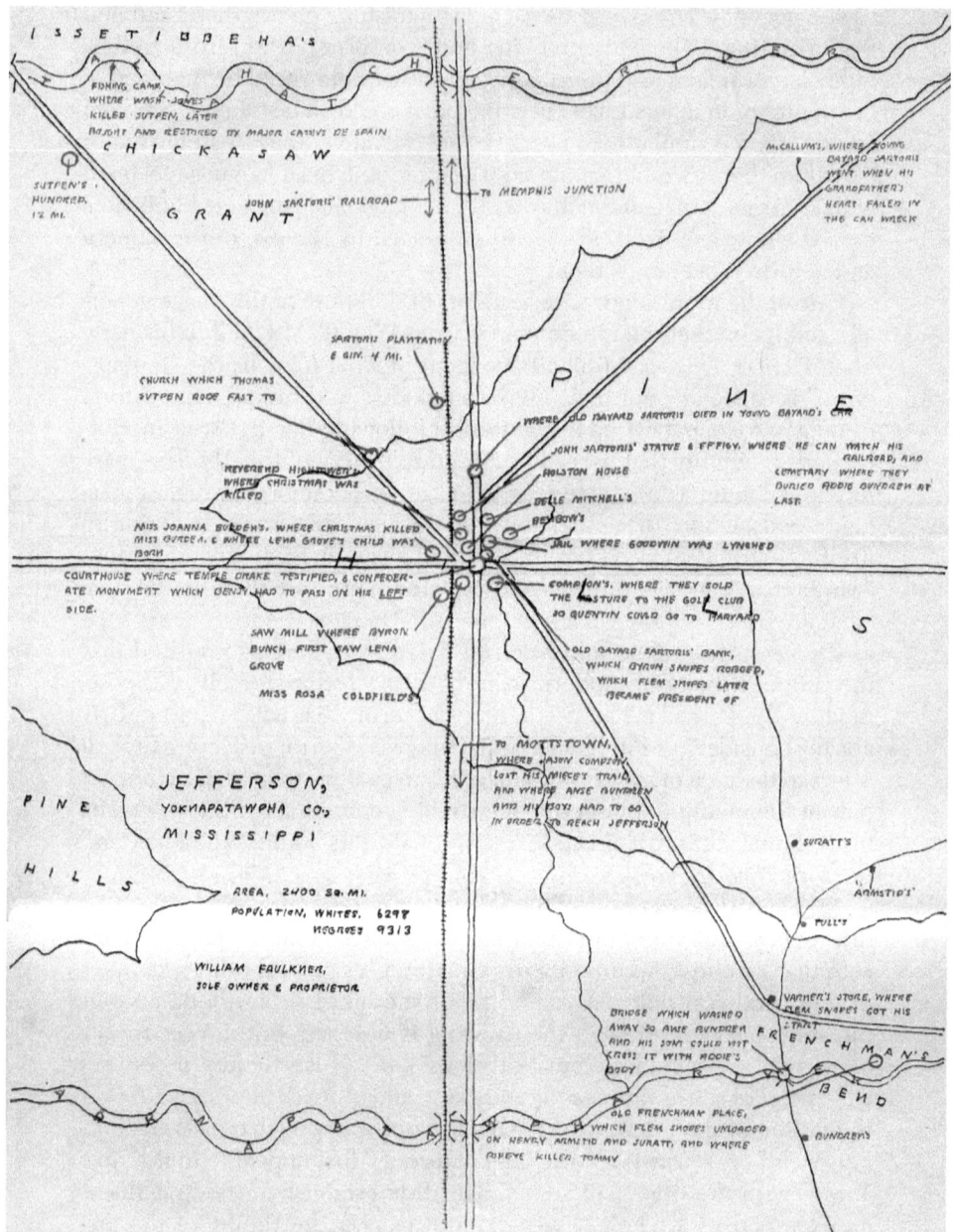

Map of Yoknapatawpha County, from *Absalom, Absalom!* by William Faulkner, copyright 1936 by William Faulkner and copyright renewed 1964 by Estelle Faulkner Summers. Used by permission of Random House, an imprint and division of Penguin Random House LLC. All rights reserved.

modern painting, one which begins with representation of the external world and moves toward pure abstraction," the fine lines of the spiral pattern. Reading and moving in the other direction, counterclockwise, "shows another history, one that has moved from the figure to abstraction to landscape to the writing at the bottom—to a 'New World' that lies beyond the circumference of the drawing" (40).

At first glance, Steinberg's cartoon may seem to have little in common with either the cinematic images Faulkner worked to produce in Hollywood or the map of Yoknapatawpha he drew for *Absalom*. Yet an even cursory examination yields some important affinities, at least with the map. To begin, like the signatory to the map, the figure at the center of Steinberg's picture draws (or is made to seem to draw) the image he fills and over which he presides. Though not identified explicitly with Steinberg, this figure may well be said to be the "sole owner and proprietor" of the landscape he surveys, some of which we see sketched and more of which is intimated in the drawing's caption, which reads, "New World." That new world in the case of Faulkner's map is of course Yoknapatawpha, or the new imaginative space it was becoming in the midthirties and beyond. If the *Absalom* map is a metapicture, a cartographic reflection on Faulkner's broader rendering of his mythical county, the "New World" it incorporates is both the US South's deeper history and the various, often violent events across his works that the map references.

This new world also encompassed the new circumstances of Faulkner's writing or, as Mitchell puts it above, "the determining conditions of the work." Those included the fact of his composing portions of the manuscript of *Absalom* while in Hollywood and in the service of an industry that produced large-scale images and that did so by incorporating the work of huge teams of laborers, many of whom, like Faulkner, arrived from other parts of the country or, in the case of the celebrated German directors, actors, and writers, from Europe.[9]

The affinities between these two drawings, however, are also figurative or, we may say in a particular manner, theoretical. Mitchell points out that the "New World" to which Steinburg's drawing refers is not only that of the artist ensnared in his own (self-) representation, a common critique of the modernist writer, but also what he refers to as "*our* world ... [of] 'America' or '1964,' as the caption puts it," the already postmodern world of 1964 that is constituted solely by images (*Picture Theory*, 41). In this way, the drawing, Mitchell says, "is a perfect illustration of ... the 'pictorial turn' in postmodern culture, the sense that we live in a world of images, a world in which, to paraphrase Derrida, there is nothing outside the picture."[10] We should admit that the world of 1936 that Faulkner knew, particularly during his time in Hollywood and in a

The Spiral (1964), by Saul Steinberg, from Steinberg's New World series. Saul Steinberg; © 1963, 1991 The *New Yorker* Magazine. Inc. Used by permission.

decade that included illustrated newspapers, *Life* magazine, other glossies, newsreels, and, of course, the movies was already, as scholarship on Faulkner's media ecology asserts, a "world of images," as per accounts of postmodernity like those of Guy DeBord or Jean Baudrillard.

Julian Murphet has described the several ways in which Faulkner's 1930s writing, and *Absalom* in particular, contends with the increasing cultural sway of motion pictures in the period, one that, Murphet contends, was consonant with Faulkner's and others' recognition of the technological and cultural obsolescence of the printed novel.[11] Of particular note is Murphet's account of the ways in which the photomechanical processes of photographic and image reproduction in mass-circulation newsprint and magazines of the period—such as those like the *Saturday Evening Post* and *Scribners*, in which Faulkner sought assiduously to publish his short fiction—infused print itself with a pictorial dimension.[12] In a reading of *Pylon* that he offers in conjunction with what he terms Faulkner's "picture writing" in *Absalom*, Murphet points to the earlier novel's scenario of the newsroom and the "subterranean crisis" of the paper's underground printing presses, the same machinery that Murphet notes also ran the *Scribner's* and *Post* stories that would later comprise *The Unvanquished* (*Faulkner's Media Romance*, 223). These consonances contribute to a profound shift in how we can conceive of the coeval relationship between visual and verbal modes in the modern period, one that Murphet suggests was underway well before Faulkner's career and the advent of literary modernism. "These presses are, like all since the collotype revolution of the 1880s, photomechanical in nature, freely able to blend symbolic type and reproduced photographs on the same page, on a mass basis."[13] More important are the implications of this new print technology for other forms of writing, including Faulkner's literary efforts of the thirties and beyond. "[T]his implies," Murphet continues, "that photography as a chemical process has stealthily infiltrated the very material underpinning of the discourse network of the Enlightenment—i.e., printing itself" (223).

Murphet's commentary on what he calls the congeries of textual and image production arises in the context of his claims about Faulkner's modernism generally and about *Absalom* in particular. While the terms of this discussion do not allow a full exploration of Murphet's approach, his emphases on the singularity of *Absalom* within the broader interdiscursive and intermedial workings of novelistic writing in the age of Hollywood are most salient to my argument. For nowhere is this mutual imbrication clearer than in the novel Faulkner wrote while in the throes of his effort to reconcile his writerly ambitions with the monetary rewards the studios offered, circumstances that Murphet claims were even more immediate in their relationship to the novel's compensation as well as its formal uniqueness than I here suggest. As he asserts, "*Absalom, Absalom!* is the greatest work of literary art to be subsidized by the new corporate form of patronage, the Hollywood studio system and magazine capital" (*Faulkner's Media Romance*, 216). Elsewhere, and in terms more consonant with my own conception of Faulkner's pictorialism, he avers, citing Mitchell, that "it would appear to have been at this precise [early twentieth century] moment in literary history that the literary world finally and irrevocably learned that writing itself, 'in its physical, graphic form, is an inseparable suturing of the verbal and the visual, the "imagetext" incarnate'" (225). It is the notion of *Absalom* the novel and its endpapers as a conjoined and similarly purposed version of Mitchell's "imagetext" that I here describe.

Rather than seeking to describe how pictorialism "works" in Faulkner's fiction, as Murphet does (2), I want to consider the ways a material history of cultural labor on Faulkner's part, in tandem with theoretical accounts of the film medium, contributes to how we understand the mid-1930s work and beyond. Even the type of historicizing that Murphet essays could be focused, it seems to me, by a sense of what the scalar dimensions of the cinematic image of Faulkner's period meant to his writerly vision for Yoknapatawpha and its variously raced and classed denizens. Mitchell's deconstructive mode may seem a long way from Yoknapatawpha or from Faulkner's literary practice in 1936. Yet as Mitchell writes of Steinberg's spiral drawing, "dissolv[ing] the boundary between inside and outside, first-and second-order representation, on which the metapictorial structure depends" (*Picture Theory*, 42) is a version of what Faulkner was doing with the series of Yoknapatawpha maps he drew beginning with *Absalom*.

This is precisely what Jay Watson, in a forthcoming article, claims the endpapers of *Absalom* perform. Watson's remarks also helpfully return us to a Faulkner who, following his sojourn in Hollywood, became part of a much more ambitious and commercially oriented publishing venture with Random House, which merged with Faulkner's former publisher, Smith & Haas, in 1936. In "Reading the *Absalom!* Endpapers: Reflections on the Poetics and Politics of Paranarrative," Watson draws attention to the variance of details in the chronology and genealogy from the main narrative of *Absalom*, differences that Noel Polk "corrected" for the Library of America edition of the novel but which Watson sees as evidence of the text's greater ambiguity and refusal of interpretive containment.[14]

In addition, and importantly to my argument, the map shows Random House's effort to market not just this novel but Faulkner's corpus generally. As Watson points out, the map was attached to the end page of the first edition, a place where publishers would ordinarily insert ads for other titles by the same author. "We might consider the *Absalom* map, and particularly the way that, in contrast to the genealogy and chronology, it expands its frame of reference beyond the narrative or even the book, as a serendipitous extension or even a canny element of Random's marketing strategy. Placed in the back of the first edition . . . and differentiating itself from unremarkable, run-of-the-mill print textuality by way of its innovative, fold-out format and colored ink, the map may help construct a 'Faulkner' who exceeded the significance of any book he authored yet lent his emerging brand prestige to all of them" ("Reading the *Absalom!* Endpapers," n.p.). Faulkner's fold-out, color insert was literally an opening out of and *from* the novel proper and its fictional world. If I offer the expanded visual field of the film image, what cinema and image theory describe as its powerful hint of "the universe" or at least of a spatiovisual (if not also historical) "repleteness," as a potential basis for Faulkner's fuller confronting of the South's ills and his more fulsome mode in doing so in the later thirties and beyond, I hope to do so in the same spirit of curiosity as Watson's own "expanding" questions.

Watson himself cagily suggests that Random would have welcomed or even encouraged a method of reminding readers of other Faulkner novels whose publishing rights the firm had recently acquired. "Since Random had acquired publishing rights to four of the other five novels that supplied material mentioned on the map . . . upon its merger with . . . Smith and Haas in 1936, any additional interest the map might help generate in the other Yoknapatawpha novels would directly benefit the firm as well. It made good business sense to present Faulkner in precisely the way the map did: as the 'sole owner and proprietor' of an imaginative territory demonstrably capable of generating book after book" ("Reading the *Absalom!* Endpapers," n.p.). Elsewhere Watson points out that despite the fact that, by the time of *Absalom*'s release, Faulkner had published nearly thirty short stories, the map largely references events from Faulkner's published novels, suggesting, as he puts it, "that a proper reckoning with the map, and with its creator, may require a deeper engagement not just with the imaginative or even the narrative ecology of Faulkner's writings but with their print culture ecology as well" (n.p.). To this look to print culture I would add a consideration of the wider media culture that surrounded Faulkner's writing efforts in this period and beyond.

As evidence of that media ecology, and true to Hollywood convention, the events the map mentions are nearly all examples of violent or sensational action from the novels Faulkner had written to that point. Among the notations and locations that appear are the following:

"Where old Bayard Sartoris died in young Bayard's car"
"Jail where Goodwin was lynched"
"Reverend Hightower's, where Christmas was killed"
"Miss Joanna Burden's, where Christmas killed Miss Burden"
"Old Bayard Sartoris' bank, which Byron Snopes robbed"
"Old Frenchman Place, which Flem Snopes unloaded on Henry Armstid and Suratt, and where Popeye killed Tommy"
"Church which Thomas Sutpen rode fast to"

This last example is notable in that, while no violence or crime occurs per se, the affront that the rough-hewn Thomas Sutpen poses to Sunday decorum in Jefferson by way of his breakneck carriage driving connotes what is objectionable about him—but also what marks his character as dangerous, modern, and, importantly from a marketing perspective, narratively interesting.[15]

Faulkner may not have been playing the marketing game I suggest here, but his choice of violent and often criminal acts to highlight on the map suggests an awareness of the ways these details would more immediately compel readers' interests. Additionally, the map's cross-referencing of various story events suggests the scenario of the film studios, on whose lots discussion of other studios' movies was common in what was, essentially, an industry town. And though Faulkner spent most of his time in Hollywood with his head down, he doubtless would have known something of the many films in production during his stay.

Certain of these films and their plots resonate suggestively with aspects of Faulkner's work from this period, particularly events from *Absalom* or aspects of the novel that the map does not mention. Joseph Blotner reports that Faulkner delivered the final screenplay for *Today We Live* to MGM on October 22, 1932, which was the release date for the studio's *Red Dust*, a film directed by Victor Fleming and starring none other than Clark Gable. Gable's character's exploits on a rubber colony in French Indochina may not have had anything to do with Thomas Sutpen's plantation experiences in another French-speaking colony in the novel Faulkner published a few years later. And Faulkner's direct familiarity with the picture isn't clear. Yet Blotner relays the famous anecdote of Faulkner's hunting trip with Gable and Howard Hawks during this same fall 1932 California stay within a page of mentioning October 22. As the anecdote archly suggests, Gable's film roles were likely not unfamiliar to Faulkner at this moment.[16]

Another, slightly earlier, release, also by MGM, was 1931's *Trader Horn*. The film is about a white trader in Africa who discovers, among other things, a "white goddess" among the "natives." Not surprisingly, it was wildly successful and was nominated for the Academy Award for best picture that year. For that reason and others, Faulkner may well have seen it.[17] Importantly, the film's colonial setting and its objectionable colonial perspective on race may have prompted Faulkner's moves toward depicting race and black characters even slightly differently in his post-Hollywood writing—differently both from the studio's patterns of racial representation and from Faulkner's own earlier, arguably limited depictions of African Americans in figures such as *Flags in the Dust*'s Simon Strother or Dilsey Gibson in *The Sound and the Fury*. MGM's and other studios' patronizing stance toward people of color on screen, that is, might have prompted Faulkner's efforts to represent black subjectivity more authentically or, at least, with more interiority. Charles Bon, Rider of "Pantaloon in Black," Lucas Beauchamp (in "The Fire and the Hearth" especially), and Nancy Mannigoe (as she appears in *Requiem for a Nun*, a novel on which Faulkner began working in December 1933 after returning home from Hollywood) offer meaningful variations on both Hollywood's racial representations and Faulkner's pre-1932 novels.[18]

In addition to Watson's suggestion that the map compels attention to the broader print culture around Faulkner in the middle 1930s, it also invites us to consider the broader media culture that it in ways resembles and in which Faulkner played a sporadic role during this period. I am less immediately interested here in the emerging Faulkner brand than I am in what was emerging in Faulkner's writing itself at this midthirties moment and beyond, namely, a sensibility and an aesthetic project that, like the map and perhaps inspired by its hints of the greater world beyond the frame (of the film screen; of his earlier novels; of white Jefferson), Faulkner increasingly pursued.

There is, thankfully and in closing, a caveat to this proposition. In conceiving Lucas Beauchamp for the novel *Intruder in the Dust*, Faulkner found a meaningful limit for his expanded spatial, novelistic, and historioracial imagination. What Esther Sánchez-Pardo and others have called Lucas's opacity—or, rather, the writerly stubbornness Faulkner manifested about trying fully to envision the character or to depict his interiority—shows a boundary beyond which, I submit, Faulkner respectfully declined to go.[19] That is, Lucas and other members of the black community, as well as their often furtive spaces, reveal Faulkner *not* opening out *all of* Yoknapatawpha to the rationalized, abstract representations of space associated with the map (or with the film industry's effort, within a year of the novel's release, to "map" the fictional

Jefferson onto the actual space of Oxford with the on-location filming of the novel, a move that, like Random House's map, sought to capitalize on a visual depiction of Faulkner's mythical county). For all of the novel's and the film's respectful treatment of Lucas, conferring upon him dignity and autonomy beyond the efforts of Beat Four or even Gavin Stevens to discipline or explain him, Lucas remains a cipher. Faulkner's efforts to depict African American experience and consciousness, which begin with Joe Christmas but extend and deepen with Charles Bon and with Rider, Mollie Beauchamp, and the other characters in *Go Down, Moses*, reveal a wider racial aperture than he'd demonstrated in his pre-Hollywood fiction. Amidst the significant changes that his exposure to the film medium effected, Faulkner was indeed able to demonstrate a richer perspective on Yoknapatawpha and its citizens—and on spatial and temporal regions beyond it. Yet even apparent exceptions to this rule, such as the characterization of Lucas I describe, are salutary. As capacious, prolix, inventive, and *full* as Faulkner's vision became as his professional and artistic prospects expanded, he still demonstrated a meaningful reticence toward a subject who he recognized was at the heart of the Yoknapatawpha dialectic—of white and black, master and slave, commerce and art, past and present—but also, and meaningfully, a subject of whom he was decidedly not the sole owner and proprietor.

NOTES

1. William Faulkner, quoted in Joseph Blotner, *William Faulkner: A Biography*, rev. ed. (1974; repr., New York: Random House, 1984), 364.

2. Joseph Blotner, ed., *Selected Letters of William Faulkner* (New York: Random House, 1977), 96.

3. Candace Waid, *The Signifying Eye: Seeing Faulkner's Art* (Athens: University of Georgia Press, 2013).

4. See Joseph R. Urgo, "*Absalom, Absalom!* The Movie," *American Literature* 62, no. 1 (March 1990): 56–73, and Charles Hannon, *William Faulkner and the Discourses of Culture* (Baton Rouge: Louisiana State University Press, 2005), 83–84.

5. Cf. Edouard Glissant, *Faulkner, Mississippi*, trans. Barbara B. Lewis and Thomas Spear (Chicago: University of Chicago Press, 1999), and his discussion of Faulkner's consistent narrative deferrals and syntactical attenuations as a means of showing the impossibility of establishing origins or a clear genealogy.

6. Stanley Cavell, *The World Viewed: Reflections on the Ontology of Film* (Cambridge, MA: Harvard University Press, 1979), 24.

7. Stephen Heath, *Questions of Cinema* (Bloomington: Indiana University Press, 1981), 25.

8. W. J. T. Mitchell, *Picture Theory: Essays on Visual and Verbal Representation* (Chicago: University of Chicago Press, 1995), 35. Hereafter cited parenthetically.

9. An only cursory list of such individuals who, like Faulkner, worked in Hollywood would include luminaries such as the Germans Thomas Mann, Bertolt Brecht, Marlene Dietrich, Ernst Lubitsch, and Erich von Stroheim and the American writers F. Scott Fitzgerald, Nathaniel West, and John Dos Passos.

10. Mitchell cites Derrida's *Of Grammatology* rather broadly when he refers to the absence of an effective border between a representation and its purported signified. Yet Derrida's now canonical essay "Structure, Sign, and Play in the Discourse of the Human Sciences" furnishes a more succinct account of what Mitchell claims of his poststructuralist thinking: "It would be easy enough to show that the concept of structure and even the word 'structure' itself are as old as the *episteme*—that is to say, as old as Western science and Western philosophy. . . . The center is at the center of the totality, and yet, since the center does not belong to the totality (is not part of the totality), the totality *has its center* elsewhere" (Jacques Derrida, "Structure, Sign, and Play in the Discourse of the Human Sciences" [1967], in *Critical Theory Since 1965*, ed. Hazard Adams and Leroy Searle [Gainesville: University Press of Florida, 1986], 83–84).

11. See Julian Murphet, "Faulkner in the Histories of Film: 'Where Memory Is the Slave'" in *Faulkner and Film: Faulkner and Yoknapatawpha, 2010*, ed. Peter Lurie and Ann J. Abadie (Jackson: University Press of Mississippi, 2014), 214–16.

12. Julian Murphet, *Faulkner's Media Romance* (New York: Oxford University Press, 2017), 223. Hereafter cited parenthetically.

13. Surprisingly, Murphet does not point out that the *Unvanquished* stories and book all, upon their original publication, included illustrations as headnotes, some in the style of woodcuts that for many readers added to the narrative's nostalgic tone and that only enhanced the intersections of image and text that, as we increasingly see, defined modernity in its cultural and technological realms.

14. Jay Watson, "Reading the *Absalom!* Endpapers: Reflections on the Poetics and Politics of Paranarrative," *Transatlantica* 2019, no. 1 (forthcoming). Hereafter cited parenthetically.

15. We might here recall the insistence of the news editor Hagood from *Pylon*—the novel Faulkner wrote during the time in which he composed *Absalom* and worked on at (this inserted "at" is necessary) both the MGM and Fox lots—that what makes for mass-market appeal is sensationalistic action of the sort Faulkner's map emphasizes. As he puts it, hectoring the reporter about his approach to covering the air meet, "You listen to me a minute. If one of them takes his airplane or his parachute and murders [Laverne] and the child in front of the grandstand, then it will be news" (William Faulkner, *Pylon*, in *Novels 1930–1935*, ed. Joseph Blotner and Noel Polk [New York: Library of America, 1985], 808).

16. Asked by Gable to list the "best living writers," Faulkner included himself, whereupon Gable hesitated and said, "Do you write?" to which Faulkner drily responded, "Yes, Mr. Gable. What do you do?" (Blotner, *Faulkner: A Biography*, 310).

17. The film enjoyed a measure of notoriety and did not escape the attention of another native Mississippi writer and Faulkner contemporary. Richard Wright refers to the film in the early scene in his 1940 novel *Native Son* when the protagonist Bigger Thomas and his friend Gus take in a matinee and *Trader Horn* is playing on the screen.

18. Deborah Barker points to the ways that *Requiem* works to dismantle plantation myths such as the black mammy and the male rapist that animated popular culture and early cinema; see "Demystifying the Modern Mammy in *Requiem for a Nun*," in *Faulkner and Film: Faulkner and Yoknapatawpha, 2010*, ed. Peter Lurie and Ann J. Abadie (Jackson: University Press of Mississippi, 2014), 71–97. Ben Robbins sees Faulkner's post-Hollywood fiction as informed by an understanding of the industry's constraining vision

of gender, one Faulkner gleaned while working on scripts for so-called "women's films" in the forties. Robbins's "William Faulkner's *Requiem for a Nun* and Cold War Hollywood Melodrama" (*Genre* 50, no. 3 [2017]: 343–70) shows the writer fashioning a character in Temple Drake who resists the era's dominant vision of domesticity, much as Faulkner had done with Temple and the image of the southern belle in *Sanctuary*. D. Matthew Ramsey also argues for a salutary or at least broadening effect that Faulkner's Hollywood work had on his conception of gender. In his "'Touch Me While You Look at Her': Stars, Fashion, and Authorship in *Today We Live*" (in *Faulkner and Material Culture: Faulkner and Yoknapatawpha, 2004*, ed. Joseph R. Urgo and Ann J. Abadie [Jackson: University Press of Mississippi, 2007], 82–103), Ramsey points to the fact that MGM's requirement that Faulkner invent a role for Joan Crawford in adapting "Turnabout" led him to contemplate women's agency and female desire in ways that shaped his approach to *Pylon*. It is a similar re-envisioning of race after Faulkner's exposure to Hollywood practices that I describe here.

19. Sánchez-Pardo posits that Lucas's "inscrutability," his "subversive self-possession . . . can operate as a form of resistance to a justice system that contains no outlet through which he can be allowed to speak for himself" ("Unraveling Race and Mystery in *Intruder in the Dust*," in *Faulkner and Mystery: Faulkner and Yoknapatawpha, 2009*, ed. Annette Trefzer and Ann J. Abadie [Jackson: University Press of Mississippi, 2014], 124). Sánchez-Pardo cites Édouard Glissant's observation in *Faulkner, Mississippi* that Lucas is "a picture-perfect portrait of a Negro's opacity" (quoted in Sánchez-Pardo, "Unraveling Race and Mystery," 124).

Financialization and Neoliberalism: A Snopes Genealogy

John T. Matthews

Faulkner charts Flem Snopes's career against the economic environments he exploits serially. If in *The Hamlet* (1940), during the decades around the turn of the twentieth century, Flem calculates a move from the dead end of his landless father's sharecropping to his landlord's speculative mercantilism, in *The Town* (1957), set in the late 1920s, Flem takes advantage of what appear to be new opportunities presented by financialization. Unlike Will Varner's capitalism, in which owner-lenders underwrite the production of real goods by extending credit, financialization bids to separate "finance from nonfinancial activity."[1] The ability to profit from intangible financial activities typifies many of the moneymaking ventures in *The Town*, from the arcane practices of insurance companies and national banks to opportunistic trade in social information. The novel's narrators, V. K. Ratliff, Gavin Stevens, and Chick Mallison, as members of Jefferson's established mercantile and professional cohort, view the emergence of such economic antics at first with bemusement, then with growing alarm. Montgomery Ward Snopes's "Atelier Monty," a studio he opens in Jefferson to exhibit pornographic photos, serves as a caricature of the alluring indecency of the sort of business in which, as Ratliff puts it enviously, "there aint no destructive consumption at all that's got to be replenished at a definite production labor cost."[2]

Yet the narrators' conviction that such financial shenanigans represent a degrading novelty in Jefferson actually indexes a more habitual misrecognition about capitalism: goods-based trade is somehow more legitimate than traffic in abstract commodities. Ratliff and Stevens marvel that the flourishing Atelier does not seem to be offering anything tangible—no actual goods, such as bootleg liquor or in-person services such as prostitution; what it does prove to be selling—looking at pornographic photographs—strikes them as strangely insubstantial, the augur of making real money from a virtual economy. As in *The Hamlet*, though, what appears to be new about Flem's financial doings turns out to involve some intensified exploitation of capitalism's plasticity. The middle novel of Faulkner's Snopes trilogy recalls the moment of what was once America's most fervent embrace of financialized forms of making money, during the 1920s, as it also, at the moment of its composition in the 1950s, limns a genealogy for a second late-century intensification of financialization arising with neoliberalism in the 1970s and lasting to the present. Faulkner in the Cold War era was positioned as a national writer to witness modern America's formation of a liberal consensus in defense of democratic capitalism. As a southern writer, however, Faulkner doubted the premises of such liberalism because he grasped the brutal lineage of a national state capitalism that had been founded on the commoditization and financialization of its laboring subjects.

Financialization

Today, we may think of financialization as accompanying the capitalist social structure of accumulation that emerged in the 1980s and became known as neoliberalism.[3] Economists have defined it as "the increasing role of financial motives, financial markets, financial actors and financial institutions in the operation of . . . economies" (Kotz, "Neoliberalism and Financialization," 15). But even during the decades around the turn of the twentieth century, New York banks were purging the corporate scene of predatory financial operators and re-entrenching goods-based finance capitalism in the "real sector" of the economy. Nonetheless, the 1920s "saw a resurgence of financial speculators," and, as a result, "a first round of [full-fledged] financialization" took hold in the United States by the second half of the decade (15). As suggested by such ebb and flow, some economists understand financialization as a "tendency" at the "core" of capitalism itself: "[S]hifting ownership of capital from real capital to financial capital is the best way to insulate against the inherent risks of the capitalist marketplace" (9). Rather than seeing present-day financialization as capitalism's destiny, then, economists such as Giovanni Arrighi characterize it as intertwined with goods-based capitalism, leading to century-long cycles that have been dominated by one tendency or the other.[4] For Arrighi, the form of finance capitalism devised in the seventeenth century to propel Europe's global trade in goods eventually gave way to an era of profit seeking through financial practices such as speculation in paper credit, investment banking, and commercial insurance. Likewise, a capitalism linked to escalated powers of production, marketing, and consumption of goods resulting from the industrial revolution of the nineteenth century was eventually overtaken by the invention of twentieth-century financial instruments for profit deriving from the paper traffic in stocks, bonds, and debt.[5]

A stricter Marxian account, however, locates financialization at the root of capitalism. If one grants that the critical move in the formation of capital is the "division of living labor time into necessary" and "surplus labor time," then the appropriation of that surplus by the owning class constitutes "the hidden basis of capitalist society."[6] Writing during the financial crisis of the 1930s, Samezo Kuruma directs readers to Marx's account of the transformation of surplus value into profit as the result of its continuing metamorphosis into financialized commodities, which distances profit from its true origin in the extraction of surplus value from labor.[7] Value, accruing from "the circulation of capital, suddenly presents itself as an independent substance, endowed with a motion of its own, passing through a life-process of its own, in which money and commodities are mere forms which it assumes and casts off in turn."[8] Profit, in its financialized forms of interest and other seemingly autonomous forms, "then seems to be independent both of the labourer's wage-labour and the capitalist's own labour, and to arise from capital as its own independent source. . . . Profit seems to be determined only secondarily by direct exploitation of labour" (Marx, *Capital*, vol. 3, 598). Although the narrators of *The Town* exhibit the sort of practical misrecognition that hides the financialized basis of mercantile capitalism, the novel offers a conflicting story, one that refuses to "forget" the origins of capitalism in the most abusive of agricultural labor economies. In *The Town*, when Will Varner surveys the remains of his life as merchant-in-chief of Frenchman's Bend, the parataxis of Faulkner's prose accurately equates trade in labor, material goods, and financial instruments: "the symbolical gnawed bones—the racks of hames and plow-handles, the rank side meat and flour and cheap molasses and cheese and shoes and coal oil and work gloves and snuff and chewing tobacco and fly specked candy and the liens and mortgages on crops and plow-tools and mules and horses and land—of his fortune" (257).

In *The Hamlet*, Flem learns the basics of agricultural capitalism in a local economy based in the real sector: land leases, labor contracts, credit for supplies, general merchandise. Flem moves on to speculation in commodities—goats, spotted horses, real estate—while learning more advanced techniques like capitalizing personal debt and investing in going businesses. When *The Town* takes up his story two decades later, in 1927, the "Snopes industry" (113) has advanced to the capitalization of immaterial goods in the novel's prominent activities: banking, insurance, investment, and even monetized gossip and rumor. Strictly financial transactions increasingly mystify profit as distinct from material substance. Think of how Ratliff in *The Town* reframes Eck Snopes's earlier dilemma over which spotted horse to chase first in language that mocks the abstract nature of fiscal calculation: Eck must decide "which represented the most net profit if he caught it," "that is, was a hundred-plus percent of a free horse worth more than just a hundred percent of a six-dollar horse?" (30–31). The horses themselves disappear into the fog of computation.

Financial schemes in *The Town* routinely appear to involve making money off nothing. For example, Mrs. Hait outmaneuvers her dead husband's partner, I. O. Snopes, by rejecting his claim of ownership of the mules killed with Lonzo in a train accident. She hires Flem to negotiate a settlement with the railroad insurance company and receives a windfall summed up as the unreal reality of having "sold her husband to the railroad company for eight thousand percent profit" (204). I. O. and Hait's original scheme had involved converting living mules into reimbursable losses by arranging their slaughter as they are herded across the rail line's most dangerous turn. Chick describes the grotesque scene of the final accident as a near-total dematerialization of objects: "What remained of Mr Hait had finally been sorted from what remained of the five mules and several feet of new manila rope scattered along the right-of-way" (204–5). Casualty registers as a matter of mathematical risk and monetary compensation.

And yet, the increasingly abstract and fictive machinations of financialized capitalism never, in Faulkner's telling, float entirely free of the laboring bodies whose capitalization yields profit. *The Town* is coated with the residue of dematerializations; financialization levies obliterative violence on bodies, language, time, and human subjectivity itself. Instantaneous disembodiment is a constant threat. Enraged that he's gotten nothing from the insurance settlement for the railroad "accident" he has himself contrived, I. O. fills Mrs. Hait's yard with mules, hoping to panic her into paying him. This unreal scene reads like a replay of the original slaughter: "Mrs Hait was just too mad to notice, rush[ing] right into the middle of the drove, after the one with the flying halter-rein that was still vanishing into the fog still in that cloud of whirling loose feathers like confetti or the wake behind a speed boat" (210). It's as if the actual accident and its financial reckoning are a single event. That's because, in a sense, Hait and the mules cease to exist at the moment they are insured, not at the moment their bodies are destroyed.[9] Their value is already a condition of their extinction. Earlier, Eck Snopes is killed when he uses a lit lantern to investigate a leak in an oil tank. His destruction nearly total, the worker's only trace is his neck brace, found hanging from telegraph wires: "But they never did find anything of Mr Snopes" (97). There does turn out to be a company insurance policy, however, so Eck's widow receives a $1,000 settlement, which she sets aside for their oldest son, Wallstreet. Eck's fate, like Hait's, is less an anecdote about the boon of life insurance than an allegory of the financial dematerialization of the laborer's body by the abstract calculus of risk and the monetization of human loss.[10]

The evolution of the Snopes industry toward speculation in derealized goods has been prepared for by Flem's experiments in detaching value from use. In Faulkner's recycling of his short story "Centaur in Brass" (1932), Flem schemes to strip out the safety valves of Jefferson's water-power plant, resell them, and, as a town superintendent, authorize replacements to turn into fresh stock. The two plant workers Flem tries to blackmail into helping him eventually defeat their boss by dumping the cache of stolen fittings into the water tank itself—in mock fulfillment of Flem's ruse about wanting to use the stashed brass to increase the weight of the float. Turl and Tom burlesque Flem's dissolving allegiance to use value, delaying Flem's first step toward financial dominance in Jefferson. The water tower remains a reminder of Flem's only defeat, but Chick understands that commemorating it will have to reflect Flem's trajectory from an economy of tangible things to one as insubstantial as "Motion" itself: "Except that it was not a monument: it was a footprint. A monument only says *At least I got this far* while a footprint says *This is where I was when I moved again*" (26).

To its settled owning classes, Jefferson in the 1920s is suffering a shift in economic practices. Montgomery Ward's Atelier constitutes, Ratliff believes, the sort of novel enterprise that makes its profit off of nothing real. Ratliff tries to explain to Chick what customers are paying for—"It's kodak pictures of men and women together, experimenting with one another. Without no clothes on much" (143). Snopes converts the photos into slides, so they can be projected by a magic lantern. What Snopes is selling is the viewing of prints: a virtual commodity. The magic lantern was a precursor of the motion picture; fed serially through the device, the slides created the illusion of movement. Montgomery Ward's "Atelier" is a liminal space between fine arts studio painting and the movies, and although such mass entertainment did appeal to working-class audiences in part because of its lewd subject matter, Monty's enterprise also suggests there's something perverse about a future of nakedly virtual economies. The episode of Jefferson's Atelier takes on greater significance because Faulkner's novel attaches it to another story about the perversity of immaterial value forms.

In chapter 7 Chick rehearses the story of Montgomery Ward's business from its origins as a canteen in wartime France to its establishment in Jefferson. In chapter 8, Gavin Stevens charts the rise of Flem Snopes to the vice presidency of the bank founded by Colonel Sartoris. Stevens relates Flem's original bargain with Will Varner to take a damaged Eula off his hands in exchange for a dowry that includes stock in the Sartoris bank. Further leveraging Eula's subsequent adultery with Manfred de Spain, Flem ultimately banishes his economic cum spousal rival and mounts to the bank presidency himself. As in *The Hamlet*, those struggling to comprehend the obscenity of Flem's economic behavior resort to sexual metaphors. In the earlier novel, Ratliff is responsible for one of the angriest and most lurid: the imagined scene of a black girl who trades her body to storekeeper Flem for lard. In *The Hamlet*, Eula's virginal sexuality fetishizes the land as unownable, untillable—the earth before it has been reduced to a monetized good; in *The Town*, Eula is violated repeatedly in her reconfigured status as an immaterial commodity whose reputation can be traded on publicly. Just as Eula's pregnancy gets monetized by Flem (Mrs. Varner thinking "he had even made sin pay by getting the start from it that wound him up vice president of a bank" [261]), so he capitalizes on Eula's adultery. It's not that such valorization of information is entirely new in Yoknapatawpha. Jody Varner, after all, wants to use Ab's expected regard for a good name against him when he tries to strike an advantageous deal with the tenant farmer/barn-burner at the outset of *The Hamlet*, and Flem is always trying to use advance or misleading information to fool Ratliff.

But *The Town* reveals a more systematic economic valuation and exploitation of knowledge. Characters in *The Town* think habitually in terms of the value form of money as the dominant social epistemology. Chick jokes that Gowan should have spied on Manfred de Spain and Eula Varner more intently, because if he'd caught the lover climbing out of a bedroom window, "he really would have had something he could have sold for a dollar or two" (46). That this might be referring to a photograph as much as an anecdote reflects Monty's sort of world. Early on, Ratliff compares Flem's as-yet-undocumented knowledge of his wife's affair to a coin waiting to be spent: "Not catching his wife with Manfred de Spain yet is like that twenty-dollar gold piece pinned to your undershirt on your first maiden trip to what you hope is going to be a Memphis whorehouse. He dont need to unpin it yet" (26). The perversion of Flem's deferred gratification as Ratliff sees it is that when he finally cashes in on Eula's infidelity, it's only to make more money. As I shall argue, such unthinking reliance on a language of monetized knowledge in modern Jefferson points surprisingly to a long history of slavery that devised, as Ian Baucom has shown, speculative epistemologies, economic institutions like banking and commercial insurance, capitalized trade in slaves, the treatment of humans as a money form, and cultural technologies like the realist novel to represent them, throughout the Atlantic world.

In *Flags in the Dust*, we get the preliminary story of Byron Snopes, the bookkeeper in Flem's bank, whose sexual obsession with Narcissa Benbow induces voyeurism, obscene letter-writing, blackmail, and intimacies fantasized around passing money hand-to-hand through a teller's window. In *The Town*, we learn of this eventual embezzler's fascination not with money itself but with "the mechanics of its recording; he had not entered crawling into the glare of a mystery so much as, without attracting any attention to himself, he was trying to lift a corner of its skirt" (38). Such cross-trafficking in fungible social data, imaginary sexual currency, and the raw erotics of "the mechanics of . . . recording" makes banking another kind of pornography. Juxtaposed, the micronarratives of the Sartoris bank and a Snopes atelier allegorize the emergence of a virtual economy ruled by a new kind of magic. Stevens imagines that "perhaps what held [Flem] thralled there was the simple solvency of the bank": "[N]o matter how much money people drew out of it, there was always that one who had just deposited that zero-plus-one dollar into it in time" (122). But it's more mysterious than that, and Flem is in a position to peek under the skirt of financialized capital. When he deliberately creates a run on his own bank, Flem must figure out what to do with his personal deposits. He chooses a big bank for his small amount, since he believed "that [because] money itself, cash dollars, possessed an inherent life of its mutual own like cells or disease, his minuscule sum would increment itself by simple parasitic osmosis like a leech or a goitre or cancer" (234). It is Byron Snopes's naivete that lets him believe bank deposits are just hard cash waiting to be stolen. Flem, instead, as Ratliff insists, comes to respect *money*; and what he respects most is the inexplicable magic of capitalism: money itself making money.

S to $: The Novel's Subject

Florence Dore has shown how *The Town* reflects a new direction in Faulkner's aesthetics, away from the modernist difficulty of his early novels, with its bid for high cultural standing of the sort promoted by the New Critics, and towards "an emerging contemporary style" hospitable to mass culture—rock and roll, the movies: the commercialized forms of entertainment that will dominate the second half of the century and inform postmodern fiction.[11] Dore understands Faulkner's move as reflecting a conviction that "capital had already obliterated cultural capital" (54). If we see *The Town* as a moment of creative destruction for Faulkner, we might appreciate how the recourse to the more traditional novel form—prospectively revived in *The Hamlet* for what we might consider Faulkner's trilogy of capital—confronts an impasse in the 1950s: the novel's relation to capital has been transformed. How does Faulkner suggest capital's obliterative effects on the genre itself in volume 2 of *Snopes*?

The realist novel's confidence in its descriptive power itself founders before the violence of more open financialization. Figurative language in *The Town* tilts toward catachresis, as in those mules in Mrs. Hait's yard "vanishing into the fog still in that cloud of whirling loose feathers like confetti or the wake behind a speed boat" (210).[12] Confetti, a speed boat's wake—shredded paper, the trace of new velocities—point to the effects of financialization but also register the violence of converting bodies to unreal financial equivalents, entities of incommensurable volume, weight, density. Advanced financialization seems to accumulate profit from ungrounded circulation, an effect reflected in I. O. Snopes's "babbling": a "steady stream of confused and garbled proverbs and metaphors attached to nothing and going nowhere" (34). Town wits try to make a joke of Snopesism by tagging it as "the horse which came home to roost" (37), a broken metaphor recalling Flem's spotted horses escapade—poor Eck being "that horse boy" (30) nearly killed in the melee that followed the auction. Continuing the conceit, Stevens says that when Byron Snopes is found to have embezzled Sartoris bank money, he might be said to have "dis-stabled" the colonel (39). Similarly, Flem's chicanery ends up having "dis-restauranted" Ratliff and his partner. Such awkward neologisms betray Stevens's anxiety that he can account for Snopes behavior only in privatives, as not-actions. The effort to describe Byron's crime as characteristic and somehow predictable—even if only as Snopesism—makes Stevens worry self-consciously over what's happening to the novel's descriptive capacities: "using, to really mix, really confuse our metaphor, an humble cane out of that same quiver" (38). The narrators register the new order as an unintelligible din, an indecipherable semiotics: ear-shattering reports of souped-up cars, two-torn horn blares, condoms circulated as messages, even toxic metaphors arriving from the future—"if they had invented wolf whistles then, Father would have been giving one" (49).[13]

Speculative capitalism also employs abstract temporalities that are functions of finance's terms and rhythms: risk, projected profit, interest maturity, investment, liquidity, transfer, the movement of paper across distances, and so on. If the novel depicts the unreal reality under which financialization enables prospective death to valorize present bodies—something Ian Baucom describes as insurance's ability to visit its consequences proleptically upon its object—other temporal effects seem equally disordering. In *The Town*, narrators struggle to relate a story that must account for the future both before and after it has happened. *The Town* begins with Chick as the future narrator of the past present to be represented; he relies on a contemporary witness, his Uncle Gavin's cousin Gowan: "I wasn't born yet so it was Cousin Gowan who was there and big enough to see and remember and tell me afterward when I was big enough for it to make sense" (3). The narrative situates the relating of the events as the past's future and the events themselves as the present's past. Capital's independent temporal velocities and vectors destabilize narrative epistemology. As Ratliff notes about Flem: "You never even wondered how he heard about things because when the time come around to wonder how he managed to hear about it, it was already too late because he had done already made his profit by that time" (260). The repetitiousness here evinces the wish to slow things down, but Flem refuses to coincide with narrative temporality.

Numerous lags behind and leaps ahead trouble the narrative, the difficulty the effect of the novel's principal motive: to divine Flem's purposes. Ratliff explains his frustration: "Confound it, the trouble is we dont never know beforehand, to anticipate him" (126). The problem is that Ratliff must predict the future on the basis of the present, but he finds he can't quite manage that "in time"—the way, he says, you would be able to predict the behavior of a rabbit bolting from a brake (126). Another way to put this is that the narrators must envision future events in order to make the present intelligible. In so formulating the novel's concern with temporality and knowledge, I wish to tie Faulkner's purposes as a novelist of capital here to the longer history of the novel as a cultural technology devised to train readers to predict the future probabilistically on the basis of composite characters who could be read for typical behavior and average predictable outcome.

Finance capital, Baucom contends, gave birth to the modern subject. Liberated from subjecthood under sovereignty, the modern subject becomes a creature both of the Rights of Man and of speculative agency—of money. He is constituted by financial and political revolutions in the eighteenth century that presented individuals with a conception of self as a function of a universal will to freedom. The self is related to abstract universal rights in a way that is analogous to "the abstract value form typical of finance capital" (Baucom, *Specters of the Atlantic*, 54). Baucom recalls Žižek's formula S to $ for this invention of the modern subject under the logic of finance capitalism. Contemporaneous developments like financialized trade in humans, commercial insurance, and speculative investment demanded new conceptual techniques for deciphering business character and new habits of mind to endorse the validity of fictional truths such as the imaginary status of property, the treatment of humans as a money form, and the crediting of the abstract or speculative. Like the burgeoning insurance industry, for example, the realist novel was based on constructing particularized composites who behaved according to type. Actuarial and realist fictions coincided in the interests of speculative forecast. Thus, the eighteenth-century realist novel emerges as a primary cultural technology for equipping the modern subject to function in a world of finance capitalism.

When Ratliff, puzzling with Stevens over Flem's inscrutability, insists, "We got to figger" (126), he is reflecting this double duty of realist fiction's origins: to "anticipate" the future, as a form of calculation. It's the same linkage apparent in "estimate," another term used to describe the difficulty of predicting Flem's course: "The trouble with us is, we dont never estimate Flem Snopes right. At first we made the mistake of not estimating him a-tall. Then we made the mistake of over-estimating him. Now we're fixing to make the mistake of under-estimating him again" (154). But the project of figuring and estimating correctly seems exhausted in *The Town* of 1957. What we see in it is the *remains* of the realist novel, or perhaps a recognition of its constitutional impossibility from the outset: the genre's ultimate realization that the averaging characterization and predictive plotting so central to its original application were just necessary fictions. The Snopes saga relies at its outset in *The Hamlet* on the realist habit of trying to decipher character, project the behavior of particularized types (sharecroppers, landlords, merchants, speculators), extrapolate the future, and generally allow readers (both those within and without the novel) to imagine capitalist thought processes for their speculative advantage. Having dramatized in Flem's evasion of fictive anticipation the futility of such a social, economic, and aesthetic project, the next novel in the trilogy realizes, under the conditions of intensified financialization, that speculative reading of character and probabilistic narrative is always-already spectral within realist epistemologies.[14] The realist novel in the age of its postmaturity at midcentury confronts the resistance of hyperfinancialized capitalism to representation.[15] As Fredric Jameson observes, late capitalism is marked by financial capitalism, itself having become the dominant mode of production: the breeding of money from money (Baucom, *Specters of the Atlantic*, 142–43). This is the haunting of present-day financialization by its origins: both a transformation and a return.

Seemingly without human intervention, modern finance capitalism reproduces itself invisibly. Once Flem rises to the bank presidency, he no longer sits in the lobby witnessing actual transactions; he disappears from view altogether. Multinational banks, insurance companies, investment institutions, and stock-and-bond markets likewise operate remotely. In the late 1920s, Jason Compson struggles futilely to locate the metropolitan center of finance in his communication network, the spatial relays distancing him from timely updates. It's Wall Street that's become an unreadable abstraction. *The Hamlet*, as a first attempt at a novelistic version of the Snopes saga, fails to sustain the genre's capacity to read the capitalist subject at the moment that hyperfinancialized capitalism may be reorganizing the subject. That is, not only is Flem on the way out of Frenchman's Bend at the end of *The Hamlet*, but he's on his way out of the realist novel itself.[16] It takes Faulkner fifteen years to concede to the postnovelistic form of *The Town*, in which narrative speculation has been converted to idleness, storytelling to the recycling of past narratives and the pooling of gossip, reading character to the doomed effort to comprehend behavior that has no motive, and realist prose to words incapable of keeping up with capitalist velocities, prose that all but stops in the face of Flem's perpetual "Motion."

If early twenty-first-century digitalization has atomized human subjects into sets of algorithms formulating investment opportunities, directing flows of capital in microseconds, extrapolating and constituting consumer desire—all the ways humanness may with the greatest banality be understood as turning into data—then it is not surprising that Flem is less a character in *The Town* than a function to be read by its effects, less a particularized type of person than an epiphenomenon of the limitless accumulation of capital. One uncanny feature of Flem in *The Town* is the mechanical impassivity with which he conducts financial transactions. When he's caught stealing the brass, he pays the auditors nearly without participating:

> "How much does it come to?" he says.
> "Two hundred and eighteen dollars and fifty-two cents, Mr Snopes."
> "Is that the full amount?"
> "We checked our figgers twice, Mr Snopes."
> "All right," he says. And he reaches down and hauls out the money and pays the two hundred and eighteen dollars and fifty-two cents in cash and asks for a receipt. (19–20)

He behaves much the same way in striking checks for I. O.'s claim and Montgomery Ward's damages—as if it is not Flem who is acting but some abstract mechanism of debt and payment. Capitalism's centuries-long dependence on treating people as money forms has produced in Flem an allegorical figure of its dehumanizations—both the reduction of others to financialized goods and the corresponding suppression of the knowledge of such dehumanization in those who profit from it. As a prefiguration of later twentieth-century hyperfinancialization, Flem no longer exhibits the characteristics of a modern liberal subject born of eighteenth-century finance capitalism. Instead, Faulkner sees Flem as exposing the fiction that was the modern liberal subject—perhaps the ultimate obliterative effect of late-century financialization.[17]

Liberal Consensus

In *The Town*, the narrators champion what they take to be an opponent of the twentieth-century turn to financialization. Wallstreet Panic Snopes changes his name to Wall, in repudiation of financial chicanery and opens a modern food market in Jefferson offering quality products at "a decent price" (132). Wall's mart even features forward-looking amenities like parking lots and consumer education. Such seemingly ethical commerce means to resist the inhumane capitalism Flem practices. Wall's wife, the most anti-Snopesist character in the novel, insists that he fend off Flem's attempt at a hostile takeover, which Flem has contrived by manipulating the business's debt. She wants "to beat Snopes from the inside" (132).

Wall Snopes serves as an avatar of possessive individualism under midcentury American liberal capitalism. He succeeds by dint of honesty and hard work, his whole family toiling to build the business. He rises by "simple honesty and industry" (129), having come up from humble origins "the hard way" and "extricated himself by his own suspenders and boot straps" (129). Wall's American success story offers itself as the template for groups such as African Americans and women whose civil rights have been deferred. His "boot-strap[ping]" suggests the path all strivers are expected to take under the aegis of liberal democratic capitalism. It's a plan successful white males can buy into, and it's no surprise both Ratliff and Stevens want to invest in Wall's enterprise.

In chronicling Wall's restrained market practices in the 1920s, Faulkner may be reflecting an economic equilibrium that continued through his writing of the novel in the 1950s. Keynesian remedies that had been prepared for interwar ills of the sort that culminated in the Great Depression continued to be administered after World War II to cure capitalism from within—at just the moment Cold War Communism began challenging it from without. Faulkner completed the last two novels of the Snopes trilogy during a period of regulated capitalism, when government oversight of the economy, cooperation between ownership and labor, and a patriotic culture of consumption yielded several decades of stable prosperity after the war. In Wall's enterprise, Faulkner depicts the need for state supervision, with federal inspectors, auditors, bonding agents, adjustors, and courts keeping an eye on things in *The Town*. Such a situation reflects the "liberal consensus" of the 1950s that government had a critical role to play in moderating the excesses of a free-market economy that otherwise embodied the ideals of American democracy and was entrusted to extend them to disfranchised populations at home and abroad. Wall envisions "self-service" markets "built on the pattern which the big chain grocery stores were to make nation-wide in the purveying of food" (131). Note the prolepsis of "were to make" that projects Wall's enterprise as already closer to the time in which the novel is written. Ratliff explains to Stevens that Wall's creditors want to be supportive because "he's helping all business" (132). That ethical values are good for business and business values good for ethics is precisely the fantasy of postwar US liberalism.

    Yet Faulkner foresaw that the social crises afflicting his own time, foremost among them desegregation, but also including agitation for greater women's rights, might prove elusive to the democratic liberalism regnant during the fifties. As a moderate southerner, Gavin Stevens wages a campaign of sentimental resistance to the mistreatment of women, as he has in *Intruder in the Dust* to racial injustice. His opposition runs from his own refusal to participate in an economy of sexual commodification—as when Eula twice offers herself to him—to his mentoring of Linda, which concentrates on her education as the way to break Snopesism's misogyny. Greenwich Village, he rhapsodizes to her, will be better even than college—a place of no boundaries, of personal expansion beyond regional narrowness, of self-fulfillment free of the obligation to marry at all. It's a doctrine of liberal self-realization arrived at via a course of individual resistance: Gavin imagines Linda becoming the sort of "woman who shapes, fits herself to no environment, scorns the fixitude of environment and all the behavior patterns which had been mutually agreed on as being best for the greatest number; but on the contrary just by breathing, just by the mere presence of that fragile and delicate flesh, warps and wrenches milieu itself to those soft unangled rounds and curves and planes" (249). Stevens champions the individual's ability to oppose the whole edifice of oppression by the mere insistence of the self's being. Turning down Eula's offer of herself because he suspects she wants to protect Flem in order to save Linda, he says: "We've all bought Snopeses here, whether we wanted to or not.... But nothing can hurt you if you refuse it, not even a brass-stealing Snopes. And nothing is of value that costs nothing so maybe you will value this refusal at what I value it cost me" (84).

    Liberalism, then, extols individual freedom as it suppresses awareness of women's systemic subjugation, its vision of increasing democratic inclusiveness consonant with expansionist capitalism in the postwar years. Growing access to well-paying jobs, consumer goods, and mass education inspires midcentury confidence. One thing that compromises Linda's initial career as sexual resistor, though, is her mother's overvaluation of higher education; when Flem finally relents, after Eula's suicide, and writes a check for his putative daughter's tuition at the state university, she springs to embrace him, crying, "Daddy!" Faulkner doubts that such education emancipates women from dependency on male canons, Temple Drake's year at Ole Miss serving as prime evidence. And the notion that America's culture of consumption somehow furthers the ends of democracy also earns Faulkner's skepticism. In the running narrative of Gavin Stevens's Humbert Humbert-like attraction to Linda, she, Lolita-like, comes to represent an indiscriminate leveling of high- and low-culture consumption—Jefferson's present nymphet compulsively indulged with "banana splits and ice cream sodas and books of poetry" (159).[18]

I contend here, and have argued elsewhere in connection with both *The Mansion* and Martin Ritt's film adaptations of *The Sound and the Fury* and *The Hamlet* in the 1950s, that Faulkner, as a southern outsider to national norms during the Cold War, represents American democracy's continuing social injustices as spectralized by a world system founded on slave capitalism.[19] The last image Gavin has of Linda before she leaves Jefferson for college involves a kind of fade from view, a loss of presence: "I watched her, through the gate and up the walk, losing dimension now, onto or rather into the shadow of the little gallery and losing even substance now. And then I heard the door and it was as if she had not been. No, not that; not *not been*, but rather no more *is*, since *was* remains always and forever, inexplicable and immune, which is its grief. That's what I mean: a dimension less, then a substance less" (293). I read this as Gavin's registering, without comprehending, the spectrality of Linda's financialized body, reduced in substance and dimension by her father-banker's purposes. As she turns away from a southern liberal's oversight, Linda's abstract form appears ghostly, her resistance fading at the threshold of an imitation antebellum mansion. It will take one more novel for Linda to discover forms of political activism inspired by leftist economic and aesthetic critique.

In *Represent and Destroy: Rationalizing Violence in the New Racial Capitalism*, Jodi Melamed has argued that official antiracisms in post–World War II America actually contributed to the perpetuation of racism; she contends that the "liberal anti-racism" dictating the federal civil rights agenda from the 1940s through the mid-1960s construed racial injustice not as a foundational illegitimacy in Western capitalism but as a flaw in a system that could be corrected by changing white attitudes. Melamed takes Gunnar Myrdal's *An American Dilemma* (1944) as the quintessential example of liberal democratic assumptions: (white) America will free itself of the ills of racism by opening its opportunities to all. Differences in status or outcome that result after that will indicate other kinds of discrepancy—between individuals' character, will, culture—that may be accepted as differential results within a fair system. Goals for social reform emphasize equal opportunity: the same education for all, uniform political enfranchisement, the reform of white attitudes, desegregation. They do not include redress of the history and present-day economic inequalities that continue in the 1950s to afflict American life.[20] Melamed contends that liberalism had the effect of overpowering more radical critiques of American injustice during this period; by obscuring an economic critique of racism, it made race itself seem to disappear.

In a novel that Faulkner organizes as pretty much a whites-only confab, the economics of race appear in *The Town* spectrally. Laboring in the cellar, the maker of Uncle Willy Christian's ice cream, Walter, is described as a "dangerous"-looking black man—"not malevolent, not savage but just dangerous if you blundered out of your element and into his," an uncanny double of his white employer and the grandson of a slave owned by Willy's grandfather (141). Another trace of unconfronted economic racism flickers in the character Turl in the first chapter of the novel: a black worker, manipulated by Flem, who succeeds in turning the tables on his white employer but who vanishes after his cameo. The snag Turl poses in the text is an apparent slip of misnaming by Faulkner; in the novel, Faulkner refers to him as "Tomey's Turl" (and also at least once as "Tomey's Turl Beauchamp").[21] Faulkner may be forgetting that *Tomey's* Turl is the child of old Carothers McCaslin and his slave daughter, born in 1833. On the other hand, what if Faulkner, in relating a story that takes place in 1909, in the midst of Jim Crow racial violence, couldn't help but name the persistence of racism as the neoslavery it was or couldn't help but see the afterlife of southern bondage haunting 1950s desegregation?

Writing from the South, Faulkner was in a position to witness more closely the economic basis of racism. He grasped the tangled roots of financialized racism in the long history of the West's speculative plantation and slave-trading economies. Indeed, the reappearance of the name "Tomey's Turl" at the moment of early twentieth-century financialization might also be recognized as the lingering name of slavery haunting centuries of Atlantic finance capitalism. Baucom takes the infamous *Zong* massacre of 1781 as the epitome of finance capitalism's embeddedness in the Atlantic slave trade. The massacre occurred when the captain of the British slave ship *Zong*, headed from Guinea to Jamaica, slowed its course as if to take advantage of optimal market timing, but in fact to create losses to be claimed against its insurers upon the disposal of 133 enslaved people thrown into the sea. Recall that Baucom notes the violence spectralized in the slave trade to be twofold: the conversion of living bodies into labor commodities and the conversion of those commodities into paper credit, debt, and profit. I. O. Snopes's slaughter of work animals for insurance purposes, which includes as collateral damage the sale of a human to the insurer, may point to a long genealogy for the Snopes economy. It's no surprise that one of the Snopes mules "came out of the fog to begin with like a hant or a goblin" (209).[22]

Financialization in the Time of Neoliberalism

Faulkner often found the voice of radical antiracism when he was condemning the historical and continuing excesses of capitalism: the unfeeling "rapacity" it unleashed, its murderous violence, and its pointless acquisitiveness. Faulkner regularly insisted in the 1950s that racism would not disappear in the South until it confronted its economics. No doubt he was also convinced that the sort of official antiracism embodied by federal initiatives to end legal desegregation and promote racial equality was a national evasion of the nation's capitalist racial history. In an essay entitled "On Fear" published in 1956 in *Harper's*, Faulkner wrote: "Nor is the tragedy the fear so much as the tawdry quality of the fear—fear not of the Negro as an individual Negro nor even as a race, but as an economic class or stratum or factor, since what the Negro threatens is not the Southern white man's social system but the Southern white man's economic system—that economic system which the white man knows and dares not admit to himself is established on an obsolescence—the artificial inequality of man."[23] Faulkner was doubtful about racial progress under the liberal assumptions of the 1950s. Much recent scholarship has demonstrated that under neoliberalism over the intervening decades, the "artificial inequality" of the present US economic system has metastasized into financialized racisms like the prison-industrial complex, eviction entrepreneurialism, and mortgage derivative speculation. In *The Town*, Faulkner was already hypothesizing that America's capitalist liberal democracy, given its self-contradictory premises, its denial of illiberal origins in the economics of slavery, could not remedy social injustices. The cures offered by capitalism harbored their own lethality: "[M]oney itself, cash dollars, possessed an inherent life of its mutual own like cells or disease," capital working to "increment itself by simple parasitic osmosis like a leech or a goitre or cancer" (234).

In *The Mansion*, Faulkner goes on to imagine a conclusive break with the mindless Motion of capital and to limn possibilities for postliberal ethics, politics, and aesthetics.

NOTES

I wish to thank Richard Godden, Theresa Towner, Myka Tucker-Abramson, and Jay Watson for invaluable help with this chapter.

1. David M. Kotz, "Neoliberalism and Financialization," paper presented at the Political Economy Research Institute, University of Massachusetts Amherst, May 2–3, 2008, 15. Hereafter cited parenthetically.

2. William Faulkner, *The Town*, in *Novels 1957–1962*, ed. Joseph Blotner and Noel Polk (New York: Library of America, 1999), 102. Hereafter cited parenthetically.

3. Costas Lapavitsas, "The Financialization of Capitalism: 'Profiting without Producing,'" *City* 17, no. 6 (2013): 792–805. Although Lapavitsas allows that financialized capitalism has been a cyclical constant throughout the history of capitalism, he sees contemporary financialization as representing a significant new stage in its development: more "sophisticated" than its nineteenth-century predecessors, the sort of financialization that led to the 2007 derivatives crisis "reflects a growing asymmetry between production and circulation" (793), with a "rise in profits accruing through financial transactions, including new forms of profit that could even be unrelated to surplus value" (794).

4. Giovanni Arrighi, *The Long Twentieth Century: Money, Power and the Origins of Our Times*, rev. ed. (1994; repr., New York: Verso, 2010).

5. Deidre Lynch discusses how the government encouragement of investment in war bonds during the First World War fostered a postwar culture of investing in stocks and bonds. See *The Economy of Character: Novels, Market Culture, and the Business of Inner Meaning* (Chicago: University of Chicago Press, 1998).

6. Anwar Shaikh, "An Introduction to the History of Crisis Theories," *US Capitalism in Crisis* (New York: Union for Radical Political Economics Press, 1978), 232.

7. Samezo Kuruma, "An Overview of Marx's Theory of Crisis," *Journal of the Ohara Institute for Social Research* (August 1936): n.p. Reprinted in *Kyoko kenju* (Investigation of crisis) (Tokyo: Otsuki Shoten, 1965), trans. Michael Schauerte for marxists.org (2006). In citing Kuruma's excerpts from Marx, which are retranslated into English for his piece, I have quoted directly from the first English translation of *Capital* (see note 8).

8. Karl Marx, *Capital: A Critique of Political Economy*, 3 vol., ed. Frederick Engels, trans. Samuel Moore and Edward Aveling (1887), Moscow, USSR: Progress, 1995–1996, 1:107–8, accessed via Marx/Engels Internet Archive (marxists.org).

9. Ian Baucom, *Specters of the Atlantic: Finance Capital, Slavery, and the Philosophy of History* (Durham, NC: Duke University Press, 2005). Baucom addresses the temporality of insurance as entirely fictive, imagined, and proleptic: insurance must posit what something will have been worth once it is no more, once it has been destroyed. Baucom argues that such a temporality is not that something will have a value when it is destroyed, but that at the instant it is valorized, in the moment of being insured, it already in effect *is* destroyed as a thing, a commodity.

10. My approach throughout my discussion of financialization's obliterative effects follows gratefully in the wake of Richard Godden's reading of Bret Easton Ellis and our discussions of the larger project on post-1945 fiction of which it forms a part. See Godden,

"Bret Easton Ellis, *Lunar Park*, and the Exquisite Corpse of Deficit Finance," *American Literary History* 25, no. 3 (Fall 2013): 588–606.

11. Florence Dore, "The New Criticism and the Nashville Sound: William Faulkner's *The Town* and Rock and Roll," *Contemporary Literature* 55, no. 1 (Spring 2014): 37.

12. In the version of the short story published in *Scribner's* in 1934 one can see the origins of this figurative language: "She rushed on after the haltered mule which was still in that arrested and wraithlike process of vanishing furiously into the fog, its wake indicated by the tossing and dispersing shapes of the nine chickens like so many jagged scraps of paper in the dying air blast of an automobile, and the madly dodging figure of a man" (William Faulkner, "Mule in the Yard," *Collected Stories of William Faulkner* [New York: Random House, 1950], 255). This surrealistic quality is intensified for *The Town*.

13. The anachronism seems topical: Emmett Till, a fourteen-year-old African American boy, was murdered in 1955 in Mississippi on the false accusation that he had wolf-whistled at a young white woman during a visit from Chicago.

14. In *The Hamlet*, Ratliff welcomes the challenge that the Snopeses present to his reputation as Frenchman Bend's sharpest trader, and he is confident he can anticipate their moves, until Flem emerges as the clan's commercial tactician. Ratliff admits to being surprised by Flem's maneuver in capitalizing on his father's threat of barn burning to launch his retail career in the Bend. Ratliff acknowledges getting "beat" in subsequent skirmishes, like the speculation in goats, then successfully retaliating. But Flem's ultimate ability to elude prediction altogether hits Ratliff hard when he realizes the newcomer has managed improbably to auction off worthless spotted horses to the Bend's farmers (successfully denying any involvement), then to culminate his career in the hamlet by ensnaring the salesman with the oldest trick in the book—a "salted mine" scheme—in which Flem demonstrates that capital value is the result of social performance, not simply intrinsic worth.

15. Baucom remarks that the "hyperfinancialized late twentieth century and early twenty-first, like Benjamin's nineteenth century, Arrighi's regimes of accumulation, and Jameson's textual object, is not contemporary with itself alone. It accumulates, repeats, intensifies, and reasserts the late eighteenth. The hour of *its* apparitions is fixed by this prior hyperspeculative moment" (*Specters of the Atlantic*, 30).

16. *The Hamlet* ends with Flem's departure from Frenchman's Bend, registered as an enigmatic announcement of the next stage of his financial ascent: "Come up," he instructs his mules, as they head out for Jefferson. The novel's realistic narration, once confident in its depiction of this first stage of the Snopes saga, breaks off, unable to follow Flem to what comes next, just as Ratliff and the other internal storytellers have proven incapable of predicting this innovative capitalist's nature, motives, or tactics. Flem beggars the realist novel's power to read character and action probabilistically. Faulkner mulls the generic consequences of writing capital in its more openly financialized, more remotely human forms, and in *The Town* he replaces any would-be omniscient narrator with character-narrators divining Flem's plotting from limited points of view.

17. Leo Panitch and Sam Gindin suggest in *The Making of Global Capitalism: The Political Economy of American Empire* (New York: Verso, 2013) that US finance policies associated with later neoliberalism actually have their origins in the post–World War II years: "The roots of 'monetarism,'" for example, "really need to be located not in the 1970s but in the 1950s, during the supposed heyday of the Keynesian era" (86–87).

18. Dore reads Stevens's and Linda's college catalog shopping for liberal arts schools in the Northeast as suggesting the reduction of elite educations to elite consumer goods by the 1950s. I speculate on the possible reflection of *Lolita* in *The Town* in "Many Mansions: Faulkner's Cold War Conflicts," in *Global Faulkner: Faulkner and Yoknapatawpha, 2006*,

ed. Annette Trefzer and Ann J. Abadie (Jackson: University of Mississippi Press, 2009), 3–23. Mauri Skinfill studies "the American conflation of the free market with social freedom" in "The American Interior: Identity and Commercial Culture in Faulkner's Late Novels," *Faulkner Journal* 21, nos. 1–2 (Fall 2005–Spring 2006): 133–44. Charmaine Eddy argues that the South's "ambivalent relationship to the nation" plays out in forms of narrative production in the later Snopes fictions, with contending stories projecting their narrators' rival desires for gratification in the face of regional denial ("Labor, Economy, and Desire: Rethinking American Nationhood through Yoknapatawpha," *Mississippi Quarterly* 57, no. 4 [Fall 2004]: 569–92).

19. John T. Matthews, "Faulkner to Film in the Fifties," in *William Faulkner in the Media Ecology*, ed. Julian Murphet and Stefan Solomon (Baton Rouge: Louisiana State University Press, 2015), 17–33.

20. See my discussion of Myrdal in "Touching Race in *Go Down, Moses*," in *New Essays on "Go Down, Moses,"* ed. Linda Wagner-Martin (New York: Cambridge University Press, 1996), 21–48.

21. Theresa M. Towner discusses Turl's misnaming in "'It Aint Funny A-Tall': The Transfigured Tales of *The Town*," *Mississippi Quarterly* 44, no. 3 (Summer 1991): 321–35. The appearance of "Tomey's" as part of Turl's name first occurs when Faulkner incorporates the earlier short story "Centaur in Brass" (1932) into the first chapter of *The Town*.

22. In *The Hamlet*, Flem has already come up with a perverse permutation of the practice of insuring African slaves when he takes to selling burial insurance at extortionate terms to black farmers in his district.

23. William Faulkner, "On Fear: Deep South in Labor: Mississippi," *Essays, Speeches, and Public Letters*, ed. James B. Meriwether (New York: Random House, 1965), 95–96.

Legacy: The Currency of Eternity

Gloria J. Burgess

Consider and act with reference to the true ends of life. This world is but a vestibule of an immortal life. Every action of our lives touches on some chord that will vibrate in eternity.
—*Edwin Hubbell Chapin*

I begin with gratitudes. I want to thank Dr. Jay Watson for being a gracious gatekeeper. The gate swings both ways, and I really appreciate your welcoming and honoring my family and me by inviting and hosting my presentation this evening. Thank you very much.

I also want to thank my family for representing, for showing up.

I want to thank my mother, Mildred Blackmon McEwen. If you would stand, mother, as you are able. Originally from right here in Oxford, thank you for traveling here all the way from Michigan.

I want to thank my sisters: Doris, Annie, Debbie, and Vera. If you would stand please.

And I want to thank my daughter. Would you stand, Quinn?

My husband, John, thank you for being here, for being my helpmate.

I want to thank my niece and nephew, Maleika and Cheo.

I also want to thank my many aunts and uncles and cousins. I'll just ask the whole row to stand up and be counted please. Thank you so much!

And friends of the family: Dr. Bramlett Murphy and his niece Grace. Would you please stand to be honored? Thank you so much.

I didn't call everyone's name because I might miss somebody. But I want you to know that some of these folks are here for a hot minute. I'm not talking about the weather. They're here tonight, and tomorrow morning they're on a dawn-thirty plane to go back home.

All of these people are part of my community, part of my personal village. I would not be here with you this evening without these broad shoulders, these broad, stout, fierce shoulders to stand on.

This is an important and historic occasion for the McEwen and Blackmon families and for our extended family. I am blessed to be in the company of so many magnificent presences.

My heart is full.

Finally, I thank my father, Earnest McEwen Jr., and William Faulkner, for they are the focal point of my presentation.

Although I'm an avid reader of Faulkner's work, I'm not here to talk about one of his literary characters. This evening I am here to talk about the character of one William Faulkner as my father and my family came to know him.

Legacy: A Covenant with the Future

Everything I know about legacy, I learned from my father, my mother, my extended family, and Faulkner. Early on, I learned that our current notions about legacy are outmoded. They are barren and too constrained to embrace the largesse and magnificence of the human spirit. Here's what I know: contrary to conventional Western ways of being and knowing, legacy is not something that happens "out there." Nor is it merely something that happens at the end of our life after we accumulate financial assets or other possessions to bequeath to others. Rather, legacy's purview is spiritual, and it is intimately concerned with our inner music, so that who we are, what we say, and what we do are in harmony. Ultimately, legacy is a summons to stewardship, calling us to be of service, calling us to make a covenant with the future by living in such a way that we make a positive difference here and now. That difference is our signature imprint, the shining inheritance we pass on daily to our children, our children's children, and our children's children's children.[1]

Each of us creates a legacy whether we are aware of it or not. Vigilant about raising me and my awareness, my mother would often admonish me, "Make yourself useful."[2] As a young girl, her words irritated me because I was already busy doing my chores or homework or otherwise engaged. Today, as an adult, my mother's words echo in my soul as the voice of legacy. As I learned and as I now share in my books, leadership courses, and keynotes, legacy unfolds moment by moment. Intimately connected to who you are, legacy is about the intentional choices you make every single day—365, 24/7. At the end of the day, legacy is about every decision you make, every phone call you take, every text message you send, and who and what you decide to include or ignore.[3]

Legacy is an invitation to reflect on and value our own experiences and family narratives. When I teach transformational leadership, I invite my students to delve into their experiences as well as their personal and family narratives. Why? Because our experiences and the narratives we create and share about those experiences hold the key to the people we are and the people we aspire to become. Like legacy, leadership is not something that happens "out there." Leadership is about who you are. Simply put, who you are and how you live is how you lead. Hence the necessity to mine your experiences and the narratives you create about those experiences. To prime the pump for my students, I share several of my own personal stories with them. I often share the story about Mr. Faulkner and my father.

Let me tell you that story.

Let me tell you a little bit about the intertwined legacies of my father and William Faulkner. I share this story because it honors their legacies and epitomizes the hopes and dreams we have for ourselves. And though it is deeply personal, I share this story because it is a universal story, an archetypal story in which I hope you can see a bit of yourself in the personhood of my father and in the personhood of Mr. Faulkner.

How It All Began

Like me, my father was born right here in Oxford, Mississippi. In 1931, the year he was born, Oxford was very different than it is today.[4] It was a small, racially segregated town, where his mother spent each spring and fall working with dozens of other men and women planting and harvesting cotton. She often worked from sunrise until sundown. When my father was a young boy, four or five years old, he had two dreams: he wanted to live in a house with running water, and, more than anything, he wanted to go to school. And here in Oxford, going to school meant going to college.

My father wished his mother didn't have to work so hard, and he often told her so. At the end of each day, he would look into his mother's eyes and say, "Someday, I'm going to live in a house in town, a house with running water." Looking at him with tired, loving eyes, his mother would smile and say, "Oh, Junior, you're always dreaming." My father would just grin. "You'll see, Mama. Someday we'll have our own house, and someday I'm going to go to college, too!" No one really knows the source of my father's dreams. No one in his family had ever lived in a house with running water, and no one in his family had ever gone to college. Some people said his dreams must have come from God. One of my father's close friends put it this way: "Some folks look out and all they can see is a mountain. But Earnest is different. When he looks out, he can see to the *other side* of the mountain."

My father knew that his were bold dreams. As a black man living in the Jim Crow South, my father was also keenly aware that articulating his dreams could endanger himself and others. Even so, he refused to let the strictures of Jim Crow define him or his vision of a radically different future. Passionately devoted to his vision of creating a better life for himself and his family, my father was the kind of person who was comfortable talking with anyone. And he did just that. He'd talk to *anyone*, anyone who would listen to his dreams. He'd talk to you in the town square and anywhere else. He wasn't supposed to, but he did. It didn't matter what you looked like: tall, short, white, black, brown, yellow—it didn't matter.

My father dreamed not only of going to college, but also of designing and building a house of his very own. His dreams were also fueled by his love of reading. Although my grandparents were too poor to buy books, that never stopped my father from reading every book he could get his hands on, borrowing them from teachers and even fishing them out of the trash. The people he read about lived in different places and led different lives from the life he and his parents knew. But how could a poor, black youth living in the South during the 1930s and 1940s be able to afford college? And even if he could, there were few opportunities for a black man to attend college, let alone become an architect.

My father knew that it would cost a lot of money to buy a house with running water, money that neither he nor his parents had. He figured that getting a good education would be his means to leave the poverty of the South behind. The first problem he faced was finding the money for college. Though he had few prospects of finding a job, he never let a lack of money deter him from keeping his faith and his vision of a brighter future, a time when he and his parents would enjoy the fruits of a better life. Each day after school, my father went from house to house selling seed packets to supplement the family's meager income. What little money he earned was barely enough to buy a few books, and there was none to set aside to pay for college or to buy a house. Determined and focused despite what seemed to be an impassable mountain, he never lost sight of his goals. Even after he married and started a family, my father remained optimistic that he would someday find or hear about a job where he could earn enough money to support his wife and daughters and still save enough to go to college.

When I was a babe in arms, my father managed to get a job as a janitor at the University of Mississippi, a job that paid a black man better than most others in town. Although he could work at Ole Miss, my father couldn't attend school there because the university was still segregated. However, unbeknownst to him, he was one step closer to realizing his dreams. He took great pride in his work; he believed that whatever the job, you should always do your best. He scrubbed the floors not once but twice, and then waxed and polished them until the white linoleum glowed. All the while, my father would talk to anyone who would listen about his dream of going to college. He never expected special treatment. He believed in devoting himself to his work—"Steady and sure; you reap what you sow; hard work pays off and has its rewards"—these were the bedrock of his values, the enduring legacy that my father's parents had passed on to him.

While working as a janitor, my father talked to the students, to the professors, to anybody who would listen. You know that little game we played as children, the game called "Telephone"? You tell somebody something, they tell somebody, and that somebody would tell somebody else. Well, one of those somebodies was Dr. Malcolm Guess, a professor at the university. Dr. Guess took notice and started a chain of events that would change my father's life, and that of our family, in a most amazing way. While my father worked as a janitor, he continued to read any books he could get his hands on. Dr. Guess offered to let my father use his office before and after work as a quiet place to read. As I remember this story so many years later, I can still hear my father's description: "One morning before work, I was reading, when the office door opened, and in walked one of the deans of the university, Dr. Leston L. Love. He wore a hat, bow tie, tan-colored suit, and his brown shoes were polished to a shine. The man spoke slowly, 'You must be Earnest McEwen.'" The professor had told Dr. Love about my father's desire to go to college and his interest in architecture. When Dr. Love heard my father's story, he was deeply moved by his passion and determination. "Mr. McEwen, I know just the person who can help you with your dream."

Did y'all hear what I just said? I said, "*Mr.* McEwen." Do you know that black men were not called mister anything back in the 1950s in Oxford, Mississippi? *"Mr. McEwen, I know just the person who can help you with your dream."* And, with that, Dr. Love put my father in touch with the writer that we're all here to celebrate: Pulitzer Prize–winning, Nobel Laureate William Faulkner; he reached in his pocket and handed my father a piece of paper with a name and address on it. Dr. Love said, "Now when you go to see Mr. Faulkner, tell him I sent you." Then he extended his hand for a hearty shake.

Even if my father's family had had a telephone, my father would not have called Faulkner. In those days, he would "call" by visiting Faulkner at his home. So, a few days later, my father walked up a long pathway to a big white house on the Rowan Oak estate, with no idea what to expect when he arrived. He had heard stories about the great writer William

Faulkner, but what was he really like? He knocked on the door and waited. A dark-skinned woman in a yellow dress and white apron greeted him: "You must be Earnest McEwen. Mr. Faulkner has been expecting you. Please wait here for just a moment."

His heart pounded when William Faulkner greeted him and invited him inside. My father hesitated, for they both knew the unspoken rule—blacks were allowed to work for whites but not to socialize with them. "No, thank you, sir," my father said. They talked for a long time in the shade of Rowan Oak's giant old oak trees. Mr. Faulkner listened intently as my father told him, "Ever since I was a boy, I've loved books. In those books, I've learned about people and places that I may never see. My wife and I have worked hard all our lives, and we want our girls to have a better life than ours. It's my dream to go to college and to give our children a life where they can learn and be able to do whatever they want to in this world."

Mr. Faulkner felt my father's excitement and saw the determination in his face. "Let me ask you, Mr. McEwen, where do you intend to go to college?" Without missing a beat, my father told Faulkner that he wanted to attend Alcorn A&M, a college located about two hundred miles from Oxford. He went on to say that it was a wonderful school that provided a solid education for black people. Mr. Faulkner knew about Alcorn and that it had a good reputation. He looked my father in the eye, and right there and then he offered to become my father's benefactor, to pay for his tuition, his books, and his room and board. And because somehow he had heard that my father was married and had three little girls, Mr. Faulkner offered to find jobs for my parents so they wouldn't have to worry about pocket money.

Now, what do you think my father said?

All those years of yearning, and now my father was about to taste the tantalizing fruit of his dreams. After a long silence, my father shook his head slowly from side to side. "Mr. Faulkner, I want to go to college more than anything in the world, but I can't accept your generous offer."

Now, I'm a little babe in arms, and I'm wondering, "What were you thinking? This was your lifelong dream!"

My father paused for a moment then continued, "Sir, I just don't see how I'd ever be able to save enough money to pay you back." As I mentioned earlier, my father expected to work hard and to earn his own way in the world.

At first, Mr. Faulkner looked surprised. Then with a twinkle in his eye, he said, "Why, I don't expect you to pay me back!" Then he smiled. "Mr. McEwen, the only thing I ask is that you pass this kindness on to somebody else when you're able to do so . . . and let it just keep on going." Mr. Faulkner told my father that he would send payments directly to the president of Alcorn College and that he would arrange to have clothing sent for our family as well. He invited my father to stay in touch and to let him know how he was doing. My father thanked him for his generosity and assured him that not only would he "pass it on," he would also stay in touch, which he did until Mr. Faulkner's untimely death almost a decade later.

As they shook hands and said good-bye, I imagine my father's face radiant, his stride strong and sure, his whole being expectant and filled with deep gratitude. When he reached the edge of Rowan Oak, my father knelt on the cool grass beneath an old oak tree and said a prayer of thanks for his family, Professor Guess, Dr. Love, and William Faulkner. As he stood, Mr. Faulkner's kind words echoed in his ear: "Pass it on." From that day forward, my father did just that, offering the blessing of Mr. Faulkner's kindness to countless others.

Whether Faulkner had asked my father to pass it on or not, he would have done just that because that's who he was. And when he was able to do so, my father encouraged and supported many family members, friends, and coworkers to pursue their education. My father would be in your face, so to speak, encouraging you to get your GED; if you had your GED, he'd encourage you to get your community college degree; if you had your community college degree, he'd encourage you to get your undergraduate degree, graduate degree, or whatever degree you didn't have. That was my father. Passionate. Tireless. Unshakeable.

Transitions

That autumn, my father moved our family to Lorman, Mississippi. There he enrolled at Alcorn A&M College with my mom and me and my two older sisters by his side. My father and mother were grateful for the blessing of being together as a family, for the compassion and kindness of Drs. Guess and Love, and for Faulkner's windfall blessing of generosity. In June 1957, four years after he enrolled, he would graduate from college with honors. However, to his credit as well as his deep sorrow, my father would graduate not from his beloved Alcorn but from Central State College in Wilberforce, Ohio.

In many ways, my father was a visionary who saw far beyond the era in which he lived. As I've already mentioned, he was very clear about and committed to his values. Among his rock-solid values was standing up for what he believed was equitable and just—no matter the consequences. A natural leader, my father became president of the Alcorn

Student Council during the black freedom struggle, those horrible, turbulent years leading up to what we now call the civil rights movement.

In March 1957, just three months before he was to graduate from Alcorn, my father took a stand against social and racial injustice when he and a number of other students were faced with the denial of their civil rights by a black faculty member and racial discrimination by the all-white board of trustees.[5] In his role as student council president, my father and the other council leaders led a peaceful protest calling for the faculty member's resignation or firing and a walkout of the entire student body. Knowing they were risking their hard-won access to education, the student body walked out. In retaliation, the trustees issued an ultimatum that all students were to return to their classes, or they would shut down Alcorn. My father and other student leaders refused to return to their classes, refused to relinquish their birthright dignity, and abandon their stand for equity and justice. For this, he and the other student leaders were expelled, or "ousted." The trustees mandated that the ousted students leave Alcorn's campus immediately and never return.

Knowing that he was endangering his lifelong dream, if not his life, my father was willing to give it all up at Alcorn for what he believed was a moral and spiritual imperative: equity and justice. With the assistance of the NAACP, my father finished the final three months of his undergraduate education at Central State College apart from our family.

After he graduated, my father moved our family from Oxford to Detroit, Michigan. Like millions of other African Americans who transitioned from the rural South to the urban North, we, too, became part of the Great Migration. But no matter where we lived—first in Detroit, then in Ann Arbor—we always remembered our foundation, and we always came back home to Oxford, at least once, if not twice, a year. Sometimes we came back three times a year. And we'd always stop at Rowan Oak, the old Bailey house, to say hello, to pay our respects to Mr. Faulkner.

In the embrace of Rowan Oak, William Faulkner became a friend to my father. When we visited, my father would talk with him while my mom, my sisters, and I would go to the side porch, where we were served lemonade. During their conversations, Faulkner told my father that with a college degree, life would be better, but it would not necessarily come easily. What he meant was that change would eventually come, but it would come very slowly for blacks.

My father soon discovered the prescience of Faulkner's words. After he graduated with his degree in building and construction (now called architecture), my father worked once again as a janitor because, in fact, during the four years he was in college, things hadn't changed all that much. In the 1950s, there were few opportunities for blacks to work as architects anywhere in the country. Disappointed but undaunted, my father turned his love of reading and learning into other arenas. By day, he worked as a janitor in a hospital. By night, he immersed himself in his books.

Even though the pace of change was glacial, Providence was still moving in my father's life. Working as a janitor in a hospital gave him access to a whole new world of people and possibilities. He was drawn into the realm of hematology, the study of the nature, function, and diseases of the blood. Fueled by his passion for knowledge, he enjoyed talking with the laboratory technicians who worked in the blood bank, and he read all the books about hematology he could find to learn as much as he could on his own. In due time, my father launched his first career as a blood-bank laboratory technician at Detroit Osteopathic Hospital.

Years later, my father launched his second career. Drawing on his knowledge of design and construction processes, he worked in engineering for many years at Ford Motor Company. Not only did he fulfill his dreams of going to college and living in a house with running water, but he created a blueprint for his very own house. However, he didn't live long enough to build it. In 1988, after a long struggle with cancer, my father died at the age of fifty-six. But his spirit lives on through the lives of the many people he touched: family, friends, coworkers, and who knows how many others. At his funeral, when the minister invited the family to enter the chapel to pay our last respects, he expected just the members of my immediate family. He was delightfully overwhelmed when several hundred people poured into and around the tiny chapel— an extended family of relatives, friends, and family of the heart.

Ripple Effect

How wonderful to witness and now to amplify the legacy created by my father's vision and faith and by Faulkner's capacity to see and support my father's potential through his generosity and kindness, intertwined legacies that continue to resound, creating a ripple effect that keeps on flowing within our family and out into the world.

Inside each of us is a glorious world longing to be born. When we serve as midwife to another soul, we extend a kindness by helping to birth that world within. When we extend a kindness, we never know how that ripple will expand, where it will flow, or how many lives it will touch. And you know what? It's not our business to know. Our business is to see and to be compassionate and generous and kind. Our business is to "make ourselves useful," to be of service, to pass our blessings on to others. In my family, in my personal village, this is a given. My mother and father taught my sisters and me that you make your living by what you choose to do for your work, and you make a life by what you choose to do for others.

I haven't always publicly shared this story about Faulkner and my father. Why? Because it was a family story. We didn't talk about family experiences, about family "business," outside of our immediate family. As a matter of fact, I rarely heard my father share the details of their relationship—in our family, let alone outside the family. But I witnessed and experienced the ripple effect of his lived experience by virtue of who he was—his character, his daily choices, his unshakeable devotion to helping others in so many ways, especially with regard to pursuing their education and, thereby, creating a better life for themselves and their families.

Thirty years ago, my father crossed over. Because I didn't know some of the details about his life, I had to do research to learn more about his history, more about his life as a young boy. I talked with his older sister, Leanna, his younger brother, Ollie, and my mom, as well as with other relatives and family friends who could tell me more about my father's life. I talked with as many people as I could who might know even the smallest detail. I contacted Ole Miss. I learned more about Dr. Love and Dr. Guess. I learned more about Faulkner. I learned more about my father's Alcorn years; I found out who Faulkner sent the money to at Alcorn. And I'm still learning myriad details about individuals, places, and moments in my father's life, and in Faulkner's.

Later this year or early next year, I plan to return to Oxford when my new book *Pass It On!* is released. *Pass It On!* is a picture book about my father and Faulkner, a picture book that I hope will inspire children from 2 to 102. Illustrator Gerald Purnell's sumptuous artwork visually augments my historic narrative.

As an educator, writer, and speaker, I've now had the opportunity to share this story about my father and Faulkner throughout the world. Humbly yet proudly, I've shared it on every continent but Antarctica; if the penguins would host me, I'd go there, too. No matter what country or culture folks are from, this story resonates with them. And the folks who witness my family's story share their family stories with me, similar stories about vision, compassion, generosity, and kindness from this particular time in our world history, the 1950s, the 1940s, the 1930s: "My family is Jewish. Years ago, my great-grandparents were helped by Germans to escape from Vienna." "Oh, did you know Eleanor Roosevelt helped my family? She gave us all winter coats."

Well . . . of course.

Closing

I'm so blessed and honored by this opportunity to share, to give you a glimpse into, my story, my father's story, my family's story, and a glimpse into another facet of the complex human being we all know as William Faulkner. I'll close with a very special poem about Faulkner and my father.

When I first began writing about my father's story, poems emerged. At that time, I was in my inaugural year as a Cave Canem Fellow.[6] While attending one of their marvelous, weeklong poetry intensives, one of my mentors, Nikky Finney, challenged and encouraged me to go all the way down into the well of my history and, if necessary, to go beneath it to excavate and explore the many presences there. With righteous vigor, she exhorted me to "Write it all down! Write it all down!" Following her sage advice, I wrote down everything I could recall about my father and Faulkner, filling up scores of pages. From that ocean of words, one of the pearls that surfaced is a poem called "Sanctuary."[7] An antiphon of courage, determination, faith, gratitude, love, perseverance, and transformation, my poem is a celebration and tribute to two ordinary men who had the extraordinary vision and resolve "to move against the tide at a time in our history when it was unfashionable for whites to extend a hand to blacks and almost unthinkable for a black man to imagine a life other than the one into which he was born."[8]

SANCTUARY
for William Faulkner and my father, Earnest McEwen Jr.[9]

Between the brush of angels' wings
and furious hooves of hell, two mortal men
fell down. How you must have looked—
white shirt stained, khakis fatigued,
smelling of sweat and smoke,
hair at odds with itself and the world.
At the threshold among your restless dead
in echo and shadow of ancient oaks,
providing sanctuary, offering shade,
you had many worlds behind you,
few yet to be born: stories of insurgence,
scorn, decay—theme and variations
of a vanquished South.

Leaning against a jamb
of antebellum brass, you watched, waited,

raised weary arm and hand, saluted
the familiar stranger. *Come. Enter. Sit. Sing.*

You reached each other across the grate.
What you two must have known of heaven and hell.

NOTES

1. Gloria Burgess, *Legacy Living: The Six Covenants for Personal and Professional Excellence* (Provo, UT: Executive Excellence, 2006), 26.

2. Gloria Burgess, *Dare to Wear Your Soul on the Outside: Live Your Legacy Now* (San Francisco: Jossey-Bass/Wiley, 2008), 3.

3. I have written, taught, and spoken extensively on legacy, legacy consciousness, legacy leadership, and legacy living in my books, including *Dare to Wear Your Soul on the Outside, Legacy Living, Flawless Leadership: Connecting Who You Are with What You Know and Do* (Edmonds, WA: Red Oak, 2016), and *Pass It On!* (Kingston, WA: Two Sylvias, 2018); in undergraduate, graduate, and postgraduate courses and seminars and in numerous keynotes.

4. The story I tell in the pages ahead draws liberally on material from Burgess, *Dare to Wear Your Soul*, 3–14, 207–08.

5. "One Way to Kill a College," *Time* 69, no. 11 (March 18, 1957): 51.

6. Founded in 1996, Cave Canem is a prestigious collective of poets and writers of the African diaspora. Toi Derricotte and Cornelius Eady started the collective to address and remedy the underrepresentation of African American poets and other voices in the literary landscape and canon. I became a Cave Canem Fellow in 2000.

7. I titled my poem "Sanctuary" for numerous reasons, including being intentional about echoing the title of the William Faulkner novel *Sanctuary* (1931; repr., New York: Random House, 1958).

8. Burgess, *Legacy Living*, 28.

9. Gloria Burgess, *The Open Door* (Edmonds, WA: Red Oak, 2001), 29.

The Friction of Money: Poverty and Failure in Early Faulkner

GAVIN JONES

Looking back on his early career, William Faulkner noticed "something missing" from his novel As I Lay Dying (1930). The same quality seemed absent from Sanctuary (1931), too, but there it was more easily accounted for.[1] Sanctuary was "deliberately conceived to make money," wrote Faulkner in the 1932 introduction to his potboiler, even if it had to be rewritten, the galleys torn down as Faulkner tried to "make something" out of the scraps.[2] Faulkner's comments on his early struggles with publication suggest the economics of his authorial selfhood, how he came "to think of books in terms of possible money."[3] In a letter to the Four Seas Publishing Company, for example, Faulkner wanted a crucial clause in the contract changed, to leave him liable not for the manufacturing cost of the printer's plates but instead for "the actual value of the melted plates."[4] Quite literally, he wanted to keep his assets liquid, to know the exact monetary value of his outlay, and to get it back if needed. Faulkner's identity as a writer grew in this impoverished economy of bargaining and reuse. Weaving a tall tale to his publisher, Horace Liveright, in 1927, to explain why he had drawn on Liveright a substantial draft to pay down gambling debts, Faulkner suggested that $200 could be deducted from his next advance for a manuscript not yet half-written.[5] His unpublished, incomplete manuscripts—even promises thereof—became a kind of currency, or chips to bargain with potential publishers. In Faulkner's mind, these personal financial struggles were at once regional struggles. They were a condition of living in the provincial South, or as he put it, living "day in day out" in a way he considered unconceivable to a northerner.[6]

This chapter revisits these economic questions during the early stages of Faulkner's career, questions that scholars have approached primarily through Faulkner's attitude to the short stories he was forced to write, and rewrite, to stay financially afloat.[7] These stories notoriously distracted Faulkner from his novel writing, generating hostile and calculating comment. "While I have to write trash," he put it bluntly in 1934, "I don't care who buys it, as long as they pay the best price I can get."[8] Faulkner was "writing trash" in another sense too. Much of this early material concerned the poor-white inhabitants of Frenchman's Bend—Flem Snopes and company—such as the story of the wild Texas horses that Snopes helps auction to gullible villagers of the Bend. This material was an important part of the "something" that Faulkner thought missing from *As I Lay Dying*. The novel was a partial failure, Faulkner wrote, because "I knew too much about this book before I began to write it."[9] Many of the novel's characters, its anecdotes, its themes, and even its techniques (its phrasal schemas, its narrative points of view) lay elsewhere, in a constellation of satellite texts that we can term broadly the Spotted Horses material.[10] This material includes a series of unpublished manuscripts and typescripts from the late 1920s and early 1930s, in addition to the published "Spotted Horses" story (*Scribner's*, July 1931), which was rewritten yet again to form the first chapter of the final part of *The Hamlet* (1940) and extracted from that novel by Malcolm Cowley to become the "Spotted Horses" of *The Portable Faulkner* (1946). These manuscripts and typescripts include "Father Abraham," "Abraham's Children," "As I Lay Dying" (not the novel but the Spotted Horses story), another version with the same title "As I Lay Dying," "The Peasants," and "Aria con Amore." The relationships among these works make up one of the most complex textual questions in Faulkner scholarship. Together, they represent a significant body of work, equivalent to a fairly long novel.[11] Some versions, begun as early as 1926, were written toward the novel that would become the first of Faulkner's Snopes trilogy, *The Hamlet;* others were early (but very different) versions of "Spotted Horses," the short story, but I follow Hans Skei in questioning the usefulness of this distinction.[12]

Dianne Cox writes that the Spotted Horses material and *As I Lay Dying* were so closely related in Faulkner's mind that the latter can be considered a "thrifty borrowing of an existing conception" to produce a new work that did not preempt publishing the Snopes novel at a later date.[13] We can describe this relationship as an *economy of composition*, without stretching far into metaphor. It represents an efficient reuse of material, a borrowing on the interest of that material while protecting its principal value. Or we can consider it a pragmatic recycling of a story that, like *As I Lay Dying*, also concerns money and the consequences of its absence. *As I Lay Dying* and the multiple stories in the Spotted

Horses material represent a traumatic return to fundamental questions about the impact of poverty on people and about the equally negative effect of money on human relationships.

Faulkner's early, unpublished novel manuscript, "Elmer," terms this effect "the friction of money." Elmer's first lesson is to learn "how quickly the friction of money can wear thin all ties, of blood or affection or whatever."[14] This friction can be felt in one of the scenes in *As I Lay Dying* that most directly connects that novel to the Spotted Horses episode: the "Armstid" chapter, in which we learn that Anse has traded with Snopes (here apparently the nephew of the Snopes of Spotted Horses) to get the span of mules he needs to continue his journey to lay Addie to rest. "Anse stands there, dangle-armed. 'For fifteen years I aint had a tooth in my head,' he says. 'God knows it. He knows in fifteen years I aint et the victuals He aimed for man to eat to keep his strength up, and me saving a nickel here and a nickel there so my family wouldn't suffer it, to buy them teeth so I could eat God's appointed food. I give that money. I thought that if I could do without eating, my sons could do without riding. God knows I did.'"[15] First and foremost, money, or attempts to get it, has a frictional effect on the human body. In addition to Anse's eroded teeth and his splayed feet described earlier in the novel—signs of his impoverished decomposition—Jewel is literally worn thin by labor. He spends flesh to earn the money to buy the horse that Anse eventually trades to secure his mules. Money thus has a corrosive impact on the ties of "blood" and family, even the limited ties between Anse and Jewel. Money becomes a universal solvent in which an action's meaning in terms of money ("it means three dollars" is the compelling reason for Darl and Jewel's journey on the eve of Addie's death) dissolves ethical obligation. Other kinds of friction are implied by the trade between Anse and Snopes (again recounted by Armstid), at the clearest point of intersection between *As I Lay Dying* and Spotted Horses: "'Sho,' Eustace said. 'All they liked was the horse. Like I said to Mr Snopes, he was letting his team go for fifty dollars, because if his uncle Flem had just kept them Texas horses when he owned them, Anse wouldn't a never—'" (112). Another kind of exchange is occurring here, an intertextual one. Anse's trade with Snopes is enabled by prior events in another story altogether. But the relation between texts remains broken: Eustace's thought is unfinished, just as the precise correspondence between the stories of *As I Lay Dying* and Spotted Horses is never fully established. If anything, the two stories are at odds. Eustace's anecdote clashes with key details underpinning the Spotted Horses story. Eustace seems on the point of saying that Anse would not have had a horse to begin with if Flem had kept the original Texas horses, but this makes little sense in regard to the Spotted Horses episode, in which Flem's ownership of the horses is never explicitly revealed.[16]

Other threads connect *As I Lay Dying* and the various texts of the Spotted Horses material to make similar yet different story worlds, their chronologies distinct yet also blurred. The Armstid of *As I Lay Dying* seems different from the Henry Armstid in the Spotted Horses episode, but not entirely so. *As I Lay Dying*'s Anse Bundren is a different character than the Bundren named in "Aria con Amore" (the version of Spotted Horses that predates the published story in *Scribner's*, the only version to name Bundren explicitly),[17] though he's not entirely separate either. The Anse of *As I Lay Dying* strongly resembles the man chewing the peach sprig throughout the Spotted Horses stories. For example, the way Anse dips snuff is a direct echo from the very first "Father Abraham" manuscript (an early draft of the Snopes novel), in a repetition of an important signifier of socioeconomic status, based on whether one chews tobacco, or dips it, or cannot afford it at all (as in the case of Henry Armstid). But Anse also strongly resembles Henry Armstid at times: "dangle-armed" is a classic descriptive schema for Henry throughout the Spotted Horses material. And if, in *As I Lay Dying*, Armstid is helping Bundren, then the relation is exactly reversed in the Spotted Horse stories, where Bundren (or his prototype, the anonymous man chewing the peach sprig) is provoked by the sight of the Armstids' poverty into lending time and labor. These worlds may be inverted, but their coordinates correspond, like the flip sides of a coin.

This frictional relationship between *As I Lay Dying* and the Spotted Horses material is part of a broader series of tensions between the various versions of the Spotted Horses episode itself. These tensions frame a window onto Faulkner's attitudes toward money, particularly at this early stage of his career, when financial hardship was relieved by considerable success with short stories, especially in 1930 and 1931.[18] What interests me, though, are not the successes but the failures: the stories surrounding the central Spotted Horses episode that did not make it into print. By describing these unpublished versions as failures, I do not mean that they should be dismissed or even relegated as experiments in service of "Spotted Horses." They are too different from one another to be considered drafts that are revised into the published short story. Some of these versions were finished enough for Faulkner to try to sell them,[19] even if others remained incomplete. Nor do I intend that easy idea of failure associated with works of high modernism: what Faulkner called the "splendid failure" of *The Sound and the Fury*, or what Pierre Bourdieu called the "autonomous principle" whereby the kind of "difficulty" that brings failure in the market signals success on an artistic level.[20] Perhaps there's a meaningful shape to a different kind of failure. Perhaps the drama of incompletion, repetition, and contradiction across multiple texts—the changing relationship between literary discourse (particularly shifts in narrative point of view) and a common story—can reveal something more about Faulkner's attitude to money and to the kind of economic failure and suffering we call poverty.

I say "common story," but really there are two stories present simultaneously in the Spotted Horses material. First, we have the story of Flem Snopes's shady dealings with the Texas stranger, the story of the auction of the horses and its hilarious aftermath when those horses break from the fold and cause mayhem throughout the neighborhood of Frenchman's Bend. This is the antic story of poor whites, a tall tale continuous with the humor of the Old Southwest. It is a story whose details change very little across the various retellings (for example, we never learn anything more definite about Snopes's relationship with the Texan and the horses, even if we can guess the answer).[21] And then we have a second story, the story of the Armstids: their interaction with the auction; Henry's impulsive bid of five dollars (the only money between the family and the poor house); his injury trying to recover his horse; and Mrs. Armstid's unsuccessful attempt to reclaim her money from Snopes, to whom Henry hands it after its initial return by the Texan. This is the tragic story of failure and poverty.[22] It is a story that changes significantly across the different versions, a story that Faulkner finds difficult to tell and to sell. For example, one version of the Spotted Horses episode, "Abraham's Children," leaves out the Armstids almost altogether).[23]

We feel the friction between these two stories already in the initial "Father Abraham" manuscripts and typescripts from 1926. The details of the first story are in place, but the story of poverty and failure is left incomplete.[24] We are presented too with Faulkner's early reaction to the "rise of the redneck," as his friend Phil Stone would come to call it.[25] Here is a passage from the ribbon typescript of "Father Abraham," with possible typos intact: "The Snopes sprange untarnished from a long line of shiftless tenantfarmers—a race that is of the soil and yet rootless, like mistletoe; owing nothing to the soil, giving nothing to it and getting nothing of it in return; using the land as a harlot instead of an imperious and abundant mistress, passing on to another farm. Porlific and rootless and clannish, they move and halt and marry and multiply and move and marry and multiply like rabbits."[26] "Porlific" may be more of a Freudian slip than an intentional coinage, but it captures perfectly Faulkner's sense of the Snopeses and his complex understanding of poverty.[27] The Snopeses are poor *and* prolific; they represent democracy run rampant. Critics have tended to read Flem Snopes as the agent of capitalist accumulation—an interpretation that Richard Godden has questioned recently with a more nuanced understanding of Flem's historical class position and class resentments, particularly as Faulkner's understanding develops later in the 1930s.[28] Further complicating a purely critical view of Snopes, the typescript page from "Father Abraham," immediately beneath the description of the Snopes clan's "porlific" multiplications, contains a series of marginal multiplications and other sums in Faulkner's hand. In all likelihood, they are financial calculations in which Faulkner seems to be multiplying small amounts, as if he's trying to scrape a larger sum together (ironically, a sum around five dollars: the amount that the Armstids presumably lose to Flem in the transaction at the heart of the Spotted Horses episode).[29] At one level, these marginal calculations are clear signs of how Faulkner's financial situation was pressuring his material (for example, he initially sent a version of the Spotted Horses story to the high-paying *Saturday Evening Post*, despite the known interest of the editor at *Scribner's*).[30] With John T. Matthews, we can read the auction of the spotted horses as an implicit critique of the market and its spectacular culture of mass consumption.[31] But in the alignment of Faulkner's marginal arithmetic with the multiplying power of the Snopeses, we might also glimpse Faulkner's longing for endless multiplication and the financial rewards it could bring (Faulkner was, after all, unusually compliant with the demands of magazine editors for changes to his work). We can glimpse this longing too in Faulkner's comments to Malcolm Cowley about the catalyzing potential within the Spotted Horses material in general: its production of a host of related and tangential tales, including stories, such as "Wash," that do not seem directly connected.[32]

The wild horses themselves become the site of this multiplied interest, as is clear in the earliest extant version of the Spotted Horses episode, "Father Abraham," and on throughout the series. The horses attract spectatorship within the story. Mrs. Littlejohn, the boardinghouse landlady, models this interest when she repeatedly stops her work to observe the Texan (Buck) and the horses. And they attract narrative attention through the descriptive energy that eddies around the horses' exotic wildness. They are "like hysterical fish," for example, or "ceaseless fluid gleams like gaudy patched calico."[33] They are described predominantly as liquid in form ("clotted and blended," "a towering parti-colored wave"), as if they represent a kind of raw narrative material, a hot mess of linguistic potential.[34] Interest in the horses redoubles through Buck's ability to describe, to pick out (or "spot") the individual horses—"that fiddle-headed hoss with most of his mane wore off"—and hence make them saleable.[35] When the horses escape the auction, their value only multiplies further through Suratt, the professional humorist, who creates tall tales based again on multiplied values: "Well, hit was the biggest drove to have jest one hoss in it I ever seen in my life," he responds when his audience notes with amusement his exaggerations.[36]

We would be mistaken to find in the hilarious energy of the Spotted Horses episode the reason for Faulkner's repeated retelling of the story. A better reason is suggested by the frayed endings of the various "Father Abraham" manuscripts. The ribbon typescript ends with the injured Henry Armstid being carried into Mrs. Littlejohn's boardinghouse, during which one of the men supporting Henry's injured head becomes distracted by the sound of an escaping horse in the distance.[37] The carbon typescript takes the story one page farther than its ribbon progenitor, to the point of Mrs. Armstid's appearance at the boardinghouse, where she is described as having "desolate dog's eyes" (in an allusion to Homer's *Odyssey*, which informs the title "As I Lay Dying," one that Faulkner applied to various texts).[38] But the bigger failure of vision seems to be Faulkner's own inability to see beyond this point of the story, which might suggest a reticence in his approach to the pain of the Armstids' poverty. The original holograph manuscript advances the story a little further by describing Uncle Billy Varner's arrival to attend to the injured Henry. But even here, we feel a competition between two discursive registers. The distant sounds of attempts to catch the escaping horses (and all the hilarious antics they imply) confront the local screams of Henry's pain and suffering, "a harsh respiratory Ah. Ah. Ah." The clash is compacted into contiguous sentences: "'Whooey . . . goes . . . .' Henry's scream consumed itself Ah. Ah. Ah." Suratt's humorous tale of a horse's antics in Mrs. Littlejohn's boardinghouse is similarly halted by speculations concerning Henry's level of impoverishment and by accusations that Flem should accordingly be ashamed of his actions.[39] But here, in the original holograph manuscript of "Father Abraham," a page is missing, its absence ironically staging the difficulty of approaching the Armstids' story, just as the manuscript subsequently wanders through disconnected episodes—Eck's unsuccessful attempt to catch his horse; Jody Varner's efforts to protect his candy store from hungry children; a poetic description of gathering twilight—toward an unsatisfying termination.

The shame of the Armstids' situation is captured in the agonizing scene that occurs in later versions of the Spotted Horses story, when Mrs. Armstid approaches Flem in sheer poverty and desperation to ask for her money back. This scene is hinted at, in the "Father Abraham" manuscripts, in the men's reluctance to fetch Mrs. Armstid to the boardinghouse, a reluctance, moreover, that necessitates a change in form.

A break into directly reported but unmarked speech—"they looked at Henry and shuffled their feet and muttered among themselves. You go. No, you better go. Let Ernest git her. Go tell her, Ernest"—effectively shows, rather than tells of, this embarrassed hesitation.[40] In familiar Faulknerian fashion, we are forced to patch the story together from its discourse. The first of the two typescripts that share a title with Faulkner's novel, *As I Lay Dying* but feature instead versions of the Spotted Horses story, is likewise told entirely through unmarked, reported speech, as if the only way to tell the story is by avoiding a direct view. Toward the end of this version of "As I Lay Dying," we are presented with the dialogue in which Mrs. Armstid asks for her money back and Flem lies about his role in the deal. But again, we can only infer the degree of the men's embarrassment—their turn away from the performed necessities of poverty and the cruel display of unequal power—from the shift in the subject of their conversation to a barely realized subplot involving characters called "Uncle Dick" and "Mitchell."[41] Flem's brazen and humiliating offer of candy for the Armstid children is likewise punctuated with digressive dialogue. The moment begins with Flem's "Wait a minute, Miz Armstid" and ends with his "Hyer's a little sweetenin fer the chaps next time you go out home." But in the middle of this dialogue, while Flem (as we come to realize from other versions) is inside Jody Varner's store buying five cents' worth of candy, we encounter the following lines, extending the subsubplot involving Uncle Dick and Mitchell:

> They wus a feller fum town offered Mitchell a good price fer that mare last year. Dont know why he never taken hit.
> He could sell hit over and over. Reckon that's why he wont.
> That's Mitchell. He dont want nothing twell he thinks some other feller wants hit too.
> Whut wus Uncle Dick's trouble?
> Dont know. Just holed up fer the winter, more'n like. A feller like Uncle Dick—[42]

The spoken discourse takes us away from the story at hand and hence correlates with a similar loss of attention in other versions, to which we will return shortly. Here we are diverted to an alternate story of a horse trade, or rather to an antistory about *not* selling a horse. The extended line of dashes, just before Flem reappears on the scene, indicates a continuation of the dialogue in the background, an abrupt break in that dialogue, a strikethrough (a correction as we pivot back to the Snopes-Armstid drama), or all three at once. The extended line, like this moment of dialogue as a whole, is a moment of failure—a failure to face the deep abjection of Mrs. Armstid's poverty, though one that ironically prolongs the moment, holding before us an agonized turning away. This moment in the first "As I Lay Dying" typescript thus focuses the overall effect of Faulkner's multiple versions of the Spotted Horses story. Through them we experience failure as a process of incomplete or faltering engagement whose meaning lies in the textual drama of a traumatic return.

The second typescript titled "As I Lay Dying" (which, we know, was rejected by *Scribner's* in November 1928)[43] may share a title with the first but could not be more different formally. We move from an all-dialogue antistory without narrative diegesis to the first-person viewpoint of a young nephew of a judge in Jefferson who is campaigning for votes at election time. If these different versions represent traumatic returns to some primal scene—each return bringing another shock to form—then the focus is again on Mrs. Armstid's poverty:

> I had seen her almost every Saturday in Jefferson, in her gray, faded, shapeless garment and canvas tennis shoes and a cloth sunbonnet and, in the winter, a man's wornout overcoat, going from house to house with a market basket on her arm, selling the objects she had knitted or woven, swapping them for old garments and rags to make yet other objects of. In our house at the time was a centerpiece she had crocheted of pieces of colored cotton string hoarded from parcels from the stores, and I have seen her with her gaunt face and her dead eyes and her gnarled hands that, motionless on her knees or moving slowly on some outgrown garment of my own—she had five children—shaped even then the handle of a plow or the helve of an axe or a hoe, sitting in the library with my mother. She did the knitting and weaving at night. She did it by firelight until mother gave her a lamp.[44]

According to his brother, Faulkner made a similar trip as a child with his uncle, J. W. T. Faulkner, Jr., during which they witnessed an auction of wild range ponies. "Bill sat there on the porch of the boardinghouse and saw it all" and retold the story to his family the following day.[45] This is the biographical point of origin of the Spotted Horses story. The description of Mrs. Armstid suggests a similar intimacy, the specific and grotesque details (say, the canvas tennis shoes) implying that *"I have seen her"*—a phrase repeated twice. The tennis shoes are described as stained in other versions, but here the stain seems to be on the memory itself, as if Faulkner is working through a real encounter, trying to find a literary form to contain his confrontation with deep impoverishment. The shoes represent a forced repurposing, full of irony compounded, perhaps, by Faulkner's own sporting interest in tennis.[46] Objects of leisure become the stigma of entrapment, a spectacular outing of poverty that is again difficult to face directly. So intense is this encounter—whether real or imaginary—with the Armstids' poverty that its details (Mrs. Armstid's sunbonnet and tennis shoes; her saving, weaving, and peddling of knitted objects; her hard work with plow in field) are saved from the Spotted Horses material and woven again into another story featuring the Armstids, "Lizards in Jamshyd's Courtyard" (1932). Indeed, the major schemas of the Armstids' poverty are here given in summary, almost like a moved block of description. This suggests again a traumatic compulsion to repeat or a dilemma of inequality that transcends the stories that attempt to contain it.[47]

If the Armstids' poverty breaks out of individual stories, then it also, in the passage quoted above, dislocates the narrator's vision. Mrs. Armstid's hands are "motionless on her knees or moving slowly on some outgrown garment of [her] own," but then they also shape "the handle of a plow or the helve of an axe or a hoe" even as she is "sitting in the library with [her] mother." Two perspectives are present simultaneously. We know from other versions that Mrs. Armstid's labor in the fields is essential to the survival of the family. The sheer physical and temporal demands of poverty—the need to work different jobs at once, to perform antagonistic tasks (laborer, mother) simultaneously—take formal shape in this bifurcated perspective. Mrs. Armstid's poverty is thus difficult to locate because of its inherent contradictions. In this version of "As I Lay Dying," as at other points, we learn that the five dollars Henry bids at the auction are Mrs. Armstid's and that Flem, the Texan, and Suratt are not the only characters selling things. If the sewing-machine salesman Suratt is selling tall tales to his avid listeners, then Mrs. Armstid is also weaving something of her own, bringing color into an impoverished world where it often seemed to be lacking.[48] For all of her deadness, her flatness of voice, her virtual nonexistence as a characterized human being, Mrs. Armstid is still a figure for the aesthetic. Her tennis shoes, after all, are *canvas*. She is a figure of skill, of improvisation; she is associated with the library, not with the kitchen; she provides an aesthetic centerpiece to the narrator's house. We learn that her five dollars are valuable because they are conjured out of selling items made from packaging and waste, during marginal hours that are stolen from the night.

During his early career, Faulkner conceived of his own authorial identity in terms close to those describing Mrs. Armstid's craftsmanship. *Sanctuary*, we might recall, was allegedly woven from galleys Faulkner "tore down." Or we can think of Faulkner's part-mythical description of writing *As I Lay Dying*, the novel, while working in the University of Mississippi power plant. Like Mrs. Armstid, Faulkner describes himself sitting with someone while he writes (the "fireman," just as Mrs. Armstid weaves by firelight); again, Faulkner is in a situation of improvisation and reuse (he invents a table from a wheelbarrow); and his act of creation also takes place at night (from midnight to 4:00 a.m.), as he, like Mrs. Armstid, gains surplus from stolen time. Again like Mrs. Armstid's crocheted centerpiece, *As I Lay Dying* is conceived as a deliberate act of craftsmanship, of technique, woven to some extent from other threads and yarns that lie within the Spotted Horses material.[49] As critics have pointed out, we can think of Faulkner's aesthetic in general as one of recycling. Strands of narrative and individual episodes tend to be repurposed and reworked between stories and novels. Again following John T. Matthews's lead, we could locate in the Mrs. Armstid of the second "As I Lay Dying" story another critique of the publication industry: she reflects the impoverished author forced to peddle her wares around the fiction market. But something more intimate and productive—not simply critical or satirical—lies in Faulkner's approach to Mrs. Armstid. The apparent contradiction of an aesthetic within desperate need seems to drive a negative capability, a process of confusion and uncertainty that yields the multiple, aborted Spotted Horses stories. Textual failure performs a polemics of poverty.

This leads us to "The Peasants," a fifty-nine-page typescript that appears to be a draft of a section of the novel that would become *The Hamlet* but that may also have been seen (or a version of it seen) as a possible short story by an editor at *Scribner's*.[50] "The Peasants" is closer in style to the final version of the Spotted Horses episode in *The Hamlet*—both feature omniscient narration, for example—but it has one enormous difference. We are given details of Mrs. Armstid's repeated journey home during Henry's rest at Mrs. Littlejohn's boardinghouse following his injury—an episode missing from other versions. Faulkner adds specifics about the brutal poverty and severe malnutrition in which the Armstids live. But more significant are the contradictions between this and other narratives, for example, concerning a basic detail: How many children do the Armstids have? Figures vary across the different versions of Spotted Horses, but the typical answer is five, with the eldest child a twelve-year-old girl who, because of her age, can help around the place and care for the younger ones. In "The Peasants," however, we discover that the Armstids have only four children and that the eldest is not twelve but eight: "She was thin. Her face might have been fourteen; it was gaunt, weary."[51] Not only do the characters in other versions of Spotted Horses get this fact "wrong" (assuming that "The Peasants" has epistemic privilege because of the extended access it offers into the Armstids' domestic life) but the situation is exactly reversed. The young girl's advanced age does not help alleviate the Armstids' poverty, but rather their poverty creates misperceptions of her age—she *looks* older as a result—and hence it leads to a crucial underestimate of the family's degree of suffering. This intertextual, ironizing effect is compounded by the version of "Spotted Horses" published in *Scribner's*. This version agrees with "The Peasants" typescript by recording the number of children at four. But the published "Spotted Horses" disagrees strongly with "The Peasants" inasmuch as the narrator (Suratt) considers the Armstids "lucky" because the girl is twelve and hence old enough to bar the door when Mrs. Armstid leaves the children alone at night. When we actually see these scenes in "The Peasants," we discover that this is the very thing the girl *cannot* do: "If I could just lock the door," she says.[52] "The Peasants" typescript contains another unique and resonant detail. We realize that Mrs. Armstid's agonizing decision to ask Snopes for her money back is not suggested by Mrs. Littlejohn (as in other versions) but is a promise of sorts that she makes to her daughter when looking directly at the girl's malnutrition, "her rib-cage serrated in blue shadows."[53]

The final prepublication version of the Spotted Horses story, the typescript "Aria con Amore," begins on the verso of a page from "The Peasants" typescript—the page on which Henry first enters the auction. This establishes the interconnectivity of different versions while again flagging significant discrepancies between them, here concerning the question of timing: When, exactly, do Henry and Mrs. Armstid arrive on the scene? This is an important question that underscores narrative attitudes toward the Armstids' poverty, whether it is caused by luck or fault. In "The Peasants" and in the published *Scribner's* version of "Spotted Horses," the Armstids arrive *before* the auction begins, and hence before the Texan offers Eck Snopes a free horse just to get the bidding started (this is true of the earliest "Father Abraham" variants too). Perhaps we are meant to think that Henry assumes this will be his own deal too—two for the price of one—hence explaining his compulsive, misguided bidding. By the time we get to the version in *The Hamlet*, however, Henry arrives just *after* the Texan offers Eck the free horse, making Henry feel that he is unlucky to have arrived at just the wrong time: "Then if you were just starting the auction off by giving away a horse, why didn't you wait till we were all here?" he asks.[54] Henry gets much more to say in this later version from 1940. He becomes a voice of protest at the unfairness of the Texan's ploy, and in the novel, he is not to blame for leaving the gate open and letting the horses escape, as he is in earlier versions.[55] We can read such changes in Henry's situation in light of Richard Godden's thesis that, through the mid- to late thirties, Faulkner's confrontation with the revolutionary impact of the New Deal on the southern economy introduced a more radicalized voice of labor into his depictions of class.[56] But in the earlier "Aria con Amore" (another narrative in which Suratt is *recalling* the story of the auction, some of it based on overheard conversation), Henry arrives at the very *end* of the auction and is not responsible for getting it going. He arrives holding and hollering, "Five dollars!" in what seems to be a compulsive fetishization of the money itself, clenching his fist, perhaps, not in protest but simply to keep the amount together (mostly coins with a few notes). Here Henry is more like the Henry Armstid of "Lizards in Jamshyd's Courtyard," driven mad by a lust for gold. The version of the Spotted Horses material in "Aria con Amore" does not stand on a continuum of revision. It is less part of a process and more of a discarded tangent in which Suratt tells a truncated, very different, and—taking the weight of evidence in the other versions—more unreliable version of events, one that blames Henry for leaving the gate open, thus presenting him as shiftless, not unlucky. There is no reference to Henry initially entering the auction ring in a failed attempt to retrieve his horse (after which the Texan returns the money in other versions). Instead, the Texan refuses to take the money because Henry, in "Aria con Amore," has not really participated in the auction at all; quite simply, he has not purchased a horse. The Texan's decision to return the five dollars seems directly motivated too by the curse that Mrs. Armstid places on her cash—a curse present across the other versions, but particularly powerful here. "If you take the money I earnt my chaps a-weaving," she says, "it'll be a curse onto you all the time of man."[57]

If the sales prices of the horses differ considerably across the different versions of Spotted Horses—a sign of the fluctuating values in the story itself—then Mrs. Armstid's five dollars is the one consistent sum. Its roundness as a number suggests intentionality, a completed amount saved up over time. As becomes clear in the court scene added to the episode in *The Hamlet*, when Mrs. Armstid unsuccessfully attempts to sue Flem, she would "know them five dollars . . . if I was to see it again" (360). The sum is made mostly of coins, collected a little at a time, coins marked by the friction of acquisition in ways that Mrs. Armstid can read to reveal an intrinsic value, an embodiment of her labor. This is why the money can rub on a conscience (or at least most consciences: not Flem's, of course), and why it can hold a curse. Mrs. Armstid's power to curse is enhanced by her ghostlike presence throughout the various versions of the story: dressed in a shapeless shroud, she moves "without visible motion, like something on a float in a parade."[58] Mrs. Armstid's phrase to describe her husband's inability to resist the auction, "he haint no more despair," describes his eroded agency and abject state, beyond emotion altogether.[59] *Haint* is also a southern colloquialism for "ghost":

contained within the Armstids' virtual deadness is a capacity to haunt, which is again brought to light through discrepancies between parallel manuscripts. In the published "Spotted Horses" and in its immediate (unpublished) antecedent, "Aria con Amore," the ghostly quality of Mrs. Armstid lies in her deadness of vision.[60] "Mrs. Armstid never looked at nothing," says the narrator of "Spotted Horses" at the moment when Flem lies that the Texan took Mrs. Armstid's money with him when he left.[61] Here's the same moment in "Aria con Amore":

> A wagon comes up the road, going on up the hill. It's MacCallum, from across the river. She turns her head like she was watching it, like she heard it and turned her head and then forgot what she turned it for.
>
> After a spell she moved, the rubber soles hissing again. "I reckon it's about time to get dinner started," she says.[62]

The version in "The Peasants" typescript—which gets incorporated into *The Hamlet*—presents a different account of events through omniscient narration:

> She raised her head and looked up the road. It went on beneath the locust trees. Across the road, beyond the rusting iron roof of the blacksmith shop, a peach tree was in bloom against a slope still green with winter wheat. Before the door of the blacksmith shop a tethered horse dozed on three legs; within the shop a measured hammer clanged. From there the road mounted in a grave red curve. At the top of the hill was the grave yard, its lean graves bordered with broken crockery; a knoll choked with cedars through the long afternoons of summer loved of doves.[63]

We can read this straying attention as a narrative avoidance of the moment of embarrassment, corresponding to the scene in the first "As I Lay Dying" when the talking men change the topic of conversation away from Mrs. Armstid's situation. But here it's Mrs. Armstid's gaze that floats away as she seems to leave her own body at the point of shaming. A power to haunt emerges within her apparent failure of vision, though one we only see by encountering the "failed" versions of "Spotted Horses," which haunt the published version with alternate possibilities that are present but not fully seen. When we realize Mrs. Armstid's out-of-body power, the fact that her tennis shoes *hiss*—a detail common to various versions of the story—becomes a sign not of emptiness but of possession. Haunted, they provide her only voice of protest.[64]

In "Aria con Amore," Suratt (the narrator) describes Mrs. Armstid's failure of vision as being "like she was holding up one of these here double barrel spy glasses with the lenses broke out."[65] This image of visual difficulty is itself difficult to visualize. Rather than an external description of Mrs. Armstid's appearance, the image seems motivated by how she herself would see, or rather *not* see clearly owing to her broken spyglass. Objective description is haunted by the subjective experience it attempts to hold at a distance. The image is unique to this version of Spotted Horses, but it does recall another moment of out-of-body experience, from *As I Lay Dying*, and hence it returns us finally to those complex ties between Faulkner's novel about the Bundrens and the "something missing" with which we began this chapter: the parallel tales about poor whites in the Spotted Horses material. In a late chapter, Darl views himself being forcibly carried to the Mississippi State Insane Asylum, on account of burning down the barn where the family was camping on the outskirts of Jefferson—a final reaction against the gaze of shame in which they have been traveling throughout:

> They pulled two seats together so Darl could sit by the window to laugh. One of them sat beside him, the other sat on the seat facing him, riding backward. One of them had to ride backward because the state's money has a face to each backside and a backside to each face, and they are riding on the state's money which is incest. A nickel has a woman on one side and a buffalo on the other; two faces and no back. I dont know what that is. Darl had a little spyglass he got in France at the war. In it it had a woman and a pig with two backs and no face. I know what that is. (146)

The spyglass reference allows us to date the novel to the years following the Great War. But the strong parallel with the spyglass image in "Aria con Amore" also blurs temporality, making the events of *As I Lay Dying* seem continuous with the earlier period of the Spotted Horses episode (referred to as "twenty-five years ago" in *As I Lay Dying* [77], but dated as 1908 in *The Portable Faulkner*). Darl's split vision of himself, in which he seems to be haunting his own body, reflects the double-barreled vision of Mrs. Armstid, both inside and outside at once. It also reflects the bifocal quality in the historical vision of *As I Lay Dying*, which looks forward as "the first quintessentially Depression novel"[66] but also looks back to the problems of rural poverty in the South, problems that emerged with Reconstruction and persisted even as the nation boomed in the 1920s.[67]

The moments of exchange between *As I Lay Dying* and the satellite texts of Spotted Horses establish the novel's place in Faulkner's broader if faltering attempts to theorize the impact of poverty on human experience. The precarious boundary between life and death, the violent intimacy between humans and animals, the ways that objects gain agency and power over human subjects—these shared realities of *As I Lay Dying* and Spotted Horses are all consequences of the dependency and disempowerment of the characters. Both story worlds share an ambivalence over causality (is Anse Bundren, like Henry Armstid, unlucky, exploited, or lazy?). If Mrs. Armstid fuses social deprivation and aesthetic creativity, then the rich mental language of the novel's monologues suggests a similar paradox. Indeed, the tonal uncertainty of *As I Lay Dying* in general—its grotesque and tragicomic excesses, its location of dark humor within social suffering—seems rooted in the difficulties that poverty posed to Faulkner's imagination in the early days of his career. If the Armstids and the Bundrens have trouble holding level glances with others, then similar problems emerge from attempts to hold these characters in a consistent narrative point of view, problems that necessitate the textual variants of the Spotted Horses story and the multiple perspectives of *As I Lay Dying*.[68]

To understand this multiplicity of viewpoint as a special kind of failure—different from textual revision or from a modernist aesthetic of incomplete retelling—is to encounter the formal drama staged between competing texts without a teleology, each one offering different, at times contradictory perspectives on the problems of money and its absence. The theoretical work performed by these complex intertextual relationships can be found again in the parallels between Mrs. Armstid's dilemma and Darl's haunting vision of himself on the train to Jackson. Echoing Mrs. Armstid and her five dollars, the moment implies an intimacy with specific coinage. Darl's vision of "the state's money" recalls a real coin, a buffalo (or Indian head) nickel, in production from 1913 to 1938. Indeed, the reason Darl mistakes the Native American head on the real coin for a woman's head may relate to the reason for the coin's eventual retirement: its indistinct striking and tendency to wear. As with Mrs. Armstid and her hoarded cash, money seems to bear the marks of its possession. But the harshest friction of money lies in its power to possess us, to erode our human ties as we seek its ghostly promises. We can read Darl's formulation, the "state's money . . . is incest," as a crazed encapsulation of money's power to break apart conventional family relations or to create equivalences that have the same result. In Darl's view, the symbolic system of the state's authority (money) is not representing but *determining* the order of things. This is why the men sit face to face, as Darl sees it, like sides of a coin. Money is a symbolic discourse that shapes a social reality according to preexisting power relationships, ones in which the Bundrens, as poor whites, are intrinsically disadvantaged. This, then, is the ultimate curse of money: its unseen, multiplying, abstract power to determine our relationships and to structure their inequality. After all, the irony of the Spotted Horses episode is that Mrs. Armstid, contrary to her assertion, would *not* know her own money, even if Flem were to produce it at the end. The various coins and notes get swapped for a single five-dollar bill by the Texan in several versions of the story,[69] turning an intimacy with money into the cold exchangeability of currency.

NOTES

1. See Faulkner's 1933 introduction to *The Sound and the Fury* (1929), unpublished during Faulkner's lifetime, reprinted in the Norton Critical Edition of *The Sound and the Fury*, ed. Michael Gorra (New York: W.W. Norton, 2014), 250–52.

2. Faulkner's introduction to the Modern Library Edition of *Sanctuary* is reprinted in William Faulkner, *Sanctuary*, rev. ed. (1931; repr., New York: Vintage International, 1993), 321–24. Faulkner wanted to create something that would not shame his modernist novels, he said.

3. Faulkner, *Sanctuary*, 322.

4. William Faulkner to Four Seas Company, November 23, 1923, *Selected Letters of William Faulkner*, ed. Joseph Blotner (New York: Random House, 1977), 6. The letter is from 1923 and concerns the manuscript of *The Marble Faun*.

5. Faulkner weaves a tall tale of buried treasure (or at least, bootleg whiskey) and its discovery worthy of the humorists of the Old Southwest: "I had about one-fifty in bank, and I knew I could dispose of my whisky and raise the balance with only the minor risk of being had by the law for peddling it. So I came home in about three days, found that one of our niggers had smelled the whisky out, dug it up, sold a little and had been caught and told where the rest of it was. So I lost all of it." Faulkner, *Selected Letters*, 37. The letter is from July 1927.

6. Faulkner to Horace Liveright, February 1928, in *Selected Letters*, 39.

7. Exemplary here is John T. Matthews's essay, "Shortened Stories: Faulkner and the Market," in *Faulkner and the Short Story: Faulkner and Yoknapatawpha, 1990*, ed. Evans Harrington and Ann J. Abadie (Jackson: University Press of Mississippi, 1992), 3–37.

8. Faulkner to Morton Goldman, August 1934, in *Selected Letters*, 84.

9. Faulkner, 1933 introduction to *The Sound and the Fury*, 251.

10. I use the term Spotted Horses, capitalized but without quotation marks, to indicate the different versions of the same episode involving the horse trade and its aftermath, versions that have varying strengths of connection to the short story "Spotted Horses" (1931).

11. This is the estimate of Hans H. Skei, in *Reading Faulkner's Best Short Stories* (Columbia: University of South Carolina Press, 1999), 167.

12. Hans H. Skei, *William Faulkner: The Short Story Career* (Oslo: Universitetsforlaget, 1981), 46. The exact chronology of these texts is not entirely clear. "Father Abraham," "Abraham's Children," and "The Peasants" appear to be drafts of a novel, while the two versions of "As I Lay Dying," along with "Aria con Amore," seem to be versions of a short story. For more details, see Thomas L. McHaney's introductions to *William Faulkner Manuscripts 1: Elmer and "A Portrait of Elmer*,*"* ed. Thomas L. McHaney (New York: Garland, 1987), xxv–xxxi, and *William Faulkner Manuscripts 15: The Hamlet*, vol. 1, ed. Thomas L. McHaney (New York: Garland, 1987), vii–xxii, in addition to James B. Meriwether's introduction to William Faulkner, *Father Abraham*, ed. James B. Meriwether (New York: Random House, 1983), 3–7.

13. Dianne L. Cox, introduction to *William Faulkner's* As I Lay Dying: *A Critical Casebook*, ed. Dianne L. Cox (New York: Garland, 1985), xx. Cox writes that when Faulkner promised Hal Smith a new novel in May or June of 1929, he may have had the Snopes novel in mind, rather than *As I Lay Dying*, as is conventionally thought (xix). Cox's point is corroborated by Faulkner's use of the title "As I Lay Dying" for two early versions of the Spotted Horses story.

14. McHaney, *William Faulkner Manuscripts 1*, 17–18.

15. William Faulkner, *As I Lay Dying*, Michael Gorra (1930; repr., New York: W. W. Norton, 2010), 111. Hereafter cited parenthetically.

16. We are told by Darl earlier in the novel that Jewel's horse descends from "those Texas ponies Flem Snopes brought here twenty-five years ago and auctioned off for two dollars a head and nobody but old Lon Quick ever caught his and still owned some of the blood because he could never give it away" (77).

17. However, Mrs. Bundren is mentioned briefly in "Spotted Horses": Suratt wants to sell her a sewing machine. There may have existed yet another, prepublication version of "Spotted Horses," also with the title "Aria con Amore," now lost; see Skei, *William Faulkner*, 47.

18. See Skei, *William Faulkner*, 13. For example, "Red Leaves" fetched $750 at the *Saturday Evening Post* (Matthews, "Shortened Stories," 6).

19. Skei points this out concerning "Aria con Amore" and "As I Lay Dying" (*William Faulkner*, 44).

20. Faulkner called *The Sound and the Fury* his "most splendid failure" in a Q&A during Frederick Gwynn's American Fiction class at the University of Virginia on February 15, 1957, and he would discuss elsewhere the process of writing that novel as one of repeated failure to tell a truth. See also Pierre Bourdieu, *The Field of Cultural Production* (New York: Columbia University Press, 1993), 39, 40, 116, 136. I take up this idea of failure in *Failure and the American Writer: A Literary History* (Cambridge, UK: Cambridge University Press, 2014).

21. Admittedly, collusion between Flem and the Texan does become clearer in some versions, for example in "The Peasants"; see McHaney, *William Faulkner Manuscripts 15*, vol. 1, 51.

22. The addition of the court scene in the second part of chapter 1 of book 4 of *The Hamlet* highlights a possible third story in the Spotted Horses material, the story of Vernon and Mrs. Tull (named Turpin in the first "Father Abraham" manuscript), who are injured in their wagon on the bridge by one of the escaping horses. But the power and agency of Mrs. Tull in the court scene only underscore the special abjection of the Armstids.

23. In this version, Henry is just a voice to get the auction started, his presence unexplained, while Mrs. Armstid is entirely absent. See the ribbon typescript of "Abraham's Children" in McHaney, *William Faulkner Manuscripts 2*, 156–203, especially 180–81.

24. This version lacks the scene in which Mrs. Armstid approaches Snopes to ask for her money back (though Faulkner may well have had it in mind).

25. As Stone would have us believe, he gave Faulkner his supposed understanding that "the real revolution in the South was not the race situation but the rise of the redneck, who did not have any of the scruples of the old aristocracy, to places of power and wealth." Stone's 1957 letter is quoted in Joseph Blotner, *Faulkner: A Biography*, vol. 1 (New York: Random House, 1984), 192. See also Faulkner's 1954 essay "Mississippi" on the dividing and parceling of land into smaller farms, in *Essays, Speeches, and Public Lectures*, ed. James B. Meriwether (New York: Random House, 1965), 11–43.

26. McHaney, *William Faulkner Manuscripts 2*, 34.

27. The word is corrected in later versions and absent from the original holograph manuscript.

28. See Richard Godden, *William Faulkner: An Economy of Complex Words* (Princeton, NJ: Princeton University Press, 2007), 17–21.

29. The calculations in three columns all seem to add up to around $5: 5.50 is the sum of the figures in the left column, 4.50 in the right column, and in the middle, 5.00 is the difference between the final figure of 9.85 and the sum (2.55 + 2.30) above it. And just above that, in the middle column, 5.00 = (7.55 - 2.55). See the bottom of page 8 of the ribbon typescript of "Father Abraham" in McHaney, *William Faulkner Manuscripts 2*, 34.

30. McHaney, introduction to *William Faulkner Manuscripts 15*, vol. 1, ix.

31. Matthews, "Shortened Stories," 16–19.

32. In his famous letter to Cowley of August 16, 1945, concerning *The Portable Faulkner*, Faulkner credits the multiplying potential of the Spotted Horses material to the character Suratt's power as a catalyst and to his own authorial desire to tell the story of the Snopes clan. See Faulkner, *Selected Letters*, 197.

33. These examples are from the ribbon typescript of "Father Abraham"; see McHaney, *William Faulkner Manuscripts 2*, 44, 63.

34. Ibid., 67, 52.

35. Ibid., 48.

36. Faulkner, *Father Abraham*, 67.

37. "Ther's one mo' of 'em," he pants. The man is described as the "head-supported" rather than the "head-supporter," but this seems to be a typo, and is corrected in subsequent editions. McHaney, *William Faulkner Manuscripts 2*, 80.

38. Ibid., 135. To his editor, Saxe Commins, in 1956, Faulkner inaccurately quotes the influential lines from Homer's *Odyssey* (Agamemnon's description of his own death) thus: "As I lay dying the woman with the dog's eyes would not close mine eyelids on mine eyes as I descended into the abode." See *Annotations to William Faulkner's As I Lay Dying*, ed. Dianne C. Luce (New York: Garland, 1990), 1. The phrase "desolate dog's eyes" is also present in the original holograph manuscript of "Father Abraham" (see Faulkner, *Father Abraham*, 60) but is not present in the source, William Marris's 1925 translation of book 11 of *The Odyssey*, where the phrase "as I lay dying" is found.

39. Faulkner, *Father Abraham*, 61, 63, 68. "That was the last dollar Henery [sic] had in the world, I reckon," Suratt comments (68).

40. Ibid., 59–60.

41. McHaney, *William Faulkner Manuscripts 15*, vol. 1, 16.

42. Ibid., 16–17.

43. McHaney, introduction to *William Faulkner Manuscripts 15*, vol. 1, viii.

44. McHaney, *William Faulkner Manuscripts 15*, vol. 1, 28.

45. See Blotner, *Faulkner*, 112. Blotner dates these events as summer 1922.

46. See *Talking about William Faulkner: Interviews with Jimmy Faulkner and Others*, ed. Sally Wolff (Baton Rouge: Louisiana State University Press, 1996), 166–67.

47. See William Faulkner, "Lizards in Jamshyd's Courtyard," *Uncollected Stories of William Faulkner*, ed. Joseph Blotner (New York: Random House, 1979), 142. This story maintains an ambivalence concerning the cause of the Armstids' poverty: "The land was either poor land or they were poor managers."

48. See Peter Nicolaison, "Rural Poverty and the Heroics of Farming: Elizabeth Madox Roberts's *The Time of Man* and Ellen Glasgow's *Barren Ground*," in *Reading Southern Poverty Between the Wars, 1918–1939*, ed. Richard Godden and Martin Crawford (Athens: University of Georgia Press, 2006), 196.

49. Faulkner, *Sanctuary*, 321–24.

50. See Skei, *William Faulkner*, 46. Skei quotes a letter dated December 30, 1930, from the editor K. S. Crichton to Faulkner: "We still think back with a great deal of pleasure on that long story of yours which had to do with the bringing of the horses from Texas, and the resultant auction."

51. McHaney, *William Faulkner Manuscripts 15*, vol. 1, 90.

52. Ibid. Suratt's comforting version of events in "Spotted Horses" (admittedly based in part on what he overhears Mrs. Armstid herself saying, just as she says, "Ina May bars the door when I leave" [William Faulkner, "Spotted Horses," *Uncollected Stories of William Faulkner*, ed. Joseph Blotner (New York: Random House, 1979), 179]), that Mrs. Armstid returns at night to "cook up a pot of victuals and leave it on the stove" (178), does not occur in "The Peasants," in which she has to return before the children wake to cook some food. In "Lizards in Jamshyd's Courtyard," we learn that the Armstids "had four children, all under six years of age, the youngest an infant in arms" (Faulkner, "Lizards," 142).

53. McHaney, *William Faulkner Manuscripts 15*, vol. 1, 91.

54. William Faulkner, *The Hamlet* (1940; repr., New York: Vintage, 1991), 322. Hereafter cited parenthetically.

55. Henry may be a voice of protest, but he is also a voice of naivety: Eck will get the free horse whatever happens.

56. Godden, *William Faulkner*, 18–19.

57. McHaney, *William Faulkner Manuscripts 15*, vol. 1, 112. In "Aria con Amore" Henry does not give the money to the Texan but hands it directly to Snopes after the Texan refuses it (113).

58. This is the description in the second version of "As I Lay Dying," McHaney, *William Faulkner Manuscripts 15*, vol. 1, 36. See also, in the same volume, parallel descriptions in "The Peasants" (94) and "Aria con Amore" (123).

59. This phrase appears, almost identically, in several versions of the Spotted Horses story, such as "Father Abraham" (see Faulkner, *Father Abraham*, 41, and McHaney, *William Faulkner Manuscripts 2*, 33), "The Peasants" (McHaney, *William Faulkner Manuscripts 15*, vol. 1, 63), "Spotted Horses" (169), and *The Hamlet* (321), although *haint* becomes *aint* in this last version.

60. See McHaney, *William Faulkner Manuscripts 15*, vol. 1, 117. In the second version of "As I Lay Dying," we again read of Mrs. Armstid's "ghost of vision turned inward, contemplating nothing there, even" (ibid., 37).

61. Faulkner, "Spotted Horses," 182.

62. McHaney, *William Faulkner Manuscripts 15*, vol. 1, 121–22.

63. Ibid., 100. Cf. Faulkner, *The Hamlet*, 349.

64. In "The Peasants," her tennis shoes are described as "not her shoes, not on her feet" (McHaney, *William Faulkner Manuscripts 15*, vol. 1, 94).

65. Ibid., 118.

66. Ted Atkinson, *Faulkner and the Great Depression: Aesthetics, Ideology, and Cultural Politics* (Athens: University of Georgia Press, 2006), 194.

67. See Richard Godden and Martin Crawford's introduction to *Reading Southern Poverty between the Wars, 1918–1939*, ed. Richard Godden and Martin Crawford (Athens: University of Georgia Press, 2006), ix–x.

68. See, for example, the moment in *As I Lay Dying* when Jewel cannot countenance the outrage at the family's poverty expressed by African American characters, directing his anger toward a white man instead (132–33).

69. This is true of the initial ribbon typescript of "Father Abraham" (McHaney, *William Faulkner Manuscripts 2*, 69) and the final version of the story in *The Hamlet* (326–27).

Too Small to Fail: Jason Compson's Precarious Self-Worth

TED ATKINSON

For Jason Compson IV in *The Sound and the Fury*, April 6, 1928, is one of those days when it seems impossible to achieve a work-life balance. In the course of the day, he goes back and forth between the Compson household, where he sees himself as a master of bedlam trying to impose some semblance of order, and the feed store, where he holds down a job as a clerk, which he finds unsatisfying and considers beneath his talents. The day also entails routine stops at the telegraph office to get expensively belated market reports and a farcical car chase in pursuit of his rebellious niece and her showman suitor that ends with a slashed tire on his prized automobile—a literal confirmation of the deflationary trend that has ruled the day. All the while, Jason delivers a screed against his perceived enemies, whether close to home or far removed, a rhetorical performance in which misogyny and white nationalism converge to express his frustration with the web of familial obligation and material decline that has ensnared him in a state of arrested development and humbling precariousness. As Faulkner shows through flashbacks of boyhood wheeling and dealing, Jason has long been one to keep tabs. On April 6, he tallies the various slights, injustices, and unforgivable transgressions suffered at the hands of family and fate and remains fixated on the bare necessities that shape his so-called life: keeping the flour barrel full; working just hard enough to prevent getting fired by his long-suffering boss, Earl; and trying to keep reins on the feckless kin whose behavior reflects poorly on him as head of the Compson household and bespeaks a once-distinguished family going to seed. Out of these circumstances Jason crafts a story to tell himself (and us as readers) in which he figures as the ill-fated protagonist—a fantasy of the capable financier thwarted by misfortune, cunning antagonists, and a system rigged by far-flung Wall Street players. As a result, Jason perceives himself as mired in a saga of familial and financial declension that has devolved from epic to mock-epic proportions and that he must escape to avoid ruin and to reap the rewards he considers his due.

Jason's sense of himself as cut out for success but cut off from it at every turn contrasts with what we see in his brother, Quentin, whose inability to function in the daily routines of modern life leads him down the path toward suicide. Faulkner famously described Jason as the "first sane Compson since before Culloden," adding credence to the notion that he is an outlier in the household he heads.[1] According to his mother, Caroline, Jason is so unlike the rest of the Compson clan that he merits a special exemption. "I know you have to slave away your life for us," she tells him in one of several displays of passive-aggressive mothering. "You know if I had my way, you'd have an office of your own to go to, and hours that became a Bascomb. Because you are a Bascomb, despite your name" (1016). What it means to "be a Bascomb," in this instance, is to have the potential to thrive in modern business. Jason's penchant for making cold calculations in service of the profit motive that has driven him since childhood provides evidence for conferring this dubious distinction upon the reluctant breadwinner. By this logic, such as it is, Caroline conveniently sets aside the countervailing example of her brother, Maury, whose purple-prose-laden requests to his sister for yet another "loan" come with assurances of a shared windfall once the next new financial scheme pans out. For Caroline, the idea that Bascomb blood runs in the veins of her favorite son feeds her belief that he can break the family free from the magnetic hold of despair and failure that steered his alcoholic father and melancholic, suicidal brother to their early graves. This fate is the Compson "curse" that the mother imagines as an explanation for the family's declining fortunes in recent generations. In materialist terms, it is a means of cloaking in the performative trappings of tragedy the family's inability to adapt to a rapidly changing modern economy driven by the shift to finance capitalism.

The notion of Jason's mind for business that Caroline clings to out of desperation is manifest in the self-image that drives his constant financial and familial scheming. While Jason's materialism is on vivid display, it masks a fragile ego beneath the surface: he relies on pure self-interest and detachment to form a carapace in his relations with family and the community and to guard against the anxieties that arise from increasing uncertainty and instability. Cast in this light, Jason stands out as a figure whose characterization resonates with contemporaneous debates about whether the much-ballyhooed prosperity of the 1920s was actually reaching middle- and working-class Americans or remaining just out of reach in a cycle of unreasonable expectations that was fueling the profit motive, driving rash financial decision making, and monetizing self-worth. The field of popular economics was particularly invested in pursuing this line of inquiry, resulting in studies that drew on insights from the burgeoning disciplines comprising the social sciences. In *Prosperity: Fact or Myth*, for example, the economist Stuart Chase set out to test the claim that the economic boom of the Roaring Twenties had registered with significant impact beyond the parameters of an elite class enriched by the flows of paper currency flooding the bullish markets. In researching the book, one of a few concerned with living in the new economy, Chase made every effort to drill down to the level of the quotidian in order to extract microeconomic evidence of macroeconomic forces at work, applying as a framework the metonymic Wall Street/Main Street paradigm that was in vogue among experts interested in the socioeconomic conditions on the ground.[2] Toward this end, *Prosperity* relied heavily on *Middletown: A Study in Modern American Culture*, the first of two influential studies published by the sociologists Robert and Merrill Lynd. Appearing in 1929, *Middletown* was an in-depth examination of Muncie, Indiana, aimed at isolating broad socioeconomic trends in the frame of one small town for the purposes of close examination and broader application. Through the popular metonymy of the moment, Chase describes a process by which "Middletown, and with it the whole nation, has been shifting from year to year to a pecuniary economy. Money has become the sine qua non of existence."[3] With all the information at Chase's disposal, however, he winds up disappointed by the end of *Prosperity* regarding the inherent limitations of the tools of his trade. Chase expresses frustration over the nagging feeling that there are depths of individual lives unfolding in local communities that the discipline of economics simply cannot fathom—a realization made plainer in the wake of the 1929 stock market crash and its immediate aftermath, which forced the author to delay publication in a hasty effort to address the sudden turn of events. Turning from the social sciences to the humanities, Chase avers that literature is ideally suited to delve into the areas of human experience that remain elusive to data-driven models. Chase reasons that the mimetic and imaginative aspects of literature enable it to deliver fictional truths about the social and economic conditions of lived experience and the affective dimensions of financial matters. "To tell the whole story," Chase concludes, "would require 27 million novels from the pens of such observers as Theodore Dreiser, Ring Lardner, or Sherwood Anderson."[4]

For the sake of argument, it is worth thinking about how Chase's lineup might be improved by the addition of William Faulkner. As Faulkner biographies and letters to his agent and publishers attest, Faulkner spent an inordinate amount of time worrying about finances, in large part because of family members, immediate and extended, and people in his domestic charge who relied on him for support. More to the point, Faulkner's fiction is deeply concerned with the workings of capital and the way money changes hands. The network of financial holdings and transactions that shape the landscape and lives in Yoknapatawpha is extensive, constituting the local economy and connecting it to broader national and global economic flows and systems. The depiction of Jason Compson in the final two sections of *The Sound and the Fury* offers an instructive case in point, seemingly answering Chase's contemporaneous call for literature to take up the task of delving into everyday human experience and consciousness during a time of rapid social and economic change.[5] This critical prospect inspires a variation on the nomenclature of the twenty-first-century crisis that assumed Depression-era proportions. In 2008, the disastrous effects of Wall Street gone wild in the form of financial monstrosities created by deregulation and deemed "too big to fail" hit close to home for those holding mortgages on a share of the lived-in American Dream. In the case of Jason Compson, the relationship between pecuniary and psychological matters—money and ego—animating Jason's rhetorical performance leaves him exposed as too small to fail. The phrase reflects a shift in focus from an institutional to an individual level and speaks to several factors that influence Jason's identity, motivation, and behavior: the fantasy of his financial acumen; anxieties about his own trajectory relative to his family's precipitous fall; fear that additional losses might mean a sort of existential annihilation; and repressed feelings of guilt and filial responsibility that return despite his professions of self-interest and a self-imposed program of detachment. Thinking of Jason as too small to fail is also helpful for exposing how he benefits from the structure of white privilege and the residual class distinction the Compsons enjoy despite the material losses they have incurred. During his narration, Jason does not acknowledge—or, more likely, does not even consider—that he benefits from such an advantage.

The threat of failure looms large over Jason, intruding on virtually every waking moment in the final two sections of *The Sound and the Fury*. Expanding the scope that Gavin Jones applies in examining failure as a preoccupation among nineteenth-century American writers and texts is useful for measuring how it factors into Faulkner's twentieth-century novel. Jones notes a tendency among historians to rely on economic criteria when defining failure. Like Chase, Jones finds literature capable of greater depth and nuance in comprehending failure as "a process of thinking, knowing, and feeling." "Failure, as it unfolds in literary pages," Jones argues, "becomes essential to an understanding of what makes us human—both within and beyond the pressures of social context."[6]

The thoughts and feelings that failure conjures in Jason are tethered to the high expectations and hopes that his mother invested in him: "Jason will make a splendid banker he is the only one of my children with any practical sense you can thank me that he takes after my people the others are all Compson" (Faulkner, *The Sound and the Fury*, 949). The argument for Jason's exceptionalism is a burst of ego inflation designed to counteract the reality of his small standing with a dose of the fantasy that he is destined for great things by virtue of his own ambition and talents. Buying into this idea, Jason espouses bootstrap philosophy and appeals to the Protestant work ethic to cast judgment on the alleged laziness and shiftlessness of others. Jason routinely laces such accusations with virulent racism and misogyny, berating the alleged freeloaders in the household who benefit from his hard work while doing none of their own. In the first paragraph of the section he narrates, Jason sets the tone, railing against his niece and members of the Gibson family to his mother, pointing out that Quentin should be downstairs instead of "up there in her room, gobbing paint on her face and waiting for six niggers that cant even stand up out of a chair unless they've got a pan full of bread and meat to balance them, to fix breakfast for her" (1015). Jason's self-described industriousness, a dubious claim if ever there was one, is a form of posturing that justifies his bitter disposition and bolsters the homegrown fantasy of his exceptionalism as a deterrent to the threat of financial and existential failure.

The fast pace of Jason's monologue reflects the state of emergency that he experiences while trying to fulfill his mission not only to survive but to thrive. The invective he delivers comes with a tone of harsh cynicism and caustic humor in alternating registers of self-aggrandizement and self-deprecation that define his role in the larger Compson saga. As Carolyn Porter observes, Jason tempts readers with a directness that holds out hope for answers to the questions that the opaqueness of the Benjy and Quentin sections invariably raises. The price for this "plainspoken and unreflective" clarity is heavy, Porter adds, because the longer Jason holds the floor, the more apparent it becomes that he is "certainly among the most repugnant figures in all literature."[7] This assessment of Jason is neither unprecedented nor unwarranted; scores of readers have found his casual racism and misogyny abhorrent. On the surface, Jason's aggrieved disposition comes across as a product of frustrated entitlement that makes it difficult to work up any sympathy for him or his cause to right the wrongs he claims have been done to him. It is not necessary to feel for Jason, however, in order to take his feelings into account—in this instance, to consider that Jason's capacity to dispense a steady stream of venom has developed partly from deep-seated feelings of inadequacy that the conditions of the modern marketplace only exacerbate. Holding grudges, lashing out at his enemies, and acting on acquisitive impulses are responses motivated by Jason's need to seek recompense. On a deeper level, though, they stem from self-doubt that jeopardizes the fantasy of business acumen that has formed the very core of his identity.

Jason is heavily invested in the belief that hitting pay dirt will enable him to get payback for the ultimate lost opportunity: the banking job promised to him by his then future brother-in-law, Sydney Herbert Head. Normally, Jason's brother, Quentin, is (psycho)analyzed as the Compson who is most firmly in the grip of the past. Quentin's melancholia becomes manifest as he clings to the youthful, virginal image of his sister, Caddy, as the object of loss that gives him a reason to exist until, in the end, it becomes the reason he ceases to exist. Jason is usually cast as Quentin's polar opposite, not least when it comes to recognizing the need to adapt to modern times. Christopher Breu describes the sibling contrast succinctly, couching it in terms of masculinity:

> If Quentin represents a melancholic version of modern masculinity, one that is retrospectively focused on the image of the antebellum planter, Jason Compson embodies a much more present-and future-oriented version of modern masculinity. . . . If Quentin turns away from the unbearable present toward the past, Jason immerses himself, obsessively, in the implacable workings of a present and future that he perceives as hostile to his interests as the twentieth-century heir to the lineage of the aristocratic past.[8]

While such readings capture Jason's desire and determination to be a creature of modernity, they elide the centrality of the past in defining Jason's orientation toward the present and future. After all, the failed prospect in banking becomes the source of a dashed alternate reality whose material consequences and symbolic meaning have accrued over time in the context of familial and personal history and experience. Accordingly, the past is a key influence on the way Jason does business, serving as a motivating factor in the ill-fated investment in cotton *futures* that leads to heavy losses on April 6, 1928, and in the ongoing scheme to bilk the money from Caddy intended for his niece. The job that never was kicks Jason's profit motive into overdrive, as he pursues an elusive windfall with a sense of desperation and reckless abandon commensurate with his belief that turning a profit will be a quick fix for his feelings of declining stature at home and in the community. In this regard, Jason is struck by the transformative potential of money that Karl Marx describes as a force of captivation. Riffing on a passage from Shakespeare's *Timon of Athens*—another instance of literature serving instructive ends in economics—Marx takes on the voice of someone held in thrall by the allure of money as a source of empowerment: "That which I am unable to do as a *man*, and of which all of my individual essential powers are incapable, I am able to do by means of *money*."[9] Chase's notion that currency functions as the prime ontological determinant of experience in the modern economy echoes Marx's observation about the healing properties it seems to hold from the standpoint of those suffering from diminished self-worth measured in terms of affective and monetary value.

The gap between Jason's desire to play the stock market for immediate financial gain so that he can wield the power of money and the reality of the heavy losses he incurs on April 6 runs along the fault line of the proverbial Wall Street/Main Street divide. In the parlance of Chase's study, Jason is caught between the myth that prosperity is (or at least should be) readily accessible to someone of his station and "natural" prowess and the fact that the bulk of new wealth remains concentrated in relatively few hands far removed from Jefferson, Mississippi. As he tries to turn a profit from Wall Street at the level of Main Street, Jason has trouble comprehending how his own life fits materially into "the total economic life of the United States," which Chase likens to an onion.[10] As the various layers—states not located in the mid-Atlantic, Pacific, or Northeast regions; farmers and small-town merchants; a large section of the middle class—are stripped away, they become separated from and lose access to the prosperity at the heart. When he receives word of his losses by telegraph, Jason cites technology as a crucial factor. He claims that traders in urban centers, whether New York or Memphis, receive crucial market updates instantaneously over the wire while their counterparts on the rural periphery take a hit due to the lag. But this assessment of market conditions gives way to financial speculations of a different order, as Jason engages in the conspiracy theory that a cabal of "eastern jews" (1024) has rigged the system such that "any dam foreigner that cant make a living in the country where God put him, can come to this one and take money right out of an American's pockets" (1024–25). Steeped in nativism, Jason denies that Jews have a claim to citizenship and blames them for robbing "real" citizens (those who hail from places like Jefferson or Middletown) of opportunities to prosper.[11] The flagrant anti-Semitism that Jason espouses in response to his bad day on the market allows him to displace the responsibility he himself bears for not being more vigilant in monitoring developments.

The extent of Jason's investment in the power of money for egoistic security and enhancement becomes readily apparent as his narration unfolds, but Faulkner provides symbolic foreshadowing earlier in the novel. Amid the fractured images and scenes comprising the Benjy section is a flashback sequence in which Jason takes scissors to Benjy's paper dolls, acting out in response to forced separation from his ailing grandmother, Damuddy. "[Jason]'s chewing paper again," Caddy says after a physical altercation with him on behalf of Benjy (932). At this stage, the boy Jason has not developed the armor of indifference that the man will rely on for protection against the complications of emotional attachment and guilt. The image of Jason eating paper, which Caddy implies is a compulsion, presages the conflation of familial and financial relations as Jason uses the manipulation of currency in an effort to gain profitable leverage in the economy of Compson dysfunction. Taking Jason's precipitous fall on April 6 into account, the flashback also works as a flash forward in that it foreshadows the paper losses Jason eats as he receives dismal market reports by paper telegram. Toward this end, Jason must keep the emotional toll of his cruelty in check, vigilantly guarding against a replay of the vulnerability exhibited in the tearful paper-chewing incident from childhood. He is able to maintain this posture, save for fleeting moments of unanticipated feeling, such as his recollected encounter with Caddy in the graveyard after their father's funeral. After reading about her father's death in the paper, Caddy came to Jefferson in secret to pay her respects. As Caddy and Jason stood over the fresh grave, Jason recalls, he held on to the grudge over the lost banking job and informed his sister that there was no inheritance, as though that were the only reason for her clandestine visit. But Jason remembers that he was unable to feel satisfaction after taking a dig at Caddy and then learning how she had found out about their father's death: "I didn't say anything. We stood there, looking at the grave, and then I got to thinking about when we were little and one thing and another and I got to feeling funny again" (1032). The response Jason remembers having is an emotion that he fails to recognize as guilt mixed with grief on another day when he experienced great loss. For the most part, the adult Jason acts out by performing an aggrieved martyrdom as a means of lording over those in his charge to compensate for feelings of inadequacy and to provide cover for profiteering aimed at bolstering a fragile ego in which self-worth and financial worth are inextricably bound up. No mention of the family's record of scandal and financial loss can pass without a reminder from the resentful breadwinner that he never had the luxury of leisure time to become a disgrace to the family.

By the time his narration unfolds, Jason's financial self-interest masked as familial self-sacrifice has reified his relations within the Compson household, as demonstrated by his repeated usage of the objective pronoun "it" in reference to his niece and the objectifying phrase "the job," which is an expression of his alienated labor. As Jason's frequently displayed resentment makes clear, Quentin represents to him the embodiment of the cruel cosmic joke that turned his dream job into a living nightmare. As a result, he tries to exercise control by making her an instrument of profit—a means to the end of vengeful recompense he has been accumulating in the elaborate scheme to seize her assets. Asserting his authority through mental and, increasingly, physical abuse, Jason berates Quentin with reminders of what she costs him in hard-earned dollars—at times calculated to the cent, as in his citing of $11.65 wasted on her books for school since tardiness and delinquency are fast becoming her routine. The potency of this tactic is waning, however, as Quentin is maturing into agency. "There's not a cent of your money on me," she says in disputing one of his line items. "I'd starve first" (1020). This moment of resistance is merely a prelude to the public show of defiance that Quentin stages later in the day as she eludes her uncle's grasp while cavorting with the showman in the red tie. Jason fixates on the tie as he pursues the couple in an effort to put a stop to his niece's embarrassing behavior, which he sees as a threat to his reputation. Two days later, in the final section of the novel, Jason suffers an even more severe blow to his ego and to his bottom line. When Quentin makes off with the stash of money her uncle has accumulated, his long game of monetizing maternal devotion is cut short by poetic justice and, given the sheriff's accusatory rebuke against Jason's plea for justice, the legal kind as well.

While Jason contends with the threat Quentin's unruliness poses to his standing at home and in the community, he encounters problems at work that compound his fear of failure. For Jason, the job in the feed store is like his niece: a reminder of the cruel hand he has been dealt and a way to take stock of what he has been denied as a result. "But as I haven't got an office, I'll have to get on to what I have got," he says bitterly before leaving home from a meal break to return to the store (1016). Jason carries the notion of his exceptionalism into the workplace to mitigate the damage to his pride that working in the tertiary economy entails. Jason's approach to the clientele is to eschew the best practices of customer service encouraged by the proprietor, Earl. Sales pitches to the "redneck[s]" (1026) Jason deigns to serve only out of necessity while biding his time—as in the failed attempt to sell a farmer a high-priced item by asserting an absolute correlation between price and quality—have less to do with closing deals to the store's benefit than with stroking his own ego by demonstrating a superior understanding of commerce. He tries to distance himself from Earl along similar lines, speculating about how taking over the business would mean a dramatically improved bottom line and criticizing Earl's lack of entrepreneurial imagination and drive in settling for a steady but uninspired annual return from the store. Unfortunately for Jason, however, Earl, like the sheriff later on, gives the lie to the hollow posturing by essentially calling Jason out for cheating his kin and lying to his mother about the thousand dollars she intended as an investment to secure Jason an interest in the feed store and thus prevent him from working as a mere sales clerk (1052–53). That money instead went toward the purchase of a status symbol—the automobile that yields petro-headaches and deflated tires as returns on the investment. It turns out that, in effect, Earl has been propping up his employee, not because he respects Jason as an individual or buys into the notion that his talents will be good for business, but because he has sympathy for Jason's mother and perhaps regard for a family name that he likely considers already too far gone for the good of the social order in Jefferson. This commitment on Earl's part shows that what Jason sees as a web of frustrating obligation to his family operates as a kind of social safety net available to him because he enjoys sufficient privilege to warrant its mobilization.

As the window onto April 6, 1928, and into Jason Compson's consciousness, draws to a close, Jason retires to his room for the night. There, as he did earlier in the day, he checks on the cash he has stowed away in a box—though not for much longer. At the end of a day filled with frustration and loss, Jason counts his money and counts on his money for compensation in a ritual of financial and psychological insecurity. In this moment, he appears cut from the mold of the Dickensian miser, exhibiting an obsessive-compulsive fixation on money that involves seeking but never quite finding a way to accumulate enough wealth to shore up a fragile identity and make up for a lack of meaningful social relations. In setting up Jason for his fall, Faulkner offers a finely observed portrait of dubious faith in the capacity of money to increase self-worth. The added value that Jason applies to the currency he possesses (and that possesses him) brings diminishing returns that eventually amount to nothing but further despair once the money is out of his hands. Jason's (mis)handling of money evinces one of the properties that Marx assigns to it by limning Shakespeare's Timon of Athens, another man who was in thrall to the power of gold and adept at parting with it. The "visible divinity" of money, Marx explains, makes it possible for estrangement to gain purchase at the level of individual consciousness: "The overturning and confounding of all human and natural qualities, the fraternization of impossibilities—the *divine* power of money—lies in its *character* as men's estranged, alienating, and self-disposing *species-nature*. Money is the alienated *ability of mankind*."[12] Accordingly, Jason completes his ritual by making sure all of the cash is accounted for and then enumerating his antagonists, among them his dysfunctional family and the "dam New York jew," to avoid admitting that what he really wants is to succeed in business without really trying. "I dont want to make a killing; save that to suck in the smart gamblers with. I just want an even chance to get my money back," Jason says, asking the gods of the market for a level playing field on which to engage in the risky game of investing for another day (1080). Jason's appeal to fairness is rich, given that he views the game solely in terms of winners and losers and extends that mentality from the marketplace to the homeplace with emotional costs he is thus far incapable of calculating. Also, Jason's claim that he wants simply an "even chance" to recuperate a short-term loss belies his long-term investment in financial scheming not as a way to break even but as a power play to get even and to validate the story he tells in an aggrieved attempt to place blame for his failure anywhere but on himself. Jason doesn't put much stock in what his boss has to say, but he would profit substantially from taking to heart Earl's admonition that "a man never gets anywhere if fact and his ledgers dont square" (1053).

NOTES

1. William Faulkner, *The Sound and the Fury*, in *Novels 1926–1929*, ed. Joseph Blotner and Noel Polk (New York: Library of America, 2006), 1137. Hereafter cited parenthetically.

2. Chase was particularly interested in consumer spending during the 1920s, as the following studies preceding *Prosperity: Fact or Myth* evince: *The Challenge of Waste* (1922); *Your Money's Worth: A Study in the Waste of the Consumer's Dollar* (1928); and *The Tragedy of Waste* (1925). The influence that Chase exerted is demonstrated by the fact that he provided the name for Franklin Delano Roosevelt's comprehensive program to end the Great Depression. In 1932, he published a *New Republic* cover story titled "A New Deal for America," expanding the article later the same year into a book, *A New Deal*.

3. Stuart Chase, *Prosperity: Fact or Myth* (New York: Charles Boni Jr., 1929), 177.

4. Ibid, 179.

5. The literary representation of everyday experience has garnered interest in modernist studies in recent years. See for example Byron Randall, *Modernism, Daily Time, and Everyday Life* (New York: Cambridge University Press, 2008), and Liesl Olson, *Modernism and the Ordinary* (New York: Oxford University Press, 2014).

6. Gavin Jones, *Failure and the American Writer: A Literary History* (New York: Cambridge University Press, 2014), 13. Although I am interested in the relationship between Jason's finances and his ego, it is worth noting that Jones treats failure not merely as a function of theme or characterization but also as constitutive of literary form. That calls to mind Faulkner's famous assessment of *The Sound and the Fury* as "the most gallant, the most magnificent failure" in his body of work and the implications of that remark for the novel's modernist form (Frederick L. Gwynn and Joseph L. Blotner, eds., *Faulkner*

in the University: Class Conferences at the University of Virginia, 1957–1958 [1959; repr., New York: Vintage, 1965], 61).

7. Carolyn Porter, *William Faulkner: Lives and Legacies* (New York: Oxford University Press, 2007), 47.

8. Christopher Breu, "Privilege's Mausoleum: The Ruination of White Southern Manhood in *The Sound and the Fury*," in Craig Thompson Friend, ed., *Southern Masculinity: Perspectives on Manhood in the South since Reconstruction* (Athens: University of Georgia Press, 2010), 117.

9. Karl Marx, "The Power of Money in Bourgeois Society," in *Economic and Philosophic Manuscripts of 1844*, trans. Martin Milligan (New York: Prometheus Books, 1988), 138–39.

10. Chase, *Prosperity: Fact or Myth*, 173.

11. For more on Jason's nativism, see Walter Benn Michaels, *Our America: Nativism, Modernism, and Pluralism* (Durham, NC: Duke University Press, 1995). For a response to Michaels's formulation, see John T. Matthews, "Whose America? Faulkner, Modernism, and National Identity," in *Faulkner at 100: Retrospect and Prospect: Faulkner and Yoknapatawpha, 1997*, ed. Donald M. Kartiganer and Ann J. Abadie (Jackson: University Press of Mississippi, 2000), 70–92.

12. Marx, "The Power of Money in Bourgeois Society," 138.

What Price a "Cheap Idea"?: Money, *Sanctuary*, and Its Intertexts

RICHARD GODDEN
For Noel Polk

A brief theoretical prelude.[1]

In a letter to Ben Wasson, dated September 1932, Faulkner suggested that were *Sanctuary* (1931) to be filmed, Popeye might best be played by Mickey Mouse.[2] *The Story of Temple Drake* reached the screen from Paramount in 1933, with Popeye renamed Trigger, played by Jack LaRue. Undoubtedly, Faulkner's preferred casting would have clashed with Disney's post-1930 sanitization of the Mouse, the better to suit him for official trademark status as Disney's first copyrighted character: an image—not a brand—but inextricably identified with the Disney Company. Perhaps Popeye, as played by Mickey, appealed to Faulkner because by 1933, he felt himself to be branded by *Sanctuary*. As "the corn-cob man," financially semisecure for the first time in his writing career, he sometimes worked the brand for all its intangible worth: asked by the playwright Paul Green which part he might play in a dramatized version of the novel, he responded, "the corn-cob."[3] To watch the all-singing, dancing, barking, biting hot dogs in *The Karnival Kid* (1929) is to recognize that in the world according to Disney, corncobs might assume a disarray of variable parts.

In a brief note on Mickey Mouse cartoons (written in 1931), the German philosopher Walter Benjamin commented, "Here we see for the first time that it is possible to have one's own arm, even one's own body, stolen."[4] He added, "These films disavow experience more radically than ever before," an observation apt to *Sanctuary*: witness Popeye, crouched above Temple's bed in Reba's Memphis brothel, "his face wrung above his absent chin, his bluish lips protruding as though he were blowing upon hot soup, making a high whinnying sound like a horse."[5] Nor are Popeye's prosthetic lips, equine by association, his most singular feature.

His suit, black and tight enough to be a second skin, becomes, by repetition, almost that—a removable skin. In *The Karnival Kid*, Minnie Mouse offers to pay for her salacious hot dog with a coin removed from her skin-tight stocking (black on white), a stocking that proves not to be her skin when lifted, black from white, to expose a second layer of white under black. To glimpse, with Temple's eyes, "one of Popeye's innumerable black suits lying across a chair" (225) is to wonder how he removed it; did he "have to shave it off at night?" (50). In contradistinction, Temple's single skin barely contains her: her "blonde" (28) legs seem always liable to carry her at a run, "out of her body" (91) at such speed that she must wait "for some laggard part to catch up" (66). Hers is a body running variously upside down and apparently on air, whose constant "spr[i]ng" (92) and "whirl" (91) might at any point elicit the clouds, dashes, and stars that attend Mickey's impacts and dispersals.

What steals physical cohesion from so many bodies in *Sanctuary*, allowing the eyeballs of Reba's maid, Minnie, to roll "out of the dusky light beside Miss Reba's door" (224), or the whole person of the Grotto's proprietor to appear "to be on the point of bursting out of his dinner-jacket through the rear, like a cocoon" (243)? Benjamin might respond, the movie camera: he famously argues in "The Work of Art in the Age of Its Technological Reproducibility" (1935–36), that while "our bars and city streets, our offices and furnished rooms . . . close relentlessly around us," the apparatus of the cinema, with its close-up expanding space and its slow-motion extending movement, "brings to light entirely new structures of matter," by which means film "explode[s] this prison world with the dynamite of the split second," sending audiences "on journeys of adventure among its far-flung debris."[6] Able to swoop, rise, disrupt, isolate, stretch, compress, enlarge, reduce, the movie camera, for Benjamin, discovers "the optical unconscious, just as we discover the instinctual unconscious through psychoanalysis."[7] To view Temple Drake's first appearance (at a run) in the dual light, first of Benjamin's claim, and second of any split-second that stretches, compresses, enlarges, and reduces Mickey's body in *The Karnival Kid*, is to recover Temple as an adventure among far-flung debris: "Townspeople . . . would see Temple, a snatched coat under her arm and her long legs blonde with running, in speeding silhouette against the lighted windows . . . vanishing into the shadow beside the library wall, and perhaps a final squatting swirl of knickers or whatnot as she sprang into the car waiting there with engine running" (28). I would pause the "explosion" only to note an affinity between Temple's and Minnie Mouse's knickers. And yet such an answer inclines to technological determinism, so to repeat my question: What steals physical cohesion from bodies in *Sanctuary*? Answer, the movie camera. Yet Benjamin knows better, as indicated by his aside on Mickey Mouse and subdivided, stolen bodies: "The huge popularity of these films is not mechanization, nor is it misunderstanding. It is simply the fact that the public recognizes its own life in them."[8] What possible "life" might be recognized in Mickey's rubbery nose, extended or retracted, or in a cow's "moo" prosthetically drawn out to fill a screen?

In 1929, the sociologists Robert and Helen Lynd noted that for the population of their representative, small American city (for their Middletown, read Faulkner's Memphis), "more and more of the aspects of living are coming to be strained through the bars of a dollar sign."[9] As bodies pass through those bars, by way of the consumption imperative, systemic distentions occur. A swift instance from Marx, but apt to Mickey, is furniture about to dance: a table, built by a carpenter for his own use, stands still so that he may sit at it. The same table, taken to market, "stands on its head . . . evolv[ing] out of its wooden brain grotesque ideas" because, as a commodity, comparable to any and "all other commodities," that is as the equivalent of all things priced, the table gets ideas above itself.[10] Originally concrete, or at least sufficient unto meal time, put on sale, it is at once concrete ("an ordinary sensuous thing") *and* abstract ("a thing that transcends sensuousness"),[11] care of "the impossible equals sign"[12] of monetary equivalency, whereby diverse and qualitatively incomparable things are rendered implausibly commensurate through the abstraction of money.

Yet, once again, my alternate response to the question of what steals cohesion from bodies in *Sanctuary*—answer: "the bars of the dollar sign"—proves reductive. Money, in and of itself, does not do it, because money, ever and always, remains a mere "form of appearance."[13] The phrase belongs to Marx, for whom money—like value, a hieroglyphic sign—is simply one point (albeit vital) in the barely visible processes through which the social relations of production generate capitalist value. Moreover, money necessarily "obliterates"[14] those processes through which it is made: as Marx famously put it, *"non olet,"* money does not smell of that from which it comes.[15] How then might the occluded relations in process, for which money is in some measure *the* measure, best be represented? Take the apparently simple formula by which Marx represents basic market exchange, $M—C—M^1$ (money—commodity—money + some, the some being profit from exchange). "Magic," "secrets," "mystery," and "necromancy" for Marx attend the dashes, as he tracks the several metamorphoses accompanying the passage of money into commodity, and of commodity into money, each dash being a "transubstantiation" that rests on a founding transubstantiation whereby labor congeals into commodity itself.[16] Of the passage of person into thing, and of thing into person, and of our initial misrecognition of those passages—the first fetish—Marx writes, "It is nothing but the definite social relation between men themselves which assumes here, for them, the fantastic form of a relation between things."[17] As a person passes into thing and thing into person, each leaves an aspect of itself in the other, producing thingified persons and personified things (note how close we are to Popeye's suit and Mickey's hot dogs), both of which are doubled and therefore troubled bodies, liable to come apart under the force of their own compressed and internalized antagonisms.[18] Take any commodity, residually human (in that it congeals from labor power), emergently abstract (in that it exists to become money by realizing its price). As Marx notes, "Not an atom of matter enters into the objectivity of commodities as values,"[19] by which I take him to mean that for the seller, the nature of the commodity (its "objectivity," or concrete materiality) is a matter of final indifference, given that, from the viewpoint of exchange, what matters is that said commodity realizes its price. For the merchant, operating under the principle of buy cheap, sell dear, price trumps merchandise, the best price being all. I would stress that the commodity retains its antagonisms, which, for Marx, are "the real form of motion in the process of exchange."[20] To sell, the commodity must *be* or have a concrete use, while simultaneously *being* an exchange value (as abstract as price). Commodities are therefore two things at once, both real and abstract (or real abstractions) whose dual and divided nature we, as subject to and subjects through a pervasive commodity fetishism, for the most part do not notice.

Faulkner, by his own account, "deliberately conceived" *Sanctuary* "to make money." By taking seriously his claim that it was "a cheap idea"[21] written in two versions between 1929 and 1931 (and therefore inextricable from *The Sound and the Fury* [1929] and *As I Lay Dying* [1930]), I do not mean to cast doubt on the scholarly work that establishes how scrupulously Faulkner revisited the ur-*Sanctuary* (1929) to produce the published novel (1931). Rather, I argue that in writing *for* money, Faulkner wrote *through* money, doing so at a time—post-Crash and during the early years of the Depression—when prevalent monetization of the real might prove problematic: or, put another way, when strains within money's mediation of "more and more of the aspects of living" might be seen to take thingified persons and personified things apart. By such reasoning, the physical incoherence characteristic of Mickey Mouse or Temple Drake could be said to result less from money than from the coming out of hiding of a monetary unconscious, immanent within the unthinkable or underthought incoherence of the monetary sign itself.

For the economists Kiyotaki and Moore, "money is strange stuff."[22] One form of that strangeness might be identified with a tension between the various purposes that it fulfils. Money, under capital, exists as a measure of value (equivalency), as a means to circulation (credit) and as an independent embodiment of value (most typically in the form of gold). How can money be at once price (the measure of a certain quantity of abstract labor time), liquidity (offered against labor as yet not undertaken), and gold (the hoarded precious, evidencing value)? Put another way, how can money be at once capital's lubricant, the motion in the system, *and* the golden mean, held static in the vault?

For Slavoj Žižek, the answer lies not in what we think about money but in what we *do* with it. Confronting one form of monetary duplicity—the persistence of the precious in the paper—he asks, "Given that we know that money, like all things, is subject to wear, tear, and decay, why do we act as though it contained a changeless body—the body of value?"[23] Or, as he has it, "I know that money is a material object, like others, but still . . . it is as if it were made of special substance over which we have no power." The "as if," informing our daily practice with money, crucially allows the coinage, the paper, the plastic, the electronic pulse (whatever our particular monetary form), a doubled body, setting a "sublime body" within the body of money (or putting the precious in the paper).[24] For Žižek, after Sohn-Rethel, what we *do* with money—the social effectivity of our exchange practices—lodges "an immutable substance, over which time has no power" within the thoroughly mutable materiality of money itself.[25] Such an account contains problems in the degree to which its focus on exchange and circulation, as those processes that put value into the symbolic representations of value, to the exclusion of production ignores Marx's fundamental insistence on labor as the sole source of value. Marx offers a labor theory of value. Žižek offers a circulationist theory of value. Nonetheless, Žižek's claim seems apt to *Sanctuary* in the degree to which the substance of the novel was conceived exactly to maximize exchange and circulation.

Faulkner, in his introduction to the Modern Library reprint of 1932, notes: "I had been writing books for about five years, which got published and not bought. . . . I began to think of myself . . . as a printed object. I began to think of books in terms of possible money."[26] Deciding that he "just as well might make some of it" himself and speculating on "what a person in Mississippi would believe to be current trends," he "invented the most horrific tale" he could imagine, at the center of whose horror lies the corncob rape of Temple Drake—Faulkner's money shot.[27] Please excuse my crudeness, but *Sanctuary* is a cleverly crude book.

Furthermore, Faulkner's preoccupation with circulation to the exclusion of production reaches beyond the novel's conception, affecting its substance. *Sanctuary*'s two key locations exhibit a conspicuous absence of labor. We approach the Old Frenchman Place via "abandoned grounds and fallen outbuildings. . . . [N]owhere was any sign of husbandry—plow or tool; in no direction was a planted field in sight" (41). Although Lee Goodwin produces liquor, we see neither his still nor his labor, much attention being paid, however, to the distribution of his product—the blocked road, the awaited truck, the loading of the vehicle—and to Popeye, his distributor, with links to Memphis, "where the money is" (21). The fields on the approach to Memphis may be "green with new cotton" (137), but they are "empty of any movement," they lack workers, while the run to Reba's, although it features "smoke-grimed frame houses" (142), offers no stacks, preferring to focus on the "rear ends of garages" and the "sound of traffic—motor horns, trolleys . . . [the] stupendous clatter" (142) of distribution. Reba's house is also "full of noises" (153), though of a different kind of traffic: a distant but shrill bell, "a swishing garment," "discreet whispers of flesh" (144)—sounds of trafficked bodies in a place whose "spent" light (144) necessarily plays between ejaculate and price-paid, where the madam's dogs "looked as though they had been cleaned with gasoline" (143), and the eyes of the doctor summoned to stem Temple's bleeding "looked like little bicycle wheels at dizzy speed" (150). Through analogy and by way of practice, circulation permeates the walls of Reba Rivers's house, "seeping" (153) into Temple's room. Sounds that seep recall Temple's blood (137), a circulatory medium ("It's still running" [139]), bleeding that must, in this place, carry a price: "That blood'll be worth a thousand dollars to you, honey" (145). Spent light, seeped sound—even the more immaterial elements of the Memphis brothel "sweat money"[28] without evident labor.

Elsewhere, similar principles apply. In Jefferson, Horace Benbow crosses alleys "choked with tethered wagons" (111); the square, "two-deep with ranked cars": "That was Saturday, in May: no time to leave the land" (112). Faulkner dwells on the hands of absentee tenants, come to Jefferson to view Tommy's body and to listen to music in the storefront doorways, "slow hands long shaped to the imperious earth," doing so in a manner that accentuates their withdrawal of their labor from the land: "on Monday they were back again," "functioning outside of time, having left time lying upon the slow and imponderable land green with corn and cotton in the yellow afternoon" (111). Labor here deserts labor time, apparently allowing cotton and corn to grow themselves. Benbow monetizes Faulkner's mystification with his earlier suggestion that "the very winds" and the "flat and rich and foul" soil of the Delta "engender money.... Like you wouldn't be surprised to find that you could turn in the leaves off the trees, into the banks for cash" (15). Where wind, tree, and soil "engender money" in the absence of labor, we are close to the financier's wildest dream, that of money "pregnant with itself": hands, for such a dream, in their redundancy tend to museum pieces, "gnarled ... lugubrious, harsh, and sad" (112).

Consumption, in these places, seems likewise geared to the service of a circulationist fantasy: a fantasy that distorts bodies to the point of barely needing them; or better, of needing them only to speed throughput. Liquor, Goodwin's liquid asset, circulates freely at the Old Frenchman Place, metonymically linked by proximity to the vehicular and sanguine fluidities soon to follow, en route to Memphis, "where the money is." Even the solid food served here by Ruby Lamar proves less than solid, displaying itself as fecally ready prior to mastication and passage through the gut: witness Pap's dish, sucked, regurgitated, mushed, and sorghumed, a sight from which Benbow averts his eyes (12). Having seen as much, the lawyer should be prepared when, in Jefferson's gaol, Ruby tells her story while "turn[ing] [a] bon-bon slowly in her hand" (275): eventually, she drops the "shapeless" candy (276) and, not wishing to soil Benbow's extended handkerchief, wipes her "chocolate-stained fingers" on her child's "discarded" nappy (275–76). The passage from hand to anus, without intervention by mouth, dispenses with digestive time. Gastrically, Popeye and Temple both embody Ruby's culinary lessons in fast-track consumption and throughput. Accordingly, for Popeye, not an atom of matter enters into Goodwin's liquor, which, since to drink it would kill him, remains for him entirely a matter of price or cash flow without use value. Flow, virtually unimpeded by substance, or in these instances by gastric interruption, also characterizes Temple, at least at Goodwin's place, where she remains digestively as pure as Popeye. She counts the hours during which she has not eaten and consumes only cold coffee: accordingly, though equipped by Ruby with advertising pages torn from a mail-order catalog with which to wipe herself, she can neither squat nor emit. Faulkner dwells on the interruption of her squat by "the squatting outline of a man," identity unknown (91): this provision of advertising copy all but carried to anus logically links exchange to defecation, perversely identifying both at once as promissory (we almost glimpse the "squatting ... knickers" [28]) and without substance (excremental air).

Once lodged in Memphis, Temple's consumption pattern obeys Popeye's logic, the logic of his medium, whereby goods (like bodies) become transitory excuses for further and unimpeded exchange. Temple hurls dresses, "a row of hats" (225), "flasks and jars ... bearing French labels," into a corner "in thuds and splintering crashes. Among them lay a platinum bag: a delicate webbing of metal upon the smug orange gleam of bank-notes" (226): without the verb, the bag stays shut, thoroughly problematizing "gleam." Perhaps the notes gleam through unlined platinum links, but whatever its circumstances, paper money does not gleam, unless the notes are very new; but even then their sheen, of itself, hardly justifies the modifier "smug." By inference at least, "wad[ded]" garments (225), broken bottles, and a clutch-bag achieve smugness in the degree that their breakage exposes a sublime and metallic body veiled within their temporary commodity form. Small wonder, in a text written to circulate ("maybe 10,000 of them will buy it"[29]), that these personified things, purchased with money made from liquor, gleam smugly, having successfully misappropriated, to items deriving from Popeye's liquid capital, the precious quality of that metallic measure more typically associated with the golden hoard.

To step briefly back from Memphis to *Capital*, under the heading "C—M. *First metamorphosis of the commodity or sale*," Marx describes "the leap taken by value from the body of the commodity into the body of gold . . . [as] the commodity's *salto mortale*," a leap (*salto*) he deems "deadly" (*mortale*)[30] because "thrown into the alchemist's retort of circulation"[31] by way of sale, the commodity "divested of its original shape" must "shape-shift," "chang[ing] its skin," in order to "transubstantiate" into the price that, from the viewpoint of exchange, was immanent within it from the first.[32] Like her accessories—the dresses, the hats, and the perfume bottles—Temple obeys the logic of her monetary form, the structural motor that keeps her "running." Witness her desire for Red: "He came toward her. She did not move. Her eyes began to grow darker and darker, lifting into her skull above a half moon of white, without focus, with the blank rigidity of a statue's eyes. She began to say Ah-ah-ah-ah in an expiring voice, her body arching slowly backward as though faced by an exquisite torture. When he touched her she sprang like a bow, hurling herself upon him, her mouth gaped and ugly like that of a dying fish as she writhed her loins against him" (238). Later, she will strain "to touch him with all of her body-surface at once" (240). Seldom can a "divestiture," for Marx "the fundamental condition . . . of circulation,"[33] have been so absolute. Temple experiences herself being taken apart: "her legs felt . . . like they were not hers" (235); "her mouth was open and . . . she must have been making a noise of some sort with it" (237). Her eyes do not simply roll back into her head; they deaden the cliché on which Faulkner's passage is modeled by articulating the skull beneath the skin, before petrifying into funereal art. Her voice expires, and her mouth, soon to be seen as a "straining protrusion, bloodless"

(238), in its prosthetic proximity to her loins recasts both apertures as fishy, recalling Benbow's expressed reason for leaving Belle: his Friday shrimp distribution. That Red's touch releases "sprang," a term recurrently applied to Temple as a preface to "whirl"—the latter describing a tight circle—intensifies the circulatory imperative informing her desire: yet "bloodless" drains her circulatory medium, perhaps because, to become money, desire must denature its vehicle. Skin, therefore, all but turns inside out, peeling back from its oral and vaginal mouths in a maximization of the tactile, but in the context of a "dying fish," the liquid effort to engulf and encircle proves inseparable from the horror of the "cheap idea" that sells *Sanctuary*.[34]

It would be accurate to describe this kind of writing as hate speech, but only if one identifies what it hates. The ready answer—Temple's desire, and by extension, female desire more generally—may at the last be insufficient. In the Grotto, drunk and waiting with Popeye for Red, Temple "thought that perhaps she had passed out and that it had already happened. She could hear herself saying I hope it has. I hope it has. Then she believed it had and she was overcome by a sense of bereavement and of physical desire. She thought, It will never be again, and she sat in a floating swoon of agonised sorrow and erotic longing, thinking of Red's body, watching her hand holding the empty bottle over the glass" (237). "It," the most prominent word in the passage, recurs five times, shifting as it recurs. If, at first usage, "it" addresses the death of Red, killed by Popeye, one might expect that by its fifth usage Red-dead (the referent) would take the personal form "he" (as in "[he who] will never be again"). Arguably, Red had always been a substitute phallus, and therefore an "it." But if so, the first "it" shifts, referring not only to Red's killing but to the scene in Reba's room. Further, given the capacity of any substitute both to fill in for and to add to that for which it is a supplement, Red's phallus ("it") necessarily carries with it Popeye's corncob. Pronouns, because they shift, may also stretch. If the semantic reach of "it" includes at its outer edge the triangle on the bed and, in a further subsemantic whisper, the pairing in the barn, then that for which Temple grieves necessarily changes. For what, in the world of "it," does she "swoon"? For Red, or for the triangle? And does her "agonised sorrow" extend agony towards cob and barn, as Temple watches her hand holding another dry prosthesis? Before attempting a troubled answer, I shall introduce a complex of intertexts that will change the nature of the question (for what does Temple grieve and long?) by shifting the subject who mourns, and therefore the object of that mourning.

Given that Faulkner conceived and revised *Sanctuary* even as he completed *The Sound and the Fury* and wrote *As I Lay Dying*, I find it difficult not to read *Sanctuary* as arising from and extending (rather than as simply alluding to) its co-texts. The first sighting of Temple's "squatting swirl of knickers" (28) exists for me in relation to "the muddy seat" of Caddy's "drawers," as the image of her undergarment initiates Benjy's consciousness.[35] Similarly, Temple's "it," in its problematic relation to a moment or moments of penetration, contains Addie Bundren's dying memory of becoming "unvirgin": "I would think: The shape of my body where I used to be a virgin is in the shape of a and I couldn't think *Anse*, couldn't remember *Anse*."[36] Temple "couldn't think [*Red*], couldn't remember [*Red*]": her "it," finally the space of her raped virginity (that "it" which "will never be again"), finds an explanatory and relational place in the space within Addie's text—the space of the hymen that for Mr. Compson, in *Absalom, Absalom!* (1936), must "depend upon its loss . . . to have existed at all," "must incorporate in itself an inability to endure in order to be precious."[37]

But I run far ahead of myself and must backtrack to "it" as a shifting reference to something that Temple has lost and for which she longs erotically. In 1933, in an unpublished introduction to a planned edition of *The Sound and the Fury* that did not appear, Faulkner describes his own experience of ecstatic loss while writing the Benjy section: "that emotion definite and physical and yet nebulous to describe: that ecstasy, that eager and joyous faith and anticipation of surprise which the yet unmarred sheet beneath my hand held inviolate and unfailing, waiting for release. It was not there in As I Lay Dying [sic]."[38] An "unmarred sheet," in the context of ecstatic writing, sets paper and bed linen in metaphoric tension, thereby easing "marr[i]ed" from marred and linking the ink that marries and mars the sheet (black on white) to racialized semen. That the release of such a semantically complex constellation waits in "anticipation" commits the sheet to an absolute contradiction: at once marred (or written upon) and "unmarred" (or blank), a contradiction that exactly catches Benjy's consciousness, blank and yet written. Moreover, the contradiction is internal to the consciousness that it structures: Benjy's first thoughts, chronologically speaking, occur in 1898 on the evening Caddy climbs the tree to view Damuddy's corpse, thereby exposing her soiled undergarment to her brothers below. From the vantage point of the text, it is as if, for the three years between his birth in 1895 and Caddy's tree-climbing, Benjy is literally blank (an "unmarred sheet"), three years presumably spent with Caddy but empty of consciousness. Faulkner ensures that the marring will be comprehensive: Caddy's drawers "release" Benjy into language and by Biblical association into a fallen state inextricable from time, sexual knowledge, and knowledge of death. Despite which, for Benjy the blank persists—just as the marred sheet remains "unmarred"—being that preferred time towards which he seeks always to work.

To read Benjy's notional blank, hidden, unmarred within its marring, as a ubiquitous hymeneal space lodges that space within the very stuff of Faulkner's writing, the ink and paper "beneath [his] hand." Logically, therefore, having violently taken the hymen in the original version of *Sanctuary* written between January and May of 1929, when Faulkner next puts pen to paper, with *As I Lay Dying*, the hymen recurs, though in a more apparent form as an iconographic figure, the space left blank in Addie's section: "The shape of my body where I used to be a virgin is in the shape of a   and I couldn't think *Anse*, couldn't remember *Anse*." The shape created by leaving a blank requires the hymen, even as Addie fingers the vaginal space that once contained it. But in not thinking or remembering "*Anse*" (the name italicized so that Anse takes written form), Addie both restores the membrane that he took, and erases the writing that might mar-by-marrying that restored purity. In effect, she perfects a regrown hymen trick: "My aloneness had been violated and then made whole again by the violation: time, Anse, love, what you will, outside the circle."[39]

As a co-text to these texts, *Sanctuary* returns to the hymen, lodged as a "sanctuary" within a "[t]emple," but in order violently to take and sell it: in doing so, Faulkner reconstitutes the materiality of his own writing by submitting it to circulatory drives. It follows that what Faulkner hates in writing Temple is his own writing, and his transubstantiation of that writing into money ($C—M^1$). Perhaps some intimation of what he has done to his medium in drafting and revising *Sanctuary* prompts him to find Mickey Mouse in Popeye and to declare in 1932 to MGM story editor Sam Marx, "I like cartoons"; adding, presumably on the basis of his expertise, "I want to write for Mickey Mouse."[40] Any viewer of cartoons—whether serious or not—having come to Hollywood in 1932 under contract to Metro-Goldwyn-Mayer, would have watched *The Karnival Kid*, since it was the first cartoon in which Mickey speaks, and therefore required a script. At one point during his account of Popeye's serial assault on Temple, Faulkner brings rape, writing, and a hint of the cartoon in question into utterly disturbing proximity. On the day after Dr. Quinn's visit to Reba's brothel, Popeye enters Temple's room to initiate his second attempt at manual penetration: "When he put his hand on her she began to whimper. 'No, no,' she whispered, 'he said I can't now he said. . . .' He jerked the covers back and flung them aside. She lay motionless, her palms lifted, her flesh beneath the envelope of her loins cringing rearward in furious disintegration like frightened people in a crowd" (159). A metaphor, a simile, and a cinematic long shot—as though taken from above, on a high boom. (At the close of the previous paragraph, Faulkner elevates Temple's "isolation" by comparing it to that of a presumably naked body, "bound to a church steeple" [158].) First, by the metaphor, "the envelope of her loins," "loins" may refer to the abdominal region in general, but typically the referent is more anatomically specific. That an "envelope" probably carries a triangular flap lodges its "semantic impertinence"[41] firmly within Temple's genitalia, recast as a source of letters. That Temple's "flesh beneath . . . her loins" cringes "rearward" shifts the writing from vagina to anus and towards an identifiable source. Mickey's first ever line, "Hot dogs! Hot dogs!" contains the euphoric echo, "Corn Cobs! Corn Cobs!" while his second line, voiced in response to Kat Nipp's efforts to draw a crowd for Minnie's hoochie-coochie dance, runs, "It's a bumhole's stand keep yer money in your pants." Given Mickey's enunciation and the status of the "coochie" as a southern slang term for vagina, the off-rhyme "stand / pants" contains, anatomically, the corrective, "It's a bumhole *dance* keep yer money in yer pants." The substitution of anus for vagina seems apt in the cartoon context of a hot dog that drops its lower skin to reveal a bum-crack. But why the cinematic long shot of a crowd exiting in fear from the lower regions of Temple's body? Within ten pages, the text posits a plausible crowd: taking a train from Jefferson to Oxford in search of information concerning Temple's whereabouts, Benbow encounters an "unmusical" gathering (169), among whom two young men "whistle . . . broken dance rhythm[s]" and exchange jokes about "natural halitosis" (170), punched tickets, and body organs, to an "ejaculate[ed]" accompaniment worthy of Kat Nipp's song. For Nipp's, "Ya da di di di," read the students' "duh-duh-duh. . . . Eeeeeeyow," heard, very specifically by Horace as a "furious" disintegration" of language: "[T]o Horace it was like sitting before a series of printed pages turned in furious snatches, leaving a series of cryptic, headless and tailless evocations on the mind." Properly printed and flicked, a "series" of "pages" may be made to make an image move. Benbow does not "read" his imagined pages; he "sit[s] before" them, as though before a screen. What he views, "on," not in, his mind comes from "furious snatches": "snatch" like "coochie" being a slang term for vulva. By bridging the ten-page gap between the two crowds, and allowing those crowds to mingle, one may recover animated and broken "cryptic" language streaming in cartoon form from "the envelope of . . . [Temple's] loins." Yet, despite a parallel "disintegration" of words, in the loins and on the train, Horace's crowd evidences no fear. The "frightened people" and linguistic debris released, by way of analogy, from within Temple's flesh seem more readily identifiable once we appreciate the nature of the place from which they exit.

I have time only for density concerning the dense matter of the hymen at the moment of its ruin. The hymen is a cultural skin that grows at the meeting point of a real prohibition (involving the maintenance of bound labor) and a fantasmal desire (involving the eroticization of the white woman). The casting of the bound African American, whether bound as chattel or as debt peon, as the "black beast rapist" necessitates the co-construction of the white woman as a particular object of desire (embodied purity or the hymen at risk). A coercive labor structure, designed to keep black agricultural workers poor and in place, benefits from the eroticization of its "legal" and extralegal methods, since real fantasies (or shared imaginings), even as they recast bodies and desires, may more effectively hold bodies in place—on behalf of a regime of accumulation—by means of labor constraints co-woven from labor necessity, anxiety, desire, and sexual prohibition. So a coercive labor structure and a class-based structuration of desire prove mutually reinforcing, each being founded on the violence of the other. By the imagined means of a real fantasy, a plantocracy sustains itself while extending a hymeneal skin into the lines of Jim Crow.

It follows that when Faulkner speaks of the "ecstasy" of writing on a blank "sheet" (never to return) or leaves a blank within a written page to conjure a hymen long gone ("because I was three now" [Faulkner, *As I Lay Dying*, 100]), he struggles to bring to figuration, in iconic form, what Mr. Compson called the "precious" center of a plantocratic regime of accumulation in its later days, historically speaking: witness the decay of the Compson house and of the Old Frenchman Place. The "disintegration" of what I would call the hymen's precious hoard releases, therefore, not simply the debris of an economic system ("frightening" and "cryptic" enough) but also that of the substance of Faulkner's writing—both thrown into circulation from within Temple's body.

Put reductively and in conclusion: for Faulkner to monetize the precious, both of his own writing and of the economic system about which he prevalently writes, involves him in a necessary transformation of his idea of himself as an author. For Benbow read Popeye; for Popeye read Faulkner, or he who casts Temple into circulation. I would suggest that Faulkner recognizes himself through these substitutions as he revises *Sanctuary*. At the core of his revisions—a reduction in, and decentering of, the Horace Benbow materials—lies the foregrounding of a figure referred to in *Mosquitoes* (1927) as "a little kind of black man."[42] *Sanctuary* repeatedly refers to Popeye as little and black (109, 219, 220), as "smell[ing] black" (7), and as a "black presence" (121). *Mosquitoes* incidentally features a Mr. "Faulkner" (149), also "a little kind of black man" (148), "a liar by profession" who "made good money at it." Perhaps by 1931 Faulkner recognized that "to make good money at it," his writing would have to become what in a letter to his literary agent, Morton Goldman, he called "orthodox prostitution."[43] By which logic, the rape from which *Sanctuary* takes final form amounts to the rape that his own writing must undergo in order to circulate. Ergo: the corncob figures Faulkner's pen; Temple's blood, the ink; the noisy shucks in the barn, the page. Popeye writes; Red reads; Temple, the written upon (or hymen marred), circulates. Aptly, corncob and corn shuck, here recast as the material elements of Faulkner's writing—pen and page—amount also to the loud waste matter of an economic regime.

NOTES

I thank Devan Bailey for conversations concerning circulation and *Sanctuary*.

1. The theoretical prelude consists in a showing, in edited form, of Walt Disney's *The Karnival Kid* (1929), featuring Mickey Mouse's first spoken lines, addressed variously to Kat Nipp, Minnie Mouse, and some hot dogs. The full version of *The Karnival Kid* is readily available on YouTube.

2. Joseph Blotner, ed., *Selected Letters of William Faulkner* (1977; repr., New York: Vintage, 1978), 65.

3. See Joseph Blotner, *Faulkner: A Biography* (New York: Random House, 1974), 739.

4. Walter Benjamin, "Mickey Mouse," in *The Work of Art in the Age of Its Technological Reproducibility, and Other Writings on Media*, trans. Edmund Jephcott et al. (London: Harvard University Press, 2008), 338.

5. William Faulkner, *Sanctuary*, rev. ed. (1931; repr., New York: Vintage International, 1993), 159. Hereafter cited parenthetically.

6. Walter Benjamin, "The Work of Art in the Age of Its Technological Reproducibility," in *The Work of Art in the Age of Its Technological Reproducibility, and Other Writings on Media*, trans. Edmund Jephcott et al. (London: Harvard University Press, 2008), 37.

7. Ibid. On the "optical unconscious," see also Walter Benjamin, "A Little History of Photography," in *The Work of Art in the Age of Its Technological Reproducibility, and Other Writings on Media*, trans. Edmund Jephcott et al. (London: Harvard University Press, 2008), 278–79.

8. Benjamin, "Mickey Mouse," 338.

9. Robert and Helen Lynd, *Middletown* (New York: Harcourt and Brace, 1929), 80–81.

10. Karl Marx, *Capital*, vol. 1, trans. Ben Fowkes (London: Penguin, 1990), 163.

11. Ibid.

12. For the idea of the "impossible equation," see Jacques Rancière, "The Concept of Critique and the Critique of the Political Economy from the *1844 Manuscripts* to *Capital*," in Louis Althusser, Étienne Balibar, Roger Establet, Jacques Rancière, and Pierre Macherey, *Reading Capital: The Complete Edition*, trans. Ben Brewster and David Fernbach (London: Verso, 2015), 104–8.

13. Marx, *Capital*, vol. 1, 179.

14. Karl Marx, *Capital*, vol. 3 (London: Lawrence and Wishart, 1984), 393.

15. Marx, *Capital*, vol. 1, 205.
16. Ibid., 169.
17. Ibid., 165.
18. See particularly Marx, "The Metamorphoses of Commodities," *Capital*, vol. 1, 199–209, especially 199.
19. Ibid., 138.
20. Ibid., 199.
21. William Faulkner, introduction to *Sanctuary* (1932), in *Sanctuary*, rev. ed. (1931; repr., New York: Vintage International, 1993), 321, 321–22, 321.
22. While the phrase appears on the third page of the first of their Clarendon Lectures (2001), the more formal version of this material omits it. See Nibuhiro Kiyotaki and John Moore, "Evil Is the Root of All Money," *American Economic Review* 92, no. 2 (2002): 62–66.
23. Slavoj Žižek, "How Did Marx Invent the Symptom?" in *The Sublime Object of Ideology* (London: Verso, 1978), 9.
24. Ibid., 13.
25. Alfred Sohn-Rethel, *Intellectual and Manual Labour* (London: MacMillan, 1978), 59.
26. Faulkner, introduction to *Sanctuary*, 322.
27. Ibid., 322, 323, 323.
28. Marx, *Capital*, vol. 1, 208.
29. Faulkner, introduction to *Sanctuary*, 324.
30. Marx, *Capital*, vol. 1, 200.
31. Ibid., 208.
32. For Marx's phrasing of the metamorphoses attendant on circulation, see ibid., 204–8.
33. Karl Marx, *Grundrisse*, trans. Martin Nicolaus (London: Penguin, 1993), 196.
34. Temple is drunk: what I describe as her liquid effort to engulf and encircle depends on her level of liquor intake. In Memphis, she drinks almost continuously, yet despite the fact that liquor distribution and consumption (though not its manufacture) feature as the novel's primary economic activities, and as major sources of bodily distortion, they represent the larger laws of capital as structures in motion towards value. To literalize those structures as liquor, in its impact on bodies (care of the novel's cartoons of drunkenness), might be to miss or underplay Faulkner's wider preoccupation with circulatory drives and their problematic representation. I thank Jay Watson for his insights in this matter.
35. William Faulkner, "Interview with Jean Stein" (1956), in William Faulkner, *The Sound and the Fury: An Authoritative Text, Backgrounds and Contexts, Criticism*, ed. Michael Gorra, rev. ed. (1987; repr., New York: Norton, 2014), 273.
36. William Faulkner, *As I Lay Dying: An Authoritative Text, Backgrounds and Contexts, Criticism*, ed. Michael Gorra (New York: Norton, 2010), 100.
37. William Faulkner, *Absalom, Absalom!* rev. ed. (1936; repr., New York: Vintage International, 1990), 77.
38. William Faulkner, "An Introduction to *The Sound and the Fury*" in William Faulkner, *The Sound and the Fury: An Authoritative Text, Backgrounds and Contexts, Criticism*, ed. Michael Gorra, rev. ed. (1987; repr., New York: Norton, 2014), 250–51.
39. Faulkner, *As I Lay Dying*, 99.
40. Cited in Otto Friedrich, *City of Nets: A Portrait of Hollywood in the 1940s* (New York: Harper and Row, 1986), 237. See also Blotner, *Faulkner: A Biography*, 772.

41. Paul Ricoeur, "The Metaphoric Process as Cognition, Imagination, and Feeling," in *On Metaphor*, ed. Sheldon Sacks (Chicago: University of Chicago Press, 1979), 146.

42. William Faulkner, *Mosquitoes* (1927; repr., New York: Liveright, 1997), 149. Hereafter cited parenthetically.

43. Blotner, *Selected Letters of William Faulkner*, 85.

Mink Snopes's *Shavasana*: Body, Relation, and Exchange in Faulkner's Economies of Being

Ryan Heryford

At the conclusion of Faulkner's Snopes trilogy, after murdering Flem Snopes and fleeing the county, Mink Snopes finally decides to lay his body down upon the earth, "because he was free now . . . [and] anytime the notion struck him to, he could lay down . . . arranging himself, arms and legs and back, already feeling the first faint gentle tug like the durned old ground itself was trying to make you believe it wasn't really noticing itself doing it."[1] And in this posture, Mink finds that

> he could feel the . . . unnecessary bother and trouble, beginning to creep, seep, flow easy as sleeping; he could almost watch it, following all the little grass blades and tiny roots, the little holes the worms made, down and down into the ground already full of the folks that had the trouble but were free now, so that it was just the ground and the dirt that had to bother and worry and anguish with the passions and hope and skeers, the justice and the injustice and the griefs, leaving the folks themselves easy now, all mixed and jumbled up comfortable and easy so wouldn't nobody even know or even care who was which anymore, himself among them, equal to any, good as any, brave as any, being inextricable from, anonymous with all of them. (720–21)

I reflect most on this passage in my own pose of rest, what in the practice of hatha yoga is referred to as *shavasana*, or "corpse pose," when, after a strenuous workout, the body releases from itself, lying flat upon the floor below, arms and legs out long, feeling its own weight supported by the earth entirely, each point of contact dissolving, free from any assembled notion of a thinking self, enmeshed into anonymity with the heat and breath of those who rest beside it.

It may seem odd to bring up yoga in a collection titled *Faulkner and Money*. And while we'd be hard pressed to imagine William Faulkner stretched out on an exercise mat, I have no doubt that he'd have relished satirizing the ironic rise of this ancient Indian meditative practice as the exercise routine par excellence in neoliberal pathways from Oxford to Hollywood. Indeed, despite an often-inflated rhetoric of minimalist asceticism, one only need check the price of membership for a local Bikram class or visit a Lululemon athletic apparel shop to recognize the networks of commodity fetishism and class privilege shaping many yogic ventures throughout the United States. Additionally, with their role in reorienting large communal spaces as capital-bearing exercise rooms, yoga businesses continue to spread across the forefront of urban gentrification. It would not be difficult to picture, perhaps, somewhere in this country, a Snopes-branded Pilates studio.

Yet, despite its entanglement in neoliberal consumer practices, the final resting pose of most yogic disciplines, *shavasana*, seems to bely the individuation underwriting our dominant economy of accumulation and exchange. To reach *shavasana*, as Mink Snopes demonstrates, is to find the body "all mixed and jumbled up," "equal to any" and "anonymous with all of them." It is this vision of the body, both *absent of* and *more than* the presumably unified self that it contains, that offers us the deepest insight into economic relations within and beyond Faulkner's Yoknapatawpha.

Echoing the sentiments of many scholars before him, André Bleikasten has argued that the body is the last site for possibility in Faulkner's fiction. In a reading of *Sanctuary*, he suggests:

> There is no point in looking to [bodies] for signs of interiority or transcendence. They contain no presence, no mystery, other than that of their reproduction and their extinction. What dignity could there be for such bags of skin riddled with holes? The bodies . . . don't know how to hold themselves up or to hold themselves back. Everything pushes them to reveal themselves shamelessly . . . to deliver their grubby secrets. Disgorging, bleeding, drooling, spitting, sweating—through all of this discharge and oozing, the skin endlessly exhibits its misery and heralds its future as carrion.[2]

Indeed, a survey of many of Faulkner's most heralded texts would lead one to concur. When Peabody visits the lifeless body of Addie Bundren, he finds not the site of an anterior humanity, but a "tenement or a town," "a bundle of rotten sticks," a lamp deserted of oil and flame.[3] Shaken from reminiscent nostalgia, Jason Compson envisions modern bodies as "diffused and scattered creatures drawn blindly limb from limb from a grab bag and assembled."[4] Quentin Compson reflects upon his own body as "an empty hall echoing with sonorous defeated names . . . not a being, an entity . . . [but] a commonwealth . . . a barracks filled with stubborn back-looking ghosts" (Faulkner, *Absalom*, 7). While they may not transcend, Faulkner's bodies do persist, offering a subaltern articulation of the human that might best be defined as flesh. And flesh is everywhere in the novels, from Thomas Sutpen's white supremacist fantasy of "bearing more than . . . any bones and flesh could or should" be asked to stand (205), to Eula Varner's monstrous grace, read as misogynist spectacle, with "too much of leg, too much of breast, too much of buttock, too much of mammalian female meat."[5]

As Maurice Merleau-Ponty reminds us, flesh "is not matter, is not mind, is not substance," but nonetheless it necessarily constitutes *being* and additionally, with its privileging of parts over wholes, urges us to reconsider mythologies of the organized body as the site for a unified and stable personhood.[6] Born in relation to its outsides, flesh creates what Elizabeth Grosz refers to as a "new ontology, which supersedes the ontological distinction between the animate and the inanimate," disrupting that segregation of reason from embodiment that aggressively "positions one kind of subject (white, male, capitalist) in the position of superiority over others."[7] Drawing from Sylvia Wynter's distinctions between a wholly decolonized humanity and the coloniality of Man, Alexander Weheliye celebrates flesh's deconstructive potential as "the ether that holds together the world of Man while at the same time forming the condition of possibility for this world's demise."[8] And in dominant Western epistemologies that often conflate the divisions of bodies and personhood, flesh, as Hortense Spillers suggests, haunts us as "that zero degree of social conceptualization that does not escape concealment under the brush of discourse, or the reflexes of iconography."[9] To *be* in one's flesh, rather than in one's body, thus implies that personhood is born from the temporal antecedents of diversification and responsive to the social and economic conditions of place.

The flesh must likewise respond to certain conditions of history and its residues, where rendering a body as flesh, far from discursive sleights of hand or the luxuries of physical exercise, often required a violent coercive apparatus, which Spillers locates within "the calculated work of iron, whips, chains, knives, the canine patrol, the bullet."[10] Borne from technologies of dispossession, forced migration and enslavement, the flesh not only testifies to this human history but demands the acknowledgment of its continued iterations. Spillers asks whether the "phenomenon of marking and branding actually 'transfers' from one generation to another, finding its various symbolic substitutions in an efficacy of meanings that repeat the initiating moments" and thus rendering black diasporic personhood as entangled within a *hieroglyphics of the flesh* "whose severe disjunctures come to be hidden to the cultural seeing by skin color."[11] If, as Merleau-Ponty suggests, flesh is neither "a color [n]or a thing, therefore, [but] a difference between colors and things,"[12] the epidermal objectification of such a phenomenology beckons us to engage the flesh within a continued history of white supremacist terrorism in the United States, which seeks to instill and naturalize "a logic of social organization that produces regimented, institutionalized, and militarized conceptions of hierarchized 'human' difference."[13]

Faulkner was intimately familiar with such histories. As Richard Godden notes, in the cultural narratives infused within Yoknapatawpha world building, "dependency cuts two ways," where the white landowning class and its inheritors in Faulkner's novels, "owing their substance to black labor, are blacks in whiteface."[14] To engage this racialized mimicry through the black feminist vocabulary of Spillers situates Faulkner's predominantly white protagonists and narrators in a crisis of ontological ambiguity, where both their individuated subjectivities and their whiteness become contested by precarious transgression into a radical new phenomenology where "the-individual-in-mass and the mass-in-the-individual mark an iconic thickness: a concerted function whose abiding centrality is embodied in the flesh."[15] Flesh expands through contact with its social and environmental surroundings and is therefore numerous. These indiscernible, overlapping assemblages that arise when reconsidering the mass-in-the-individual present a direct challenge to economies of exchange that would otherwise rely on contained and fixed units of difference, hierarchy, and, subsequently, value, as well as the presumably stable and discrete subjects who perform them. As Monique Allewaert puts it, to exist in the flesh "challeng[es] capitalism within the realm of the quantitative by treating quantity as an expression of a physical, rhythmic, and fundamentally relational singularity that exceeds and also disrupts the money form's claim that a quantity is a flatly numeric measure."[16] Like the act of *shavasana*, considering the body as flesh helps us recognize ourselves embroiled in processes of touch, feel, and the overlapping proximity of our immersive environs. Relation, in this case, no longer amenable to narratives of exchange, emerges as a practice where bodies and their parts infiltrate the broader terrain of networks that they both comprise and decompose. Relation is an enmeshment that disavows all opportunities for exchange, and the act of *shavasana* dissolves any concentrated subject positions acquiescent to capitalist logic, as the body now lays itself down beside, among, and within its socioecological environs.

I want to be cautious here—when building a theoretical register that appears to occlude subjectivity in the name of collective, anticapitalist ontologies—not to obscure the very real histories of loss and violence that constitute the canon from which I draw. To be clear, I am not suggesting that yogic practices of *shavasana*, Faulkner's fiction, and the violent mechanisms of enfleshment embedded in colonization and human enslavement can be placed into any relation of equivalence. Rather, by applying the revisions of black feminist theorists and scholars of decolonization like Wynter, Weheliye, and Spillers to the embodied phenomenology of Merleau-Ponty, I hope to engage Faulkner's narrative histories of Yoknapatawpha through a theoretical lens that considers "what it means to be human during and in the aftermath of the transatlantic slave trade, and the imagination of liberation in the future anterior tense of the NOW."[17] To find Faulkner's characters in *shavasana* is not, then, to find them at rest. Rather, *shavasana*, in this revisionist phenomenology, entails a rigorous engagement with the archives of personhood in hopes of excavating another vision of humanity, an undertaking that, amidst the current crises posed by our expansionist economies of hierarchy and exchange, appears ever more urgent.

While we find Mink Snopes in *shavasana* only at the conclusion of *The Mansion*, there are many other instances in Faulkner's fiction where characters experience their bodies as flesh, in scenes both horrifying and illuminating, disrupting the economies of containment, difference, and exchange in which their subjectivities were implicated. In the remainder of this chapter, I will consider a few distinct instances occurring over a century apart in Faulkner's narrative history, including Thomas Sutpen's voyage to Haiti in 1824 and Darl Bundren's crossing of the Yoknapatawpha River during the Mississippi Flood of 1927, with the hopes of illustrating the long-spanning and continuous role of what I call "bodies in *shavasana*" as precarious sites of possibility, where characters are forced to redefine and reinhabit new modes of personhood amidst the historical shifts from economies of relation to economies of exchange.

In his arguably ludicrous suppression of a plantation revolt in postrevolutionary Haiti, Thomas Sutpen subdues the rioters, not with his body, but with his flesh,

> maybe by yelling louder, maybe by standing, bearing more than they believed any bones and flesh could or should (should, yes: that would be a terrible thing: to find flesh to stand more than flesh should be asked to stand); maybe at last they themselves turning in horror and fleeing from the white arms and legs shaped like theirs and from which blood could be made to spurt and flow as it could from theirs and containing an indomitable spirit which should have come from the same primary fire which theirs came from but which could not have, could not possibly have. (Faulkner, *Absalom*, 205)

There exists a compelling body of commentary on Faulkner's historical inconsistencies in this scene whose arguments I won't reiterate here other than to acknowledge that Sutpen's improbable Haitian voyage—undertaken twenty years after the revolution—continues to inspire productive insights from historical materialist scholars engaging late-modernist visions of a hemispheric South.[18] What I am most interested in, rather, are the analytics of existence in postrevolutionary Haiti that seem to force Thomas Sutpen's flesh to endure "more than flesh should be asked to stand."

As a legal body in Haiti, Thomas Sutpen, in the flesh, would have been subject to Jean Baptiste-Riché's 1816 constitution, which revived much of the language from Toussaint L'Overture's original document, including the opening declaration, which acknowledges "the Supreme Being, before whom all mortals are equal, and who has scattered so many species of beings over the surface of the earth, with the sole goal of manifesting his glory . . . through the diversity of works."[19] As many scholars of the Haitian revolution have noted, L'Overture's preamble, despite obvious reflections on other transatlantic Enlightenment-era texts, uses particular language to articulate a measure of equality for a diversity of "species of beings," detouring from the liberal humanism of other early nationalisms as it demonstrates awareness of the colonial legacy on which Western human rights ultimately relied.[20] Additionally, while it is popularly known that the Haitian Constitution of 1801 forbade white male ownership of any land or property, it also exempted German and Polish citizens, as well as white women, from this clause and designated that all Haitians, regardless of physiognomic signification, would henceforth be known by "la dénomination générique de noirs" or the now-cultural and national term "black."[21]

While Quentin Compson muses over the "white arms and legs" and the "indomitable spirit" that he traces to some other primary fire, I would argue that such rhetorical renderings may have more to do with what Aliyyah Abdur-Rahman has referred to as the white narrators' refusal to face histories that would challenge their faith in racial caste.[22] If we read against such fantasy, we might come to a different interpretation of Sutpen's flesh, where yelling and screaming spawn not from an indomitable spirit but as result of what he unconsciously recognizes as the crisis posed to colonial ontology by postrevolutionary Haiti.

Inspired by Colin Dayan's writings on vodou and the formation of Haitian civil subjectivities, Monique Allewaert argues that the legal persons of Haiti's first constitutions were constructed from spiritual practices that refused "the expectation that a body is an empty vessel whose animation is secondary and effected through the exterior and dematerialized force of the spirit" in favor of a concept of the body "in relation to physical and historical forces" in "a rhythmic plenitude that syncopates with other rhythms."[23] To consider the body as such negates the Cartesian dualism of Enlightenment humanism and in turn offers a vision of personhood that acknowledges the flesh's entanglement in its social, economic, and ecological environs. These ontological analytics of diasporic African communities in Haiti also influenced a range of American and European botanists, naturalists, and medical scientists, like Alexander von Humboldt, Benjamin Rush, and Benjamin Barton, who reframed them into a philosophy called vitalist materialism, which suggested that atoms, heretofore invisible tissue particles, and bodily fluids like phlegm, urine, menstrual blood, and semen could be attributed to an agency apart from and superseding their organization within bodies. Vitalist materialism would radically challenge both the humanist dimensions of liberalism and the value-exchange paradigms of capitalism, proposing instead "an ontology in which *combining* and not *being* was the first principle."[24] In the plantation economies of the early United States, however, where capital circulated through the violent maintenance of difference, vitalist materialism was quickly demoted from existential philosophy to sham science, and its Haitian antecedents, insofar as they were not absorbable into "end-oriented" and commercially driven global trade networks, were deemed "'fetishistic' in the pejorative sense."[25]

Nevertheless, and contrary to Barbara Ladd's account of racial ambiguity in southern literature as representing the recalcitrant South's inability "to accomplish the transcendence of history that was required before [it] could be effectively redeemed,"[26] I would offer an alternate reading of Sutpen's journey to postrevolutionary Haiti as a productive site for meditation on the possibilities afforded by vitalist materialism, the Haitian constitution, and other archived visions of ontological uncertainty, wherein we are drawn toward communities of entangled relation apart from the violent transactions of exchange, accumulation, and collapse that structure the remainder of *Absalom, Absalom!*

This is not to suggest that Thomas Sutpen finds any sort of *shavasana*. If there exists some newly startled consciousness, some terrifying recognition of the entangled relationality of his own flesh—what Spillers might call a "second birth"—it takes the form not of creative political imaginings but rather of an entrenchment in the orthodoxy of difference and hierarchy.[27] He responds to this unsettling ambiguity by standing and yelling louder than all those surrounding him, a stance still evidently popular in white supremacist politics today.[28] In flight from this moment of *shavasanic* terror, Sutpen fully installs himself in the reactionary terrorism of white American identification and dedicates himself to realizing that iconic monument to the human-as-Man, Sutpen's Hundred. Finding *shavasana* in Faulkner's fiction instead requires the courage to confront uncertain relations that exceed our economies of fixed subject positions, enforced via our strict culture of coercion. To seek out such bodies in Yoknapatawpha, one might look toward the outskirts of town: the hospitals, the prisons, the asylums, the bottom of a riverbed.

Over a century after Sutpen's Haitian voyage, journeying toward Jefferson to bury his mother already "dead these ten days" (Faulkner, *As I Lay Dying*, 43), Darl Bundren is swept downstream in the Great Mississippi Flood of 1927. Later, watching the bodies of Jewel and Vernon from the shore as they wade through half-torn currents, Darl discovers that they "do not appear to violate the surface at all; it is as though it had severed them both at a single blow, the two torsos moving with infinitesimal and ludicrous care upon the surface. It looks peaceful, like machinery does after you have watched it and listened to it for a long time. As though the clotting which is you had dissolved into the myriad original motion, and seeing and hearing in themselves blind and deaf; fury in itself quiet with stagnation" (163–64). In this emergent space between Eric Sundquist's reading of *As I Lay Dying* as "obsessively concerned with problems of disembodiment" and Jay Watson's commitment to "the recalcitrant materiality" of bodies across the broad register of southern fiction, there exists a vision of the (extra)embodied, *shavasanic* body, lying severed beneath the flood.[29] Darl, whose eyes we are told were once "full of the land all the time" (36), materializes the fluid rush over and across his body as "something huge and alive" (141), with the power to dissolve his being "into the myriad original motion" where "seeing and hearing" become "blind and deaf." Susan Scott Parrish marks this experience as Darl's "contact with an intense vitalism" in which his flesh unravels into networked ecologies and environmental histories reaching across and beyond Yoknapatawpha County.[30] That he sees bodies in parts as opposed to wholes, much like the vital materialists and the authors of the Haitian constitutions, is not, I would argue, a negation of Darl's own historical moment but rather reflects many of the anxieties generated by shifting bodily visions and concurrent economic relations in the United States during the early twentieth century.

Following Ross Granville Harrison's first artificial tissue culture in 1907 and Harrison's declaration that "each of the elements . . . of our bodies lives without doubt a little for us, but . . . above all for themselves," American medical science once again began to see bodies not as contained, organized units but as loose assemblages comprised of hyperindividuated cells to be altered and rearranged like peaceful machinery.[31] Patricia Chu has argued that Faulkner's fiction, like that of many of his contemporaries, worked to address these new views of organic life as amenable to emergent technologies of governance.[32] Where Chu invokes early twentieth-century biopolitical science in order to situate Faulkner as a distinctly *modern* writer, however, I hope by juxtaposing Darl's underwater immersion with Sutpen's Haitian voyage to suggest that these bodies in *shavasana* have continued to haunt American cultural politics during moments of economic upheaval, signaling subaltern routes apart from our reiterated economies of exchange.

As Thomas Sutpen struggles to revive his design in a declining postbellum plantation economy where difference and hierarchy must once again reconfigure, Darl Bundren is likewise enveloped in changing conditions of being and belonging, which, as Jay Watson notes, came in the modern era "to emphasize forms of abstract personhood and disembodied or 'anesthetized' subjectivity," reflecting both the ideological mandates of liberalism and the coming agrarian transformations of the Agricultural Adjustment Act, which rapidly shifted southern economics from the management of physical labor to the management of speculative markets.[33] As Richard Godden notes, "to modernize itself the southern landowning class, and Faulkner as its contemporary and historian, had to experience its lived forms—face, skin, sex, land, language—as archaic limits, available either for recuperation (modernity refused) or negation (modernity accepted as 'creative destruction')."[34] With his body *already* negated as flesh, Darl Bundren cannot modernize through passive acceptance of these aggressive exchange economies. He is not interested in new teeth, bananas, or graphophones. Rather, like the disillusioned Ike McCaslin before him, Darl comes to view property ownership as always already incompatible with any true economics of relation. Unlike Ike, however, Darl doesn't stop with disavowal. Rather, with his body in *shavasana*, Darl begins to develop a powerful and destructive anarchy culminating in that other disaster underwriting Faulkner's self-proclaimed tour de force, fire.

Darl's *shavasanic* act situates him within a longer turn-of-the-century Mississippi history of an anticapitalist populism that was clandestinely, if not explicitly, racialized. As southern historians have shown, Mississippi barn burnings between 1880 and 1930 quickly became iconic signifiers of a dispossessed tenantry's revolt against property ownership, including, necessarily, its racialized architecture of social relations, first drafted within the plantation system and later realigned to the economies of value and exchange underwriting the reconstructing South.[35] Coercive retaliation against these rebellious acts would conversely galvanize the militancy of white supremacist state infrastructure, from the extralegal but nevertheless juridically sanctioned lynchings of black bodies to an exorbitant rise in prison and asylum populations. Like Thomas Sutpen before him, Darl Bundren's vital enfleshment situates him in a relationality of being that is unamenable both to the exchange paradigms of market capitalism and to the entailed networks of racial interpellation. Unlike Sutpen, however, Darl refuses to repress willfully this newly enfleshed, expansive body, signaling a transgression incompatible with Jefferson's civil society. For Yoknapatawphans to continue the mythology of Man, Darl must be locked away.

To consider *As I Lay Dying* only so far as the novel's ominous conclusion would situate Darl's act of "creative destruction" within strict Marxian parameters, as "the violent destruction of capital, not by relations external to it, but rather as a condition of its self preservation . . . in which advice is given to be gone and to give room to a higher state of social production."[36] Under this reading, the already contained flames and their well-disciplined suppression enact what Richard Godden might refer to as an autochthonous peasantry's transition from land relations undermediated by capital to a fully infiltrated and integrated economy of exchange.[37] Darl, as an agent of both radical possibility and abject disability becomes what Godden, via Antonio Gramsci, diagnoses as a "morbid symptom" of the *interregnum*, whose temporal and existential dilemma is generated "precisely [by] the fact that the old is dying and the new cannot be born."[38] Yet just as the flesh asks us to reconsider the presumably unified constitution of bodies, I wonder what possibilities arise when we disassemble the linearity of Faulkner's novels and privilege instantaneous moments like Sutpen's Haitian uprising and Darl's burning barn as independent elements in the cosmology of Yoknapatawpha.

To read *As I Lay Dying* as beginning with Darl's immersion in the flooded river bottom and ending with the ignition of Gillespie's property affords a more utopian vision, what Georges Bataille once referred to as poetry's "creation by means of loss," wherein destruction necessarily entails a magnificent release of "radiance," a waxing flame across the Mississippi hillside.[39] Darl's telepathic musings throughout the journey might therefore invoke manifestations of what Deleuze and Guattari call the minor narrative, which "a minority constructs within a major language" to effect the "deterritorialization of languages, the connection of the individual to a political immediacy, and the collective assemblage of annunciation."[40] If this reading of Darl's *shavasanic* act of radiantly destructive property disavowal is not convincingly utopian, I do hope that, at the very least, it represents a crack in the sealed ontologies of Man and offers a critical questioning of self-contained theories of capitalism that, even at their most ardently contested, seem to reiterate and reinforce the exchange economy as a totalizing, foregone conclusion.

In spite of my attempts to reimagine Gillespie's burning barn as a site of political possibility, any reader by this point will likely note that bodies in *shavasana* do not usually fare well in the work of William Faulkner. Thomas Sutpen is cut down, Darl is locked away, and we can only imagine what strange torments await the traveling Mink Snopes. Nevertheless, if, as Sharon Cameron has argued, one of the most important themes in American literature is the relation of a body to its surroundings, Faulkner's bodies offer us a window into precarious ontological economies beyond systems of exchange.[41] In these fragile and momentary glimpses, we see states of being dispersed, envisioned as flesh, and radical possibility shines through, before the fire is extinguished and the revolution suppressed.

But how do such radical instantaneity and precarious fluctuation align with what appears to be one of Faulkner's most restive, tranquil, and conclusive passages, Mink Snopes's final *shavasana*? As close readers of the Snopes cosmos have likely already noted, Mink's corpse pose reflects the residues of an earlier moment in the ledgers of Yoknapatawpha, where another member of the prolific clan, Ike Snopes, while traversing the hillsides on an amorous voyage with his bovine companion, sees the recurrent sunrise over the flatlands below, only to discover that

> dawn, light, is not decanted onto earth from the sky, but instead is from the earth itself suspired. Roofed by the woven canopy of blind annealing grassroots and the roots of trees, dark in the blind dark of time's silt and rich refuse—the constant and unslumbering anonymous worm-glut and the inextricable known bones—Troy's Helen and the nymphs and the snoring mitred bishops, the saviors and the victims and the kings—it wakes, up-seeping, attritive in uncountable creeping channels: first, root; then frond by frond, from whose escaping tips like gas it rises and disseminates and stains the sleep-fast earth with drowsy insect-murmur; then, still upward-seeking, creeps the knitted bark of trunk and limb where, suddenly louder leaf by leaf and dispersive in diffusive sudden speed, melodious with the winged and jeweled throats, it upward bursts and fills night's globed negation with jonquil thunder. (Faulkner, *The Hamlet* 200–1)

The prelapsarian currents entwining these two scenes, separated by over four decades, demand our attention, as do the gravitational contrasts between the two *shavasanas*, which offer interesting revelations about the ground upon which each body lies. Where Mink feels a "faint gentle tug" that creeps and seeps "down and down into the ground" (Faulkner, *The Mansion*, 720), Ike finds a light suspiring, which "rises and disseminates" from the earth itself, "upward-seeking." Like Darl's baptismal submersion, Ike's mid-dawn revelations depict a nonhuman ecology that is far from fixed or passive, neither idyllic canvas nor sealed chest. In a "corporeal" reading of Ike's transspecies affair, Colin Dayan notes that "in order to exhume and put back into history whatever had been ignored or denied, Faulkner surrenders his prose to the *excrescence.*"[42] Ike, as both historian and historiographer, bears witness to epochal, accumulative history as an "upseeping," vital force, dynamic and alive, whose dispersive speeds, "unslumbering" and staining gasses, and negating "jonquil thunder" suggest a hospitality toward human inhabitants that remains tenuous.

These spatial and temporal inversions could simply be read as perceptual indicators of Ike's "idiocy," and indeed, the disorientation here is reminiscent of Benjy Compson's narrative passages in *The Sound and the Fury.* Likewise, Ike's sensuous idiosyncrasies align him with Darl Bundren, whose perceptual abilities create discomfort for those other Yoknapatawphans reliant on the clean divisions between self and other. Vernon Tull's anxieties in returning Darl's gaze, for example—which Tull says feels "like he had got into the inside of you, someway. Like somehow you was looking at yourself and your doings outen his eyes" (Faulkner, *As I Lay Dying*, 123)—are echoed by V. K. Ratliff's own horror when peeping through the hole in the back of Mrs. Littlejohn's barn, where "it was as though it were himself inside the stall with the cow, himself looking out of the blasted tongueless face at the row of faces watching him who had been given the wordless passions but not the specious words" (Faulkner, *The Hamlet*, 217). Such transgressive, vital sensuality marks Ike, like Darl, as already outside recognizable networks of accumulation and exchange. As Joseph Gold suggests, Ike situates himself as "the antithesis of Snopesism. Not only is the episode an idyll, and a tribute to love, which exists only in an idiot in a Snopes world, but it is also a portrait of the innocent, the anti-materialist."[43] Indeed, if we hold true to Marx's assessment of exchange as lobotomizing the sensuous from commodities, to the point where "not an atom of matter enters into the objectivity of the commodity," then Ike's affair with Houston's cow, an animal whose domestication prefigures its role in the market economy, suggests that while money may not buy love, one can make love to that which was previously viewed within the realm of the monetary.[44] We see this most clearly when I. O. Snopes, in attempting to dodge the financial burdens necessary in disciplining Ike back into a world of exchange—forcing him to consume his lover as flesh—offers a bizarre inversion of Merleau-Ponty's original precepts, suggesting that "a cow is a heap different things besides the meat. Yet it's all that same cow. It's got to be, because it's some things that cow never even had when it was born, so what else can it be but the same thing?" (Faulkner, *The Hamlet*, 224).

Ike's "mowing head turned backward" (90) and "thick thighs about to burst from the overalls" nod uncomfortably both toward trans-species ontologies and toward aesthetic partnerships with other human characters, most notably Eula Varner, whose "flesh itself," according to Charles Mallison in *The Town*, "would burn her garments off," and whose aggressive commodification by the Jefferson patriarchy leads to her forlorn realization that in the networks of sexual exchange one of the few possible routes to reflective being is the very negation of the body itself.[45] But there are less-noted parallels between Ike's interspecies romance and other human-animal relationships in *The Hamlet*. Consider Ike's primary persecutor, Jack Houston, whose own Man-hound partnership signals an inverse ontology, wherein "his very savageness toward the dog had recalled him to something like sanity" (208), leading him, much like Thomas Sutpen before him, to curse out loud, not in rage but in "savage contempt and pity for all blind flesh capable of hope and grief" (208). As Houston hunts Ike across the Yoknapatawpha countryside, the lines drawn between autochthony and habitation, indigeneity and colonization, savagery and civility seem to twist, entangle, deflate. And when he comes to his own *shavasana*, Houston finds not a pose of rest and release, but a violent repudiation from the earth itself, where "pain blast[ed] like lightning across the gap . . . from the other direction: not from himself outward, but inward toward himself out of all the identifiable lost earth. Wait, wait, he said. Just go slow at first, and I can take it. But it would not wait. It roared down and raised him, tossed and spun" (241). That Jack Houston, a character so violently entrenched within the networks of hierarchy, difference, and exchange constituting his own economic privilege, should feel the vital "pain blast like lightning" from an "identifiable lost earth" seems to suggest that imposed crises of the flesh force human bodies into relation not only with other human bodies but also with the very earth itself, an earth that, while identifiable, has been transformed, "lost," or altered by its own dynamic relations.

While Mink feels an earth tug "easy as sleeping" (Faulkner, *The Mansion*, 720), and Ike senses his own body atop the "anonymous worm-glut and the inextricable known bones" (Faulkner, *The Hamlet*, 200), there are other narrative ellipses throughout the Snopes trilogy where non-human ecologies offer a less mythic, less anonymous account of their socioenvironmental relations. For instance, before Ike finds his interspecies *shavasana*, he must first traverse

> the rich, broad, flat river-bottom country and [enter] the hills—a region which topographically was the final blue and dying echo of the Appalachian Mountains. Chickasaw Indians had owned it, but after the Indians it had been cleared where possible for cultivation, and after the Civil War, forgotten save by small peripatectic sawmills which had vanished too now, their sites marked only by the mounds of rotting sawdust which were not only their gravestones but the monuments of a people's heedless greed. (190)

Ike's odyssey reflects the earth's own genealogical movement across different social relations underlying various stages of capitalism. As Chickasaw "ownership" is denied through the clearing practices of settler colonialism, the labor-bound relations of agricultural production are likewise supplanted by what anthropologist Anna Tsing calls "salvage" capitalism, a process of accumulation that relies not on production or labor alone but also and more importantly on the extraction of what is often deemed *nonlife* (oil, gas, coal, wood): a regime here marked by its own residual archeology of "peripatectic saw mills" and other monuments of "heedless greed."[46] To attend to these shifting dynamics of socioecological relation requires that our attention turn from the labor-specific foci of traditional historical materialism to what Elizabeth Povinelli describes as the recognition that "life is not, after all, merely in labor or, for that matter, in life. The key to the massive expansion of capital was the discovery of a force of life in dead matter, or life in the remainders of life: namely, in coal and petroleum. Living fuel (human labor) was exponentially supplemented and often replaced by dead fuel (the carbon remainders of previously alive entities) even as the ethical problems of extracting life from life ha[ve] been mitigated."[47] To release oneself upon the earth, "inextricable from, anonymous with all of them" (Faulkner, *The Mansion*, 721), rather than affording utopian visions of relationality, further entangles us in the heretofore unseen assemblages of extractive capitalism. Thus, when Mink surrenders to the "durned old ground itself" (721), he rests not only upon the decomposing bones of Chickasaw inhabitants, a dispossessed tenantry, and the heedless monuments of decaying sawdust, but also upon the hollowness now habiting the earth's own identifiable loss. Mink having journeyed two days south from Jefferson after killing Flem, the ground upon which he lies would likely sit along the edges of the Tinsely Oil field, a series of wellsprings discovered in

1939, one year before the publication of *The Hamlet*, that continues to emblemize Mississippi's place in the increasingly apocalyptic narratives of salvage capitalism.[48]

Far now from the luxurious, restive posture that closes most contemporary yogic practices, Faulkner's bodies in *shavasana* have led us through violent mechanisms of subjugation, coercive regimes of suppression, the entangled power structures of extractive capitalism, and into tangible, ecohuman histories that demand a repositioning of these cultural narratives within the deep time of the Anthropocene, a geological epoch wherein human activity has irreversibly impacted conditions for life on earth.[49] *Shavasana*, as a political ethic or critical analytic, directs us toward both social and geologic time scales, accompanied always by the overwhelming odds we face in our enfleshed, related lives. But, like the other, rigorous poses preceding it, *shavasana* is neither a culminating bookend nor a definitive final note. Rather, like all poses, it exists as one moment in an assembled sequence, somewhere between being and becoming, where possibility might still reside. In that instant when the body meets earth, floodtide, violent nightscape, prior to the yelling, the cursing and other sirens of the world of Man, Faulkner's bodies in *shavasana* suggest a vision of the self that is born in relation to its outsides, that cuts across the hierarchies of difference, refuses the habitation of capital, and in so doing watches the individuated body "creep, seep, flow easy as sleeping" (720) into a more expansive ethic of being.

In enfleshing and dispersing the citizens of Yoknapatawpha, I've run the risk of what Jay Watson refers to as "appealing to an abstract, monolithic theoretical body and thus in effect disembodying" Faulkner's characters and with them his fiction.[50] Despite the porosity and fungibility of flesh, the bodily assemblages that it tenuously forms are not homogeneous or universal. Rather, as my yoga teachers continue to remind me, every body is unique. I suspect they sometimes remind me of this more than my classmates. With creaky joints and shoddy coordination, my body often feels uniquely unfit for yoga. Even after a few years of practice, I still struggle to bend over and touch my toes. But, with any exercise, the goal ought never rest on pregiven ideals. Rather, in exercise, we sift through the litany of our limits, the reiterated histories of the actual, in hopes of finding those subtle and instantaneous moments of *otherwise*, the communities of being that should or could have been and that might still become. As socialists, we might call this a realistic demand for the impossible; in yoga, we call it stretching, which is, I would argue, what any great body of fiction is all about.

NOTES

1. William Faulkner, *The Mansion*, in *Novels 1957–1962*, ed. Joseph Blotner and Noel Polk (New York: Library of America, 1999), 720. Hereafter cited parenthetically.
2. André Bleikasten, *William Faulkner: A Life through Novels*, trans. Miriam Watchorn (Bloomington: Indiana University Press, 2017), 159.
3. William Faulkner, *As I Lay Dying*, rev. ed. (1930; repr., New York: Vintage International, 1990), 43. Hereafter cited parenthetically.
4. William Faulkner, *Absalom, Absalom!* rev. ed. (1936; repr., New York: Vintage International, 1990), 71. Hereafter cited parenthetically.
5. William Faulkner, *The Hamlet*, rev. ed. (1940; repr., New York: Vintage International, 1991), 111. Hereafter cited parenthetically.
6. Maurice Merleau-Ponty, *The Visible and the Invisible; Followed by Working Notes*, ed. Claude Lefort, trans. Alphonso Lingis (Evanston: IL Northwestern University Press, 1968), 139.
7. Elizabeth A. Grosz, "Merleau-Ponty and Irigaray in the Flesh," *Thesis Eleven* 36, no. 1 (1993): 54.
8. Alexander G. Weheliye, *Habeas Viscus: Racializing Assemblages, Biopolitics, and Black Feminist Theories of the Human* (Durham, NC: Duke University Press, 2014), 40.
9. Hortense J. Spillers, "'Mama's Baby, Papa's Maybe': An American Grammar Book," *Diacritics* 17, no. 2 (Summer 1987), 67.
10. Ibid.
11. Ibid.
12. Merleau-Ponty, *The Visible and the Invisible*, 132.
13. Dylan Rodriguez, *Forced Passages: Imprisoned Radical Intellectuals and the US Prison Regime* (Minneapolis: University of Minnesota Press, 2006), 3.
14. Richard Godden, *William Faulkner: An Economy of Complex Words* (Princeton, NJ: Princeton University Press, 2007), 7.
15. Spillers, "'Mama's Baby,'" 67.
16. Monique Allewaert, *Ariel's Ecology: Plantations, Personhood, and Colonialism in the American Tropics* (Minneapolis: University of Minnesota Press, 2013), 8.
17. Weheliye, *Habeas Viscus*, 39.
18. See Valérie Loichot, "Faulkner's Caribbean Geographies in *Absalom, Absalom!*" in *Faulkner's Geographies: Faulkner and Yoknapatawpha, 2011*, ed. Jay Watson and Ann J. Abadie (Jackson: University Press of Mississippi, 2015), 112–28; Farah Jasmine Griffin, "A Daughter's Geography: William Faulkner, Zora Neale Hurston, and a New Mapping of 'The Black South,'" in *Faulkner's Geographies*, 129–42; and Ryan Heryford, "Thomas Sutpen's Geography Lesson: Environmental Obscurities and Racial Remapping in Faulkner's *Absalom, Absalom!*" in *Faulkner's Geographies*, 97–111. See also Richard Godden, *Fictions of Labor: William Faulkner and the South's Long Revolution* (New York: Cambridge University Press, 1997), and John T. Matthews, "Recalling the West Indies: From Yoknapatawpha to Haiti and Back," *American Literary History* 16, no. 2 (2004): 238–62.
19. I am quoting from Sibylle Fischer's translation of the Constitution of Saint-Domingue (1801) in Fischer, *Modernity Disavowed: Haiti and the Cultures of Slavery in the Age of Revolution* (Durham, NC: Duke University Press, 2004), 275.
20. See Fischer, *Modernity Disavowed;* Laurent Dubois, *Avengers of the New World: The Story of the Haitian Revolution* (Cambridge, MA: Harvard University Press, 2004); Susan Buck-Morss, *Hegel, Haiti, and Universal History* (Pittsburgh: University of

Pittsburgh Press, 2009); and Michel-Rolph Trouillot, *Silencing the Past: Power and the Production of History* (Boston: Beacon, 1997).

21. Fischer, *Modernity Disavowed*, 275.

22. Aliyyah I. Abdur-Rahman, "'What Moves at the Margin': William Faulkner and Race," in *The New Cambridge Companion to William Faulkner*, ed. John T. Matthews (New York: Cambridge University Press, 2015), 44–59.

23. Allewaert, *Ariel's Ecology*, 139.

24. Ibid. 62.

25. Srinivas Aravamudan, *Tropicopolitans: Colonialism and Agency, 1688–1804* (Durham, NC: Duke University Press, 1999), 273.

26. Barbara Ladd, *Nationalism and the Color Line in George W. Cable, Mark Twain, and William Faulkner* (Baton Rouge: Louisiana State University Press, 1996), 31–32.

27. See Hortense J. Spillers, "'Born Again': Faulkner and the Second Birth," in *Fifty Years after Faulkner: Faulkner and Yoknapatawpha, 2012*, ed. Jay Watson and Ann J. Abadie (Jackson: University Press of Mississippi, 2016), 57–79.

28. See Donald Trump's 2016 Republican National Convention Speech, retitled by *The Atlantic*'s Yoni Appelbaum as the "I Alone Can Fix It" speech, https://www.theatlantic.com/politics/archive/2016/07/trump-rnc-speech-alone-fix-it/492557/.

29. See Eric J. Sundquist, *Faulkner: The House Divided* (Baltimore: Johns Hopkins University Press, 1983), 29; and Jay Watson, *Reading for the Body: The Recalcitrant Materiality of Southern Fiction, 1893–1985* (Athens: University of Georgia Press, 2012).

30. Susan Scott Parrish, "*As I Lay Dying* and the Modern Aesthetics of Ecological Crisis," in *The New Cambridge Companion to William Faulkner*, ed. John T. Matthews (New York: Cambridge University Press, 2015), 83. See also Susan Scott Parrish, *The Flood Year 1927: A Cultural History* (Princeton, NJ: Princeton University Press, 2017), 209–29.

31. Quoted in Hannah Landecker, *Culturing Life: How Cells Became Technologies* (Cambridge, MA: Harvard University Press, 2007), 29.

32. Patricia E. Chu, "Faulkner and Biopolitics" in *The New Cambridge Companion to William Faulkner*, ed. John T. Matthews (New York: Cambridge University Press, 2015), 59–74.

33. Watson, *Reading for the Body*, 10.

34. Godden, *William Faulkner*, 17.

35. See Richard Godden, "*As I Lay Dying*, a Horse, a Fish, Telepathy, and Economics," in *William Faulkner in the Media Ecology*, ed. Julian Murphet and Stefan Solomon (Baton Rouge: Louisiana State University Press, 2015), 240; and Albert C. Smith, "'Southern Violence' Reconsidered: Arson as Protest in Black Belt Georgia, 1865–1910," *Journal of Southern History*, 51, no. 4 (November 1985): 527–64.

36. Karl Marx, *Grundisse: Foundations of the Critique of Political Economy*, trans. Martin Nicolaus (New York: Penguin Classics, 1973), 749–50.

37. Godden, "A Horse, a Fish, Telepathy, and Economics," 256.

38. As cited in Godden, "A Horse, a Fish, Telepathy, and Economics," 244.

39. Georges Bataille, "General Economy," in *The Bataille Reader*, ed. Fred Botting and Scott Wilson (Malden, MA: Wiley-Blackwell, 1997), 171.

40. Gilles Deleuze and Felix Guattari, *Kafka: Toward a Minor Literature*, trans. Dana Polan (Minneapolis: University of Minnesota Press, 1986), 18.

41. Sharon Cameron, *The Corporeal Self: Allegories of the Body in Melville and Hawthorne* (New York: Columbia University Press, 1991), 1–13.

42. Colin Dayan, "Salvific Animality, or Another Look at Faulkner's South," in *Faulkner and History: Faulkner and Yoknapatawpha, 2014*, ed. Jay Watson and James G. Thomas, Jr. (Jackson: University Press of Mississippi, 2017), 24.

43. Joseph Gold quoted in Taylor Haygood, *Faulkner, Writer of Disability* (Baton Rouge: Louisiana State University Press, 2015), 113.

44. Karl Marx, *Capital*, vol. 1, ed. Frederick Engels, trans. Samuel Moore and Edward Aveling (London: Lawrence and Wishart, 1984), 138.

45. William Faulkner, *The Town*, in *Novels 1957–1962*, ed. Joseph Blotner and Noel Polk (New York: Library of America, 1999), 13.

46. See Anna Lowenhaupt Tsing, *The Mushroom at the End of the World: On the Possibility of Life in Capitalist Ruins* (Princeton, NJ: Princeton University Press, 2015), 63–66.

47. Elizabeth Povinelli, *Geontologies: A Requiem to Late Liberalism* (Durham, NC: Duke University Press, 2016), 167.

48. See Dudley J. Hughes, *Oil in the Deep South: A History of the Oil Business in Mississippi, Alabama, and Florida: 1859–1945* (Jackson: University Press of Mississippi, 1993), 155–70.

49. My use of the term *Anthropocene* is drawn from atmospheric chemist Paul Crutzen. For more information on this epochal concept and its uses in literary studies, see Will Steffen, Jacques Grinevald, Paul Crutzen, and John McNeill, "The Anthropocene: Conceptual and Historical Perspectives," *Philosophical Transactions of the Royal Society A: Mathematical, Physical, and Engineering Sciences* 369, no. 1938 (March 2011): 842–67; and Dipesh Chakrabarty, "The Climate of History: Four Theses," *Critical Inquiry* 35, no. 2 (Winter 2009): 197–222.

50. Watson, *Reading for the Body*, 25.

Faulkner's Stores: Microfinance and Economic Power in the Postbellum South

David A. Davis

After his encounter with the balloon-faced butler, Thomas Sutpen determines to become a powerful planter, so he goes to the West Indies, makes a fortune, and then develops a massive plantation in Mississippi with an enormous big house. This is his design, and the house is essential to its execution because it symbolizes his power. After the Civil War, he returns to his plantation to find his crops ruined, his slaves gone, most of his land sold for taxes, and his house in disrepair, and he determines to rebuild, so he opens a store. Amid the drama of the novel, the store may seem less significant than the big house, but it is critically important within the power structure of the postbellum South. Charles Aiken writes in *The Cotton Plantation South since the Civil War* that while the "big house" is the most important building on a plantation in the antebellum South, in the postbellum South "the headquarters often is an office building or is located in a related business such as a store."[1] Sutpen's store is a signifier for the postbellum southern economy. In the antebellum South, the primary forms of capital investment were land and slaves, and banks used these assets for collateral. Cotton and other commodity crops were mediums of exchange, and liquid assets, such as cash, were scarce. After the war, capital in the form of slaves was gone, but land confiscated from Confederates was returned to its previous owners, and factories in the United States, England, and Germany were desperate for cotton. Without capital to use as collateral, however, banks were reluctant to finance a new crop. While baled cotton had tangible exchange value, cotton in the field was an inherently risky investment, susceptible to drought, pests, poor management, rot, and a host of other losses. A new system of microfinance and labor exploitation developed after the war to re-establish the cotton economy, and it shifted the center of power from the plantation house to the store.

Before the Civil War, stores were not centers of power. In *Pills, Petticoats, and Plows*, a history of southern country stores, Thomas D. Clark writes, "[T]here were country stores in the antebellum South, but as a part of the whole economic picture they were of relatively minor significance."[2] Before the war, planters purchased goods and provisions through cotton factors, and most crossroads stores conducted trade with poor-white landowners on a cash basis, so they did not conduct a sufficient volume of business to negotiate deals with major East Coast wholesalers and importers, and they did not have enough political clout to leverage favorable legislation through state governments. Clark concludes that "antebellum stores never did become a functional part of southern agriculture and industry" (12). Faulkner depicts the antebellum country stores' diminished social significance in *Absalom, Absalom!* in the story of Goodhue Coldfield. Coldfield moves to Yoknapatawpha County in 1828 with his family to open a store, and while his family becomes thoroughly entangled with Thomas Sutpen, he maintains a socially marginal role in the community, according to Quentin's father. "And as he had brought his entire business to Jefferson in one wagon," Jason says,

> and this at a time when he had mother sister wife and children to support out of it, and weighed along with this that profound disinterest in material accumulation which had permitted conscience to cause him to withdraw from that old affair in which his son-in-law had involved him not only at the cost of his just profits but at the sacrifice of his original investment, his stock which had begun as a collection of the crudest necessities and which apparently could not even feed himself and his daughter from its own shelves, had not increased, let alone diversified.[3]

His store is not a lucrative concern, and Coldfield, with the exception of being a Methodist steward, is not an important member of the community. This is typical, because, as Ted Ownby explains, "store owners often seemed and felt themselves to be outsiders in the communities where they lived, and planters and farmers, especially in the antebellum period, tended to see selling goods as a frivolous and perhaps untrustworthy profession."[4]

The novel does not clearly explain how or why Sutpen becomes entangled with Coldfield. A student at the University of Virginia once asked Faulkner about the business relationship between the two characters, but Faulkner evaded the question, so we are left to speculate about the specifics of their arrangement.[5] We know that Sutpen brings two wagons full of goods to his plantation, the first filled with French-speaking slaves and the second filled with furnishings for his big house, which arouses the suspicions of the people of Jefferson. We also know that he spent his last money purchasing his land from Ikkemotubbe, so we don't know how he got the money to purchase these slaves or furnishings. Jason Compson tells Quentin that "Sutpen did not need to borrow money with which to complete the house, supply what it yet lacked, because he intended to marry it" (31), but rather than targeting the daughter of a wealthy man, he sets his sights on Goodhue Coldfield's daughter. This seems curious because Coldfield "obviously could do nothing under the sun for [Sutpen] save give him credit at a little cross-roads store" (32). Sutpen and Coldfield apparently develop a lucrative business relationship that involves some form of smuggling, which troubles Coldfield's conscience. Quentin tells Shreve that this scheme made Sutpen rich, but "nobody ever did know for certain" what they were doing (208). He explains, "It was something about a bill of lading, some way he persuaded Mr Coldfield to use his credit: one of those things that when they work you were smart and when they dont you change your name and move to Texas." A bill of lading certifies that a person is transporting goods to sale, but the core of this mysterious relationship is the type of goods that were being transported and why the goods needed to be certified.

Sutpen and Coldfield may be smuggling slaves into the country and selling them in the Delta. The book does not specifically state this as a fact, but the evidence suggests that it is likely. Article 1 section 9 of the US Constitution prohibited the importation of slaves as of 1808, and the Act Prohibiting Importation of Slaves went into effect in that year, which made slave smuggling a federal offense. It also created a lucrative black market for slaves as the rapid westward expansion of cotton plantations through Alabama and Mississippi in the 1830s created a demand for slaves. For the most part, this demand was met through the domestic slave trade, and thousands of slaves were sold from Virginia and the Carolinas to the Old Southwest. In *Freebooters and Smugglers: The Foreign Slave Trade in the United States after 1808*, Ernest Obadele-Starks estimates that between 192,500 and 786,500 slaves were smuggled into the United States between 1808 and 1863.[6] The huge range in the estimate reflects the fact that smuggling was illegal, so the numbers were not scrupulously recorded, but they indicate clear evidence that slaves were being smuggled into the country in large numbers, particularly through New Orleans, the South's largest port and busiest slave market. We know for certain that Sutpen smuggled a coffle of "imported slaves" (28) into Mississippi to build his plantation, and we know that Sutpen and Coldfield had a nefarious, secretive business relationship, and it only requires a small degree of speculation to surmise that they were using

Coldfield's bill of lading as a cover for smuggling slaves into Mississippi. If this is the case, we have to wonder why the text does not state the fact. Considering that we know almost nothing directly from either Coldfield or Sutpen, it is reasonable that it is not mentioned because none of the characters who narrate the story is personally aware of the smuggling. Nonetheless, the opening of the Civil War brings an end to Sutpen and Coldfield's business arrangement, changing the structure of southern commerce in the process.

The end of the war created an economic crisis that reshaped the southern system of finance and placed significant social and economic power in the country store. Sven Beckert describes the situation in *Empire of Cotton*: "Just as slaves had revolutionized the cotton empire, emancipation forced cotton capitalists toward their own revolution—a frantic search for new ways to organize the cotton-growing labor of the world."[7] The pressure to redevelop the system of cotton production was intense. In the nineteenth century, cotton production was the world's leading industry, cotton was America's top export, and nearly 80 percent of the world's raw cotton came from the US South. With the end of the war, global markets were clamoring for cotton, and the US treasury urgently needed to restart exports to begin paying war debts, but the infrastructure and labor markets of the cotton-producing regions were ruined. The Freedman's Bureau interceded for a time to develop new labor arrangements based on wages, but for a host of complicated reasons, sharecropping contracts became standard. Faced with the urgent need to produce a crop, southerners had land but little capital and labor but little cash.[8] When Thomas Sutpen returns to his ruined plantation, he recognizes the crisis, and he immediately sets to work rebuilding— "he would not even pause for breath before undertaking to restore his house and plantation as near as possible to what it had been" (129; emphasis removed)—but he is not the virile man he was when he ripped the plantation from the earth thirty years earlier. He "realised that he was old (he was fifty-nine) and was concerned (not afraid: concerned) not that old age might have left him impotent to do what he intended to do, but that he might not have time to do it in before he would have to die" (129; emphasis removed). Sutpen is, in effect, a synecdoche for the southern cotton economy in the wake of the war: defeated, committed to rebuild, and facing urgent pressure to produce.

Like most former planters, Sutpen converts his plantation to sharecropping to cultivate cotton. Although sharecropping is only barely mentioned in the text—specifically, when Charles Etienne Saint-Valery Bon goes to live with his wife in a cabin and "farm[s] on shares a portion of the Sutpen plantation" (169)—the evidence is apparent in how Sutpen manages the plantation. Rather than working alongside his laborers or using physical violence to coerce work as he did before the war, he uses a different means of manipulation: material goods and debt. He opens a store, but the postbellum store is completely different from the antebellum store. In the sharecropping system, the rural merchant became a financial intermediary.[9] Where planters had provided slaves with rations and paid for their own seed, tools, and other implements, postbellum landowners passed the costs for these and all other necessary items on to their laborers on credit, and the store became the nexus for labor control. The mechanism for control was the crop lien, a legally binding contract that gave the merchant control of the crop as collateral for a loan for provisions and furnishings needed to produce the crop. A sharecropper would be obligated to give the landowner, who might also be the merchant, a portion of the crop he or she produced and then pay off the loan, with interest often above 50 percent, to the merchant.[10] This payoff was called "settlement," and many sharecroppers found themselves in debt to the merchant after settlement, which obligated them to add the debt to the following year's loan. This cyclical debt is called peonage, and it effectively bound many sharecroppers into involuntary servitude. Small farmers who owned their own land also signed crop liens, mortgaging their land as collateral, and many merchants became landowners through foreclosure on these mortgages.

In the antebellum South, mastery was control, but in the postbellum South, debt was control. "As the merchant consolidated his economic power," Roger Ransom and Richard Sutch write in *One Kind of Freedom*, "he began to be viewed in a different light. The storekeeper came to be seen as an oppressor who exploited and coerced his customers and who displaced the landowner as the leader of the community."[11] Before the war, slaves were sources of labor, revenue, and capital, but after the war, sharecroppers were sources of labor and revenue. Merchants had every incentive to force workers into debt and to minimize their own costs, and merchant-landowners had every incentive to maximize their share of the crop and to force laborers into debt, which kept them in thrall to the landowners. For many landowners, furnishing charges were a major source of cash income.[12] Merchants assumed a degree of risk, however, as failed crops due to drought, infestation, or low prices on the commodities market could wipe out a year's production, but they transferred as much of their costs as possible onto the laborers to minimize their own risk. Ownby concludes that "plantation stores were thus tools that landowners used less for selling goods than for maintaining power relations" (*American Dreams in Mississippi*, 68). The crop lien system was insidious and pervasive in the postbellum South.

Quentin and Shreve, however, fail to understand the significance of Sutpen's store. As they retell Sutpen's story more than forty years later in a Harvard dorm room, Shreve picks up the narrative and portrays Sutpen after the war as pathetic, "running his little crossroads store with a stock of plowshares and hame strings and calico and kerosene and cheap beads and ribbons and a clientele of freed niggers and (what is it? the word? white what?—Yes, trash) with Jones for clerk and who knows maybe what delusions of making money out of the store to rebuild the plantation" (147). The boys are correct that the fall from largest landowner in Mississippi to crossroads merchant is immense, but they do not recognize the power inherent in the goods in Sutpen's store. Whether he is delusional or not, the store is his most realistic means of rebuilding some semblance of his plantation, and the goods he sells and the debt he leverages there give him power over the former slaves and poor whites who constitute the postbellum laboring class. Sutpen, in fact, uses the ribbons and beads in his store in a final effort to secure an heir for his plantation and complete his design, but the plan fails when Wash Jones's granddaughter, Milly, gives birth to a girl. Sutpen insults Milly, and Jones, the store clerk, murders him with a scythe. Two years later, Judith sells the store to purchase a gravestone for Charles Bon (155). Altogether, Sutpen's store lasts less than five years, from the end of the war to 1870, tumultuous years of economic disarray in the South, and the relative brevity of his foray into shop keeping may explain why Quentin and Shreve fail to recognize its significance. Sutpen's store, nonetheless, illustrates a crucial point about the economy of the postbellum South. Even after the end of slavery, plantations still exploited manual labor to produce cash crops. Cotton was a crop that required a huge labor force, so landowners could not afford to lose control over their laborers. Richard Godden states that "*Absalom, Absalom!* is a novel about dependency both as a fact of labor and as a consequent mental fact for the owning class."[13] Cotton producers like Sutpen were dependent upon cheap labor, so they had an urgent need to manufacture their workers' dependency upon them. Debt acted as the linchpin in this arrangement of forced mutual dependency.

Faulkner makes the power dynamics of the postbellum southern economy more easily discernible in *The Hamlet*. The novel is set at Will Varner's country store in Frenchman's Bend, a crossroads community built on the ruins of an antebellum plantation, the Old Frenchman Place. The plantation is gone, but Varner has acquired most of the land, primarily by leveraging mortgages on the "small shiftless . . . farms" of the area.[14] He is "the chief man of the country" (5), and "he owned most of the good land in the country and held mortgages on most of the rest. He owned the store, the cotton gin, and the combined grist mill and blacksmith shop in the village proper and it was considered, to put it mildly, bad luck for a man of the neighborhood to do his trading or gin his cotton or grind his meal or shoe his stock anywhere else" (6).[15] The plot centers on the store as the site of struggle between Varner and his son, Jody, who embody the postbellum power structure, and Flem Snopes, the son of a sharecropper, who usurps their power. As John T. Matthews explains, "Will's success owes to sharp dealing" in exploiting workers and taking advantage of their debt, but "Flem identifies a counter vulnerability, offering himself as clerk-in-training to the Varners in exchange for keeping their property off his father's hit list. The Varners lose this preliminary round."[16] The action is subtle, based on deals, debts, chicanery, and literal horse-trading, with peddler V. K. Ratliff observing and commenting on the events, and the key issue underlying the plot is the problem of class mobility in the South. Flem's rise is remarkable not only for his adroit manipulation of the economic system but also for his improbable rise from sharecropper's son to eventual bank president. His story is the postbellum equivalent of Sutpen's design.[17]

Flem Snopes is the most famous literary character to make the difficult journey from rags to riches in the literature of the early twentieth-century South. Faulkner's account of Flem Snopes corresponds with his younger brother John Faulkner's novel *Dollar Cotton*, the story of a Tennessee hill farmer, Otis Town, who builds and loses a vast alluvial empire encompassing thousands of acres of the Delta. Both stories in turn echo Stribling's Pulitzer Prize–winning novel *The Store*, in which Miltiades Vaiden swindles his business partner to take control of a store and several plantations. Critics have noticed the connections among these texts, which share a similar narrative arc from poverty to bourgeois success to tragedy.[18] Vaiden and Town are the unambiguous protagonists of their stories, which invite the reader to identify with their success and failure. Snopes's story, in contrast, is told indirectly from the perspective of the community at Varner's crossroads, foreclosing the reader's ability to identify with Flem and making him appear manipulative and callous. In most narratives of sharecropping, the landowner or furnish merchant appears as the antagonist embodying the socioeconomic forces that exploit the sharecroppers. In these three novels, however, the landowners and furnish merchants exploit the laborers, but they are also protagonists who are themselves subject to socioeconomic forces.

When the Snopes family arrives in Frenchman's Bend, Ab Snopes, Flem's father, negotiates a contract with Jody Varner, and their conversation reveals how debt operates as a form of power. Ab comes into the store to ask about a farm to rent, and he and Jody begin a calculated negotiation. Jody happens to have a new farm acquired through a foreclosure sale the week before, but he doesn't know Snopes—"he had never even heard the name before" (9)—so he knows nothing of his reputation, and Snopes is deliberately elusive. Jody asks how many hands he can put into the field, and Snopes responds, "six." This answer is a bit misleading, and "Varner sensed it even before the lifeless voice seemed deliberately to compound the inconsistency." Snopes lists his hands as, "Boy and two girls. Wife and her sister," and Varner responds that this equals five hands, but Snopes includes himself in the count, after which Varner says, "A man dont usually count himself among his own field hands." The number of hands is important for a few reasons. First, it illustrates that families were units of labor in the sharecropping system. Second, the number of hands determines the size of the farm that might be rented. Third, it indicates the amount of furnish that might be allowed. Snopes then asks, "What do you rent for?" Varner responds, "Third and fourth. . . . Furnish out of the store here. No cash." Snopes says, "I see. Furnish in six-bit dollars" (10).

This is the conversation of two people well versed in the microfinance principles of the postbellum economy. Varner charges one-third of the cotton crop and one-fourth of the corn crop as rent, and he requires the renter to purchase all necessary staples to raise the crop and provide for his family from the store. All purchases must be made on credit and paid off at settlement. The term "six-bit dollars" means that a dollar, which is eight bits, only buys seventy-five cents worth of goods, so Varner effectively includes a 33 percent surcharge on all purchases, and he doubtless charges interest on the accumulated debt as well. Given these terms, one can easily see how a sharecropping family could go into debt and how the store exerts control over their lives. "Everyone knew merchants squeezed every drop of profit that could be had from every minor purchase," Edward Ayers writes in *The Promise of the New South*. "Everyone knew that merchants' ledgers hid shady bookkeeping. . . . Everyone knew storekeepers made a good living without getting their hands dirty. . . . Everyone knew that the men behind the counter appeared friendly and warm while the credit bill grew, but revealed another face when settling time arrived."[19]

This particular contract becomes a bit more complicated when Varner learns that Ab Snopes has a reputation for burning barns when he feels a grievance against a landowner. Jody considers adding a fire clause to their contract, but Flem manipulates Varner into making him a clerk in the store as a means of insuring his property. As a clerk, Flem is a spectacle specifically because he does not fit the stereotype that Ayers describes. Where Varner, like a typical storekeeper, is often careless with accounts, usually erring in his own favor, Flem is scrupulously accurate. The customers expected

> mistakes of [Varner], just as they knew he would correct them when caught with a bluff, hearty amiability, making a joke of it, which sometimes left the customer wondering just a little about the rest of the bill. But they expected this too, because he would give them credit for food and plow gear when they needed it, long credit, though they knew they would pay interest for that which on its face looked like generosity and openhandedness, whether that interest showed in the final discharge or not. But the clerk never made mistakes. (62–63)

According to Ratliff, the customers found Flem's accuracy unnerving, but his attention to detail and his consistency demonstrate fine business acumen. He is also much more circumspect than Varner about credit. According to Godden, "Flem's first significantly independent act on entering Varner's store in 1887" is to "refuse credit" (*Economy* 18).[20] Flem "flatly refused further credit to a man who had been into and out of the store's debt at least once a year for the last fifteen" (63), and when Will Varner hears of this, he comes "galloping up on the old fat grumble-gutted white horse and storm[s] into the store, shouting loud enough to be heard in the blacksmith's shop across the road: 'Who in hell's store do you think this is, anyway?'" As Godden notes, Flem seems initially to misunderstand the purpose of debt. It's about profit and about power, but Flem proves to be a quick learner, graduating from the arithmetic of clerking to the calculus of debt, and he is soon running the store's accounts *and* a usurious lending scheme of his own.

Flem, in fact, quickly passes Jody as heir apparent to the store. When the cotton gin opens in September to begin ginning the year's harvest, it is Flem, not Jody, who runs the gin and processes the crop. Then, "after the crops were in and ginned and sold, the time came when Will Varner made his yearly settlement with his tenants and debtors. He had used to do this alone, not even allowing Jody to help him. This year he sat at the desk with the iron cash box while Snopes sat on a nail keg at his knee with the open ledgers" (67). As noted earlier, settlement is an important event on a postbellum plantation, when the landowner-merchant and the laborer culminate their contract. The crop is divided according to shares, then the store account for the season is tabulated, interest is calculated, and the total is subtracted from the laborer's remaining share of the crop. The landowner-merchant has nearly complete authority in this arrangement and can manipulate the accounts with relative impunity, giving him the ability to determine if the laboring family finishes the year with a profit or in debt. Varner allows Snopes to calculate the settlements with him, which gives the latter a tremendous amount of power, and the next year, "it was Snopes who did what Varner had never even permitted his son to do—sat alone at the desk with the cash from the sold crops and the account-books before him and cast up the accounts and charged them off and apportioned each tenant his share of the remaining money" (98). The people of the community, specifically Ratliff, recognize that this means that Flem has eclipsed Jody in authority—"the usurpation of an heirship." Indeed, by the end of the novel, Flem will marry Varner's daughter, own the Old Frenchman Place, and become notorious for his trading skills, and by the end of the trilogy, he will be the most powerful man in Yoknapatawpha County. His story illustrates the role of credit as a means to power in the postbellum South.

Flem's rise contrasts with the story of Jason Compson IV in *The Sound and the Fury*. Where Flem uses the store plus his own amoral cunning to rise from poverty to wealth, Jason flounders as the clerk of a store in Jefferson. The Compson family included successful planters before Emancipation, but, unlike the Varners and the Snopeses, they fail to adapt to the postbellum economy, and Jason chafes at a position that he considers demeaning, showing utter resentment toward the store owner, Earl, and contempt for the customers, such as the man he sells a cheap hame string.[21] Jason resents his position in part because he has been promised a job in Herbert Head's bank, but the bank job never materializes, so his mother gives him money to invest in Earl's store, which should make him part owner, but he spends the money on an automobile and extorts additional funds from his sister, ostensibly to provide for his niece. Rather than using microfinance as a means to economic power, Jason invests in the cotton commodities market, participating in the system of macrofinance that underwrites the plantation economy. The fact that he works in a store but does not directly hold debt over the laborers highlights the economic utility of debt. Owning debt is a means of both earning income and exerting power. Trading commodities, however, is solely a means of making profit, one that moreover comes with considerable risk. Jason buys cotton futures and short sells them, gambling that the price of the commodity will fall, and he will thus retain the difference in price. "Viewed in the 1920s as a 'parasitic' practice," Brendan Shapiro writes, "short selling allows Jason to transform investable cash into larger amounts of money without physical asset ownership."[22]

Rather than develop wealth *and* power through the established system of indebted labor, Jason buys and sells cotton on the commodities market in an attempt to make money through speculation. "Cotton is a speculator's crop," he says. "They fill the farmer full of hot air and get him to raise a big crop for them to whipsaw on the market, to trim the suckers with. Do you think the farmer gets anything out of it except a red neck and a hump in his back? You think the man that sweats to put it in the ground gets a red cent more than a bare living[?]" (191). Jason's comment is not an expression of solidarity with the laborers, however. It is an expression of contempt because he believes that he "gets inside information" from "one of the biggest manipulators in New York" (192). His comments about the market anticipate the climactic scene of *Dollar Cotton*, in which Otis Town goes to the commodities exchange in New York to argue about the price of cotton and accuses the president of the exchange of manipulating the price (229–31). On April 6, 1928, Jason takes a catastrophic loss on the market, losing more than $4,000, which compounds with the loss of the nearly $7,000 that his niece took from his bedroom. Wayne Westbrook explains that Jason's loss would actually have been impossible because the trading rules of the period limited daily fluctuations, so either Faulkner misunderstands the complicated rules of the commodities market, or he greatly exaggerates the impact of Jason's loss.[23] The former case is entirely possible, but Faulkner specifically revised the magnitude of Jason's loss, which suggests that the loss is intentional and invites us to wonder why his loss matters. Jason has a small loss in the 1929 edition of the book, published the same year as the stock market collapse, but the corrected edition of the text, based on an earlier version of the manuscript, shows a significantly greater loss. The fact that Faulkner revised the loss to conform more closely with actual market conditions suggests that Jason's loss on the commodities market critiques the system of cotton macrofinance, the international system of trade that determined prices paid for cotton and, thus, the amount of money that landowners and merchants would have available to pay laborers.

The southern economy was ultimately dependent on a global network of finance. One could, in fact, draw parallels between the crop lien as a means of exploiting labor and the commodity market as a means of exploiting cotton production. Cotton buyers used debt to manipulate cotton landowners, and landowners used debt to manipulate laborers, so the entire system was a pyramid scheme based on maximizing profits and minimizing risks. The people who benefit from the system, in Faulkner's novels, are those who find ways to manipulate these arrangements in their favor by exploiting other people. Jason's story illustrates the inherent volatility in the system of production. He attempts to manipulate the system, but the system manipulates him. His loss on the commodities market thus magnifies the loss of the money that he has taken from him by his niece, Quentin. Even though Jason does not exploit the labor directly by holding workers in debt, he is implicated in the more expansive system of exploitation inherent to the plantation economy.

Faulkner's stores are at once symbols and vehicles of economic power in the postbellum South. Godden asserts that "southern planters effectively refused emancipation, choosing to perpetuate a premodern labor system."[24] This is a problematic statement. The system of microfinance developed after the war that used debt to control labor proved to be entirely compatible with modernity. Agricultural production may be intrinsically different from industrial production in terms of the time scales involved, but modern capitalism minimizes labor cost while maximizing consumer debt. In this sense, sharecropping was a sophisticated and efficient means to produce a commodity and to leverage the consumer potential of the labor force—agricultural Fordism. The system made laborers simultaneously disposable and dependent while converting them into a form of revenue by extending them credit. Embedded in a complicated matrix of legal and extralegal controls that pivoted on the crop lien, sharecropping defined the modern South, and the store epitomizes the complications and contradictions of that modernity.

NOTES

1. Charles Aiken, *The Cotton Plantation South since the Civil War* (Baltimore: Johns Hopkins University Press, 1998), 7.

2. Thomas D. Clark, *Pills, Petticoats, and Plows: The Southern Country Store* (Norman: University of Oklahoma Press, 1944), 12. Hereafter cited parenthetically.

3. William Faulkner, *Absalom, Absalom!* rev. ed. (1986; repr., New York: Vintage International, 1990), 60–61. Hereafter cited parenthetically.

4. Ted Ownby, *American Dreams in Mississippi: Consumers, Poverty, & Culture, 1830–1998* (Chapel Hill: University of North Carolina Press, 1999), 20. Hereafter cited parenthetically.

5. See Blotner and Gwynn's Classes, February 13, 1957, tape 1, *Faulkner at Virginia*, http://faulkner.lib.virginia.edu/display/wfaudi006_1#wfaudi006_1.5.

6. Ernest Obadele-Starks, *Freebooters and Smugglers: The Foreign Slave Trade in the United States after 1808* (Fayetteville: University of Arkansas Press, 2007), 9–10.

7. Sven Beckert, *Empire of Cotton: A Global History* (New York: Knopf, 2014), 275.

8. After the war, Sutpen's property is returned, but much of it is sold for taxes and for immediate expenses. Rosa Coldfield mentions that Sutpen proposed to her on "the very day on which he knew definitely and at last exactly how much of his hundred square miles he would be able to save and keep and call his own . . . though a better name for it would now be Sutpen's One" (136; emphasis removed).

9. For background on the sharecropping system, see Roger L. Ransom and Richard Sutch, *One Kind of Freedom: The Economic Consequences of Emancipation*, rev. ed. (1977; repr., New York: Cambridge University Press, 2001), and Gavin Wright, *Old South, New South: Revolutions in the Southern Economy since the Civil War* (Baton Rouge: Louisiana State University Press, 1986).

10. In its 1938 *Report on Economic Conditions in the South*, the Roosevelt administration labeled the South "the Nation's No. 1 economic problem" (National Emergency Council, *Report on Economic Conditions in the South* [1938; New York: Da Capo, 1972], 1). One of the key reasons for this assessment was the system of credit. Seventy years after the Civil War, the region still had little access to financing from major banks, so the system of microfinance remained in place. According to the report, the system of microfinance forced the planter-merchant to exploit tenants "in order that he may himself survive" (51).

11. Ransom and Sutch, *One Kind of Freedom*, 126.

12. Arthur F. Raper and Ira De A. Reid, *Sharecroppers All* (1941; repr., New York: Russell and Russell, 1971), 38.

13. Richard Godden, *Fictions of Labor: William Faulkner and the South's Long Revolution* (New York: Cambridge University Press, 1997), 119.

14. William Faulkner, *The Hamlet*, rev. ed. (1940; repr., New York: Vintage International, 1991), 4. Hereafter cited parenthetically.

15. Faulkner's Snopes trilogy has much in common with T. S. Stribling's Vaiden trilogy, particularly the second novel in the series, *The Store* (1932), which, as its title suggests, focuses on the postbellum economy and the social uplift of a farmer who becomes a clerk.

16. John T. Matthews, *William Faulkner: Seeing through the South* (2009; repr., Malden, MA: Wiley-Blackwell, 2012), 129.

17. Corrine Dale explores the similarities between Thomas Sutpen's rise and Flem Snopes's rise in "*Absalom, Absalom!* and the Snopes Trilogy: Southern Patriarchy in Revision," *Mississippi Quarterly* 45, no. 3 (Summer 1992): 321–37.

18. Ted Atkinson points out the connections between *Dollar Cotton* and William Faulkner's work, particularly *Absalom, Absalom!* ("Testing the Limits of Tragedy: History and Ideology in John Faulkner's *Dollar Cotton*," *Mississippi Quarterly* 54, no. 4 [Fall 2001]: 527–39). Matthew Lessig describes the Nashville Agrarians' displeasure with Stribling's work and their preference for Faulkner in "*The Store*, or T. S. Stribling's Paragraph in the History of Critical Race Studies," *Southern Quarterly* 41, no. 3 (Spring 2003): 137–55. Judith Bryant Wittenberg traces Stribling's influence on Faulkner in "William Faulkner, T. S. Stribling, Trilogistic Intertextuality and the Politics of the Canon," *Faulkner Journal* 13, nos. 1–2 (Fall–Spring 1997–1998): 149–62.

19. Edward Ayers, *The Promise of the New South: Life after Reconstruction* (New York: Oxford University Press, 1992), 93.

20. Richard Godden, *William Faulkner: An Economy of Complex Words* (Princeton, NJ: Princeton University Press, 2007), 18.

21. William Faulkner, *The Sound and the Fury*, rev. ed. (1929; repr., New York: Vintage International, 1990), 195. Hereafter cited parenthetically.

22. Brendan Shapiro, "Jason Compson's Invisible Life: Illocutionary Logic in *The Sound and the Fury*," *Textual Practice* 30, no. 5 (2016): 907.

23. Wayne W. Westbrook, "Skunked on the New York Cotton Exchange: What Really Happens to Jason Compson in *The Sound and the Fury*," *Southern Literary Journal* 41, no. 2 (Spring 2009): 53–67. Taylor Hagood explores the global reverberations of cotton in Faulkner's work in "Taking 'Money Right out of an American's Pockets': Faulkner's South and the International Cotton Market," *European Journal of American Culture* 26, no. 2 (2007): 83–95.

24. Godden, *William Faulkner*, 5.

The Gifted Presence of *Intruder in the Dust*

Michael Wainwright

The murder is to the murderer, and comes back most to him,
The theft is to the thief, and comes back most to him,
The love is to the lover, and comes back most to him,
The gift is to the giver, and comes back most to him—it cannot fail.

—"A Song of the Rolling Earth," Leaves of Grass, Walt Whitman

In 1948, banking on his publisher's continued interest in his work, and apparently speculating on the possible award of the Nobel Prize for Literature, the gifted William Faulkner, struggling with the atypical *A Fable* and with a perilously low bank balance, temporarily but concertedly reinvested himself in Yoknapatawpha County. The first major publication from this creative expenditure, which Faulkner would initially describe as "the best [thing] I have ever written," was *Intruder in the Dust*.[1] Published in 1948, the novel repaid Faulkner's reinvestment not only artistically, as its author's own appraisal testified, but also financially, as his bank balance attested, with the $40,000 that MGM paid for the film rights supplemented by the 25 percent on sales of the 37,040 copies that Random House printed of the first edition. *Intruder in the Dust*, as Michael Millgate reports, "sold more copies (about 18,000 in the first year) than any of his previous books."[2] At last, as Patrick H. Samway remarks, "Faulkner began to know a sense of financial security."[3]

Beyond these considerations, *Intruder in the Dust* reasserted Faulkner's literary presence, helping to secure him the 1949 Nobel Prize for Literature. In addition to the esteem of this award, the prize carried a substantial honorarium, which secured Faulkner's financial future for good.[4] As *Intruder in the Dust* suggests, however, this combination of rewards is fundamentally unstable: while the conferral of esteem engages the *economy of the gift*, the transfer of capital engages the *economy of money*. Jacques Derrida, whose *Given Time: I. Counterfeit*

Money (1992) capitalizes on the notion and possibilities of the gift, confirms this basic instability: each economy describes a figure of circulation, but unlike the economy of money, the economy of the gift demands neither exchange nor return of payment; indeed, the attempted transference of the gift seems to annul that very gift. The following analysis of the intractable relationship between the gift and money in *Intruder in the Dust* owes, therefore, an outstanding debt to Derrida's philosophical gift. By anchoring the resultant intellectual exchange to the accredited history of the American foundation to which *Intruder in the Dust* occasionally but unarguably defers, a historical lineage spawned by the financial transactions encompassing the Middle Passage, economic concepts circulate between Faulkner's novel and Derrida's philosophical treatise. This circulation helps to parse the account of gifting opened at the beginning of *Intruder in the Dust* and intentionally never closed by the novel. The result is a valuable account of a work that Faulknerians have hitherto underappreciated, a work that effectively sees beyond what Jean-Luc Marion (in both *Being Given* [2002] and *The Visible and the Revealed* [2008]) laments as Derrida's reductive fixation with the "horizon of exchange."[5]

"Among its irreducible predicates or semantic values," expounds Derrida, "economy no doubt includes the values of law (*nomos*) and of home (*oikos*)."[6] *Nomos* signifies not only "the law in general, but also the law of distribution (*nemein*), the law of sharing or partition [*partage*], the law as partition (*moira*), the given or assigned part, participation."[7] *Oikos* signifies not only the "home," but also "property, family, the hearth, the fire indoors."[8] The social standing of Lucas Beauchamp in *Intruder in the Dust*, as an African American farmer of mixed-race lineage, who lives and works in Yoknapatawpha County, is contentiously defined by these irreducible predicates, and his socioeconomic circle becomes personally enmeshed with that of Chick Mallison at the outset of the novel.

Chick's breaking through the ice when accidentally falling head over heels into a creek is the tipping point that will turn his racially inculcated thoughts "upside down," and Lucas is the agent who will underwrite this inversion.[9] Aleck Sander's attempts to help Chick out of the creek—"Aleck Sander rammed down at him the end of a long pole, almost a log whose first pass struck his feet out from under him and sent his head under again"—actually keep him immersed (287). It requires a disembodied voice, like that of God, to dissolve the two boys' antics: this "voice said: 'Get the pole out of his way so he can get out'—just a voice." This announcement comes from Lucas, who does not intervene physically, but whose passive involvement nonetheless enables Chick to make dry land. The inversion of racial assumptions in this tableau, with the African

American man standing above and looking down on the American boy, is obvious: events have contrived to upset the accustomed socioeconomic order. To Chick, annoyed with Lucas's passivity, Aleck's pole was "the one token toward help" (287); in consequence, he inserts Lucas and Aleck into the economy of money and the economy of the gift, respectively, with what Derrida calls "the relation of the gift to the 'present,' in all the senses of this term," coming to the fore (*Given Time*, 9–10).

Unlike a present, which is monetary, fiduciary, or commercial, a gift recognizes its recipient with a different form of presentation. This acknowledgment is one of the necessary conditions for the act of gifting. "For there to be gift," explains Derrida, "it is necessary that the gift not even appear, that it not be perceived or received as gift" (*Given Time*, 16). Chick does not consciously realize this truth—accidental immersion and subsequent restitution have not broken through the socioeconomic ice of his majoritarian pretensions—but his use of the word "token" does reveal a subconscious recognition of false symbolism: the pole, as token, is a counterfeit gift; therefore, Lucas's alternative offering, his gift and its bestowal of responsibility, has not been entirely wasted.

Having rationalized his denial of Lucas's help in extracting him from the creek, Chick has simply to turn into Edmonds's drive when following the homeward-bound Lucas, but with his world turned upside down, Chick does not "even check when they passed the gate" (288). That failure implies that Chick is both prepared (he does not check or interrupt his movements) and unprepared (the accompanying narration is grounded in the discourse of the economy of money) to accept Lucas's prolongation of gifting. For, on entering Lucas's home, Chick at once partakes of the economy of the gift and the economy of money, but he seemingly recognizes only the latter. "He could smell that smell which he had accepted without question all his life as being the smell always of the places where people with any trace of Negro blood live" (290). This odor, which "was a part of his inescapable past" (291–92), "a rich part of his heritage as a Southerner" (292), signifies the sweat of surplus value extracted from African Americans, a legacy that dates back to the days of the Middle Passage. Chick's assumption of narratorial control, despite his own admission of lacking such mastery ("he knew Lucas Beauchamp . . . as well that is as any white person knew him" [285]), reinforces this significance, which the novel underwrites by withholding the gift of narratorial interiority from Lucas.

Despite subconscious reservations, Chick offers to pay for Lucas's gift: "his dumb hand open and on it the four shameful fragments of milled and minted dross" (294). Silence is Lucas's initial response to this attempt to exchange gift for money. Lucas then asks, "What's that for?"

Each of these responses to the manner in which Chick "extended the coins" prolongs (or extends) Lucas's gift of extended presence: "In the same second in which [Chick] knew [Lucas's wife, Molly] would have taken [the money] he knew that only by that one irrevocable second was he *forever* now too late, *forever* beyond recall, standing with the *slow hot blood as slow as minutes* themselves up his neck and face, *forever* with his dumb hand open," with Lucas "not even moving, not even tilting his face downward to look at what was on his palm . . . for another *eternity*" (emphasis added). With his incipient enlightenment eclipsed, Chick finally reacts in an inculcated fashion to the extended presence of Lucas's denial: he drops the coins on the floor. Lucas, however, remains firm in rejecting the exchange between two related but distinct economies, ordering the two other youths present (Aleck Sander and Edmonds's boy) to pick up and return Chick's money.

Chick had tried to repay; Lucas had refused that repayment; and repayment remains at the economic heart of the novel. Faulkner states as much in his February 1, 1948, letter to Harold Ober: "The story is a mystery-murder though the theme is more [the] relationship between Negro and white, specifically or rather the premise being that the white people in the south, before the North or the govt. or anyone else, owe and must pay a responsibility to the Negro."[10] In effect, as Erik Dussere relates, "Faulkner was worrying about how the debt of what James Baldwin called 'more than two hundred years in slavery and ninety years of quasi-freedom' would be paid back, and by whom."[11] Faulkner's friendship with (William) Hodding Carter, whom he entertained at Rowan Oak while composing *Intruder*, partly shaped his immediate response to these issues.[12] Two years earlier, Carter had won a Pulitzer Prize for "his editorials condemning racial injustice and inequality," and Faulkner tacitly acknowledged his fellow Mississippian's influence.[13] "Carter's a good man," he told John K. Hutchens in October 1948, "and he's right when he says the solution of the Negro problem belongs to the South."[14]

The cycle of presents, by which Chick seeks to repay Lucas's positively unredeemable gift, and counterpresents, by which Lucas checks Chick's desire for the foreclosure of that gift, relates to another of the necessary conditions for the act of gifting. "For there to be gift," states Derrida, "*it is necessary [il faut]* that the donee not give back, amortize, reimburse, acquit himself, enter into a contract, and that he never contracted a debt" (*Given Time*, 13). An exchange of gifts breaks this necessity. "An exchanged gift is only a tit for tat," as Derrida insists, "an annulment of the gift. By underscoring this, we do not mean to say that *there is no* exchanged gift. One cannot deny the *phenomenon*, nor that which presents this precisely phenomenal aspect of exchanged gifts.

But the apparent, visible contradiction of these two values—gift and exchange—must be problematized" (37). The reciprocation of exchange, as *Intruder in the Dust* affirms, translates gifts into presents. The immediacy of money in Chick's act within Lucas's home attempts to prosecute this translation. "If the other *gives* me *back* or *owes* me or has to give me back what I give him or her," as Derrida maintains, "there will not have been a gift, whether this restitution is immediate or whether it is programmed by a complex calculation of a long-term deferral" (12). A gift silently presents an excess beyond the presentation of a present, an excess that any measured, calculated, or moderated present cannot reimburse.

One can surmise the excessiveness of Lucas's gift, and something of the nature of that excessiveness, from the white community's desire for Lucas's payment of his racial dues: "Every white man in that whole section of the county had been thinking about him for years: *We got to make him be a nigger first. He's got to admit he's a nigger. Then maybe we will accept him as he seems to intend to be accepted*" (296). Yet, the majoritarians of Yoknapatawpha County fail to recognize, let alone acknowledge, that Lucas proffers a gift of enlightenment. Lucas continues, therefore, to look at white men "with a calm speculative detachment" (297), with a gaze that relates to, but is at the same time separate from, the economics of speculation; in other words, with a gaze that concerns a reward that is beyond the monetary, a foresight that oversees the horizon of exchange.

In the meantime, Chick acts according to inculcation, with his attempt at psychological repression provoking a symbolic acknowledgment of his onetime host's detached disregard for the economy of money. Repression operates either systemically or topologically. "It always consists of keeping by exchanging places," as Derrida states. "And, by keeping the meaning of the gift, repression annuls it in symbolic recognition" (*Given Time*, 16). Chick's psyche tries to exchange Lucas's gift for a monetary symbol, one that nonetheless retains the significance of that gift in attempting to cancel it, and one whose inflated size recalls the asymmetric racial foundation of American capital:

> Now not only his mistake and its shame but its protagonist too—the man, the Negro, the room, the moment, the day itself—had annealed vanished into the round hard symbol of the coin and he would seem to see himself lying watching regretless and even peaceful as day by day the coin swelled to its gigantic maximum, to hang fixed at last forever in the black vault of his anguish like the last dead and waneless moon and himself, his own puny shadow gesticulant and tiny against it in frantic and vain eclipse: frantic and vain yet indefatigable too because he would never stop, he could never give up now who had debased not merely his manhood but his whole race too. (298–99)

That debasement involves a specific relation to southern propriety. Gift giving was central to the code of honor. On the one hand, the exchange of gifts cemented kith and kin relations. On the other hand, presenting an unrequitable gift confirmed the social status of both the giver (superior) and the recipient (inferior). "The language of the gift," avers Kenneth S. Greenberg, "was frequently the language of mastery," and this usage even mitigated the act of manumission.[15] "The gift relation was just as deeply imbricated in emancipation as it was in slavery," asserts Greenberg; "masters could liberate individual slaves only by awarding them freedom as a gift. Slaves could never purchase themselves in market transactions because they could give nothing to their masters. Masters might permit slaves to purchase themselves, but that was only a roundabout way of giving slaves a valuable gift."[16]

According to Chick's conscious speculation, this racial history demands redress; and Chick maintains his determination to pay Lucas back. His initial tactic comprised "the four two-for-a-quarter cigars for Lucas and the tumbler of snuff for his wife" (299) that he sent as "Christmas presents" (302). Yet in exemplifying conspicuous consumption, these items retained exchange value within the monetary economy; consequently, "there still remained the dead monstrous heatless disc which hung nightly in the black abyss of [Chick's] rage and impotence" (299).[17] Chick's subsequent tactic—for three months he saves "the twenty-five cents his father gave him each week as allowance and the twenty-five cents his uncle," the lawyer Gavin Stevens, "paid him as office salary," so that "in May he had enough and with his mother helping him chose the flowered imitation silk dress and sent it by mail to Molly Beauchamp"—provides "something like ease." Certainly, "the disc still hung in the black vault," but that coin was "almost a year old now and so the vault itself was not so black with the disc paling and he could even sleep under it" (300).

Chick's sense of relaxation has emerged, however, from Lucas's gift of time. "The gift only gives to the extent it *gives time*," as Derrida elucidates:

> The difference between a gift and every other operation of pure and simple exchange is that the gift gives time. *There where there is gift, there is time.* What it gives, the gift, is time, but this gift of time is also a demand of time. The thing must not be restituted *immediately and right away*. There must be time, it must last, there must be waiting—without forgetting [*l'attente—sans oubli*]. It demands time, the thing, but it demands a delimited time, neither an instant nor an infinite time, but a time determined by a term, in other words, a rhythm, a cadence. (*Given Time*, 41)

Hence, Lucas waits four months before undermining Chick's sense of ease: Chick returns home one afternoon to find "a gallon bucket of fresh homemade sorghum molasses" from the farmer (300). What is more, as if to emphasize the detachment between his initial gift and this present, Lucas had paid "a white boy" to deliver it. In terms of southern honor, Chick is now in a position of social inferiority to an African American. In terms of cyclical economics, the two agents are "right back where they had started," with Lucas's act of gifting still unsullied, unassuaged, and unredeemed.[18]

Chick repeatedly thinks he has laid the economy of the gift to rest by bringing it full circle, but Chick's repeated presents to Lucas simply express his repression of donee status; and repression, to repeat, does not erase but retains through exchange. For Chick, who remains inculcated into a monetary economics once sustained by slavery, the gift of time means not only that "it was all to do over again" but that "it was even worse this time," because "Lucas had commanded a white hand" to "give it back to him" (300). Chick cannot help but feel a slave to Lucas's whims: "Whatever would or could set him free was beyond not merely his reach but even his ken" (300). The necessary solution eludes Chick's current grasp because the economy of the gift is beyond the economy of money, with part of Lucas's gift to Chick involving ratiocinative time for his thoughts to circulate. Whereas Lucas's gift, to borrow the Derridean formula, "must not circulate, it must not be exchanged, it must not in any case be exhausted, as a gift, by the process of exchange, by the movement of circulation of the circle in the form of return to the point of departure," circular figuration is "essential to economics" (*Given Time*, 7). Yet, the *aneconomic* gift, according to this seemingly contradictory logic, does not remain "foreign to the circle" but keeps "a relation of foreignness to the circle, a relation without relation of familiar foreignness"; and Lucas, as an African American, embodies the familiarly foreign to the almost, but not completely, exhausted Chick.

In an economics that exploits racial difference, masters evaluate subalterns in the conferral of use and exchange value, but the complementary economics that shadows these evaluations places subalterns in the ideal position to offer a complimentary gift. This freedom under duress enables Lucas to invert the existing constructs of binary logic. The circulation put in motion by the gift, as Derrida states, "allows all the values to be inverted: The gift of life amounts to the gift of death, the gift of day to the gift of night" (*Given Time*, 54), so Chick's "four shameful fragments of milled and minted dross" (Faulkner, *Intruder*, 294), the "four two-for-a-quarter cigars" (299), and Molly's (albeit imitation) silk dress find their complement in the "four years" (291) that elapse before he realizes "the extent of its ramifications and what it had done to him and he would be a man grown before he would realise, admit that he had accepted it" (291), that "whatever" (300) of Lucas's gift.[19] That acceptance will amount to a denial (however tacit) of self-sufficiency. "For a gift to be given," to draw on John McAteer's summary of Marion's thoughts, "we must reject our view of ourselves as self-sufficient subjects. For me to give you a gift, I must admit that I have some surplus, something given to me from outside myself (otherwise I have nothing to give)."[20] One such surplus is the legacy of slavery, and the ledgers of all southerners, whatever their ethnicity, carry this external debt.

Lucas's apparent murder of Vinson Gowrie seemingly calls in that debt. Chick now believes that he can settle his outstanding balance with Lucas. Uncovering the body of evidence will prove the farmer's innocence, but entering the Jefferson jail in which Lucas is held, Chick and his uncle Gavin pass "out of the world of man"—white men, that is, "people who worked and had homes and raised families and tried to make a little more money than they perhaps deserved" (325). Indeed, the interior of the jail, which Chick associates almost exclusively with the incarceration of African Americans, is alien to the economy of money: the prisoners form a self-contained collective, and this environment is the site of Lucas's ultimate gamble. "Beauchamp and not the county attorney holds the cards" (114), as Jay Watson remarks, but in exploiting Vinson's murder, and in braving a possible lynching, Lucas is willing to risk the noose, willing to "risk entering into" what Derrida calls "the destructive circle" of the untranslatable gift (*Given Time*, 30).[21]

Lucas appears to have kept some gifting in reserve, or in the black, for this emergency, but that appearance is deceptive in partaking of the economy of money, and Lucas, as his verbal exchange with Stevens underlines, carefully separates the economy of the gift from the *nomos* of his legal defense. Lucas, who appreciates rational calculation as Stevens's supreme quality, plays on that asset: "I'm gonter pay you," he assures the attorney. "You dont need to worry" (328). Retaining an economic reserve of the gift would open that gift to the prospect of a countergift; such an annulment encapsulates payment and discharge; that discharge would be the negative gift by which Vinson's family would repay Lucas. "For there to be gift," as Derrida avers, "there must be no reciprocity, return, exchange, countergift, or debt." Otherwise, "from the moment the gift puts the other in debt," that gift is "bad, poisonous." Giving amounts to harming. "Here one need hardly mention the fact that in certain languages, for example in French, one may say as readily 'to give a gift' as 'to give a blow' [*donner un coup*], 'to give life' [*donner la vie*] as 'to give death' [*donner la mart*], thereby either dissociating and opposing them or identifying them" (*Given Time*, 12).

In the problematic logic of indebtedness, "the circulation of a good or of goods is not only the circulation of the 'things' that we will have offered to each other, but even of the values or the symbols that are involved there [*qui s'y engagent*] and the intentions to give, whether they are conscious or unconscious" (Derrida, *Given Time*, 12–13). Although social anthropologists "have *quite rightly and justifiably*, treated *together*, as a system, the gift and the debt, the gift and the cycle of restitution, the gift and the loan, the gift and credit, the gift and the countergift, we are here *departing*, in a peremptory and distinct fashion, from this tradition" (13). Lucas constantly prosecutes this departure. He has already done so in annulling Chick's Christmas presents, because that tradition relegates African Americans to subalterns for whom presents are carnivalesque, masterly sleights of hand intended to offset temporarily without alleviating permanently the burden of suppression. For "there is gift, if there is any," as Derrida observes, "only in what interrupts the system as well as the symbol, in a partition without return and without division [*répartition*], without being-with-self of the gift-counter-gift" (*Given Time*, 13).

Lucas effects such an interruption while incarcerated by exploiting that exemplar of both forced African American production and conspicuous consumption, tobacco, to engineer Chick's return to the jail without Stevens. "You might send me some tobacco," he tells the boy, "if them Gowries leaves me time to smoke it" (332). Chick reciprocates Lucas's feint in returning to the jail empty-handed. Now, sealed in an exchange of looks between Chick and the imprisoned Lucas, the transference of the gift overwrites the economy of money, translating Chick's search for Lucas's innocence into an acceptance of further tuition. In effect, the gifted Lucas passes on (rather than exchanges) the economy of the gift, which Chick's maturation into "Charles Mallison junior" (335), a moniker used nowhere else in the novel, acknowledges. Charles, who "wasn't even thinking anymore" (335) like Chick, has passed Lucas's latest test. Although separated by racial constructs, as symbolized by the bars of the prison cell, Charles can accept Lucas's gift. This transference goes beyond a reductive obsession with the horizon of exchange. "Givability," as Marion expounds in *The Visible and the Revealed*, "arises around the potential giver when [he], first of all in relation to [himself] alone, recognizes that the principle 'I owe no one anything' may (and must) admit at least one exception. The gift begins and in fact ends as soon as the giver envisions that he owes something to someone, when he admits that he could be a debtor, and thus a recipient. The gift begins when the potential giver suspects that another gift has already preceded [him], to which [he] owes something, to which [he] owes [himself] to respond."[22]

What maintains Charles's attention in Lucas's gaze is that "whatever" (300), that divine immanence (or *quidditas*) of the gift, and "that something—whatever it was—[holds] him [t]here" (335). Lucas's transference of the gift occupies an elongated present that unhinges the common (or majoritarian) notions of Chick's upbringing. What Charles must credit, as Lucas intends, goes beyond the economics of a single agent to the wider and profounder implications of racial politics. Faulkner's synesthetic description of Charles "hear[ing] the mute unhoping urgency of [Lucas's] eyes" (335) connotes the resulting derangement of socioeconomic norms. Agreeing to disinter Vinson Gowrie is lunacy; insanity "is a certain excess of the gift," as Derrida warns (*Given Time*, 45), and the intensity of this madness "begins to burn up the word or the meaning 'gift' itself and to disseminate without return its ashes" (47)—or, in the related Faulknerian discourse, its dust. This dissemination exposes the ongoing cost of colonial history. Charles's initiation into the economy of the gift has exposed the lingering shame of the Middle Passage and everything related to that economic cycle, with the prominence of Lucas's absence throughout the central portions of the text being of related significance. His ever-present disappearance hints at a divide between the metaphysical (even the theological) economy of the gift and the secular (even the atheistic) economy of money. No wonder the gifted Charles feels "responsible for having brought into the light and glare of day something shocking and shameful out of the whole white foundation of the county" (388), the South, and the United States. The young Charles is, then, the only viable trustee of "the gift of his time" in "man's enduring chronicle" (430), as this, the sole use of the word "gift" in the novel, confirms. As a trustee, "a locus of giving-and-receiving" who rejects "the ontology of will in favor of an ontology of gift" (McAteer, "The Gifts of God," 65), Charles experiences a positive advancement beyond the horizon of exchange.

The evidence uncovered by Charles, Aleck, and Miss Habersham in Lucas's defense exposes Crawford Gowrie as the guilty party.[23] Crawford, who was cashiered (or discredited) by the army for desertion, but who remains dedicated to the economy of money and usurps the right of gifting by stealing timber, murders his brother, Vinson, because he cannot afford to be discredited a second time. Indeed, with his murders of Vinson and the "timber buyer" (370), Jake Montgomery, double homicide has paid out on Crawford's double-dealing. With this confirmation of Crawford's guilt, the majoritarians of Jefferson try to draw Lucas back into the monetary economy by regularly and unendingly recompensing him with an item that is neither a gift nor a present but a reminder of the colonial past: tobacco. Stevens understands this aspect of masterly behavior: "Lucas will ultimately get his can of tobacco," he tells Charles. "[T]hey will insist on it, they will have to. He will receive installments on it for the rest of his life in this county whether he wants them or not and not just Lucas but *Lucas: Sambo*" (434). Unwittingly recalling the incident at the creek that overturned Chick's worldview, Stevens adds, "He wont want it of course and he'll try to resist it. But he'll get it and so we shall watch right here in Yoknapatawpha County the ancient oriental relationship between the savior and the life he saved turned upside down." As Charles comes to realize of the wider picture, Lucas's freedom remains *"in check going on a hundred years after Lee surrendered"* (447) because the economy of money guarantees that check. Charles "had no more expected Lucas to be swept out of his cell shoulder high on a tide of expiation and set for his moment of vindication and triumph on the base say of the Confederate monument (or maybe better on the balcony of the postoffice building beneath the pole where the national flag flew) than he had expected such for himself and Aleck Sander and Miss Habersham" (429–30). Indeed, Charles "not only had not wanted that but could not have accepted it since it would have abrogated and made void the whole sum of what part he had done which had to be anonymous else it was valueless" (430). Like Lucas, the trustee before him, Charles eschews the economic circularity of auto-recognition, self-approval, and narcissistic gratitude.

Despite his disengagement from Jefferson's white majority, Charles "hadn't expected . . . the grudging pretermission of a date" for the "all *now*" of the gift (430): "Because you escape nothing, you flee nothing; the pursuer is what is doing the running and tomorrow night is nothing but one long sleepless wrestle with yesterday's omissions and regrets." That "all *now*" is the "going to begin" of a gifted dissemination that would return America to the unsullied dream, "the moment in 1492 when somebody thought *This is it*: the absolute edge of no return, to turn back now and make home or sail irrevocably on and either find land or plunge over the world's roaring rim" (431). The economy of the gift remains, therefore, autotelic in the contradictory manner of never returning to its origin: "It was still there or at least his unfinished part in it which was not even a minuscule but rather a minutecule of his uncle's and the sheriff's in the unfinishability of Lucas Beauchamp and Crawford Gowrie" (433). The unfinishability of a gifted dissemination heralds the ultimate, self-effacing character of the gift, which Derrida describes as "an absolute forgetting—a forgetting that also absolves, that unbinds absolutely and infinitely more, therefore, than excuse, forgiveness, or acquittal" (*Given*

Time, 16). "Some things," as Stevens counsels Charles, "you must always be unable to bear": "injustice and outrage and dishonor and shame. No matter how young you are or how old you have got. Not for kudos and not for cash: your picture in the paper nor money in the bank either. Just refuse to bear them" (439). While this advice reveals the partial extent of Stevens's enlightenment, his middle-aged resignation to the unrealizable nature of the gift confronts yet encourages Charles's determination to reach for the unattainable—unattainable because the act of absolution in forgetting rests with African Americans alone.

With no case to answer, Lucas visits his defense team, his appearance in Stevens's office in the presence of both Charles and his uncle insuring and ensuring the continued circulation of the economy of the gift. Lucas first invokes the gift that sparked the slow emergence of Chick's release from prejudice: "You aint fell in no more creeks lately, have you?" he asks (465). In answer to Charles's rejoinder, "I'm saving that until you get some more ice on yours," Lucas reminds him of the enduring immanence of that gift: "You'll be welcome without waiting for a freeze" (465). Lucas then changes the subjective focus of the economy of the gift, not only freeing himself from a specific instance of the economy of money but also indicting Stevens for the latter's lack of sociopolitical perception. Thinking himself a man of enlightenment, Stevens admits that Americans "are willing to sell liberty short at any tawdry price" (467); yet justice, *nomos*, the law as equal partition, should eschew the economy of money and should be within the economy of the gift.

"I believe you got a little bill against me," states Lucas. "I didn't do anything," replies Stevens. As Lucas insists, however, as if accepting *and* resisting Stevens's check, or unenlightened state, "I authorised you." At the outset of his incarceration, Lucas had intentionally inserted both client (himself) and lawyer (Stevens) into the economy of money, and the small charge Lucas assumes of "two dollars to have a new point put in" Stevens's fountain pen is a fee that demands reimbursement. Lucas first covers this charge in monetary kind, then with a bodily gesture, doing "something with his breath: not a sigh, simply a *discharge* of it" (emphasis added). With this act, which attempts to close his financial account with Stevens, Lucas repays the lawyer for the "expense [of] sitting here last Tuesday trying to write down all the different things you finally told me in such a way that Mr Hampton could get enough sense out of it to *discharge* you from the jail" (emphasis added) (468).

Lucas extends this recompense in a timely fashion, taking back a quarter from his original payment and exchanging it for fifty pennies, which come from "a knotted soiled cloth tobacco sack" (469). The significance of this bag is twofold: expressing both conspicuous consumption and Lucas's freedom, as an African American, to fill the colonial sign with his own choice of signifying content. This compound worth fails, however, to strike the lawyer, who makes Lucas count the coins out individually.[24] Only then, when Stevens finally assumes that this "business" (469) transaction is over, does Lucas emphasize Steven's enslavement to an economy of which he himself has "wiped his hands" (470). "What are you waiting for now?" asks the exasperated lawyer. "My receipt," replies the equitable farmer. Lucas's denial of Chick's payment for his hospitality at the beginning of *Intruder in the Dust* has found its counterpart, but while the economy of money has come full circle, the economy of the gift remains open. That conspicuous consumption, as signaled by the "uproar" (470) that washes over Stevens's office from the "valueless enough" (463) automobiles that fill the town square, accompanies the quietus of Lucas's settling of his monetary debt to Stevens is entirely apt. Stevens, as the temporary exchange (or hierarchical inversion) in sociopolitical order sealed by this spoken exchange implies, ought to think over or outside or without the economy of money. Stevens must, but fails to, take responsibility.

"On what condition is responsibility possible?" asks Derrida in *The Gift of Death* (1996). "On the condition that the Good no longer be a transcendental objective, a relation between objective things, but the relation to the other, a response to the other; an experience of personal goodness and a movement of intention."[25] In *Intruder in the Dust*, that conditional relationship involves the gift of forgiveness, a gift that demands the acknowledgment of an original sin. For America, the realm of Manifest Destiny, the capital chance (offered by a supposedly *de novo* site) for the expansion of Western capital, that sin pertains to the horrific assumptions and acts of colonialism. "The deed of gift," as Robert Frost acknowledges in "The Gift Outright" (1941), "was many deeds of war."[26] "The doctrine of original sin suggests an ancient and infinite guilt that requires rectification," writes Eric R. Severson.[27] "Finite human beings are incapable of compensating for infinite guilt, and must instead receive justification as the miracle of a gift. The idea of *grace* therefore functions as the cornerstone for any Christian theology of forgiveness. The origin of this gift is God, who is also the origin of responsibility. In this way, responsibility is wrested from the cult of reason and returned to the realm of secrecy and mystery, but not without first being radically transformed."[28] By analogy, the origin of this gift in *Intruder in the Dust* is the substantially insubstantial Lucas Beauchamp, whose Godlike voice dominates the opening scene and who wrests responsibility from the figure of rational deliberation, Gavin Stevens; and the mystery of the novel emerges from its philosophical transformation of mystery-murder conventions. Neither the ratiocination of a Gavin Stevens nor the enthusiasm of a religious zealot can elicit such a gift. "Goodness happens *to* the self," observes Severson, "but it is not a performance or achievement of the self" (5). Just as "the murder is to the murderer, and comes back most to him," to requote Walt Whitman from the epigraph to this chapter, so the African American gift must turn toward the African American giver.[29] The present imminence of the accumulated interest on that gift, as figured at once in Charles Mallison's ability and Gavin Steven's inability to accept the trusteeship of the economy of the gift, encapsulates the tragedy of postbellum America, with African Americans seeking through the gesture of the gift to constitute the identity and unity born of self-possession.

Intruder in the Dust renders the gifted William Faulkner's account of that gesture to posterity. As the novel foretells at an authorial level beyond, but in relation to, its narrative levels, Faulkner's gift to literature engaged the economic cycle from which it, like its author, would have preferred to remain apart. The Nobel Prize for Literature exacerbated the resulting conflict. The excess and dislocation of the gift repaid the gifted Faulkner with a madness that was, to borrow the Derridean phrasing, "at once reason and unreason" (*Given Time*, 36). That insanity manifested the "madness of the rational *logos* itself, that madness of the economic circle the calculation of which is constantly reconstituted, logically, rationally, annulling the excess that itself . . . entails the circle, makes it turn without end, gives it its movement, a movement that the circle and the ring can never comprehend or annul" (36–37). This incomprehension is always a matter of psychic expenditure. The economic dislocation of the gift "folds back in a contradictory manner toward the subject who utters it (for example, 'do not listen to me,' 'do not read me'), it engenders that schism in the response or the responsibility in which some have sought to recognize the schizopathogenic power of the double bind" (56–57). Four years after Faulkner's death, when Helen Tartakoff coined the term "Nobel Prize complex" to describe narcissistic analysands, "she undoubtedly," as Des Jardins states, "had scientists rather than poets or peace activists in mind," but the 1949 Nobel Prize for Literature, as Faulkner's continuing struggles with *A Fable* evinced, undoubtedly stimulated a contradictory folding back for its recipient, too.[30] The Nobel Prize Committee had presented an unrequitable predicament to the gifted author's psychological ledger, an entry indebted to the ongoing cost of the colonial past, an entry that no amount of esteem or money could ever repay.

NOTES

1. James Webb and A. Wigfall Green, eds., *William Faulkner of Oxford* (Baton Rouge: Louisiana State University Press, 1965), 142. Although Faulkner completed "Notes on a Horsethief" in November 1947, some two months before he started work on *Intruder in the Dust*, this episode from the forthcoming *A Fable* would not appear in print until 1951.

2. Michael Millgate, *The Achievement of William Faulkner* (1963; repr., New York: Random House, 1966), 47. "Random House sold the movie rights of *Intruder* to M-G-M for $50,000," Patrick H. Samway explains, "with Faulkner receiving $40,000 of this. The rest being Random House's commission" (*Faulkner's "Intruder in the Dust": A Critical Study of the Typescripts* [New York: Whitson, 1980], 36). Lawrence H. Schwartz documents the number of first editions printed (*Creating Faulkner's Reputation: The Politics of Modern Literary Criticism* [Knoxville: University of Tennessee Press, 1990], 70). "Each copy of this edition [. . .] cost $2.50," details Samway, and Faulkner received "25% of that" (*Faulkner's "Intruder,"* 25).

3. Samway, *Faulkner's "Intruder,"* 36.

4. When "MGM came to town to film *Intruder in the Dust*," Faulkner told Robert N. Linscott in 1953, "that made some difference because it meant I'd brought money into Oxford. But it wasn't until the Nobel Prize that they really thawed out. They couldn't understand my books, but they could understand thirty thousand dollars" ("Faulkner without Fanfare" [1953], in *Conversations with William Faulkner*, ed. M. Thomas Inge [Jackson: University Press of Mississippi, 1999], 102).

5. Jean-Luc Marion, *Being Given: Toward a Phenomenology of Givenness* (Stanford, CA: Stanford University Press, 2002), 82; Jean-Luc Marion, *The Visible and the Revealed* (New York: Fordham University Press, 2008), 88. The critical undervaluation of *Intruder* has held relatively firm since the 1950s. "*Intruder in the Dust*," writes William Van O'Connor in *The Tangled Fire of William Faulkner* (1954), "has many of the virtues, although in a lesser degree, of Faulkner's earlier work: the wit, the virtuosity in language, the quality of living figures, the luminous scenes. But the reader does not feel that the true center of the novel is in the relationship between Lucas Beauchamp [. . .] and the white citizens of Jefferson. He may feel that the novel is a brief for the defense, not a novel written for a later as well as a present generation" (*The Tangled Fire of William Faulkner* [Minneapolis: University of Minnesota Press, 1954], 141). Although Donna Gerstenberger excludes the novel from "Edmund Wilson's condemnation of Faulkner's carelessness in constructing the design of his books," her study of "Meaning and Form in *Intruder in the Dust*" (1961) still dismisses Faulkner's creative framework as a "somewhat-contrived murder mystery" ("Meaning and Form in *Intruder in the Dust*," *College English* 23, no. 3 [December 1961]: 223). While finding much to praise in the novel, John E. Bassett cannot help classifying it as "a transitional work in Faulkner's career" ("Gradual Progress and *Intruder in the Dust*," *College Literature* 13, no. 3 [Fall 1986]: 208), with Bassett aligning the evolution of the novelist's approach to literary creation with the slow emergence of majoritarian enlightenment in the South. "*Intruder*, correctly grouped with Faulkner's lesser works," opines Robert W. Hamblin in *A William Faulkner Encyclopedia*, "is a very uneven novel, partly because the Hollywood-style 'whodunit' action (Faulkner had spent much of the early 1940s writing screenplays in Hollywood) seems incompatible with the stream-of-consciousness, high modernist style that is Faulkner's hallmark and partly because the story is frequently set aside (as in chapters 7, 9, and 10) for the effusive propagandizing of Gavin Stevens on the issues of race and sectionalism" ("*Intruder in the Dust* (novel)," in *A William Faulkner Encyclopedia*, ed. Robert W. Hamblin and Charles A. Peek [Westport, CT: Greenwood, 1999], 200).

6. Jacques Derrida, *Given Time: I. Counterfeit Money*, trans. Peggy Kamuf (Chicago: University of Chicago Press, 1992), 6. Hereafter cited parenthetically.

7. "As soon as there is law," explains Derrida, "there is partition: as soon as there is *nomy*, there is economy" (*Given Time*, 6).

8. "In Faulkner's previous stories and novels," notes Samway, "there are certain elements which seem to find further expression in *Intruder*" (*Faulkner's "Intruder,"* 236). These motifs (or *figurations*) come back with renewed interest. The term *"oikos,"* for example, immediately recalls "The Fire and the Hearth" section of *Go Down, Moses* (1942), in which Lucas Beauchamp's earlier engagement with the economy of money comes to a head. For at least a generation, Lucas had treated majoritarians with "cold and deliberate calculation" (William Faulkner, *Go Down, Moses*, in *Novels 1942–1954*, ed. Joseph Blotner and Noel Polk [New York: Library of America, 1994], 81). What is more, as "The Fire and the Hearth" makes clear from the outset, Lucas "already had more money in the bank now than he would ever spend" (26). His twenty-first birthday had secured his "financial independence" (81) because Theophilus (Buck) and Amodeus (Buddy) McCaslin had "made an especial provision (hence a formal acknowledgement, even though only by inference and only from his white half-brothers) for their father's negro son. It was a sum of money, with the accumulated interest, to become the negro son's on his verbal demand but which Tomey's Turl, who elected to remain even after his constitutional liberation, never availed himself of" (82).

"The Fire and the Hearth" recounts Lucas's related actions on coming of age. Isaac McCaslin, who has transferred the relevant account, accompanies Lucas to the bank. Lucas immediately writes a check, withdraws the entire sum, counts the money, and then returns it all to his account (84–85). Nonetheless, the chance discovery of "a single [gold] coin" (30), which Lucas links to a hoard that "old Buck and Buddy had [supposedly] buried almost a hundred years ago" (31), is enough to destabilize his circulation. Lucas's febrile thoughts induce nightly perambulations in search of gold. Only Molly's determination to divorce Lucas cures him of this obsession. "I reckon to find that money aint for me," he concedes (101). The motif of extended presence—so prominent in *Intruder in the Dust*—precedes this admission. When Lucas finally decides against a divorce, he tells Edmonds to wait outside the county courthouse from which they have just emerged, so that he can buy Molly "a nickel's worth" (100) of candy. "'Wait a minute?' Edmonds said. 'Hah!' he said. 'You've bankrupted your waiting. You've already spent—' But Lucas had gone on. And Edmonds waited" (99–100). Importantly for a reading of *Intruder in the Dust*, not only are Chick Mallison, Gavin Stevens, and the Gowries outside the domestic and familial contexts that circumscribe "The Fire and the Hearth," but thanks to Molly, Lucas's gold fever is also spent by the end of this episode.

9. William Faulkner, *Intruder in the Dust*, in *Novels 1942–1954*, ed. Joseph Blotner and Noel Polk (New York: Library of America, 1994), 286. Henceforth cited parenthetically. See also 387, 434.

10. Joseph Blotner, ed., *Selected Letters of William Faulkner* (London: Scolar, 1977), 262.

11. Erik Dussere, "The Debts of History: Southern Honor, Affirmative Action, and Faulkner's *Intruder in the Dust*," *Faulkner Journal* 17, no. 1 (Fall 2001): 43. The Baldwin quotation comes from his essay "Faulkner and Desegregation," *Nobody Knows My Name* (New York: Doubleday, 1961), 100–6.

12. See Robert W. Hamblin, "Teaching *Intruder in the Dust* through Its Political and Historical Context," in *Teaching Faulkner: Approaches and Methods*, ed. Stephen Hahn and Robert W. Hamblin (Westport, CT: Greenwood, 2001), 153–54.

13. Ibid., 154.

14. William Faulkner, "Interview with John K. Hutchens," in *Lion in the Garden: Interviews with William Faulkner, 1926–1962*, ed. James B. Meriwether and Michael Millgate (New York: Random House, 1968), 60.

15. Kenneth S. Greenberg, *Honor and Slavery: Lies, Duels, Noses, Masks, Dressing as a Woman, Gifts, Strangers, Humanitarianism, Death, Slave Rebellions, the Proslavery Argument, Baseball, Hunting, and Gambling in the Old South* (Princeton, NJ: Princeton University Press, 1996), 66.

16. Ibid.

17. From Stevens's "burning cob pipe" (342) to "the neat trim colored maids in frilled caps" (374) to the "valueless enough" (463) motorcars, *Intruder in the Dust* repeatedly illustrates the circumambience of conspicuous consumption.

18. Samway's study of the typescripts of the novel emphasizes Faulkner's growing interest in the unanswerable gift: "The second chapter of the setting copy, which had also been part of the first chapter of the original draft, structures more carefully Chick's [attempts at] repayment and Lucas' gift of molasses delivered to Chick by a white boy" (*Faulkner's "Intruder,"* 257).

19. In this sense, being gifted involves its counterpart in ineptitude, with the brilliance of Faulkner's literary creativeness illuminating his personally destructive relations with money, women, and alcohol.

20. John McAteer, "The Gifts of God for the People of God: Communion as Derrida's Impossible Gift," in *God, the Gift, and Postmodernism*, ed. John D. Caputo and Michael J. Scanlon (Bloomington: Indiana University Press, 1999), 61.

21. Jay Watson, *Forensic Fictions: The Lawyer Figure in Faulkner* (1993; repr., Athens: University of Georgia Press, 2008), 114.

22. Marion, *The Visible and the Revealed*, 91. The gifted Molly's cure of Lucas's gold fever in "The Fire and the Hearth" (see note 8 above) is one of these preceding gifts.

23. All told, Miss Habersham proves to be an eccentric figure of circulation, as her journey home after the townsfolk's acceptance of Lucas's innocence attests. She pulls her pickup truck into the traffic leaving the town square, but the weight of vehicles carries her out of Jefferson, and she must ask for return directions. In effect, she describes a circle, one with its center offset from the town square.

24. Stevens's request and Lucas's willing response are profoundly beyond the "absurd" of which Samway writes (*Faulkner's "Intruder,"* 270).

25. Jacques Derrida, *The Gift of Death*, trans. David Wills (Chicago: University of Chicago Press, 1996), 50.

26. Robert Frost, "The Gift Outright" (1941), *Robert Frost: Collected Poems, Prose, and Plays*, ed. Richard Poirier and Mark Richardson (New York: Library of America, 1995), 316.

27. Eric R. Severson, "Introduction: Economy, Gift, and Mystery," in *Gift and Economy: Ethics, Hospitality, and the Market*, ed. Eric R. Severson (Newcastle upon Tyne: Cambridge Scholars, 2012), 5.

28. Ibid.

29. Walt Whitman, "A Song of the Rolling Earth," in *Leaves of Grass* (Philadelphia: McKay, 1891–92), 179.

30. Julie Des Jardins, *The Madame Curie Complex: The Hidden History of Women in Science* (New York: Feminist Press at CUNY, 2010), 175.

Racial Debts, Individual Slights, and Sleights of Hand in Faulkner's *Intruder in the Dust*

MARY A. KNIGHTON

> *Horkheimer and Adorno enable us to see that the southern instance conforms to the general condition. The brutality internal to the project of enlightenment—the violence inherent in abstraction and equivalence-making—makes southern racialist ideology, like an otherwise so different European fascism, a conceptual product of Western idealism. . . . Put bluntly, as Enlightenment reason depends on anti-Semitism, according to Horkheimer and Adorno, so American capitalism depends on racism.*
> —John T. Matthews

> *Whar's the rest of that money old Carothers left? I wants it. All of it.*
> —Lucas Beachamp to Ike McCaslin in Go Down, Moses

However one reads *Intruder in the Dust* (1948), money motives come into play.[1] A twelve-year-old white boy owes a debt to a black man who saves his life, but when he tries to pay it back with a few coins, his offer is spurned. Aggrieved for four years, the boy finally gets his chance to pay it back in kind by saving the man from a lynch mob. Money here represents Chick Mallison's hasty, inadequate response to an abstract debt that he owes Lucas Beauchamp. A more straightforward account stresses the novel's action-oriented murder mystery. Chick and his motley crew of amateur sleuths—including his black friend Aleck Sander and seventy-year-old Miss Eunice Habersham—dig up graves and displace bodies in a shell game "read" at a distance by Lucas Beauchamp in jail who, it turns out, has known all along who the murderer is. The reader too learns this halfway through the novel: Crawford Gowrie, in a series of cover-ups, killed his brother and Jake Montgomery, his partner in stealing lumber. Lucas's impending murder by lynch mob, including his accusation in the first place, constitutes a further cover-up. Despite such machinations, *Intruder* comes across as a mystery whodunit minus the whodunit.[2] For Donald Kartiganer, *Intruder* manipulates genre conventions to reach a predictably happy ending; that is, despite serious racial conflict and a few comic twists, *Intruder* conclusively redeems mainstream society and its boy hero.[3] Hollywood itself could make hay with this version of *Intruder*'s plot.

And while both plots may well depend on Chick's mediating consciousness, what does it mean that their structural fulcrum and the narrative's beating heart can only belong to Lucas Beauchamp? Lucas's stubborn silence torques *Intruder*'s plots into one painfully contorted personal and collective racial debt that Chick can only resolve by taking up Lucas's shovel and walking in Lucas's shoes, so to speak. After all, digging up gravesites is linked not only to the stills and gold coin that Lucas alternately buries and digs up in other stories, but also to Lucas himself fallen into the old Indian burial site in *Go Down, Moses*; all function as instances of Lucas Beauchamp showing us where the bodies of history are buried.[4] Digging up the past along with money signifies his obsession with reclaiming what belongs to him in the profit-taking and moneymaking game. William Faulkner's ostensible murder mystery distracts us from Lucas's key role, obfuscating the significance of the final body stolen from the grave—Lucas Beauchamp's—in the real shell game here of story plots and burial plots.

The cipher that is Lucas gets tangled in a series of substitutions along a chain of debt: Chick Mallison's claim to a personal slight tinged with racial insults exacerbates his financial debt to Lucas, and then it gets magnified beyond mere money until it transforms into a surprising ultimatum of debt resolution as racial kinship. By *Intruder*'s end, Chick's abstract racialized debt appears to be far from incalculable, finally equated to a specific sum that neatly pays off the debt that structures the opening of the novel: Chick saves Lucas's life in repayment and exchange for Chick's life already saved. But the text's neat conclusion and circulation of bodies, formulaic in detective murder mysteries, in Faulkner's "sleight-of-hand" begins to expose something less predictable: Chick makes a painful choice to act counter to his white community—or rather, he leads by taking reparative steps in a direction community members refuse to face.[5]

The racial debt as reparations thematized in *Intruder* circulates outside of the text when received in 1948 as a response to contemporary civil rights activity and an antilynching bill.[6] The story further hardens into the contours of that historical present when the film version is shot in Faulkner's own Oxford, Mississippi, the following year using local citizens as actors.[7] In a murder mystery without a mystery, a novel about lynching where no lynching takes place, something else is going on, abetted by Faulkner's notoriously elliptical and occlusive storytelling. As *Sanctuary* (1931) perhaps epitomizes, Faulkner's style enables vital story events to be left out completely or narrated only indirectly when not operating recursively and obliquely. In this chapter, I aim to repair to legibility the aphasic story of racial reparations in *Intruder* yet to be adequately heard. Lucas Beauchamp serves structurally to link two kinds of plots: as a character with a disproportionately larger intertextual significance than his offstage role in *Intruder* suggests, he disrupts the novel's bounded form and the detective genre's formulaic circulation of burial plots, bodies, and money. Meanwhile, Chick stands in for the physically absent Lucas, simultaneously mediating our access to Lucas and magnifying what Lucas means. Chick serves as the reader's white paranoid interlocutor and co-conspirator in calibrating the costs of racial kinship ties.

Individual Slights: Family Plots, Burial Plots

In *Shadow and Act*, Ralph Ellison interprets Chick's fall into Lucas Beauchamp's creek as his "[plunge] into the depth of a reality which constantly reveals itself as the reverse of what it had appeared before his plunge. Here the ice—white, brittle, and eggshell thin—symbolizes Chick's inherited views of the world, especially his Southern conception of Negroes."[8] Chick inherits white society's views, as this baptismal scene suggests, and his profits in whiteness add up in material reality, too. However fragile its legitimacy, whiteness as inviolable property confers rights and privileges for those who can claim it and risks for those who threaten it. Aleck Sander aptly sums up what the black community thinks, trying not to get caught up in Lucas's drama even as he and Chick are embroiled in it: "It's the ones like Lucas makes trouble for everybody" (85). In Faulkner's cosmos, making trouble is Lucas's *raison d'être*.

Chick's trouble with Lucas is debt. Humiliated by his rescue from the creek and then warmed and fed in Lucas's home, Chick extends money to Molly to pay the Beauchamps back. Lucas rejects it. Slighted, Chick drops the coins on the floor, insulting Lucas's right to extend hospitality in his own home. Chick hereby compounds his monetary debt in racial terms. Paying the debt grows increasingly elusive and becomes its own parody, mutating from this point into Chick's failed bartering, extended further into a shell game of grave digging, grave swapping, and quicksand. Only later, when Chick recognizes that the debt he owes is for his life, not just for food and shelter, does he make headway. In giving Chick the tools to solve the murder of Vinson Gowrie and confront his debt, Lucas shows him the path to his own manhood, a masculinity bound up in money as a way to form, reinforce, and master patriarchal community and family bonds.

If all this suggests that Lucas serves as father figure to Chick, it is because Lucas alone marks Chick's obsession with masculinity. Although his Harvard-educated uncle, Gavin Stevens, appears to replace Chick's rarely seen father, Stevens merely serves as an intellectual sounding board for Chick's developing social conscience, not as a model of manly action and resolve. Uncle Gavin offers his nephew a southern liberal's running commentary on race relations, but at times, Chick turns away from the tortured apologies, "the significantless speciosity of his uncle's voice" (80–81).[9] Lucas, however—in rescuing him and bringing him back to life in a warm, domestic home as if his own son—haunts him and serves as a proud, unapologetic, and unattainable model for Chick. That Chick repeatedly sees his grandfather in Lucas solidifies the latter's paternal role: "he could no more imagine himself contradicting the man striding on ahead of him than he could his grandfather, not from any fear of nor even threat of reprisal but because like his grandfather the man striding ahead of him was simply incapable of conceiving himself by a child contradicted and defied" (8).

Black and white family figures interpenetrate Chick's developing social conscience, and Ikuko Fujihira persuasively maps out his surrogate family made up of Miss Habersham, Aleck Sander, and Lucas.[10] Repeatedly likening Lucas to his grandfather and Miss Habersham to his grandmother, Chick constructs the pair as his cross-racial (grand)parents. Eunice Worsham Habersham grew up alongside Lucas's wife as, in effect, Molly Worsham's sister, and hence "family" to Lucas too; she easily substitutes for Molly in Chick's surrogate family. Rounding out the family portrait, Chick regularly joins his black "brother," Aleck Sander, at Paralee's table in the Mallison family's backyard, as "at home" there as at his own family's table.

Part sentimental, part comical, Chick's unlikely cross-racial family begins to take metaphorical shape with his rebirth in Lucas's home, warmed back to life after his near death in the icy creek. For the first time, Chick identifies a smell that he had unconsciously lived with like the very air he breathes but that suddenly emerges when he loses his innocence:

> *that unmistakable odor of Negroes* . . . which if it were not for something that was going to happen to him within a space of time measurable now in minutes he would have gone to his grave never once pondering speculating if perhaps *that smell were really not the odor of a race nor even actually of poverty but perhaps of a condition: an idea: a belief: an acceptance, a passive acceptance.* . . . But the smell meant nothing now or yet; it was still an hour

yet before the thing would happen and it would be four years more before he would realise the extent of its ramifications and what it had done to him and he would be a man grown before he would realise, admit that he had accepted it. So he just smelled it and then dismissed it because he was used to it.... [H]e *could not even imagine an existence from which the odor would be missing to return no more.* He had smelled it forever, he would smell it always; it was a part of *his inescapable past*, it was *a rich part of his heritage as a Southerner.* (11–12; emphasis added)

The "odor of Negroes" marks Chick's prelapsarian innocence; his awakening racial superiority raises a suspicious new stench here. As Chick turns to black-or-white logic to rationalize racial hierarchy by basing it in biology, Faulkner's colons mimic philosophical analogy but dwindle into progressively weaker formulations: "a condition: an idea: a belief: an acceptance, a passive acceptance." A more elusive smell gets bound up in his own "inescapable past" as Chick mourns the color line now cutting him off from those once so close to him that the smell of their skin, their existential presence, and their kinship were indistinguishable from his own. The crass stereotype of a racial Other's body odor camouflages the pathos of Chick's white grief for lost kinship, a "condition" and "idea" of equally given human ties.

The fact that Gowrie murders his own brother dramatizes the role of kinship in *Intruder*. Face to face with fratricide in the name of property and greed—a crime of family—Chick is forced to put a price on his membership in the "We" of the white community. He must weigh it against Lucas's imminent lynching:

> He remembered again the faces myriad yet curiously identical in their lack of individual identity, their complete relinquishment of individual identity into one We.... [H]e now recognised the enormity of what he had blindly meddled with ... because it seemed to him now that he was responsible for having brought into the light and glare of day something shocking and shameful out of the whole white foundation of the county which he himself must partake of too since he too was bred of it, which otherwise might have flared and blazed merely out of Beat Four and then vanished back into its darkness or at least invisibility with the fading embers of Lucas's crucifixion. (137–38; emphasis added)

The stakes here are writ large: Will Chick allow Lucas's "crucifixion" and erasure despite his respect for the latter's "solitary independent and intractable" (8) manhood? Will Chick be complicit in the "shameful" and fratricidal white masculinity not only sanctioned by his community but also endorsed by the laws of the land? Unable and unwilling to change his racial identity, Chick nonetheless struggles to make it all tally with his larger "heritage as a Southerner," treating racial identity and manhood as ciphers inseparable from his personal debt to Lucas in society's larger racial account ledgers.

Chick's shock at realizing that fateful day that he had never really been a guest on Edmonds's property but rather on McCaslin's signifies more than we, or Chick himself, understand at the time: Lucas is a Beauchamp McCaslin, no longer tenant but rather master of his domain, and his family and racial history extend beyond Chick's ken and *Intruder*'s story.[11] Lucas stubbornly stakes his rightful claim to McCaslin land as black Beauchamp heir over that of the distaff line, the Edmondses. Chick's recognition of the value of Lucas's history instantiates the metaphor of a moon-shaped coin hanging over his head like the sword of Damocles.

> Because there was the half-dollar. The actual sum was seventy cents of course and in four coins but he had long since during that first few fractions of a second transposed translated them into the one coin one integer in mass and weight out of all proportion to its mere convertible value; there were times in fact when, the capacity of his spirit for regret or perhaps just simple writhing or whatever it was at last spent for a moment and even quiescent, he would tell himself *At least I have the half-dollar, at least I have something* because now not only his mistake and its shame but its protagonist too—the man, the Negro, the room, the moment, the day itself—had annealed vanished into the round hard symbol of the coin and he would seem to see himself lying watching regretless and even peaceful as day by day the coin swelled to its gigantic maximum, to hang fixed at last forever in the black vault of his anguish like the last dead and waneless moon and himself, his own puny shadow gesticulant and tiny against it in frantic and vain eclipse: frantic and vain yet indefatigable too because he would never stop, he could never give up now who had debased not merely his manhood but his whole race too. (20–21)

What is this monstrous coin that "eclipses" Chick's claim against Lucas for seventy cents so thoroughly? His appreciation of Lucas's history "in mass and weight out of all proportion to its mere convertible value," a history pregnant with the sins of the McCaslin fathers as scions of Yoknapatawpha County, predates his puny debt added to its sum now. As Chick's miscalculated personal reparations to Lucas swell to encompass Yoknapatawpha's historical reparations, the debt appears incalculable, monumentally heavy, and even absurd after so much time and whatever the rationales of Yoknapatawpha's Founding Fathers. This sentiment of absurd impossibility measures the gap between the actual coin of reparations and the irreparable acts of history depicted in Faulkner's monstrous coin. Although

Chick's "own puny shadow gesticulant and tiny" is eclipsed against the backdrop of a history that overwhelms his deeds alone, he refuses to turn his back on this vision of his race's, and his nation's, collective debt.

Chick serves as the reader's interlocutor of the novel's various "plots," reading Lucas's face, interpreting his cryptic words, and doing his bidding. Though physically absent in much of the novel, Lucas's full and valuable life hangs over it as surely as the monstrous coin. Faulkner has Lucas orchestrate a metanarrative of racial debt and reparations via Chick since a black man's voice discussing topics of racial debt and reparations would have little purchase with his readers. An "innocent" white boy serves Faulkner and Lucas both as a prosthetic tool to reach their respective white audiences. When Chick's developing sense of white superiority impedes Lucas's story, his advancement of Lucas's reparations plot despite himself enhances his authenticity. Meanwhile, Lucas paternally guides Chick in walking where he would walk, seeing what he would see, and finally solving the crime. Chick even repeats Lucas's nocturnal digging and still-swapping from "The Fire and the Hearth," but this time with graves and real bodies. By throwing his rejected coins from that fateful day into the creek from which he had been saved, Chick unwittingly contributes his share to Lucas's dream of material compensation, directing our attention to Lucas's offstage presence in the intertextual story. After all, Lucas was long convinced that the creek area held buried treasure, an obsession initially primed by the gold coin he found when trying to hide his still—now swollen into Chick's monstrous coin. The creek area acts as a ghostly repository of cross-racial violence and broken dreams across Faulkner's texts, harboring coins, stills, metal detector, and possibly even the drowned body of Lucas's enslaved great-grandmother, Eunice, who committed suicide upon learning of Old Carothers McCaslin's rape and begetting of Tomey's Turl on their daughter, Tomey (Tomasina).[12] This process of walking in Lucas's footsteps walks Chick, and us, through Lucas's cross-racial history into his present-day treasure hunts. Lucas drags him literally and figuratively through dark woods and quicksand, where Chick learns more about his racial debt than about the means to pay it. Instead of repudiating Lucas Beauchamp and his debt, Chick begins to figure the cost of his manhood while stumbling through piecemeal reparations on his own, cobbling together cross-racial family ties, responsibilities, and allegiances.

Collective Racial Debts: Re-membering Family

Treasure hunter and bootlegging entrepreneur, comical and righteous in his stubborn pride, Lucas Beauchamp is at the heart of what Faulkner talks about when he talks about race and money. Beauchamp's intertextual history precedes his adventures in *Intruder*, and he embodies his unspeakable racial and family background in the Jim Crow South of 1948 as it extends back to slavery and his emergence from the black and white family lines of the McCaslin-Edmonds-Beauchamp genealogy. At a time when "mixed race" meant illegal interracial marriage and the sins of miscegenation, Lucas Beauchamp proclaims a possessive investment in his own whiteness.[13] He takes an interest in the property rights due him as a descendant of L. Q. C. McCaslin, marking thereby the financial debts and assets of his family ties. Lucas insists on his rights as a citizen in the face of a history of disenfranchised shadow families and poll taxes that disqualified would-be voters who were not landowners.

Wealth accumulation, of course, has long been a family matter. A racial wealth gap confronts black families split up during slavery, marking their difficulty in amassing wealth in modern times even after freedom and citizenship.[14] New Deal policies affected tenant and sharecropping whites and blacks differently, and systemic twentieth-century laws and institutional practices regarding housing loans, redlining, and white flight cast very long, modern shadows on that long-ago broken promise of forty acres and a mule.[15] The disavowed shadow families in Faulkner's Dark Houses complicate this narrative still further.[16] Ike McCaslin makes explicit the family-as-property storyline in attempting to give up his birthright once he understands how his family's wealth and power were attained: a black family line enslaved, raped, incestuously violated, its suicides unmourned. Ike refuses to play his role as medium for the transfer of such disavowal and white family wealth—sacrificing his future heirs and past inheritance—in attempting to deliver thousand-dollar legacies to Tomey's Turl's descendants in a final act of atonement. As my epigraph makes clear, Lucas does not hesitate to accept the money. Lucas hereby trains a light on white families as corporate entities that convey and accumulate wealth—and he wants his share. Home ownership functions as a vehicle to wealth accumulation via intergenerational succession, and Lucas Beauchamp's searches for buried treasure and stills on his property show him, in effect, digging up and reassembling, on his own land, the wealth properly due him as a McCaslin.

If the dust that Faulkner's *Intruder* kicks up takes the form of open family secrets in the interconnected stories of Faulkner's Yoknapatawpha saga, at a deeper level, dust also indexes past white manipulations of wealth and meddling in family plots in efforts to *alter* in one's favor (not strictly *repair*) outcomes for the future. One example, of course, is Old Carothers's attempt to erase his violent sexual intrusion first into the enslaved Eunice's life, and then into their daughter's life, by paying off his black descendants. Another is how a poker game in "Was" decides the marital and family fates for white Sophonsiba Beauchamp and Buck

McCaslin and for the enslaved Tomey's Turl and Tennie Beauchamp. The racially crossed white and black McCaslins and Beauchamps, as with other Yoknapatawpha leading families, tell a larger, more resonant story about wealth in the hands of those in power and how that wealth has shaped what families and history itself could look like.

Defiantly refusing to erase history, Lucas dramatizes it as the son of Tomey's Turl and Tennie Beauchamp. He amends his first name from "Lucius" to "Lucas" and insists on his Beauchamp family name even as he stubbornly traces his lineage back to Old Lucius Carothers and proudly asserts his property rights as a male McCaslin.[17] As de facto head of the Beauchamp line, Lucas reclaims home and family. In "The Fire and the Hearth," Lucas resolves never to let the fires in his family hearth go out after marrying Molly, inspiring in turn Rider's marital ideal in "Pantaloon in Black." *Intruder* meticulously details Lucas's actual house as, in effect, the "House of Beauchamp":

> [N]ow they were in no well-used tended lane leading to tenant or servant quarters and marked by walking feet but a savage gash half gully and half road mounting a hill with *an air solitary independent and intractable too* and then he saw the house, the cabin and remembered the rest of the story, the legend: how Edmonds' father had deeded to his Negro first cousin and his heirs in perpetuity the house and the ten acres of land it sat in . . . *an oblong of earth set forever in the middle of the two-thousand-acre plantation like a postage stamp in the center of an envelope* . . . the four of them walking in what was less than walk because its surface was dirt yet more than path, *the footpacked strip running plumbline straight between two borders* of tin cans and empty bottles and shards of china and earthenware set into the ground, *up to the paintless steps and the paintless gallery* . . . and beyond this *the house itself, gray and weathered and not so much paintless as independent of and intractable to paint so that the house was not only the one possible continuation of the stern untended road but was its crown too as the carven ailanthus leaves are the Greek column's capital.* (8–9; emphasis added)

Long a sharecropper, by *Intruder*, Lucas emerges as a landowner, his ten-acre plot of land with its small cabin "like a postage stamp in the center of an envelope," inconveniently carved out of the very center of the McCaslin-Edmonds property. The home of Lucas Beauchamp is described in the same language as Lucas himself: "solitary independent and intractable." The repetitions of "paintless" conclude with a modification, "not so much paintless as independent of and intractable to paint," establishing a masculine analogy between the man and his castle, both direct and unvarnished. Most striking, a "plumbline" drops upwards to the house, rather than straight down as one would expect. Just as Lucas's home "crown[s]" the inversion from bottom to top of the plumbline that ends the path, it effectively monumentalizes Lucas's rise from slave family origins to the head of the Beauchamp lineage and property owner of his family's enslaver's land. The defiant racial and family ties that Lucas Beauchamp represents on his postage stamp of McCaslin land arguably anticipate, amend, and reconfigure Faulkner's entire Yoknapatawpha "postage stamp."[18]

But how, one might well ask, can Lucas—ever "solitary"—be about family? By *Intruder*, Molly Beauchamp is dead, present only in Chick's memories. Even earlier, in "The Fire and the Hearth," Lucas and his wife were on the verge of divorce, and Lucas was at odds with his daughter, Nat, and George Wilkins. In *Intruder*, Lucas is alone, marked by grief and fierce independence. He hardly belongs to any community, black or white. And yet, just as he guides Chick, it is Lucas who cobbles together their surrogate family—a reminder, perhaps, of the way black families have long consisted of kin reassembled and re-membered out of necessity after being unacknowledged and forcibly dispersed under slavery.

In his studies of black kinship among the enslaved of the upper mid-Atlantic South, historian Calvin Schermerhorn looks at the mobile assemblages and networks of alliances they forged based not necessarily on blood or skin color but on ties of affection, loyalty, and usefulness.[19] Such reconfigurations of family recall too the classic essay wherein Hortense Spillers describes the "American Grammar Book" of white and black family lines.[20] For white American families, family syntax gets represented by vertical patrilineage, with heritage and property passed down through the name of fathers. The syntax of African American families, however, takes on horizontal family structures resulting from displacement and dismemberment; ancestors' names were erased by bodily theft from Africa and white ownership while the condition of the enslaved as chattel property legally followed the condition of their mothers. During and after slavery, ceaseless attempts to reassemble families sold, escaped, and dispersed far and wide ensured that such horizontal inflections would persist across generations into the twentieth century. Lucas's McCaslin lineage, forged in slavery's rape and incest, is both dramatized and exposed in its distortion through the Beauchamp name, passed down through enslaved women.

Contemporary historians Edward Baptist, Sven Beckert, and Schermerhorn show us the peculiar institution's formative stamp not only on families but on America's version of capitalism, marking money and economies of exchange not as universal and timeless but as highly specific, changing over time as global and local commerce for commodities expanded. As banks developed, currency itself took different forms, widely local and questionable, printed up regionally, with letters of credit and so-called "notes of hand" backed by their issuers' reputation that circulated in lieu of cash for transactions involving bodies and commodities.[21] Baptist and Ian Baucom detail how African Americans were made "bondsmen" not only in the sense of bondage and enslavement but as embodied, marked instruments of financial exchange, insurance, collateral, and letters of credit in the global economy.[22]

This groundbreaking scholarship documents slavery not merely as some errant stage on the way to today's system of political economy but rather as incipiently structuring finance capitalism as we now know it. Enslaved people's constitutive contribution to our economic system's development and growth, past and present, can be seen in the differential ways in which white and black families could function as corporate entities for the accumulation and conveyance of wealth across generations. Spillers' racialized family syntax, we might say, ironically annotates the commonsense voice of Benjamin Franklin's *The Way to Wealth*, just as Faulkner's fictional Yoknapatawpha families originate with a Franklin character, "Father Abraham" (1926). The biblical patriarch given contemporary form serves both Faulkner and Franklin in their respective advocacy of the American values of industry and capital accumulation, and surely Faulkner found Franklin's homespun homilies irresistible for modern parody.[23] With Father Abraham standing for the Snopes family line, and with both Ab and Flem Snopes arguably white analogues to Lucas Beauchamp, each turning the tables on Yoknapatawpha's established family clans to claim his financial due, Faulkner slyly comments on history's disenfranchised finding their "way to wealth" under capitalism, by hook or by crook.

Ta-Nehisi Coates's 2014 essay, "The Case for Reparations," and Faulkner's *Intruder* both raise pressing questions about debts spawned by past violations of human and family value, but it is the modern violations of the rules under American capitalism for wealth accumulation that stand out.[24] A tangle of modern laws forged and amended in favor of white families, long after the enslavement and theft of black families and bodies for unfree labor and for national as well as regional profit, creates present-day structural inequalities enforced by twentieth-century racial terrorism and lynching, the Jim Crow regime, and *Plessy v. Ferguson*'s investment in whiteness as property. Repairing the American family sundered in the name of the "way to wealth," in short, will require digging up these displaced bodies and paying material as well as abstract debts to re-member them.

One such real body pertains to *Intruder*'s story: the lynching of Elwood Higginbottom less than two miles from Oxford, Mississippi, on September 18, 1935. Besides the 1908 murder of Nelse Patton in Oxford when Faulkner was a boy, Higginbottom's was one of several such mob crimes that likely inspired Faulkner's tales of lynching, from "Dry September" (1931) and *Light in August* (1932) to *Intruder*.[25] Higginbottom's lynching occurred closer to *Intruder*'s writing, and its story made national newspapers; moreover, a Faulkner family member allegedly witnessed it.[26] The outline of Higginbottom's story haunts that of *Intruder*: despite a trial resulting in rumors that he would be freed after being accused of killing a white timber man in Beat Two, Higginbottom's was dragged from jail and lynched by a mob that would not wait for a jury verdict.[27]

Higginbottom's buried story puts Coates's reparations argument into dialogue with Faulkner's *Intruder* because it highlights modern and contemporary crimes rather more than slavery-era ones. (Lucas represents, of course, both.) Today's diverse reparations movements also seek to repair America's racial kinship ties by digging up *recent* unmemorialized, unmourned, and still untold stories.[28] Such efforts may well open, as *Intruder* does, by acceding that money alone is inadequate and an insult, and indeed obscures incalculable racial debts; and yet, money also remains vital to the dirty open secret of race relations under capitalism that must be told. *Intruder* thematizes individual and national reparations by opening and concluding with cross-racial financial transactions between a white boy representing the present and future and an elderly black man insisting on an accounting for the past. Part of that accounting in *Intruder* is its staging of the contemporary and strikingly banal terrorism of lynching in Faulkner's time, thereby vindicating Lucas's manhood and repairing to our memory Higginbottom's story.

John T. Matthews and Robert H. Brinkmeyer Jr. argue that Faulkner, like many southern writers between the 1930s and 1950s, actively engaged in his fiction and as a cultural ambassador with contemporary cultural and political debates about American democracy and race relations under capitalism.[29] Particularly after World War II, with the advent of civil rights and decolonization movements around the world, US Jim Crow terrorism no longer signified as a mere domestic matter; rather, as Matthews's epigraph to this chapter indicates, a flagrant contempt for human rights and supposed democratic institutions led to comparisons of southern apartheid to race-based European fascism and northern or federal intervention to totalitarianism. Going forward, it is hard to imagine US reparations for a national debt to African American families being able to avoid an international frame for modern crimes committed against humanity, in violation of the nation's own rules of modern wealth accumulation as every citizen's right.

Intruder's Sleights of Hand: "Strange Fruit"

Faulkner's letters and biographies more than hint that money and family—specifically, his constant struggle for money as his extended family grew and he accepted responsibility for supporting them—shaped his approach to money matters in his fiction. After a long career of peddling his wares in the literary marketplace, Faulkner began his path to financial security when *Intruder* was published amidst the fanfare surrounding its Hollywood adaptation by MGM. Soon after, the Nobel Prize for Literature cemented Faulkner's financial and cultural success. Faulkner's take from the MGM film contract just as *Intruder* was coming out reached $40,000 and helped his book to gain greater sales and royalties than Faulkner had ever received.[30] Random House made sure that advertisements for the film came out virtually simultaneously with the book announcements, giving the impression of the successful adaptation of a successful novel even before the book had its first real reader.

For critic Regina Fadiman, it is a puzzle how the book could be such a financial success while the film was, despite critical praise, such a commercial failure.[31] Nonetheless, Faulkner reaped in the profits and cultural capital that accompanied advance film rights. Film scholars then and now noted the timing and theme of *Intruder* as remarkable considering heightened race relations on the brink of the civil rights era, not to mention film censorship and Jim Crow retrenchment.[32] How could a film that critiques white southerners' barbarity while a black man lords it over would-be lynchers even get made in 1949? Certainly, the idea of both book and film as so-called "message" works did not sit well with the advertising plans of Random House or MGM's plan to film *Intruder* in Faulkner's Oxford and market it to whites North and South. But director Clarence Brown, raised in the South, was drawn to the book for its focus on lynching, traumatized by one that he himself had once witnessed.[33] Brown read the novel while it was still in galleys, and prepublication went out of his way to make sure it became a film, trading on friendships to get a reluctant Louis B. Mayer at MGM to support the project.[34]

Faulkner described his starting premise for writing *Intruder* in a letter to his agent, Harold Ober, in early 1948, saying it was about the "relationship between Negro and white, specifically or rather the premise being that the white people in the south, before the North or the govt. or anyone else, owe and must pay a responsibility to the Negro."[35] Although Faulkner espouses here a doctrine of noninterference in the South's racial affairs by the federal government, just as important is his insistence on debt and compensation in this well-known statement. Faulkner's words complicate the complex alchemy of the racial debt outside the text as well as the one inside between Chick and Lucas, anticipating too Brown's motive for making the film. But Faulkner did not stop there in his letter to Ober: "I may have told you the idea, which I have had for some time—a Negro in jail accused of murder and waiting for the white folks to drag him out and pour gasoline over him and set him on fire, is the detective, solves the crime because he goddamn has to to keep from being lynched, by asking people to go somewhere and look at something and then come back and tell him what they found."[36] This is what Faulkner wanted to say with *Intruder* but had to dissemble in order to meet the marketing needs of MGM and Random House, concerned about white sensibilities and film censorship. Correspondence between Random House and MGM, as well as between Faulkner and Random House, certainly shows these concerns, as does Faulkner's occasional willingness to adopt his editors' language centered on Chick as a Huck Finn character rather than on Lucas or lynching.[37]

Quite telling in this regard, and comical too, is the exchange between Bennett Cerf of Random House and Faulkner over the title of *Intruder in the Dust*. Cerf wanted to change the title to *Beat Four*, ostensibly to avoid antagonizing either whites or blacks by stressing the redneck Gowries as the novel's real villains, but Faulkner resisted:

> BEAT FOUR doesn't strike my ear in this case, anymore than Range Four or Township Four would. COUNTY would come nearer fitting.
> I wish we could think of a pleasanter word than JUGGLERY. But lacking any short word for substitution, swap, exchange, sleight-of-hand, I think INTRUDER IN THE DUST is best. I am not bound to it, but I dont think Beat Four is right at all. As it is, it means nothing. Then if you let the story give it a significance, you foist the wrong significance on it. Beat Four did no more than all the rest of the county would have in those circumstances.[38]

Faulkner prevaricates, then he parries; he feigns difficulty in coming up with a better word than Cerf's, exhausting a list of "their" possible synonyms for "intruder" while comically pretending to be open to changing it; finally, he resigns himself to the original title he wanted all along. He refuses to scapegoat the Gowries in exchange for the more complex cross-racial story he wants to tell in *Intruder*, and he preserves the focus on "a Negro in jail" under threat of lynching. Striking in these lines is how these metonymic substitutions move the cogs and belts of the novel's machinery, its "sleight-of-hand" cover-ups extending to the novel's cover art.

The first-edition jacket of *Intruder* designed by E. McKnight Kauffer speaks to Random House's marketing goals and its target audience.[39]

Faulkner too paid attention to book jackets and to this artist's work in particular, as we know from editor and friend Saxe Commins' letter to Faulkner, pleased to have Kauffer as *Intruder*'s cover artist.[40] In the published cover's condensed symbolic imagery (see fig. 1), a recently opened grave appears before a highly stylized house, representing both the novel's grave-digging "intruders" and Lucas's robbing the lynch mob of his own grave.

Kauffer's cover artwork for Richard Wright's 1942 Modern Library edition of *Native Son* (see fig. 2) visually anticipates his preliminary studies for *Intruder* (see fig. 3) eight years later.[41] In this context, how striking that the 1951 "problem picture" adaptation of *Native Son*, banned outright in most states for encouraging racial misunderstanding, was unfavorably compared to the uncensored *Intruder* film.[42] Anticipating the publisher's eagerness to gain market share and avoid fomenting racial resentments, Kauffer appears to have revised the traces of Wright's jacket art in his roughs for Faulkner's *Intruder*, replacing the realistic "problem picture" of a black man trapped in the jail of Jim Crow society with a more elusive, even surreal, cover. Only after looking more closely might we discern why. For here (see fig. 4), encoded in the tree's Spanish moss, are strange fruit indeed: faces emerge from the tangles to speak the aphasic story of lynching and racial debt that *Intruder* tells despite the self-censorship and other artistic "cover-ups" of author, illustrator, and publisher alike.[43]

We should not underestimate the evasive tactics required to get this cover, this book, or this uncensored film about lynching out into the public in 1948–49. Obfuscating Faulkner's story of Lucas's imminent fate may be a boy-led murder mystery but, make no mistake, lynching hangs over the story of *Intruder* as surely as a lighted, manshaped, ghostly apotheosis threatens the Big House in Kauffer's first-edition jacket art. The novel's real suspense stems less from discovering the true murderer already revealed midnovel or from Chick's racial grudge than from the atmospheric suspense of a lynching in foment, taking shape and ever about to happen: Lucas's innocence is never a guarantee of safety from a lynch mob eager from the start to make him a "nigger" (18; emphasis removed). The lynching tension around Lucas offstage deepens the darkness around the gravediggers' search and amplifies the silence in their held breaths; even after the real criminal's motive and crime are exposed, the threat of lynching remains, and white mob racism emerges as a greater terror than any individual outlaw.[44] Continuing its patterns of substitution and evasion, the novel's heavy atmosphere lifts only with payment of a blood debt, when murderer Crawford Gowrie takes the grave intended for Lucas Beauchamp. What first appears as Gowrie

Fig. 1. First edition Random House dust jacket for William Faulkner's *Intruder in the Dust*, by E. McKnight Kauffer (1948). Copyright © Simon Rendall. Courtesy of Penguin Random House LLC.

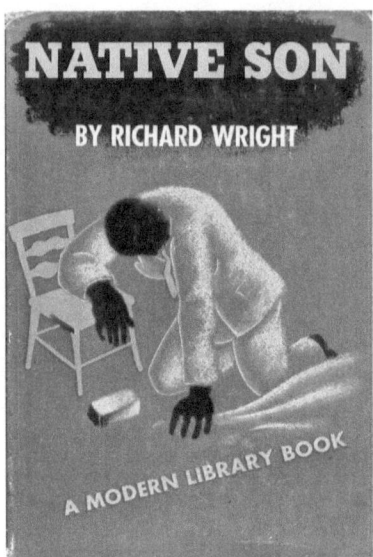

Fig. 2. First Modern Library edition dust jacket for Richard Wright's *Native Son*, by E. McKnight Kauffer (1942). Copyright © Simon Rendall. Courtesy of Penguin Random House LLC.

Fig. 3. Rough drawing and design for the book cover of *Intruder in the Dust* (1948). E. McKnight Kauffer Archive. Copyright © Simon Rendall and Smithsonian Institution. Permission of the Cooper Hewitt, Smithsonian Design Museum / Art Resource, NY.

being allowed to save face and a vestige of manhood by committing suicide is actually Faulkner's decision to satisfy the novel's bloodlust in having the white man's body replace the black man's: a final grave-swapping. Faulkner's aggressive substitution explains why Crawford Gowrie, too, is mostly absent as a character in the novel; in this way, he can serve as a functional abstraction, individualized only indirectly through the Gowrie clan and reports of his own deeds. The novel's blood debt paid with his life warns about white refusal to face up to reparations, and Crawford's suicide might well be read, then, as cowardice. The "composite Face of his native kind his native land, his people his blood his own" (194) that Chick had earlier agonized over as the many faces of a communal "We" has, by novel's end, transformed into the back of a head, as the mob averts its collective face and slinks away without apology or even gifting Lucas with a ten-cent "package of tobacco" (192).

Intruder's concluding film scene shows Lucas paying John Stevens, the Gavin Stevens figure, for his expenses with a bag of pennies that

Fig. 4. Close-up of first edition Random House dust jacket for William Faulkner's *Intruder in the Dust* by E. McKnight Kauffer (1948). Copyright © Simon Rendall. Courtesy of Penguin Random House LLC.

Stevens, after Lucas, will have to painstakingly count; at the very least, it reinforces the structural parallel between the start and the end of the novel as Chick's debt and its apparent payment. And yet, this is not the paying back of a debt Lucas owes either to Stevens or even indirectly to Chick. Rather, Lucas's payment acts as a figure for recalculating and taking painstaking account of the past at each step in a history of partial reparations. Lucas pays only for the incidental expenses of Chick's help in pretending to pay for Stevens's broken fountain pen, just as Chick had once tried to pay not for his saved life but for the expenses of a dinner and warm blanket; in this way, Lucas gently mocks Chick's earlier gesture.

Drawing objects from his deep, many-pocketed tobacco pouch like a magician before an audience, in the novel Lucas counts change, breaks his own bills into coins, tallies pennies, and adds everything up to reach two dollars. Lucas's legerdemain transforms the money into "bits," breaking money's abstraction down into its "parts" even as the word "bits" evokes the currency of an earlier time, another country. The tobacco pouch itself slyly references the money inside as far from universal but rather marked in specific and historical ways, as the cash crop of a more aristocratic Upper South with whose first families Lucas would proudly associate himself, tied by family as he already is to Yoknapatawpha's earliest white settlers.[45] Lucas's pantomime of payment from his tobacco pouch at the end of *Intruder* echoes Chick's plaintive cry that his community at least owes Lucas a ten-cent package of tobacco. Far from free or innocent at the end of *Intruder*, Chick gains the yoke of social conscience with the acknowledgment of his share of a collective debt, prompting the reader to ask in turn what conscience's token price should be.

In Hollywood movie fashion, Chick's overturned white world may get righted by novel's end, but Lucas literally gets the final word. He demands his "receipt" from Stevens (247), transforming hard specie into the abstraction of paper: a slip that in the future will ensure a continuing chain of debt and asset exchange between him and the Stevenses. The receipt will solidify their family ties much as finance capitalism in our contemporary debt economy magically registers debt not as liability but as asset—a source of future credit. For a black man whose word and family name are not redeemable as his bond, Lucas demands a receipt not only to keep accounts and mark past debts settled but also to call upon such evidence of his credit-worthiness in the future. He had already called in one such chit, we might say, in asking Chick's help when first locked up in jail. *Intruder*'s suspended IOUs and diverse sleights of hand offer us some estimate of what repair to broken fratricidal white and horizontal black family bonds might cost, in financial as well as moral and social terms, inviting us to entertain notions of how, and why, we might want to stumble in that direction.

NOTES

Grateful acknowledgments for material and intellectual support are due to the Virginia Foundation for the Humanities; the Albert and Shirley Small Special Collections at the University of Virginia, with special thanks to George Riser and Hoke Perkins; Simon Rendall of the E. McKnight Kauffer estate; Caitlin Condell, associate curator, Cooper Hewitt, Smithsonian Design Museum; and Grace Schulman.

The first epigraph is from John T. Matthews, "Touching Race in *Go Down, Moses*," in *New Essays on* Go Down, Moses, ed. Linda Wagner-Martin (New York: Cambridge University Press, 1996), 40.

The second epigraph is from William Faulkner, *Go Down, Moses*, rev. ed. (1942; repr., New York: Vintage International, 1990), 269.

1. William Faulkner, *Intruder in the Dust* (1948; New York: Vintage, 1972). Hereafter cited parenthetically.

2. André Bleikasten uses the term "whodunit" to describe *Intruder* after noting that Faulkner uses the same language in a letter to Robert Haas on April 20, 1948: "It started out to be a simple quick 150 page whodunit but jumped the traces" (Faulkner quoted in Bleikasten, *William Faulkner: A Life through Novels* [Bloomington: Indiana University Press, 2017], 340). Samway notes that Faulkner appears to lose interest in conveying the mystery plot: "The clues begin to mount up—but, in the final analysis, they seem

to indicate that the author has lost sight of the finer dimensions of crafting a detective story" (Patrick Samway, S.J., *"Intruder in the Dust:* A Re-evaluation," in *A Gathering of Evidence: Essays on William Faulkner's* Intruder in the Dust, ed. Michel Gresset and Patrick Samway [Philadelphia: Saint Joseph's University Press, 2004], 202).

3. Donald Kartiganer, "Faulkner's Comic Narrative of Community," in *A Gathering of Evidence: Essays on William Faulkner's* Intruder in the Dust, ed. Michel Gresset and Patrick Samway (Philadelphia: Saint Joseph's University Press, 2004), 142–44.

4. Lucas finds himself in the Indian mound after first seeing archaeologists "intruding" in sacred ground, reinforcing a digging-for-history trope. Lucas's intertextual story before *Intruder* appears in "The Fire and the Hearth" in *Go Down, Moses,* "Gold Is Not Always" (1940), and "A Point of Law" (1940).

5. See Erik Dussere, "The Debts of History: Southern Honor, Affirmative Action, and Faulkner's *Intruder in the Dust," Faulkner Journal* 17, no. 1 (Fall 2001): 37–57. Dussere writes compellingly about the concept of debt in southern history, particularly debts of honor and business, in order to argue that *Intruder* implicitly points toward redistributive justice, such as affirmative action.

6. Robert Hamblin, "Teaching *Intruder in the Dust* through Its Political and Historical Context," in *A Gathering of Evidence: Essays on William Faulkner's* Intruder in the Dust, ed. Michel Gresset and Patrick Samway (Philadelphia: Saint Joseph's University Press, 2004), 57–74.

7. Timeframe inconsistencies persist across Faulkner's works. Some critics take Faulkner at his word that *Intruder* is set around 1935–40; many assume a late-1940s setting and note Gavin's reference to the "atom bomb" (149). See Frederick L. Gwynn and Joseph L. Blotner, eds., *Faulkner in the University* (1959; repr., Charlottesville: University Press of Virginia, 1995), especially 141.

8. Ralph Ellison, "The Shadow and the Act," *Reporter* (December 6, 1949): 17.

9. Faulkner cautioned his audience in Nagano, Japan, not to confuse him with Stevens. See Regina Fadiman, Intruder in the Dust: *Novel into Film: The Screenplay by Ben Maddow as Adapted for Film by Clarence Brown* (Knoxville: University of Tennessee Press, 1978), 5, 8.

10. Ikuko Fujihira, "Eunice Habersham's Lessons in *Intruder in the Dust,*" in *A Gathering of Evidence: Essays on William Faulkner's* Intruder in the Dust, ed. Michel Gresset and Patrick Samway (Philadelphia: Saint Joseph's University Press, 2004), 50–55.

11. Significantly, Lucas's intertextual family history is left out of the film.

12. See Jay Watson, *Forensic Fictions: The Lawyer Figure in Faulkner* (Athens: University of Georgia Press, 1993), 110; and Eric J. Sundquist, *Faulkner: The House Divided* (Baltimore: Johns Hopkins University Press, 1983), 136.

13. The term derives from George Lipsitz's *The Possessive Investment in Whiteness: How White People Profit from Identity Politics* (Philadelphia: Temple University Press, 1998), arguably revising C. B. Macpherson's notion of "possessive individualism" in *The Political Theory of Possessive Individualism: Hobbes to Locke* (1962; repr., New York: Oxford University Press, 2010).

14. See Laura Shin, "The Racial Wealth Gap: Why a Typical White Household Has 16 Times the Wealth of a Black One," *Forbes Magazine*, March 26, 2015, https://www.forbes.com/sites/laurashin/2015/03/26/the-racial-wealth-gap-why-a-typical-white-household-has-16-times-the-wealth-of-a-black-one/#83ae8e01f45e.

15. On redlining, see Emily Badger, "How Redlining's Racist Effects Lasted for Decades," *New York Times* (August 24, 2017), https://www.nytimes.com/2017/08/24/upshot/how-redlinings-racist-effects-lasted-for-decades.html. See also Michael Rogin, "The Two Declarations of American Independence," *Representations* 55 (Summer 1996):

13–30. For discussions of Faulkner's literature in the context of labor and New Deal policies, see Richard Godden, *Fictions of Labor: William Faulkner and the South's Long Revolution* (New York: Cambridge University Press, 1997) and Ted Atkinson, *Faulkner and the Great Depression: Aesthetics, Ideology, and Cultural Politics* (Athens: University of Georgia Press, 2005).

16. For "Dark Houses" in Faulkner's fiction and family, respectively, see Noel Polk, *Children of the Dark House: Text and Context in Faulkner* (Jackson: University Press of Mississippi, 1996) and Joel Williamson, *William Faulkner and Southern History* (New York: Oxford University Press, 1993).

17. See Sundquist for Lucas's structural likeness to Ike McCaslin in taking control of his family line and name (*Faulkner: The House Divided*, 157).

18. As Faulkner put it in his 1956 interview in the *Paris Review*: "I discovered that my own little postage stamp of native soil was worth writing about and that I would never live long enough to exhaust it" (*Lion in the Garden: Interviews with William Faulkner 1926–1962*, ed. James B. Meriwether and Michael Millgate [1968; repr., Lincoln: University of Nebraska Press, 1980], 255).

19. Calvin Schermerhorn, *Money over Mastery, Family over Freedom: Slavery in the Antebellum Upper South* (Baltimore: Johns Hopkins University Press, 2011), 3–21, 207–11. Also see Schermerhorn, *The Business of Slavery and the Rise of American Capitalism, 1815–1860* (New Haven: Yale University Press, 2015); Edward Baptist, *The Half Has Never Been Told: Slavery and the Making of American Capitalism* (New York: Basic Books, 2014); and Sven Beckert, *Empire of Cotton: A Global History* (New York: Knopf, 2014).

20. Hortense J. Spillers, "Mama's Baby, Papa's Maybe: An American Grammar Book," *Diacritics* 17, no. 2 (Summer 1987): 64–81.

21. On "notes of hand," see Baptist, *The Half Has Never Been Told*, 89.

22. Baucom describes in detail how Liverpool merchants and traders in 1781 were behind the captain of the *Zong* slave ship, who threw 132 enslaved people overboard in order to collect insurance on them, effectively disembodying the enslaved as chattel commodities to quantify them abstractly as instruments of finance capital instead. See Ian Baucom, *Specters of the Atlantic: Finance Capital, Slavery, and the Philosophy of History* (Durham, NC: Duke University Press, 2005); and Sven Beckert and Seth Rockman, eds., *Slavery's Capitalism: A New History of American Economic Development* (Philadelphia: University of Pennsylvania Press, 2016).

23. See Sophus Reinert, "*The Way to Wealth* around the World: Benjamin Franklin and the Globalization of American Capitalism," *American Historical Review* 120, no. 1 (February 2015): 61–97.

24. Ta-Nehisi Coates, "The Case for Reparations," *Atlantic* (June 2014), https://www.theatlantic.com/magazine/archive/2014/06/the-case-for-reparations/361631. See also Randall Robinson, *The Debt: What America Owes to Blacks* (New York: Dutton, 2000).

25. Joseph Blotner, vol. 1 of *Faulkner: A Biography* (New York: Random House, 1974), 113–14, 1246.

26. Kinney describes hearing the story of Higginbottom's lynching from Faulkner's nephew Jimmy Faulkner, who witnessed it. See Arthur F. Kinney, "Unscrambling Surprises," *Connotations: A Journal for Critical Debate* 15, nos. 1–3 (2005–6): 17–29, especially 19; and "Mob Lynches Negro," *New York Times*, September 19, 1935, 21.

27. See Patrick Samway, S.J., *Faulkner's "Intruder in the Dust": A Critical Study of the Typescripts* (Troy, NY: Whitston, 1980), 233–35.

28. Part of that recent history involves descendants learning the truth about lynchings and how and why they happened to their family members, such as at the project of the Equal Justice Initiative's National Memorial for Peace and Justice in Montgomery,

Alabama. For Higginbottom's own family story, see Vanessa Gregory, "A Lynching's Long Shadow," *New York Times Magazine* (April 29, 2018): MM34.

29. Robert H. Brinkmeyer Jr., *The Fourth Ghost: White Southern Writers and European Fascism, 1930–1950* (Baton Rouge: Louisiana State University Press, 2009); Matthews, "Touching Race," 21–47.

30. Blotner, vol. 2 of *Faulkner: A Biography*, 1257.

31. Fadiman, Intruder in the Dust: *Novel into Film*, 7.

32. Ibid., 26, 85n1.

33. Brown witnessed the lynching of several African Americans grabbed at random in revenge for an alleged rape in the summer of 1906 in Atlanta. Fadiman, who interviewed Brown for her book, notes that it was evident that he would never get over the trauma of witnessing these events at age sixteen, Chick's age in *Intruder* (ibid., 27–28). See also Robert Jackson, *Fade In, Crossroads: A History of the Southern Cinema* (New York: Oxford University Press, 2017) 187.

34. Fadiman, Intruder in the Dust: *Novel into Film*, 28–29.

35. Joseph Blotner, ed. *Selected Letters of William Faulkner* (New York: Vintage, 1977), 262–63. The letter is dated 1 February 1948.

36. Ibid., 262.

37. In one letter, Faulkner offers Harold Ober talking points "if editors balk at mss. for popular consumption as is" (ibid., 267).

38. Ibid., 268; emphasis added. Blotner dates the letter as "possibly 5 May 1948."

39. On the relationship between Faulkner and E. McKnight Kauffer, see Mary A. Knighton, "William Faulkner's Illustrious Circles: Double-Dealing Caricatures in Style and Taste," in *Faulkner and Print Culture: Faulkner and Yoknapatawpha, 2015*, ed. Jay Watson, Jaime Harker, and James G. Thomas, Jr. (Jackson: University Press of Mississippi, 2017), 28–50; and Mary A. Knighton, "Lines of Correspondence: E. McKnight Kauffer's Original Dust Jacket Art for William Faulkner's *Requiem for a Nun*," *Notes and Queries* 64, no. 4 (December 2017): 665–68.

40. "I particularly like the jacket, done by MacKnight [sic] Kauffer, and I hope you approve of the jacket copy I wrote." Saxe Commins to William Faulkner, September 3, 1948, Albert Erskine Random House Editorial Files, 1930–1993, Accession #13497, folder 4, box 2. Albert and Shirley Small Special Collections Library, University of Virginia, Charlottesville, VA.

41. There are actually two studies for the final cover of *Intruder* in the Cooper Hewitt Design Museum's E. McKnight Kauffer collection in New York City. Besides the one reproduced here, the other shows a similar figure scrambling after coins on the floor; however, in the novel, that figure would not have been Lucas but rather Aleck Sander or the boy from the Edmonds estate. This sketch may well be more preliminary than the one shown here or may more directly place Lucas and money/debt at the heart of *Intruder* as I do in this chapter.

42. See Ellen C. Scott, *Cinema Civil Rights: Regulation, Repression, and Race in the Classical Hollywood Era* (New Brunswick, NJ: Rutgers University Press, 2015), 220n114.

43. "Strange Fruit" (1939) is the title of a Billie Holiday song written by Jewish songwriter Abel Meeropol upon witnessing race riots and seeing a photograph of a lynching. Lillian Smith's bestselling novel of the same name about interracial love appeared in 1944.

44. Walter White, documentarian of lynching in the United States (*Rope and Faggot: A Biography of Judge Lynch* [1929]) and secretary of the NAACP in 1949, said he felt "exultant" at the film and its courage in even taking up the topic of lynching (quoted in Fadiman, Intruder in the Dust: *Novel into Film*, 41).

45. I am grateful for Jay Watson's probing questions about the tobacco pouch's possible meanings in this scene.

Answering the Call: Telephonic Fascism and Faulkner's Angel of History

Myka Tucker-Abramson

> He was the Fascist galahad who saved the white race by murdering Christmas. . . . I didn't realise until after Hitler got into the newspapers that I had created a Nazi before he did.
> —William Faulkner on Percy Grimm, in a letter to Malcolm Cowley

> "Aid to the disinherited countries," says Truman. "The time of the old colonialism has passed." Which means that American high finance considers that the time has come to raid every colony in the world.
> —Aimé Césaire

As Nazism was securing its grip on Germany and much of Europe, Walter Benjamin wrote of the "necessity of a theory of history from which Fascism can become visible."[1] With the election of Trump and the resurgence of hypernationalist and racist groups both in the United States and globally, we too need such a theory that can bring the present into relief. And while Nazi Germany is a necessary referent, it is not a sufficient one. Where Nazism emerged in a society rooted in industrial capitalism, Fordism, the central urbanization of Haussmann, European imperialism, colonial science, mass culture spectacles like the Tiller Girls, Wagner's *Gesammtkunstwerk* (total artwork), and the new mass communication culture of film and telephones,[2] Trumpism is emerging in a society of what is alternately called financial, neoliberal, or platform capitalism, one marked by post-Fordism, dispersed urbanization and decentralization, and a US-backed neocolonialism that eschews racial science for a racial regime rooted in the interlocking ideologies of development and, more recently, the return of the discourse of clashing civilizations.[3] Our mass spectacles are contemporary pop music and its "resilience,"[4] reality TV shows, and the new mass-communication technologies of the Internet and the cell phone.

This chapter suggests that Faulkner can offer us the beginning of such a theory, one that can explain how we got from the postwar consensus to the neo-Fascism of Trumpism. Not only did Faulkner wrestle with both the meaning of Fascism and his reputation with regards to it, but there have been numerous attempts to grapple with Faulkner's relationship to Fascism. This chapter continues that scholarly tradition but argues that while Faulkner's early work—most notably *Light in August* (1932)—has much to tell us about the relationships between the US South and Nazi Germany, his later works are even more important for what they tell us about Fascism's transfiguration as its base shifts from the European imperialism of the nineteenth century to the US neocolonialism of the twentieth.

"To view southern society alongside Nazi Germany was a widespread practice, coming from respectable commentators, southerners and northerners alike," Robert Brinkmeyer notes.[5] And while the question of this relationship was itself a topic of debate, the dominant narrative held that Nazi Germany and the US South were linked by their backwardness. As President Franklin Roosevelt famously put it in a 1938 speech, the South was "feudal," and "there is little difference between the feudal system and the Fascist system" (quoted in Brinkmeyer, *The Fourth Ghost*, 167–68). This account of Fascism—in which the US-led Allied forces defeated Nazism abroad, while also defeating Fascism at home through a new form of "racial liberalism"—became a touchstone of Cold War ideology.[6] Against the black radical tradition, in which intellectuals like George Padmore, Aimé Césaire, Claudia Jones, and groups such as the Black Panthers continued to insist on Fascism's fundamental link to capitalist imperialism or Western enlightenment thought, Cold War ideology stripped Fascism of its imperialist and class-based character. It did so, as Nikhil Pal Singh forcefully outlines, in part, by replacing the term "Fascism" with "totalitarianism," which in turn became "defined as a Soviet and implicitly anti-Western phenomenon."[7] US capitalist democracy and its postwar program of development and modernization thus became Fascism's antithesis and antidote.

Faulkner is often understood to be part of the cultural vanguard of this process. As Brinkmeyer argues in his influential book on Fascism and southern writing, Faulkner saw World War II "pit[ting] individual freedom against the modern-day equivalent of the Old South slave system: Fascist totalitarianism" (*The Fourth Ghost*, 191) and thus ceased to be a regional author, becoming a national writer committed to the "American dream of democracy" and its "desire for freedom" (190).[8] But if this is the case, how does one account for Trump and the resurgence of an ultra-right nationalism? What is the relationship between this current moment and the American dream of democracy, which ostensibly defeated Fascism in the 1950s? To answer this question, we need to revisit the relationship between the "backward" South and a "feudal" Nazi Germany.

To do so, we need to draw on a very different analysis of Faulkner's post-Reconstruction South, one based not on the South's backwardness but rather on its timeliness. Hosam Aboul-Ela argues that the "post-Reconstruction South experience"—in which "Northern industry in the US managed to reintegrate the South into the nation, succeeding where the Northern military during the Civil War, and the general government, during Reconstruction, had failed"—acted as a model for "coloniality's specific character after World War II," in which the United States relied upon "expanded investment" to build its global empire.[9] Read thus, it was not the South's backwardness that linked it to Nazi Germany—or even offered a "model" for it, as James Whitman suggests—but rather its contemporary neocolonial character.[10]

Writing in 1950, Aimé Césaire drew a similar conclusion. In *Discourse on Colonialism*, Césaire argued that Fascism was a result of the "savagery" of colonial policies—violated treaties, lies, torture—that acted as a "poison," "distilled into the veins of Europe."[11] Though Césaire was referring to European colonialism, the essay's ultimate focus is not historical, but contemporary: the Truman Doctrine. After the "hideous mess" of Europe, Césaire argued, it was tempting to turn to America's promise that "the time of the old colonialism has passed" and to embrace its "aid" in the form of "bulldozers! The massive investments of capital! The roads! The ports!" (*Discourse on Colonialism*, 43). But, he warned, when the United States spoke of "progress, about 'achievements,' diseases cured, improved standards of living," this meant only a new round of colonization, one carried out not through direct colonial control but through development. In the coming decades, Césaire's claims were borne out as development turned into the land grabs, stolen elections, structural adjustment programs, and coups of which Chile and Iran were only two notable examples and Iraq a more recent and even more intense one. Colonialism, Césaire warned, begets Fascism, and neocolonialism would fare no better.

The wager of this chapter is twofold. First, that just as Benjamin located the primal scene of Fascism in Haussmann's "strategic beautification" of Paris under Napoleon's larger imperialist project (Buck-Morss, *The Dialectics of Seeing*, 90), postwar urban planning within the larger framework of US neocolonialism is the primal scene of contemporary

Fascism. Second, that Faulkner's location in the post-Reconstruction South (Aboul-Ela's locus of neocolonialism) and his fascination with postwar urbanization in his later works suggest that his work might provide us with an ideal standpoint from which to analyze this primal scene and shine a light onto our present Fascist threat. In this chapter, I compare Faulkner's prewar thinking about Fascism in *Light in August* (1932) against his postwar fiction, particularly *Intruder in the Dust* (1948), and "Hog Pawn" (1954, revised as part of *The Mansion* [1959]), ultimately arguing that the postwar writings are no less interested in Fascism than his earlier fiction. I track this changing relationship through Faulkner's fascinating, though unstudied, use of the telephone. The telephone, as Avital Ronell has shown, was enmeshed in the operations and fantasies of Fascism, so it is perhaps unsurprising that the telephone, now the cell phone, has seen a resurgence in meaning and import with the rise of Trump.[12] In framing this argument through the telephone, however, I don't aim to fetishize the telephone as intrinsically having either a Fascist or anti-Fascist character. Rather, I argue that because the telephone was, and now the cell phone is, what Nicole Aschoff calls "the defining commodity" of their respective eras, it remains a foundational object through which phantasms and fantasies of modern life emerge.[13] The telephone thus offers us a persistent, if shifting, object through which to track Faulkner's thinking about Fascism and to illuminate his theory of history.

I

Let's begin in the beginning, with the most obvious place where Faulkner, Fascism, and telephones come together: *Light in August*, a novel that tracks the interwoven stories of Lena Grove, a woman looking for her lover and baby's father, and Joe Christmas, who ends up working and living with that father. Not only are telephones a key feature of the landscape Lena views as she travels across the South, but they appear at key moments in the text. In one scene, for example, a black man goes to Reverend Hightower's house to phone a doctor for his wife, whose labor has taken a turn, but because Hightower has no telephone, and the father-to-be is terrified of Hightower's white neighbors, he ends up walking thirty minutes into town, resulting in the baby's death. In another, a couple comes across Miss Burden's nearly beheaded body, and the wife hurries "to the nearest telephone [to] call for the sheriff."[14] And in a third, the sheriff calls a nearby town for bloodhounds to track the fugitive Joe Christmas, ultimately leading to his death at the hands of Percy Grimm, the character whom in 1945 Faulkner would describe as a "Fascist galahad who saved the white race by murdering Christmas," a "Nazi" created "before" Hitler created his.[15] Here, the telephone is ghostly, uncanny, out of time, connected to births—most often deathly births—and to racialized deaths. The telephone delivers news of Miss Burden's murder, summons the bloodhounds to initiate the long manhunt that ends in Joe's lynching, and fails to bring the doctor in time to save the black baby.

Faulkner was not alone in his uncanny depictions of the telephone. Ronell reminds us that from Franz Kafka to the movie *Scream*, the telephone has been represented as the bearer of the "apocalyptic call. It turns on you: it's the gun pointed at your head," she writes (*The Telephone Book*, 6). This uncanniness is embedded within the history of the phone itself: we can think of Watson consulting spiritual mediums throughout its development or the numerous reports of early telephone demonstrations where audience members wondered whether it was a man or ghost on the line.[16] But for Ronell, the telephone's uncanniness more profoundly expresses the social and political nexus in which it was enmeshed: Nazism. It was, she argues, "the supertechnical power [of the Nazis] whose phantasms of unmediated instantaneity, defacement, and historical erasure invested telephone lines of the state.... Calls for execution were made by telephone.... Hence the trait that continues to flash through every phone call in one form or another" (*The Telephone Book*, 6). For Ronell, the telephone didn't just enable or expedite the mass genocide carried out by the Nazis. Rather, her point is that the Nazis' "supertechnical" abilities lay in their fusing together the fantasies of "unmediated instantaneity" promised by both the telephone and ethnic nationalism. And yet, while Ronell argues that it was Nazism that "invested" the telephone with its deathly trait—"the call as verdict, the call as death sentence"—it seems that the post-Reconstruction South again got there first. Telephone poles, after all, were frequently used as platforms for lynchings.[17]

But Faulkner's engagement with telephones and Fascism goes beyond the objects' appearances in his texts. Instead, the telephone often acts as a formal or aesthetic principle, one that, perhaps, drew the great theorizer of Fascist aesthetics, Walter Benjamin, to Faulkner. In May of 1940, Benjamin wrote to Theodor Adorno that he was "reading ... *Lumiere d'aout*."[18] In this same letter, Benjamin discusses his theses on the philosophy of history.[19] A gesture, Julie Napolin writes, toward "the lost possibility of an essay on Faulkner never written, a reverberation."[20] One such reverberation: both *Light in August* and Benjamin's "Concept of History" essay are often read as their authors' signal theorizations of Fascism. Benjamin's essay famously opens, via another US southerner,

Edgar Allan Poe, with the description of a chess-playing automaton that anticipates its opponents' moves. The game, of course, is a ruse; as Benjamin explains, there is actually an expert chess player sitting inside and pulling the puppet's strings.[21] But Benjamin is not really talking about chess. He's talking about history, and the seductive ruse of history as determined and controlled by the ruling classes, who make history—and the class structure of society—appear natural, unmediated, inevitable.

Return to the chess player inside the machine, guiding the puppet's hand. For Benjamin, we are the puppets, and it is Fascism guiding our hands. This is the closest we get to Benjamin's theory—or better, image—of Fascism: an arena in which the working class has been anaesthetized, made to blindly answer the deathly commands of the ruling class, unable to see or sense and thus to engage in the political struggle necessary to redeem history. This image is ultimately a telephonic one, of "tradition and its *receivers*" (Benjamin, "On the Concept of History," 255; emphasis added). In her lucid extension of Benjamin's theorizations of Fascism, Buck-Morss unpacks the process by which this anaesthetization occurs: through a mobilization of the fears of bodily destruction and fragmentation associated with industrialization, mechanization, and militarization in the wake of World War I. As she explains, not only did Hitler assiduously "practice his facial expressions in front of a mirror" in order to reflect the fear of the mob, but Fascism's mass rallies and aesthetics—in Leni Riefenstahl's 1935 film *Triumph of the Will* and elsewhere—more generally worked to excite and sublimate this fear by creating a pleasing "surface pattern" and "design of the whole" that masked, and inured the subject to, the violence, fragmentation, and subjective shattering of modernity (*The Dialectic of Seeing*, 38). What makes this process so nefarious, Buck-Morss argues, is that the aesthetic experience of the self-shaping and shaped crowd is explicitly designed to let "the viewer forget the purpose of the display, the militarization of society for the teleology of making war" (38). In Benjamin's account, the antidote to this anaesthetization is the organization of the working class, which must disrupt this seemingly smooth and unmediated transmission between sender and receiver, chess player and puppet, past and present, ruling class and workers.

Benjamin wasn't the only one thinking about chess, class, history, and Fascism. At the center of the famous "Percy Grimm" episode in *Light in August*, in which Grimm lynches Christmas, we find another automaton: Grimm himself. Moreover, as Sacvan Bercovitch has pointed out, Faulkner deploys a "chess analogy" to "explain" or at least enact "the lynching of Joe Christmas."[22] Faulkner describes Grimm as moving "with that lean, swift, blind obedience to whatever Player moved him on the Board" (Faulkner, *Light in August*, 462). The language of the Player is repeated obsessively. The Player gives Grimm "breath," places the car where He "desire[s] it to be" (463), and moves him not just to shoot Joe but to stab him in a bloody frenzy, proclaiming, "Now you'll let white women alone" (464). As the ruling class issues its commands in Benjamin's essay, so the Player issues His. One way to read this direct link between Grimm and the Player is as the repressed and uncanny other of the telephone, telepathy: the transmission not of voices but of feeling. The Player speaks to Percy instantaneously, from mind to mind, telepathically.

And it is this telepathic transmission that also marks the turning of a crowd into a lynch mob that precedes Grimm, the mob that forms around the fire that stands in place of Miss Burden's body. The cause of neither the fire nor the murder is known at this point, yet quickly, as if forged out of the fire, a collective understanding forms. The novel describes the bystanders' "faces" becoming "identical with one another" (291) and their ideas forming insensibly, "as if all their individual five senses had become one organ of looking, like an apotheosis, the words that flew among them wind-or airengendered *Is that him? Is that the one that did it? Sheriff's got him. Sheriff has already caught him.*" Then the fire "roar[s], filling the air though not louder than the voices and much more unsourceless *By God, if that's him, what are we doing standing around here? Murdering a white woman the black son of a* " (291). What Faulkner depicts here, in strikingly Benjaminian terms, is the precise process through which a crowd becomes anaesthetized into violence.

These Benjaminian resonances are particularly relevant if we consider what else is unifying the members of the crowd, their economic position as workers in an economy governed by lumber. That Byron, Lucas, and Joe Christmas all work in the lumber industry is not incidental. Susan Willis has argued that the motif of lumber in Faulkner's fiction illuminates the shifting neocolonial relationship between the North and the South. In her reading of Faulkner's story "The Bear," Willis argues that whereas the forest had functioned as a frontier space of "wilderness" under plantation capitalism, as the US entered industrial capitalism, southern forests became a source of lumber and other raw materials.[23] Within *Light in August*, lumber is also prominent. As Jay Watson notes, "*Light in August* is extraordinarily overinvested . . . in a material economy involving the production and distribution of timber, lumber, and other wood products."[24] It is lumber, Watson argues, that subtends both the "social plot" and "economic subplot" of the novel, producing "the ordinary, the everyday, the unremarkable—that sense of the uneventful that is so crucial to the felt experience of small-town social life" (41). While the crowd's rage, then, appears to occur at the level of the "felt experience" of the town—it is ostensibly directed by the sexual politics of the South—this felt experience is overdetermined by the economic and colonial relations of lumber that saturate the text. As a center of southern employment, the lumber mill is a key site where what John T. Matthews identifies as "the tried-and-true Southern method of deflecting economic resentment by uniting rich and poor whites around racial hostility" took place.[25] In this too, the South's alignment with Nazi Germany is not a result of its feudalism but rather of its thoroughly modern, neocolonial industrial system and equally modern use of racial hostility to displace class resentment.

In direct contrast to the immediacy that Grimm experiences with the Player, that the mob experiences seemingly with itself, and that the crowd experiences together is the novel's own structure and temporality, which offer anything but a smooth, unmediated march through "homogeneous and empty" time (Benjamin, "On the Concept of History," 395). The novel's time is fragmented, broken, and circuitous, a piling up of wreckage. For an illustration, we can turn either to Joe Christmas's past or to Joanne Burden's family history, in which generations, wars, and racial violence spanning Mexico, New Hampshire, Washington DC, Mississippi, and the Promised Land tumble over each other, often without even a paragraph break or a full stop.

One term for this catastrophic experience of time and history is "southern gothic," which, as Leigh Anne Duck notes, is marked by "claustrophobia-inducing repetitions," "lyrical and folkloric alienations," and "haunting remembrances," all of which make the South's temporality incommensurable with, and place it behind, capitalist modernity.[26] And yet if, as Stephen Shapiro suggests, the southern gothic, like all earlier iterations of the gothic, seems to inhabit a past, or at least to record an anxiety about "the return of repressed social collectives" such as "agrarian (folk) populations, seeking revenge for the traumas they suffered in the name of modernity," the very backwardness of gothic narratives also proves "prophetic about oncoming crises": thus Faulkner's surprised musings that he had, in a sense, created Hitler before Germany had. In the past-futurity of the South we can see both a residual slave economy and an anticipatory neocolonial one.[27]

While Faulkner clearly ties Fascism to modernization and to colonization, however, his solution ultimately seems to align with Roosevelt's: a more perfect modernization, one premised on replacing Shapiro's "repressed social collectives" with citizens, the region with the nation, the mob with the law. Here the dream is to create a more perfect telephone, one that reports births before they become deaths and reports crimes so that justice can be served, one that is available to all—black and white alike—and that makes telepathy unnecessary.

It is this image that concludes *Light in August*: the evenly distributed telephone poles that Lena sees while riding across the South, heralding a new, democratic nation, one symbolized in the pieced-together family of Lena, her child, and Byron as they pass the "roads and trees and fields and telephone poles" (Faulkner, *Light in August*, 505; emphasis removed). The fight against Fascism, in this reading, is not rooted in the technologies of modernization itself but lies in perfecting and expanding modernization, a project that becomes an important focus in Faulkner's postwar fiction.

II

If *Light in August* ends with the hopeful vision of a modern and telephonized South that stands as an alternative to the lynch mob, *Intruder* interrogates that modernized society and the urban crowd it engenders. This transitional South is registered at once generically and spatially. Generically, *Intruder* fuses together gothic and noir through the road novel. It repeats the lynch tropes of the gothic through the story of Lucas Beauchamp, who is falsely accused of murdering a white man, and the unlikely trio of Chick Mallison, Aleck Sander, and Miss Habesham, who try to save him. But it enacts this gothic through the motifs of the noir: it is set on the outskirts of a rapidly developing "urban" center in a world of phantasmagoric mass culture; and it involves cover-ups, a race against time, and a set of characters who must solve a crime despite being positioned outside both mainstream society and the state.[28] And it brings both genres together through the road novel's modern yet nostalgic temporality of nation-and empire-building. This uneven and overlapping temporality is also present spatially, within the built environment.

We see this perhaps most clearly through Miss Habersham, a character who, like the space of the novel itself, is at once a relic of the plantation era and a symbol of suburban modernity. Among "the old big decaying wooden houses" set "deep in shaggy untended lawns of old trees" that "seemed still to be spellbound by the shades of women, old women still spinsters and widows waiting even seventy-five years later for the slow telegraph to bring them news of Tennessee and Virginia and Pennsylvania battles," Miss Habersham's residence marks her as part of "Jefferson's long-ago foundation."[29] Yet her house itself is quite literally overlaid with the "subdivision" (120) of "neat small new one-storey houses designed in Florida and California set with matching garages in their neat plots of clipped grass and tedious flowerbeds" (119–20), homes inhabited by "prosperous young married couples . . . with two children each and (as soon as they could afford it) an automobile each" (120), along with "patented electric gadgets for cooking and freezing and cleaning" and, of course, the "telephone," used by "the neat trim colored maids in frilled caps" who "talk to one another . . . from house to house while the wives in sandals and pants and painted toenails puffed lipstick-stained cigarettes over shopping bags in the chain groceries and drug stores" (118).

The telephone's role in *Intruder* is clearly different from its function in *Light in August*, where telephones are both unevenly distributed and out of the hands of African Americans. Here the telephone is more ubiquitous and, significantly, in the hands of black domestics. Moreover, where the telephone in *Light in August* is in itself uncanny, in *Intruder* it is the technology that moves us from the gothic register in which the novel begins to its propulsive noir register, a shift that occurs at the moment in which news of the murder is transmitted: "Word had come for the sheriff about three oclock and had been relayed on by another party-line telephone down into the opposite corner of the county where the sheriff had gone this morning on business and where a messenger might quite possibly find him some time between now and tomorrow's sunup: which would make little difference since even if the sheriff had been in his office he would probably be too late since Fraser's store was in Beat Four" (27). *Intruder* is full of passages like this one, long descriptions of the paths taken for a message to get from sender to receiver or the route taken to walk, ride, or drive from point A to point B. These descriptions, much like Miss Habersham's surroundings, overlay the circular and "socially indexical language address[ing the] traumatic secret" of white dependency on black labor that Richard Godden identifies in the plantation economy of *Absalom, Absalom!* with an equally indexical language that registers the industrial dispersal of labor across time and space.[30] Because of this dispersal of labor, the mob in *Intruder* isn't—indeed, can't be—composed of workers but rather of consumers who gather in the town center.

Jay Watson has astutely observed the novel's interest with the ways in which mass communication technology—the "white noise" of radios, automobiles, jukeboxes, and amplifiers—comes to shape and reflect the "primal throb . . . pulse and hum" of the crowd, which speaks only in "babble."[31] What interests me here is Faulkner's depiction of this urban crowd as it fades in and out of the lynch mob, a link the novel develops through its repeated returns to the image of the face. Consider the following passages: "not faces but a face, not a mass nor even a mosaic of them but a Face: not even ravening nor uninsatiate but just in motion, insensate, vacant of thought or even passion: an Expression significant-less and without past" (182); "They were there of course nose-pressed to the glass but there were not even enough of them to block the pavement let alone compound a Face" (183); "[he] saw them again crossing the mouth of the alley like across a stage—the cars and trucks, the faces in invincible profile not amazed not aghast but in a sort of irrevocable repudiation" (185). What to make of this Face-mob, described entirely via absence and negation: not ravening, not uninsatiate, not aghast, not amazed, only vacant, absent. And what to make of the fusing of the Face with the automobile, in which both come to express the same "irrevocable repudiation," a fusion that is all the more striking if we consider the novel's peculiarly mechanical tone. This is, after all, a novel obsessed with mileage, time, and speed: constantly calculating the number of miles the sheriff has to traverse to stop Lucas from being lynched, the number of miles that Aleck Sander, Charles, and Miss Habersham need to go to exhume the body, the amount of time it will take on foot versus horseback versus car. *Intruder in the Dust* is a novel about the road that often reads like a test drive.

We return again to Buck-Morss's description of Fascism's anaesthetization of the crowd—only the anaesthetization that Faulkner gives us takes a slightly different cast, because it is linked not to the pleasing image of the militarized crowd but to another pleasing pattern, one in which militarization seems farther away but is nonetheless present: the planned highways and suburban subdivisions being built at the time, whose landscapes are the backdrop of *Intruder*. That is, it is not bodies here that are being organized but the cars and new subdivisions in which the masses—often veterans returning home from World War II—are now encased. But like the Fascist rallies that created pleasing designs, letting the viewer forget the true "purpose of the display" (the militarization of society), this new form of urbanism, organized around dispersion, mass consumption, single-family homes, and the reassertion of separate domestic and racial spheres, became the ideological touchstone of an era, in this case the Cold War.[32] Much like the actual Cold War, postwar urban policy's "war against the center," along with its arguments about the need for the "defensive dispersal" of industries and housing in order to make American cities resilient to nuclear threats, obfuscated the *offensive* war being waged by the state against working-class and often-racialized urban dwellers, a war that depended on the seduction of the white working and middle classes by the promise of home and automobile ownership and access to other consumer goods.[33]

Read within this context, Faulkner's revision of the lynch mob of the Jim Crow South in *Light in August* into the car-mob of *Intruder in the Dust* offers a crucial and often overlooked analysis of the American empire's new primal scene of capitalist urbanism—one replacing that of Haussmann—in its aesthetic, political, and economic forms, and of the threat of Fascism lurking therein. And yet, alas, the novel retreats from a critique of modernization programs to one of state-induced desegregation. The mob's "cause"—at least if Uncle Gavin is to be believed—is neither the backwardness of the South nor postwar development but rather the US state's increasingly insistent mandate of desegregation, a point Gavin makes by aligning the postwar national state's threat to impose "legislation to set Lucas Beauchamp free" with the Civil War, in which "Lucas Beauchamp's master was not merely beaten to his knees but trampled for ten years on his face in the dust to make him swallow it" (155). Uncle Gavin's critique is often read as an echo of Faulkner's own critique of northern interventionism. As Ticien Sassoubre has argued, Faulkner was highly critical of federal intervention because he thought "the result would be, if not a second civil war, a reactionary response on the part of Southerners answered by federal occupation."[34] This is why, she suggests, the novel is organized around an attempt "to prevent both a lynching and a trial": to neutralize both the lynch mob and the state.[35]

From this perspective, it's difficult to imagine a novel *less* in line with the Cold War strategy of racial liberalism that sought to make the US (appear as) a racially harmonious, democratic, and free nation, and even more difficult to make sense of Faulkner's tours of duty for the nation as literary Cold War ambassador. And yet, perhaps Faulkner's Cold War role and particularly *Intruder*'s reputation as a liberal race novel make more sense if we consider the alignment between the novel's solution to the problem of Lucas's imminent lynching and the United States's own desired image-transformation. The difficulty Faulkner faces in *Intruder* is how to reconcile the uncle's recasting of the racially liberal state as an imperialist one (a critique that Faulkner by all accounts supported) with Faulkner's own critique of segregation, lynch mobs, and racial violence. How, in other words, to escape what the novel locates as the twinned loci of Fascism: the overarching state and the lynch mob?

The solution takes the form of what Matthews terms a "confederacy" that marks the novel's hopeful ending, one composed of three characters largely outside the ideological pressures imposed by segregation: a spinster removed from anxieties about white femininity, a white boy who is too young to need work, and a black boy who is too young to represent a sexual or economic threat (*William Faulkner*, 237). It is neither the state nor legal reform that saves Lucas, but individuals who, following the trio's lead, spontaneously act as a democratic assemblage against the mob and the state, an assemblage that, as Matthews points out, comes together on the sidewalk in a "dense and massed" crowd—notably consumers—both "black and white." This is the crowd freed from the lynch mob. And in this context it is perhaps worth recalling Walt Whitman Rostow's anti-Communist development classic, *The Stages of Economic Growth* (1960), in which mass consumption forms the "highest" stage of social development.[36] *Intruder* enacts the South's movement through Rostow's stages: from "traditional" society, based in agriculture or subsistence farming through a capitalist take-off into a more industrialized, urbanized, and more manufacturing-focused society, and into "the high age of mass consumption" (5–9).

No wonder, then, that the novel concludes with Gavin telephoning home to get Lucas flowers to give Miss Habersham, with Stevens then driving him to her house, and finally with Lucas settling his debts. The telephone and the car shift from anxious objects mediating space and danger to symbols of consumer goods exchanged between color-blind consumer-citizens, in a perfect embodiment of Rostow's theory of development. This is the cold warrior Faulkner that Lawrence Schwartz gives us, whose literary modernism became "an instrument of anti-Communism and an ideological weapon with which to battle the 'totalitarianism' of the Soviet Union."[37] I want to suggest, then, that if we are to implicate Faulkner in Fascism, we need to do so not in the context of his writings of the 1930s and their resonances with German Nazism, but rather here, in the active role he plays in contributing to what Singh usefully terms "the post-WWII ideology of a US-led 'break' from the logic of empire and, by extension, Fascism," a role that places him in complicity with the neocolonialism that was being rolled out across Africa, Asia, and Latin America as he was writing his late-career works.[38]

But there is reason to distance Faulkner from such a reading or to credit Faulkner with a canny awareness that Uncle Gavin's critique of federal intervention misreads the nature of US neocolonialism. Not only do the novel's murders take place within the lumber industry, as we've seen a crucial southern site of neocolonialism, but *Intruder*'s entire landscape—from the subdivisions, to the highway linking the beats to Jefferson, to the new forms of mass culture and notably the car itself—is underpinned by the fossil-fueled and distinctly US suburban modernity that would underpin this neocolonial regime.[39] In fact, Gavin's entire discussion of the temporality of segregation is juxtaposed against the vertiginous temporalities of his driving—the car "whining in second gear" (150), for instance, or slowing with Gavin's "declutching." Faulkner's positioning of the uncle's anachronistic speech within this automotive space highlights the ways in which Gavin is already subsumed within this new Cold War modernity. In this context, it's hard not to read the novel's hopeful ending, with its vision of a somewhat racially integrated mass culture of consumers, as ironic. Simply put, mass culture is no third way at all but rather the seductive new form of US colonialism and working-class pacification.

If the mass culture of the novel's ending doesn't offer an alternative to the racism of the Jim Crow South or to the mass cultural sentimentalism of neocolonialism, *Intruder* does offer us a tantalizing glimpse of such an alternative, one that is, however, as hidden as the bodies of Gowrie and Montgomery, an alternative that returns us once again to the telephone: the maids on the phone in the subdivisions that are consuming Miss Habersham's house. The question this raises is, what are they talking about?[40] Premilla Nadasen offers one possible answer in the history of domestic workers' movements, which she traces from Communist-led organizing against the Depression-era domestic labor "slave market" in the Bronx through the civil rights and Black Power eras.[41] Not only were domestic workers active in fighting for their own rights, however, but as Nadasen shows, they played an important role in key civil rights struggles such as the Montgomery Bus Boycott, much of which was organized through phone trees.[42] *Intruder*'s domestics and their muted conversations offer a glimpse of this working-class history, one whose model of grassroots and transformative collective organizing represents an alternative to the false choices of mob action, state intervention, or individual-yet-mass cultural feeling. It is an alternative that Faulkner deposits into the text but isn't able to unearth explicitly.

III

The story of working-class women does return in Faulkner. It does so, however, not in the form of African American women making calls but rather in the figure of a white woman who presumably connects the calls: Essie Meadowfill, the main character of the short story "Hog Pawn" (a story that is also, intriguingly, filled with references to chess), who turns down a scholarship to take a job with a telephone company. "Hog Pawn" is about an oil company trying to buy real estate in order to open a filling station. "At the end of the War," the story recounts, "[p]rogress reached Jefferson too; the almost unused back lane on which Meadowfill's property abutted, now became an intersecting corner of an arterial highway—as soon that is as the oil company could persuade old Meadowfill to sell his orchard-late-vegetable patch which, with a strip of the next adjoining lot, comprised the site of the proposed filling station."[43] The company's attempt to buy the land from Meadowfill is complicated to say the least. Not only does Meadowfill refuse to sell, but he *can't* sell. As we learn, "during the early second Roosevelt days," Meadowfill wanted to get government relief, but the "finicking and bureaucratic federal government declined utterly to allow him to be a pauper and property-owner at the same time," so he had to transfer the deed to his daughter, Essie, who now holds it. Moreover, that narrow piece of land is only conditionally owned by Essie. It is really owned by a Snopes (named "Res" in *The Mansion*) who has made a business in "buying and selling small parcels of real estate" (315). The short story proceeds to narrate the war of attrition carried out between Snopes and the Meadowfills over this sliver of land.

This struggle, however, is in many ways less important than the narrative's registration of the new suburban sensoria that the plot allows, a registration that continues the critique of neocolonialism that Willis located in Faulkner's earlier fiction. Again, this critique occurs through lumber: only now the lumber is no longer connected to the wilderness or lumberyard but rather to the new site of profitability that emerges as the forest industry dries up: real estate. This shift receives additional emphasis when Faulkner revises the "Hog Pawn" material for *The Mansion*, where Essie and her husband move into a "subdivision of standardised Veterans' matchboxes" named "Eula Acres."[44] As has often been pointed out, Eula Varner Snopes "symbolizes nature itself, the land, fertility, fecundity."[45] By the time we get to *The Mansion*, however, that land is no longer fertile, or in Aboul-Ela's formulation, no longer able to "yield the wealth that once sustained the agricultural sector."[46] Instead, what is fertile, what does yield wealth, is real estate, so Eula becomes reborn as a subdivision.

If Eula, however, represents the vision of woman as land, as the raw material of wealth production, Essie comes to stand in for the US capital that profits off the land, and particularly such capital's emasculation of traditional southern masculinity. Not only does Essie gain control over Meadowfill's land thanks to Roosevelt's policies, but it is because the land is hers, and then her husband McKinley's, that Uncle Gavin is ultimately able to facilitate the sale of land to the oil company. The point is made even more clearly once Meadowfill retreats to his wheelchair—an all too on-the-nose symbol of impotence—as soon as Essie takes her job at the telephone company, which, to make the point still more clearly, she does with the goal of using her earnings to modernize the family house by installing a bathroom. In *The Mansion*, Faulkner tightens the relationship between Essie and finance when Mr. Holland, the president of the Bank of Jefferson, ultimately takes over and has "the bathroom installed despite old Meadowfill's outraged fury" (957) and then offers Essie "a job for life in his bank," where she presumably meets her future husband, the former Texas tenant farmer and Marine corporal McKinley Smith. Here as throughout *The Mansion*, Faulkner twins the seductions of modernization with its emasculating of the older South.

The atrocious gender politics at play in Faulkner's alignment of Essie with northern capital, however, were not Faulkner's invention but, as Molly Geidel has shown, a key facet of neocolonialism and its discontents. In *Peace Corps Fantasies*, Geidel argues that what she terms the "development imaginary" emerged in response to two postwar crises: "the crisis of capitalism brought on by decolonization and fears of masculine atrophy in the face of affluence, suburbanization, and allegedly increasing female power."[47] This development imaginary worked, she contends, both by giving US suburban men a new masculine purpose and by inducing Third World leaders to modernize through an alignment of "underdevelopment with passive femininity" (Geidel, *Peace Corps Fantasies*, 2) and "modernity with full masculinity" (xv). It achieved the latter aim, she argues, both through threats "of penetration and humiliation" for countries that refused US modernization programs and through the promise of belonging in a "US-controlled global brotherhood" for countries that acceded (xv).

By the late fifties, Faulkner's South is, interestingly, aligned with both the developers and the developed, with Essie uniting the two. Where Essie's job and the modernization of her family home emasculate her father, Essie also threatens to emasculate her boyfriend by selecting for him a house in Eula Acres and thus putting him at risk of joining the numerous other male war heroes who "a year ago [were] rushing hand grenades and . . . [are] now rushing baskets of soiled didies out of side-and backstreet Veterans Administration tenements" (Faulkner, *The Mansion*, 960), or who in Gavin's terms were "pushing the perambulator" with their "ruptured duck[s]" (961). It is ultimately only by marrying Essie, taking possession of her land, and willingly engaging in modernization by selling off Meadowfill's property to the oil company that McKinley's masculinity is restored and he is able to buy his farm.

This alignment between Essie and northern capital, along with the gender politics involved, can help explain why Faulkner chooses telephone operator as Essie's job. The telephone played a crucial role in US military operations during World War II. As John Brooks explains, "with Pearl Harbor the Bell research, development, and manufacturing arms instantly became among the most vital of national resources," and the radar technology developed by Bell was crucial to the allies' victory.[48] The military arm of telephony didn't end with World War II, however, but became key to the development of the computer industry and the consolidation of US power during the Cold War era. Women were crucial to this history, as they have been throughout the history of the telephone. In large part because of the war, women's employment at Bell skyrocketed from 20 percent in 1941 to 54 percent in 1944, and this increase also brought a resurgence of anxious fantasies about what telephone work would do to gender relations in the United States.[49]

Thus, while Faulkner falls prey to the gendered ideology of development, he also gets much right in his understanding of the tightly woven links between development and militarization, particularly as "Hog Pawn" is revised for *The Mansion*. While war is present in "Hog Pawn"—McKinley is a Korean War vet, for instance—the entire plot of *The Mansion* is saturated with this new round of midcentury militarization. Beyond the sheer volume of references to World War II within the updated material, the Snopes-Meadowfill property squabble is also recontextualized into the larger story of the Snopes-Compson battle, which the novel makes clear is nothing but a struggle over the relationship between the southern economy and the US military and over how best to profit off of that relationship. Flem Snopes wins this battle because he understands that the war economy is not limited to the "production and expansion of airplanes and tanks and cannon" (955) but rather operates within the American economy writ large. He sees that "won it or lost it wouldn't matter, in either case population would compound and government or somebody would have to house it." And it's just such a housing project that Snopes undertakes in his building of Eula Acres. What Faulkner rightly notes here is the extent to which postwar housing developments were themselves military operations that should be understood as a barracks for past and potentially future soldiers.

But perhaps more important than the suburb's role as barracks is how the new suburban sensorium militarizes all aspects of daily life, such that the patently absurd conflict between Snopes and Meadowfill over a teeny piece of land that neither actually wants becomes depicted as a military battle, with Snopes described as engaging in "an active kind of guerrilla feud" (956). Again, the South is refigured not in national terms but rather on analogy with the decolonizing countries that would come to fight the United States using guerrilla tactics and other forms of asymmetric warfare. Like Césaire, Faulkner too recognizes that US neocolonialism—and its not-so-unique formula of nationalism, consumerism, and patriotism—was not really the end of war but the beginning of a new cycle of wealth extraction that would be launched on the battlefields of real estate and oil.

This is the call that Donald Trump answered, one whose blueprint and history Faulkner's postwar fiction provides. But the call was not unmediated, and it did not, and does not, lack the possibility of being refused. Writing in the 1930s, Benjamin observed that "the totalitarian states drive everything out of individuals that stands in the way of their complete assimilation into a massified clientele. The only unreconciled opponent . . . in this connection is the revolutionary proletariat. The latter destroys the illusion of the crowd with the reality of the class" (quoted in Buck-Morss, *The Dialectics of Seeing*, 307). *The Mansion* is one of Faulkner's grimmer pieces of writing, in large part because of its ruthless depiction of the success of the drive by the United States to subsume and assimilate all facets of southern life, space, and sensoria within this "massified clientele." But this grimness is also ideological, because while Faulkner recognizes the failure of mass culture, the crowd, and the democratic individual to stand in the way of the nation's totalitarian drive, what he can't or won't see is the potential of the forms of collective organizing that he nonetheless again deposits into his novel, this time in the form of the telephone operator whom, in a final erasure, Faulkner has turn down her job in *The Mansion* to become, revealingly, a white-collar worker in a bank. Faulkner's refiguring of postwar woman from laborer to northern shill for finance capital is complete.

I want to conclude, however, by returning to the Essie of "Hog Pawn," who indexes a key yet buried history, that of the role of women workers in the postwar labor struggles over the telephone. During the same period in which the telephone became an increasingly important tool for the US military, the militancy of telephone unions was on the rise, particularly the National Federation of Telephone Workers (NFTW), whose organizational efforts culminated in 1947 in a nationwide strike that was part of a wave of militant worker organizing, which suburbanization and the postwar compromise sought to defuse. Women were crucial in this strike, comprising over 60 percent of NFTW members.[50] In fact, as Dorothy Sue Cobble notes, "The 1947 telephone strike was the largest walkout of women in US history."[51] The strike was eventually defeated, and through a mixture of the intermingled carrots and sticks of containment—notably suburban domesticity and the Red Scare—these women were absorbed into the limited postwar compromise or expelled from it. Nonetheless, like the maids on the phone in *Intruder*, these telephone operators bespeak another history of the postwar United States: the militant labor struggles of the 1950s, in which women played a key role, and the ongoing struggles of women, and particularly of women of color, who continue to organize in call centers, in homes, and in the streets. This is the history, and the Faulkner, we must redeem.

NOTES

1. Quoted in Susan Buck-Morss, *The Dialectics of Seeing: Walter Benjamin and the Arcades Project* (Cambridge, MA: MIT Press, 1991), 303. Hereafter cited parenthetically.

2. See Siegfried Kracauer, *The Mass Ornament: Weimar Essays* (Cambridge, MA: Harvard University Press, 1995); Theodor Adorno, *In Search of Wagner*, trans. Rodney Livingstone (London: Verso, 2009); Walter Benjamin, "The Work of Art in the Age of Its Technological Reproducibility: Third Version," *Selected Writings, Volume 4, 1938–1940*, trans. Rodney Livingstone (Cambridge, MA: Harvard University Press, 2003), 251–83; and Susan Buck-Morss, "Aesthetics and Anaesthetics: Walter Benjamin's Artwork Essay Reconsidered," *October* 62, no. 1 (1992): 3–41.

3. Nikhil Pal Singh, "The Afterlife of Fascism," *South Atlantic Quarterly* 105, no. 1 (2006): 77.

4. See Robin James, *Resilience and Melancholy: Pop Music, Feminism, Neoliberalism* (London: Zero Books, 2015).

5. Robert H. Brinkmeyer Jr., *The Fourth Ghost: White Southern Writers and European Fascism, 1930–1950* (Baton Rouge: Louisiana State University Press, 2009), 4. Hereafter cited parenthetically.

6. Jodi Melamed, *Represent and Destroy: Rationalizing Violence in the New Racial Capitalism* (Minneapolis: University of Minnesota Press, 2011), 2.

7. Singh, "The Afterlife of Fascism," 79.

8. In recent years, there has been a series of challenges to Brinkmeyer's anti-Fascist Faulkner, most prominently Jeanne A. Follansbee, who raises "the very real possibility that democracy itself might spawn Fascism" ("'Sweet Fascism in the Piney Woods': *Absalom, Absalom!* As Fascist Fable," *Modernism/modernity* 18, no. 1 [2011]: 86), and Daniel Spoth, who suggests that *Light in August*'s and particularly *Absalom, Absalom*'s anti-Fascist aesthetics might be more ambivalent than is often suggested ("Totalitarian Faulkner: The Nazi Interpretation of *Light in August* and *Absalom, Absalom!*" *ELH* 78, no. 1 [2011]: 239–57). Nonetheless, while both try to complicate this Cold War Faulkner, neither is able to draw out the consequences for how we understand Fascism or how this more complicated view of Fascism might shape our reading of Faulkner's postwar writing.

9. Hosam Aboul-Ela, *Other South: Faulkner, Coloniality, and the Mariátegui Tradition* (Pittsburgh: University of Pittsburgh Press, 2007), 11.

10. James Whitman, *Hitler's American Model: The United States and the Making of Nazi Race Law* (Princeton, NJ: Princeton University Press, 2017), 2.

11. Aimé Césaire, *Discourse on Colonialism* (1950), ed. Robin D. G. Kelley, trans. Joan Pinkham (New York: Monthly Review Press, 2000), 36. Hereafter cited parenthetically.

12. Avital Ronell, *The Telephone Book: Technology—Schizophrenia—Electric Speech* (Lincoln: University of Nebraska Press, 1989), 6. Hereafter cited parenthetically. I was reminded of this link while listening to an episode of National Public Radio's *This American Life* shortly after Donald Trump issued his so-called "Muslim Ban." The episode, "It's Working Out Very Nicely" (February 3, 2017), featured an interview with Beca Heller from the International Refugee Assistance Project, who was at an airport with many refugees who are now in limbo as the ban came into effect. Describing her experience at the airport, she explained that every time the refugees asked for information, "Customs and Border Patrol just kept telling them, we're waiting for a call from DC to tell us what to do." *Waiting for a call.* In the following weeks, telephones seemed to appear everywhere. The *New York Times* published an article detailing Trump's enamoured reaction to the White House phones, one of which he described as "the most

beautiful phone I've ever used in my life" (Maggie Haberman, "A Homebody Finds the Ultimate Home Office," *New York Times* [January 25, 2017], 14). And shortly thereafter, news broke that Hitler's bunker phone had just been sold to an anonymous buyer in the United States for $243,000; see "Adolf Hitler's Phone Sells for More than $240,000," *Al Jazeera* (February 20, 2017), www.aljazeera.com/news/2017/02/adolf-hitler-phone-sells-240000-170220063354390.html.

13. Nicole Aschoff, "The Smartphone Society," *Jacobin Magazine*, March 17, 2015, www.jacobinmag.com/2015/03/smartphone-usage-technology-aschoff.

14. William Faulkner, *Light in August*, rev. ed. (1932; repr. New York: Vintage International, 1990), 92. Hereafter cited parenthetically.

15. Faulkner to Malcolm Cowley, September 20, 1945, *Selected Letters of William Faulkner*, ed. Joseph Blotner (New York: Random House, 1977), 202.

16. "In 1877 when Bell and Thomas Watson were giving public demonstrations of the telephone in New England and New York, the newspaper reports were full of forebodings of witchcraft. 'It is difficult,' said the *Providence Press*, 'to really resist the notion that the powers of darkness are in league with it.' The Boston *Advertiser* spoke of a 'weirdness' never before felt in that city; and the New York *Herald* found the telephone 'almost supernatural'" (John Brooks, "The First and Only Century of Telephone Literature," *The Social Impact of the Telephone*, ed. Ithiel de Sola Pool [Cambridge, MA: MIT Press, 1977], 209–10).

17. Eula Biss, "Time and Distance Overcome," *Iowa Review* 38, no. 1 (Spring 2008): 85–87.

18. Theodor W. Adorno and Walter Benjamin, *The Complete Correspondence, 1928–1940* (Cambridge, MA: Harvard University Press, 2001), 333.

19. Ibid., 327.

20. Julie B. Napolin, "The Fact of Resonance: An Acoustics of Determination in Faulkner and Benjamin," *Symploke* 24, no. 1 (2016): 172.

21. Walter Benjamin, "On the Concept of History," *Selected Writings 1939–1940*, ed. Howard Eiland and Michael W. Jennings, trans. Harry Zohn (Cambridge, MA: Harvard-Belknap, 1999), 253. Hereafter cited parenthetically.

22. Sacvan Bercovitch, "The Function of the Literary in a Time of Cultural Studies," in *"Culture" and the Problem of the Disciplines*, ed. John Carlos Rowe (New York: Columbia University Press, 1998), 80.

23. Willis reads Faulkner through the frame of dependency theory, and central to her reading is lumber. She argues that the wilderness (the forest) functions as a site of narrative investment for "Indians, 'swampers,' plantation owners and their retainers, townspeople and businessmen" because it is a site of economic investment for the two systems that are clashing in the novel: "the industrial capitalist system which manifests itself in the city, village and wilderness," and the "older plantation system whose chain of domination includes the wilderness, the rural hinterland, and the plantation." See Susan Willis, "Aesthetics of the Rural Slum: Contradictions and Dependency in 'The Bear,'" *Social Text* 2 (1979): 94. "The Bear," Willis argues, stages the transition from one system to the other, as lumber becomes subsumed by industrial capitalism, as is most evidently seen by the logging company's buyout of Major de Spain, "formerly the most powerful representative of the plantation system" (92).

24. Jay Watson, "The Philosophy of Furniture, or *Light in August* and the Material Unconscious," in *Faulkner and Material Culture: Faulkner and Yoknapatawpha, 2004*, ed. Joseph R. Urgo and Ann J. Abadie (Jackson: University Press of Mississippi, 2007), 33–55. Hereafter cited parenthetically. See also Lawrence Buell, "Faulkner and the Claims of the Natural World," in *Faulkner and the Natural World: Faulkner and Yoknapatawpha, 1996*,

ed. Donald M. Kartiganer and Ann J. Abadie (Jackson: University Press of Mississippi, 1999), 1–18.

25. John T. Matthews, *William Faulkner: Seeing through the South* (Hoboken, NJ: John Wiley & Sons, 2009), 232. Hereafter cited parenthetically.

26. Leigh Anne Duck, *The Nation's Region: Southern Modernism, Segregation, and US Nationalism* (Athens: University of Georgia Press, 2006), 82.

27. Stephen Shapiro, "Transvaal, Transylvania: Dracula's World-System and Gothic Periodicity," *Gothic Studies* 10, no. 1 (2008): 33.

28. For a reading of *Intruder in the Dust* as a noir, see Robert Jackson, "Grayscale Summation, 1948: *Intruder in the Dust* and Its Noir Contexts," *Faulkner Journal* 28, no. 1 (2014): 37–53.

29. William Faulkner, *Intruder in the Dust* (1948; repr., New York: Vintage, 1972), 119. Hereafter cited parenthetically.

30. Richard Godden, *Fictions of Labor: William Faulkner and the South's Long Revolution* (New York: Cambridge University Press, 1997), 6.

31. Jay Watson, *Forensic Fictions: The Lawyer Figure in Faulkner* (Athens: University of Georgia Press, 1993), 130.

32. For more on the relationship between the suburbs and Cold War ideology, see Amy Kaplan, "Manifest Domesticity," *American Literature* 70, no. 3 (1998): 581–606; Elaine Tyler May, *Homeward Bound: American Families in the Cold War Era* (New York: Basic Books, 2008); and Kate Baldwin, *The Racial Imaginary of the Cold War Kitchen: From Sokol'niki Park to Chicago's South Side* (New Hanover, NH: Dartmouth College Press, 2016).

33. Peter Galison, "War against the Center," *Grey Room* 4 (2001): 6, 24. Urban renewal, especially the 1949 Housing Act that enabled the widespread development of US cities, was based on the creation of long-term and low-cost mortgages provided by the Federal Housing Authority. These mortgages, however, were based on ranking systems of insurability and risk. In both policy and practice, these systems prioritized white, suburban communities while they undervalued and effectively redlined urban neighborhoods that were older, racially mixed, and densely populated. For more on the relationship between postwar federal policies and race, see Kenneth T. Jackson's groundbreaking *Crabgrass Frontier: The Suburbanization of the United States* (New York: Oxford University Press, 1987); Thomas J. Sugrue, *The Origins of the Urban Crisis: Race and Inequality in Postwar Detroit* (1997; repr., Princeton, NJ: Princeton University Press, 2005); Arnold J. Hirsch, *Making the Second Ghetto: Race and Housing in Chicago 1940–1960* (Chicago: University of Chicago Press, 2009); Hirsch, "Searching for a 'Sound Negro Policy': A Racial Agenda for the Housing Acts of 1949 and 1954," *Housing Policy Debate* 11, no. 2 (2000): 393–441; and Robert O. Self, *American Babylon: Race and the Struggle for Postwar Oakland* (Princeton, NJ: Princeton University Press, 2005). For more on the connections between suburbanization and nuclear policy, see Galison, "War against the Center"; Kate Brown, *Plutopia: Nuclear Families, Atomic Cities, and the Great Soviet and American Plutonium Disasters* (New York: Oxford University Press, 2013); David Krugler, *This Is Only a Test: How Washington DC Prepared for Nuclear War* (New York: Palgrave Macmillan, 2006); and Matthew Farish, "Another Anxious Urbanism: Simulating Defense and Disaster in Cold War America," *Cities, War, and Terrorism: Towards an Urban Geopolitics*, ed. Stephen Graham (Malden, MA: Blackwell, 2004), 93–109.

34. Ticien M. Sassoubre, "Avoiding Adjudication in William Faulkner's *Go Down, Moses* and *Intruder in the Dust*," *Criticism* 49, no. 2 (2007): 199. As examples, she gives Roosevelt's 1941 Fair Employment Practices committee, which "initiated the desegregation of the civil service" (198); Truman's subsequent desegregation of the military; and

a "series of Supreme Court decisions in the early 1940s regarding public accommodations and voting rights" as well as the "rash of violence against blacks in the South in 1947 perpetrated by returning veterans surprised by blacks' rise in social and economic status" (199).

35. Sassoubre, "Avoiding Adjudication," 186.

36. Walt W. Rostow, *The Stages of Economic Growth: A Non-Communist Manifesto* (New York: Cambridge University Press, 1990), 8.

37. Lawrence H. Schwartz, *Creating Faulkner's Reputation: The Politics of Modern Literary Criticism* (Knoxville: University of Tennessee Press, 1988), 201.

38. Singh, "The Afterlife of Fascism," 81.

39. Mathew Huber argues not only that suburbanization was enabled by newfound access to fossil fuels but that it became a model through which the American-run fossil-fuel industry was exported globally, expanding and consolidating US international dominance and helping "power what others have called 'the real subsumption of life under capital,' where subjectivity itself mirrors the entrepreneurial logics of capital" (Matthew Huber, *Lifeblood: Oil, Freedom, and the Forces of Capital* [Minneapolis: University of Minnesota Press, 2013], xv). See also Jason Moore, *Capitalism in the Web of Life: Ecology and the Accumulation of Capital* (New York: Verso, 2015); Stephanie LeMenager, *Living Oil: Petroleum Culture in the American Century* (New York: Oxford University Press, 2013); and Frederick Buell, "A Short History of Oil Cultures; or, the Marriage of Catastrophe and Exuberance," *Journal of American Studies* 46, no. 2 (2012): 273–92.

40. I am grateful to Robert Jackson and Jay Watson for pressing me on this question.

41. Premilla Nadasen, *Household Workers Unite: The Untold Story of African American Women Who Built a Movement* (Boston: Beacon, 2016), 14.

42. Beatrice Charles, for example, talks about learning of the bus boycott in response to Rosa Parks's arrest and notes, "I said this is what we should do. So I got on the phone and called all my friends and told them, and they said they wouldn't ride" (quoted in Nadasen, *Household Workers Unite*, 21).

43. William Faulkner, "Hog Pawn," *Uncollected Stories of William Faulkner*, ed. Joseph Blotner (1979; repr., New York: Vintage, 1981), 314. Hereafter cited parenthetically.

44. William Faulkner, *The Mansion*, in *The Snopes Trilogy* (New York: Modern Library, 2012), 960. Hereafter cited parenthetically.

45. Joseph Gold, "The 'Normality' of Snopesism: Universal Themes in Faulkner's *The Hamlet*," *Wisconsin Studies in Contemporary Literature* 3, no. 1 (1962): 30. See also Diane Roberts, "Eula, Linda, and the End of Nature," in *Faulkner and the Natural World: Faulkner and Yoknapatawpha, 1996*, ed. Donald M. Kartiganer and Ann J. Abadie (Jackson: University Press of Mississippi, 1999), 159–78.

46. Aboul-Ela, *Other South*, 87.

47. Molly Geidel, *Peace Corps Fantasies: How Development Shaped the Global Sixties* (Minneapolis: University of Minnesota Press, 2015), 4–5. Hereafter cited parenthetically.

48. Brooks, "The First and Only Century," 208.

49. There is a much longer history of both the labor struggles of women telephone operators and the role they played in the cultural imaginary: they were hired for their feminine charm and were seen as in need of protection from the men who might lurk in the telephone networks they accessed. They were also feared because of their increased independence and power. Carolyn Marvin, for instance, describes the operator of this era as "independently employed, saucy in her pursuit of the slightly racy recreations of the young and unobligated, and possessor of a free-floating social identity that was particularly suspicious in women. In short, she was in need of control. Her voice, symbol of both her work and her gender, was the handiest extension of her for that purpose" (*When Old*

Technologies Were New: Thinking about Electric Communication in the Late Nineteenth Century [New York: Oxford University Press, 1990], 29).

50. Dorothy S. Cobble, *The Other Women's Movement: Workplace Justice and Social Rights in Modern America* (Princeton, NJ: Princeton University Press, 2005), 21.

51. Ibid.

Contributors

Ted Atkinson is associate professor of English at Mississippi State University, editor of *Mississippi Quarterly*, and president of the William Faulkner Society. He is the author of *Faulkner and the Great Depression: Aesthetics, Ideology, and Cultural Politics* (2006) and of articles published in *Journal of American Studies, Southern Quarterly, Southern Literary Journal*, and the *Faulkner Journal*. Previous appearances at Faulkner and Yoknapatawpha resulted in contributions to *Faulkner and Formalism, Fifty Years after Faulkner*, and *Faulkner and the Black Literatures of the Americas*. Atkinson's current project is a book manuscript titled "Monumental Designs: A Cultural History of the Tennessee Valley Authority."

Gloria J. Burgess is professor of transformational leadership at Seattle University and visiting faculty at the University of Washington and University of Southern California. Her books include *Dare to Wear Your Soul on the Outside: Live Your Legacy NOW* (2008) and *Legacy Living* (2006). She coedited *Leading in Complex Worlds* (2012) and *The Embodiment of Leadership* (2013) and has several chapters forthcoming on the intersectionality of leadership and the arts. A fellow at Cave Canem, a prestigious collective of poets and writers of the African Diaspora, she has published her work in diverse collections, including *The Ringing Ear: Black Poets Lean South* (2007).

David A. Davis is director of fellowships and scholarships, associate professor of English, and associate director of the Spencer B. King Jr. Center for Southern Studies at Mercer University. He is the author of the forthcoming book *World War I and Southern Modernism* in addition to numerous essays on southern literature and culture. Currently, he is writing a book about sharecropping and southern literature.

Sarah E. Gardner is professor of history at Mercer University. Her most recent publications are *Reviewing the South: The Literary Marketplace* *and the Southern Renaissance, 1920–1941* (2017) and *Reassessing the 1930s South*, edited with Karen L. Cox (2018).

Richard Godden teaches in the English Department at the University of California at Irvine. He is the author of *Fictions of Capital* (1990); *Fictions of Labor: William Faulkner and the South's Long Revolution* (1997); and *William Faulkner: An Economy of Complex Words* (2007). He currently works on the relation between finance capital and late twentieth-/early twenty-first-century fiction. His manuscript, "Paper Graveyards: Towards a Narrative Poetics of the Financial Turn," approaches completion.

Ryan Heryford is assistant professor of environmental literature at California State University, East Bay, where he teaches courses in nineteenth- and twentieth-century American literary and cultural studies with a focus on narratives of environmental justice. His current manuscript, "Preservation and the Production of Bare Life," explores late nineteenth- and twentieth-century American literary negotiations of the dominant discourses of environmental preservation emerging under the shadow of a rapidly expanding US empire. His article on *Absalom, Absalom!* and the 1914–34 United States occupation of Haiti can be found in *Faulkner's Geographies* (2015).

Robert Jackson is James G. Watson Professor of English at the University of Tulsa, where he is also affiliated with programs in film studies and African American studies. Among his publications in literature, film and media studies, and social history are numerous articles and reviews, as well as two books, *Seeking the Region in American Literature and Culture: Modernity, Dissidence, Innovation* (2005) and *Fade In, Crossroads: A History of the Southern Cinema* (2017).

Gavin Jones is the Frederick P. Rehmus Family Professor of Humanities at Stanford University. He is the author of *Strange Talk: The Politics of Dialect Literature in Gilded Age America* (1999); *American Hungers: The Problem of Poverty in US Literature, 1840–1945* (2007); and *Failure and the American Writer: A Literary History* (2014). He is completing a book about John Steinbeck and is beginning a study of the rise of the short story in American literature.

Mary A. Knighton is professor of literature at Aoyama Gakuin University in Tokyo. Her publications include "Hearing Secret Voices in Twain's Personal Recollections of Joan of Arc" (2017); "William Faulkner's

Illustrious Circles: Double-Dealing Caricatures in Style and Taste" (2017); and "Swinks and Snopeses: The Germ of the 'Global Provincial' in Twain and Faulkner" (2009).

Peter Lurie is the author of *Vision's Immanence: Faulkner, Film, and the Popular Imagination* (2004) and of *American Obscurantism: History and the Visual in US Literature and Film* (2018) as well as the coeditor, with Ann J. Abadie, of *Faulkner and Film: Faulkner and Yoknapatawpha, 2010* (2014). He is associate professor of English and film studies coordinator at the University of Richmond and in 2015 was the Fulbright Distinguished Chair in American Studies at the University of Warsaw. With Theresa M. Towner, he is the coeditor of *The Faulkner Journal*.

John T. Matthews is professor of English at Boston University. His previous books include The *Play of Faulkner's Language*; *"The Sound and the Fury": Faulkner and the Lost Cause*; and *William Faulkner: Seeing through the South*. He is the editor *of A Companion to the Modern American Novel, 1900–1950*; *William Faulkner in Context*; and *The New Cambridge Companion to William Faulkner*. His articles on Faulkner and southern literature have appeared in *ELH*, *boundary 2*, *NOVEL*, *American Literary History*, and *Philological Quarterly*.

Myka Tucker-Abramson is a lecturer at King's College London. Her work has been published in *Modern Fiction Studies*, *Modern Drama*, and *Edu-Factory* and is forthcoming in *PMLA*. She has recently completed a book manuscript on urban redevelopment, midcentury US novels, and the rise of neoliberalism.

Michael Wainwright is an honorary research associate with the English Department at Royal Holloway, University of London. His five monographs include *Darwin and Faulkner's Novels: Evolution and Southern Fiction* (2008); *Faulkner's Gambit: Chess and Literature* (2011); and *Game Theory and Postwar American Literature* (2016). His readings at international symposiums include two previous appearances at Faulkner and Yoknapatawpha.

Jay Watson is Howry Professor of Faulkner Studies at the University of Mississippi and the director of the Faulkner and Yoknapatawpha conference. He is the author of *Forensic Fictions: The Lawyer Figure in Faulkner* and *Reading for the Body: The Recalcitrant Materiality of Southern Fiction, 1893–1985*, which received Honorable Mention for the 2013 C. Hugh Holman Award sponsored by the Society for the Study of Southern Literature. He is also the editor of *Faulkner and Whiteness, Conversations with Larry Brown*, and coeditor of six volumes of the Faulkner and Yoknapatawpha conference proceedings.

Michael Zeitlin, associate professor of English at the University of British Columbia, is former coeditor of the *Faulkner Journal*. Recent essays include "Faulkner, Adorno, and 'the Radio Phenomenon,' 1935" and "Faulkner and the Royal Air Force Canada, 1918." His current work in progress includes a study of Faulkner's aviation stories, novels, and screenplays.

Index

Page numbers in *italics* refer to illustrations.

Abdur-Rahman, Aliyyah, 143
Aboul-Ela, Hosam, xxiii, 210
"Abraham's Children" (Faulkner), 91, 94
Absalom, Absalom! (Faulkner), xii, xv, xvi, xxi, 35, 42, 45–46, 51–52, 131, 217, 226n8; Faulkner's map in, xvi, 45, 47, *48,* 49, 52–56, 142–46, 156–61
Act Prohibiting Importation of Slaves (1807), 158
"Ad Astra" (Faulkner), 20
Adorno, Theodor, 212
Africa, 220
agrarianism, 35
Agricultural Adjustment Act, 146
Alabama: cotton plantations in, 158; illiteracy in, 9
Albert and Shirley Small Special Collections at the University of Virginia, 204
Alcorn A&M College (Alcorn College), xvii, 83, 84, 87
Alcorn Student Council, 85
Algonquin Hotel, 15
Allewaert, Monique, 141, 143
"Ambuscade" (Faulkner), 3
American Association of University Presses, xxx
American Dilemma, An (Myrdal), 73

Anderson, Daniel, xxx
Ann Arbor, Michigan, 85
Anthropocene, 152
anticapitalist ontologies, 141–42
anticapitalist populism, 146
antimaterialism, 149
antiracism, 74
anti-Semitism, 116, 120
"Aria con Amore" (Faulkner), 91, 101–4
Arrighi, Giovanni, 60
As I Lay Dying (Faulkner), xviii, 34, 35, 45, 90–106, 107n13, 130–32, 145, 147, 149
"As I Lay Dying" (Faulkner), 91, 96, 98, 99–100, 103, 107n13
Aschoff, Nicole, 211
Asia, 220
Atkinson, Ted, xix, xxix, xxx

Bailey, Devan, 135
Bailey Woods, xxx
banks, New York, 60
Baptist, Edward, 195–96
Baptiste-Riché, Jean, 143
Barker, Deborah, 57n18
barn burnings, 146, 163
Barton, Benjamin, 144
Bassett, John E., 183n5
Bataille, Georges, 147
Baucom, Ian, 66–67, 76n15, 196

236   INDEX

Baudrillard, Jean, 51
"Bear, The" (Faulkner), 214
Beardsley, Aubrey, 45
Beckert, Sven, 195
Being Given (Marion), 170
Benjamin, Walter, xv, 122–23, 208, 210, 212–14, 225
Bercovitch, Sacvan, 213
Berg, Norman, 11
Berner, Seth, xxix
Bible, 15
black freedom struggle, 85
"Black Music" (Faulkner), 16, 19
Black Panthers, 209
Black Power, 221
Bleikasten, André, 139, 204n2
Blotner, Joseph, vii, 39, 40, 54
Bolton, Matthew, xxix
Bonaparte, Napoleon, 210
Boni and Liveright, viii
Bookman, The, 8
Book-of-the-Month Club, 10
books: buying and borrowing, 4–12; stores and sales, xiv, 9
Bourdieu, Pierre, 93
Brecht, Bertolt, 57n9
Breu, Christopher, 115
Brinkmeyer, Robert H., Jr., 197, 209, 226n8
Brooks, Cleanth, 16
Brooks, John, 223
Brown, Clarence, 198–99
Buck-Morss, Susan, 213, 218
Burgess, Gloria J., xvii, xxix

Cameron, Sharon, 148
Camp Taliaferro, 23
capitalism and capitalists, ix–x, 59–75, 111, 129, 144, 147, 151, 152, 167, 195, 197, 222
Capitalism in the Twenty-First Century (Piketty), xxiii–xxiv

"Carcassonne" (Faulkner), 15–16, 19, 21, 23, 24
Carothers, James B., xxx, 36, 39
Carter, Hodding, 172
Cartesian dualism, 144
"Case for Reparations, The" (Coates), 196–97
Cave Canem, 88
Central State College (Wilberforce, Ohio), 84, 85
Cerf, Bennett, 199
Césaire, Aimé, 208, 209–10, 224
Chapin, Edwin Hubbell, 78
Chesapeake Bay region, xxii
Chile, 210
Chu, Patricia, 145–46
civil rights movement, 85, 187, 198; Montgomery Bus Boycott, 221
Civil War, xxi, 40, 42n12, 43n25, 156–57, 159, 210, 219
class mobility, 162
Cleary, Rebecca, xxix
Coates, Ta-Nehisi, xxiii
Cobble, Dorothy Sue, 225
Coindreau, Maurice Edgar, 15
Cold War, xiii, 60, 70, 72, 209, 218–20, 223
Collected Stories (Faulkner), 36, 40
Commins, Saxe, 108n38
commodity crops and market, 156, 166
Communism, 35, 221, 225
Condell, Caitlin, 204
"Concept of History" (Benjamin), 212–13, 215
consumerism, 224
Cooper Hewitt, Smithsonian Design Museum, 204
Corrigan, John Michael, xxx
cotton economy, 156; antebellum, xxi; post-Emancipation, xxi
Cotton Plantation South since the Civil War, The (Aiken), 156

INDEX

Couch, William, 10
Cowley, Malcolm, 91, 108n32, 208
Cox, Dianne, 91
Crawford, Joan, 58n18
crop lien system, 160, 166

Daniels, Jonathan, 10–11
Davis, David A., xxi, xxix
Dayan, Colin, 143, 149
De Bord, Guy, 51
de Duve, Thierry, 47
"Death Drag" (Faulkner), 39
Deleuze, Giles, 147
democracy, American, 71–72
Derrida, Jacques, xxi, 49, 57n10, 170–71, 173–79
Des Jardins, Julie, 182
desegregation, 71, 219
Detroit, Michigan, 85
Detroit Osteopathic Hospital, 86
Deutsch, James, xxx
Devine, Eric, 15
Dietrich, Marlene, 57n9
Digital Yoknapatawpha project, xxx
Dillon, Richard T., 37
Discourse on Colonialism (Césaire), 210
Disney Company, 122
Doctor Martino and Other Stories (Faulkner), 36
Dollar Cotton (Faulkner), 162, 166
domestic labor, Depression-era, 221
Dore, Florence, 65
Dos Passos, John, 57n9
"Dry September" (Faulkner), 197
Duck, Leigh Anne, 215
Dussere, Erik, 172
Duvall, John N., xxx

Economic Survey of the Book Industry (Cheney), 5–6
Elmer (Faulkner), 15

"Elmer" (Faulkner), 92
Emancipation, xxi
Empire of Cotton: A Global History (Beckert), 159
Engels, Friedrich, 23
Enlightenment, ix; thought, Western, 209
Enlightenment humanism, 144
Eudora Welty Awards in Creative Writing, xxix
eviction entrepreneurialism, 74

Fable, A (Faulkner), 46, 169, 182
Fadiman, Regina, 198
Falkner, Maud, 15
Fascism and neo-Fascism, 35, 208–25. *See also* Nazism
Father Abraham (Faulkner), vii, 21
"Father Abraham" (Faulkner), xviii, 31, 91, 93–96, 196
Faulkner, J.W. T., Jr., 98
Faulkner, William: as capitalist, 32; fear of New Deal, 42; and/in Hollywood, 34, 49, 54, 58n18, 198; market pressures on, 34; in New Orleans, 21; Nobel Prize for Literature, 169, 182, 183n4, 198; as poet-tramp, 32; post–Royal Air Force experiences, 27n12; race in post–Hollywood writing, 55; segregation and institutionalized racism, stance on, xviii; as studio writer, 45–56; at University of Virginia, 16, 33, 157
Faulkner and Print Culture (Watson, Harker, and Thomas), 4
Faulkner and the Great Depression: Aesthetics, Ideology, and Cultural Politics (Atkinson), 35
Federal Housing Authority, 228n33
Federal Works Progress Administration, 10

INDEX

femininity, white, 219
Ferguson, Niall, x
feudalism, 215
financialization, xvii, 59–75, 75n3, 196, 225
Finney, Nikky, 88
Fitzgerald, F. Scott, 57n9
Flags in the Dust (Faulkner), vii–viii, xv, 3, 15, 17, 19, 24, 55, 65
Flood, 1927 Mississippi River, xi
Florida, book sales index, 6
Follansbee, Jeanne A., 226n8
Ford Motor Company, xviii, 86
Fordism, 35, 208
Fort Worth, Texas, 23
Four Seas Publishing Company, 90
Fourth Ghost, The (Brinkmeyer), 209
Fox Studios, xvi, 45
Freebooters and Smugglers: The Foreign Slave Trade in the United States after 1808 (Obadele-Starks), 158
Fried, Michael, 47
Fujihira, Ikuko, 189
Fuqua, Joy Van, 31

Gable, Clark, 54
Gardner, Sarah E., xiv, xxx
Geography of Reading, The (Wilson), 9, 10
Gerstenberger, Donna, 183n5
Gesamtkunstwerk (Wagner), 208
Gift of Death, The (Derrida), 181
"Gift Outright, The" (Frost), 181
Given Time: I. Counterfeit Money (Derrida), 169–70, 177
Gleeson-White, Sarah, 34
Go Down, Moses (Faulkner), 46, 56, 186, 187; "Fire and the Hearth," 184n8, 192, 194–95; plantation ledgers in, xi

Godden, Richard, xiii, xix, xxix, 75, 95, 101, 141, 146–47, 161, 164, 167, 215
Gold, Joseph, 149
gold standard, xxiv
Goldman, Morton, 33, 135
Goodwin, Lee, 127
Graeber, David, vii
Gramsci, Antonio, 147
Great Depression, xi, xiii, xiv, xv, xx, 12, 21, 31–41, 70, 85, 113, 125
Greece, vii
Green, Paul, 122
Greenberg, Clement, 47
Greenberg, Keneth S., 174
Greenwich Village, 71
Grosz, Elizabeth, 140
Guattari, Felix, 147
Guess, Malcolm, 81, 84, 87
Gwynn, Frederick, 107n20

Haas, Robert, 33, 36, 204n2
Haiti, xii; Constitution, 143–45
Hamlet, The (Faulkner), xi, xiii, xvii, xviii, xxi, 31, 59–75, 91, 100–103, 148–50, 152, 161
Hannon, Charles, 46
Harcourt, viii
Harker, Jaime, 4
Harper's, 74
Harrison, Ross Granville, 145
Harvey, David, ix, xxiv
Hatha yoga, xx
Haussmann, Georges-Eugène, 208, 210, 219
Hawks, Howard, 54
Hegel, Georg Wilhelm Friedrich, x
hematology, 86
Hempstead, David, 45
Heryford, Ryan, xx, xxix
Higginbottom, Elwood, 196–97

"Hill, The" (Faulkner), xv, 21, 27n12
"Hog Pawn" (Faulkner), xxiii, 211, 221–22, 224, 225
Hollywood, xvi, 35, 45, 46, 52, 132, 139, 187. *See also* Faulkner, William: and/in Hollywood
homo oeconomicus, x–xi
"Honor" (Faulkner), 35–36
Hopkins, Harry, 10
Hutchens, John K., 172

illiteracy, 5, 9
imperialism: capitalist, 209; European, 208–9
industrialization, 213
International Refugee Assistance Project, 226n12
Internet, 209
Intruder in the Dust (Brown), 186–204
Intruder in the Dust (Faulkner), xi, xiv, xxi, xxii–xxiii, 4, 46, 55, 71, 169–82, 183n5, 186–204, *201, 202, 203,* 204, 208–25
Iran, 210
Iraq, 210

Jackson, Robert, xv, xxix, 21
Jameson, Fredric, 68
Jews, xv
Jim Crow, 81, 134, 193, 196, 197–98, 200, 220–21; racial violence, 73, 146, 200, 218–19
John W. Hunt Scholarship, xxix
Jones, Claudia, 209
Jones, Gavin, xviii, xxx
Jones, Howard Mumford, 8

Kafka, Franz, 212
Karl, Frederick R., 31
Karnival Kid, The, xix, 122–23, 132
Kartiganer, Donald, 187

Kauffer, E. McKnight, 199–204, *201*
Keynesianism, 70
Kiyotaki, Nibuhiro, 126, 136n22
Knighton, Mary A., xxii, xxx
Kotex, 33
Kuruma, Samezo, 61
Kuzmanovich, Zoran, xxx

Lafayette County, xii
LaRue, Jack, 122
Latin America, 220
liberalism, 144
libraries, public, xiv, 10
Life, 51
Light in August (Faulkner), xiii, xxiii, 37, 45–46, 197, 209, 226n8; Fascism in, 211–17
Linscott, Robert N., 183n4
Literary Guild, 10
Liveright, Horace, vii–viii, 90. *See also* Boni and Liveright
Liverpool, England, xii
"Lizards in Jamshyd's Courtyard" (Faulkner), xviii, 99, 109n52
"Lo!" (Faulkner), xiii
London, England, xii
Lorman, Mississippi, xvii, 84
Louisiana: book readership in, 6; illiteracy in, 9
Love, Leston L., 82, 84, 87
Love = Love (Rogowski), xxix
L'Overture, Toussaint, 143
Lubitsch, Ernst, 27n9
Lurie, Peter, xvi, xxix, 41
Lynd, Helen, 124
Lynd, Robert, 124

"MacGillicuddie, The" (Bellah), 37
Macmillan (publisher), 11
macroeconomics and macroeconomists, xi, xii

Mallison, Charles, 150
Manchester, England, xii
Manhattan, New York, xii
Manifest Destiny, 181
Mann, Thomas, 57n9
Mansion, The (Faulkner), xxiii, 72, 75, 142, 148, 150–51, 211, 222–25
Marionettes, The, 18, 45
market individualism, xiv, 70
Marshall Plan, xiii
Martinique, xii
Marvin, Carolyn, 229n49
Marx, Karl, 23, 115–16, 119, 124–25, 129, 149
Marx, Sam, 132
Marxist economics, ix, 61
masculinity, southern, 221, 223
mass culture, 221
Massachusetts, book readership in, 6
Matthews, John T., xiii, xvii, xxix, 34, 95, 100, 162, 186, 197, 215, 219
Mayer, Louis B., 198
McAteer, John, 176
McDonald, Brian, xxx
McEwen, Earnest, Jr., xvii–xviii, 79–89
mechanization, 213
Mencken, H. L., 11
Merleau-Ponty, Maurice, 140–42, 149
MGM Studios, xvi, 45, 46, 54–55, 132, 169, 183n2, 183n4, 198–99
middlebrow fiction, 3
Middletown: A Study in Modern American Culture (Lynd and Lynd), 112
Miles, Caroline, xxx
militarization, 213
Millgate, Michael, 169
Mississippi, 35; book readership in, 6; book sales in, 9, 12; book sales index, 6; bookstores in, 10; cotton plantations in, 158; cultural index, 6; economic index, 6; illiteracy in, 9
"Mississippi" (Faulkner), 31
Mississippi State Insane Asylum, 104
Mississippi Valley, xii
Mitchell, W. J. T., xvi, 47, 52
modernism, literary, 220
modernization, 215, 219
"Moonlight" (Faulkner), 27n12
Moore, John, 126, 136n22
mortgage derivative speculation, 74
Mosquitoes (Faulkner), vii–vii, xv, 35, 134
Mouse, Mickey, xix, 122–25, 132–33
Mouse, Minnie, 123, 133
"Mule in the Yard" (Faulkner), xvii
Muncie, Indiana, 112
Murphet, Julian, 51, 52

Nadasen, Premilla, 221
Nagano, Japan, 205n9
Napolin, Julie, 212
"Narrative Space" (Heath), 47
National Association for the Advancement of Colored People (NAACP), 85
National Association of Book Publishers, 5
National Federation of Telephone Workers (NFTW), 225
nationalism, ultra-right, 210
Native Son (Wright), 57n17, 200, 202
Native South, xii
nativism, 116, 121n11
Nazism, 23, 208–10, 212, 215, 220; Adolf Hitler, 212, 215, 227n12. *See also* Fascism and neo-Fascism
neocolonialism, 208–10, 215, 220, 224
neoliberalism, American, xiv, xvii, xviii, 59–75, 76n17, 139, 208
New Critics, 65

New Deal, xiii, 35, 42, 101, 193
New World colonialism, xii, 221
New York (state), 6; book readership in, 6
New York, New York, xii, publishers in, 8
New Yorker, 47
1949 Housing Act, 228n33
Nobel Prize Committee, 182
North Carolina: book market, 8, 10–11; illiteracy in, 9
"Nympholepsy" (Faulkner), 27n12

O. Henry Memorial Award Prize Stories of 1931, 36
Ober, Harold, 172, 198–99
Odum, Howard, 9
Odyssey (Homer), 96, 108n38
Old Southwest, 158; humorists, 106n5
"On Fear" (Faulkner), 74
One Kind of Freedom: The Economic Consequences of Emancipation (Ransom and Sutch), 160
Ownby, Ted, 157, 160
Oxford, Mississippi, 15, 35, 56, 80, 82, 139, 187, 196–98

Padmore, George, 209
"Pantaloon in Black" (Faulkner), 194
Paris, France, 210
Parrish, Susan Scott, 145
Pass It On! (Burgess), 87
patriotism, 224
Patton, Nelse, 197
Peace Corps Fantasies (Geidel), 223
"Peasants, The" (Faulkner), 91, 100–101, 103, 109n52
Peek, Charles A., xxix
"Pennsylvania Station" (Faulkner), xiii
peonage, xiii

Perkins, Hoke, 204
Picture Theory (Mitchell), 47
Pills, Petticoats, and Plows (Clark), 157
Plessy v. Ferguson, 196
Poe, Edgar Allan, 212
Polk, Noel, 52
Portable Faulkner (Faulkner), xviii, 91, 104, 108n32
Porter, Carolyn, 114
Povinelli, Elizabeth, 151
prison-industrial complex, 74
Promise of the New South, The (Ayres), 163
Prosperity: Fact or Myth (Chase), 112, 116
Protestant Ethic, The (Weber), 21
Protestant work ethic, 114
Publishers' Weekly, 5, 11
Purnell, Gerald, 87
Pylon (Faulkner), xiii, 35, 39, 46, 51

Qiqun, Han, xxx

Railton, Stephen, xxx
Raleigh News and Observer, 10
Ramsey, D. Matthew, xxx
Random House, viii, xvi, 52–53, 56, 169, 183n2, 198–99, *201*
"Reading as a Southern Problem" (Round), 8
"Reading the *Absalom!* Endpapers: Reflections on the Poetics and Politics of Paranarrative" (Watson), 52
Reconstruction, 104
Red Dust (Fleming), 54
"Red Leaves" (Faulkner), 35–36
Red Scare, 225
Rendall, Simon, 204
Report on Economic Conditions in the South, 168n10

Represent and Destroy: Rationalizing Violence in the New Racial Capitalism (Melamed), 72–73
Requiem for a Nun (Faulkner), xiii, xiv
Rhode Island: bookstores in, 9–10
Rieger, Christopher, xxx
Riser, George, 204
Roaring Twenties, 112
Roncesvalles, Battle of, xv
Ronell, Avital, 211–12
Roosevelt, Franklin, 209, 215, 222
"Rose for Emily, A" (Faulkner), 35–36
Rowan Oak, xxx, 4, 82, 84–85
Rush, Benjamin, 144

Samway, Patrick H., 169, 183n2, 184n8, 185n18
Sánchez-Pardo, Ester, 55, 58n18
Sanctuary (Faulkner), 12, 18, 34, 90, 99, 122–35, 188; Modern Library introduction to, 126
"Sanctuary" (Burgess), 88–89
Sartoris (Faulkner), viii, 34
Sassoubre, Ticien, 219
Satterfield, Jay, 4, 12
Saturday Evening Post, 35, 37–40, 51, 95
Saturday Review of Literature, 6, 7, 7, 8, 10; "A Bookman's Idea of United States of America," 6, 7, 12
Schermerhorn, Calvin, 195
Schulman, Grace, 204
Schwartz, Lawrence, 220
Scotland and Scotsmen, xv, 39
Scream (Craven), 212
Scribner's, 51, 91, 93, 95, 98, 100–101
Severson, Eric R., 181–82
Shadow and Act (Ellison), 188
Shakespeare, William, 15
Shapiro, Stephen, 215

sharecropping, xiii, xxi, 159–60, 162–63, 193
shavasana ("corpse pose"), 138–52
Signifying Eye, The (Waid), 45
Silicon Valley, xii
Simon and Schuster, 5
Singh, Nikhil Pal, 209, 220
Skei, Hans H., 36–38, 91
slave trade and slave capitalism, xii, xiii, 73–74, 142, 156, 196, 209, 215; Middle Passage, 170–71, 178
Smith & Haas, 52, 53
Smith, Adam, ix–x
Smith, Hal, 107n20
Smith, Harrison, 32
Snopes Trilogy (Faulkner), vii, 46, 59–75. See also *Hamlet, The* (Faulkner); *Mansion, The* (Faulkner); *Town, The* (Faulkner)
So Red the Rose (Young), 5
Sohn-Rethel, Alfred, 126
Soldiers' Pay (Faulkner), vii–viii, xv, 18, 21
Song of Roland, xv, 17
Sorcerer's Apprentice, The, xx
Sound and the Fury, The (Faulkner), xxi, 34, 40, 45, 55, 93, 107n20, 110–20, 120n6, 125, 130, 131, 149, 165; introduction to, 26n8, 131
Sound and the Fury, The (Ritt), 72
South Carolina: book sales index, 6, 12; cultural index, 6; economic index, 6; illiteracy in, 9
Southern Regions (Odum), 9
Southerner Discovers the South, A, 11
Spillers, Hortense, 140, 142, 195
Spiral, The (Steinberg), 47, 49, 50, 52
"Spotted Horses" (Faulkner), xviii, 91, 93, 101, 103

Spotted Horses material, 90–106, 108n32
Square Books, xxx
Stages of Economic Growth, The (Rostow), 220
Standard Oil Company, 26n11
Stokes, Elsie W., 5
Stokes and Stockwell Bookstore, 5
Stone, Phil, 94
Store, The (Stribling), 162
storekeeping, 156–67
Story of Temple Drake, The (Roberts), 122
suburbanization, 223
Sweden, 33

Tangled Fire of William Faulkner, The (O'Connor), 183n5
Tannehill, Robin, xxix
Taylorism, 35
Tebbetts, Terrell L., xxix, xxx
telephones, 211–25, 226n12; telephone operators, women, 229n49
"There Was a Queen" (Faulkner), 39
These 13 (Faulkner), vii, 18, 36, 40
"Thrift" (Faulkner), xv, 35–39
Till, Emmett, 76n13
Timon of Athens (Shakespeare), 115, 119
Tinkcom, Matthew, 31
Today We Live (Hawks), 54
Town, The (Faulkner), xiv, xvii, 59–75, 150
Towner, Theresa M., xxx
Trader Horn (Dyke), 55, 57n17
Triumph of the Will (Riefenstahl), 213
Trotter, Cham, xxix
Trotter, Ike S., xxix
Truman Doctrine, 210
Trump, Donald, 208, 210–11, 224; "Muslim ban," 226n12

Trumpism, 208–9
Tsing, Anna, 151
Tucker-Abramson, Myka, xiv, xxiii, xxx
"Turnabout" (Faulkner), 58n18
"Two Dollar Wife" (Faulkner), xiii

Uncollected Stores (Faulkner), 36
University of Mississippi, xvii, 81–82, 87; Center for the Study of Southern Culture, xxix, xxx; Department of English, xxx; J. D. Williams Library, xxx; power plant, 99; University of Mississippi Museum, xxix
University of North Carolina, 7–8, 9
University of Virginia, 107n20
University Press of Mississippi, xxx
Unvanquished, The (Faulkner), 3, 35, 51, 57n13
urbanization, 211
Urgo, Joseph, 46
US Constitution, 158

"Victory" (Faulkner), 40
Villarejo, Amy, 31
Virginia, 158
Virginia Foundation for the Humanities, 204
Virilio, Paul, 17
Visible and Revealed, The (Marion), 170, 177
vitalist materialism, 144–45
von Humboldt, Alexander, 144
von Stroheim, Erich, 57n9

Wainwright, Michael, xxx
Wall Street, xix; Crash, 34, 125; stock market, 116; "too big to fail," 113; Wall Street/Main Street paradigm, 112, 116
Wallace, Harry A., 10
war bonds, 75n5

"Was" (Faulkner), xi, 193
"Wash" (Faulkner), 95
Wasson, Ben, 122
Watkins, Lorie, xxx
Watson, Jay, 4, 39, 52–53, 55, 78, 146, 152, 176, 212, 214–17
Way to Wealth, The (Franklin), 196
Weber, Max, xv, 21, 24
Weheliye, Alexander, 140, 142
West, Nathaniel, 57n9
white supremacist terrorism, 142
Whitman, James, 210
Whitman, Walt, 169, 182
"Wild Palms" (Faulkner), xiii
William Faulkner Encyclopedia, A (Hamblin), 183n5
William Faulkner Society, xxix
Willis, Susan, 214
Wilson, Louis Round, 7–10
women's rights, 71
Woodruff, Kathleen, xxx
"Work of Art in the Age of Its Technological Reproducibility, The" (Benjamin), 123–24
World Viewed, The (Gavell), 47
World War I (Great War), xiii, 75n5, 104, 213
World War II, xiii, 12, 70, 209, 218, 223
Wright, Richard, 57n17
Wynter, Sylvia, 140, 142

Yankees, xv
Yoknapatawpha County, vii, ix, xii, xvi, 39
Yoknapatawpha River, xx

Zeitlin, Michael, xv, xvi, xxix, 41
"Zero Times Zero Equals Zero" (Daniels), 11
Žižek, Slavoj, 126
Zong, 74, 206n22
Zong massacre, 73–74

www.ingramcontent.com/pod-product-compliance
Lightning Source LLC
Chambersburg PA
CBHW030338240426
43661CB00052B/1675